THE
SYNODICON VETUS

TEXT, TRANSLATION, AND NOTES

by

JOHN DUFFY and JOHN PARKER

Dumbarton Oaks
Center for Byzantine Studies
Trustees for Harvard University
Washington, District of Columbia
1979

Manufactured in the United States of America by
Sheridan Books, Inc., 450 Fame Avenue, Hanover, PA 17331 | (717) 632-3535

In accordance with the rules adopted by the International Commission for the Edition of Sources of Byzantine History, the text and translation of this volume have been verified by Ihor Ševčenko and L. G. Westerink

The Synodicon Vetus
Text, translation, and notes
by John M. Duffy and John Parker

(Dumbarton Oaks texts ; 5) (Corpus Fontium Historiae Byzantinae ; 15)
In Greek; with English translation.

Includes bibliographical references and index.

ISBN 978-0-88402-088-2 (first clothbound: alkaline paper)
ISBN 978-0-88402-446-0 (first paperbound: alkaline paper)
LCCN: 79-52935
LCCN permalink: https://lccn.loc.gov/79052935

EU GPSR Authorised Representative
LOGOS EUROPE, 9 rue Nicolas Poussin, 17000, La Rochelle, France
E-mail: Contact@logoseurope.eu

DUMBARTON OAKS TEXTS

V

THE *SYNODICON VETUS*

CORPUS FONTIUM HISTORIAE BYZANTINAE

CONSILIO SOCIETATIS INTERNATIONALIS
STUDIIS BYZANTINIS PROVEHENDIS DESTINATAE
EDITUM

VOLUMEN XV

SYNODICON VETUS

EDIDERUNT, ANGLICE VERTERUNT
ET ADNOTAVERUNT
JOHN DUFFY et JOHN PARKER

SERIES WASHINGTONENSIS
EDIDIT IHOR ŠEVČENKO

In aedibus Dumbarton Oaks
Washingtoniae, D.C.
MCMLXXIX

FOREWORD

The idea of preparing a critical edition of the *Synodicon Vetus* came from Fr. Francis Dvornik whose interest was aroused by the discovery of a complete version of the text in a Sinai manuscript. He always supported the project and would have been pleased at its completion.

In the course of their research the editors received help of various kinds from a number of scholars; we are grateful to E. Chrysos, V. von Falkenhausen, J. Howard-Johnston, R. Jenkins, E. Kitzinger, W. Loerke, G. Moravcsik, J. Munitiz, B. Narkiss, G. Ostrogorsky, P. Schmidt, G. Soulis, A.-M. Talbot, and P. Topping.

A special tribute is due to Professor Cyril Mango who, among other things, collated *Metochion 410.* Our greatest debt is to Professors Leendert Westerink and Ihor Ševčenko whom we heartily thank for reading the work and for making numerous improvements. To Professor Ševčenko too must go a large share of the credit for deciphering the scholia presented in Appendix I.

We are also indebted to several members of the Dumbarton Oaks staff: to the Librarians for help in acquiring microfilms, to Mary Lou Masey for some expert typing, to Dr. Timothy Miller who guided the work through printing with a scholar's care, and to Associate Editor Julia Warner who over the years spent many hours on the welfare of the *Synodicon Vetus.**

John Parker
York

John Duffy
Washington

* The work of the editors was carried out in relay and the division of labor was roughly as follows: the Greek text was established by Parker (prior to his leaving the field of Byzantine studies for other areas of interest); it was slightly revised by Duffy in the light of more complete manuscript evidence. Duffy prepared the translation, notes, introduction, and indices, making considerable use of commentary matter collected by his partner.

TABLE OF CONTENTS

DUMBARTON OAKS TEXTS

V

THE
SYNODICON VETUS

INTRODUCTION

1. GENERAL

The *Synodicon Vetus,* as this work is now usually known,[1] is an anonymous, brief history of Church councils which claims in its title to describe all synods,[2] orthodox and heretical, from the time of the Apostles to the so-called Eighth Ecumenical Council (869–70). The text, however, goes beyond this, giving in four short chapters (163–66) the headlines of Patriarch Photius' career from 870 to 886, the year of his final deposition.

We have no way of knowing precisely when the *Synodicon Vetus* (hereafter *SV*) was compiled, though the text itself yields the date after which it must have been written, for the last event mentioned is the accession of Stephen I to the patriarchal throne of Constantinople, which took place in 886 or 887.[3] No such help is available to fix the second terminus, which can only be approached by guesswork. Still, the following points may be worth some consideration: (a) If the work were written after 920, we could reasonably have expected a description of the important synod of that year which issued the Tome of Union.[4] (b) Assuming that the title is original, the *SV* should end at the Eighth Council; however, the writer, an undisguised partisan of Ignatius, is not content to stop there but brings the story of Photius' career to its conclusion and shows that the Patriarch's second departure from the throne was nothing less than he deserved.[5] The author's strong anti-Photian bias, then, may indicate that the work was composed not long after 887 and before the Byzantine Church became embroiled in the affair of Leo VI's four marriages. More than this cannot be said with any usefulness.

[1] In the past it has often been referred to as the *Libellus Synodicus,* the title given by Johannes Pappus in his translation for the first edition, Strasbourg, 1601.

[2] With a few exceptions (e.g., chaps. 133–36), the only non-Eastern synods mentioned after the fourth century are those held by popes in Rome.

[3] See G. Ostrogorsky, *History of the Byzantine State* (New Jersey, 1969), 241 note 1.

[4] This synod is the last included in an anonymous council treatise in *Sinaiticus gr. 482* (311^{r}–324^{v}).

[5] Note the last words of chap. 165 and the connecting γάρ of chap. 166 line 1; cf. F. Dvornik, "The Patriarch Photius in the Light of Recent Research," in *Berichte zum XI. Internationalen Byzantinisten-Kongress* (Munich, 1958), 39 note 134.

In his search for synods the writer looked into a variety of works, not all of which can be identified. On the whole, however, it is possible to detect the sources which helped him most and which form the backbone of his account, as will be seen in the following brief analysis.

Chapters 1–32 describe the synods of the first three centuries, and as might be expected, most of the information comes from the *Church History* of Eusebius; in a few cases treatises against heretics may have been consulted, such as those by Irenaeus and Epiphanius. Working from the meager details in Eusebius, the compiler composes a kind of catalog, giving for each council the number of participants, the place where it convened, its leader or leaders, and the problem discussed along with the decision issued.

Arianism, the Council of Nicaea, and the synods provoked by the Nicene Creed until the end of the fourth century are dealt with in chapters 33–82. The main works used are the *Church History* of Theodoret and the *Epitome* of Theodore Anagnostes' *Tripartite History*,[6] though in places the writer may have taken material directly from Socrates and Sozomen. There are also occasional similarities to Photius' *Homilies* XV and XVI on Arianism, which, if they do not show familiarity with the sermons, at least suggest use of a common source.

Chapters 83–126 list the synods of the fifth and sixth centuries concerning Nestorianism, Monophysitism, and the Council of Chalcedon. Here the writer has drawn heavily from the *Epitome* of Theodore Anagnostes' *Church History* and, to a lesser extent, from Theophanes' *Chronographia*. There are indications that he may have looked at the letters of Leo I (chap. 90), the forged letters to Peter the Fuller (chaps. 106–7), the *Vita Sabae* of Cyril of Scythopolis (chaps. 113 ff.), and the *Vita Eutychii* by Eustratius (chaps. 124–25). But often we cannot know who is providing the information. For example, the account in chapter 118 of an abortive synod at Thessalonica is not to be found in any extant text.

For much of the Monothelete heresy (chaps. 128–46) the account in *SV* is close to the one given by Theophanes and both appear to be relying on the same source.[7] The description of the Sixth Ecumenical Council (chap. 141), on the other hand, is quite similar to the version in the *Chronicle* of George the Monk.

For the period of Iconoclasm (chaps. 147–56) the compiler has used the *Chronographia* of Theophanes and other, mostly unknown, texts. The account of the Seventh Council (chap. 152) is close to that of George the Monk; still, it could also have come directly from the Acts. The story of the presbyter Joseph's mediation during the revolt of Bardanes Turcus (chap. 153) seems to

[6] Edited by G. C. Hansen, GCS 54 (Berlin, 1971).

[7] The two texts have been compared by J. L. van Dieten, *Geschichte der Patriarchen von Sergios I bis Johannes VI* (Amsterdam, 1972), 179–218; see also chap. 128 note 154 *infra*.

be confirmed elsewhere only by a *Vita* of Theodore the Studite,[8] though there is no direct connection between the two texts.

Chapters 157–62 deal with the synods which took place during the patriarchates of Ignatius and Photius, and here there are striking similarities in content and expression between *SV* and the *Vita Ignatii* of Nicetas David the Paphlagonian. This relationship, if determined exactly, might have provided some evidence for dating, but none of the three possible explanations can be ruled out entirely. On the whole, however, the chances are good that both were drawing from a common source, for the fact that *SV* (chap. 159 lines 12–13) is able to give precise data on the length of Ignatius' patriarchate (see note 206) reduces the possibility that the compiler was using the biographer, and a comparison of the otherwise scanty descriptions of *SV* with the detailed account of the *Vita Ignatii* makes it difficult to think that Nicetas was relying on our author for any of his information.[9]

The last four chapters relate very briefly the main events of Photius' career after the council of 869–70 until his abdication in 886; these share some points of resemblance with the so-called anti-Photian collection.[10]

Within the genre of council histories *SV* is a unique work. All the other accounts deal either with the ecumenical councils exclusively or with these councils and a small number of synods which issued canons.[11] By contrast, *SV* tries to identify and describe every synod up to the ninth century. The compiler has tackled his task with enthusiasm and has succeeded in ferreting out from an array of texts nearly every council to be found in Greek sources. In his zeal, however, he has come up with some which are at least doubtful (e.g., chaps. 94, 99, 103, 105) and others almost surely imaginary (e.g., chaps. 16, 91, 114, 116); moreover, it was not beyond him to fabricate a few details.[12] As will be clear from the notes accompanying this edition, the writer was anything but a careful researcher, and though in places his sources, or copyists, may be at fault, he himself must be held responsible for most of those numerous errors which in the past have prevented scholars from treating the *SV* as a historical document above suspicion.

[8] PG, 99, 265D.

[9] Furthermore, a comparison of *SV* chap. 158 lines 4–5 (καὶ συναθροίσας πονηρευομένων . . . συνέδριον) and *Vita Ignatii,* PG, 105, 513D (τὴν κατ' αὐτὸν ἐκκλησίαν τῶν πονηρευομένων συναγαγών) with the words of Ps. 21:17 (συναγωγὴ πονηρευομένων) and Ps. 25:5 (ἐκκλησίαν πονηρευομένων) shows that the *Vita Ignatii* is echoing the psalmist more exactly and is, therefore, more likely to be independent of the *Synodicon.* This idea is due to Professor Ševčenko.

[10] Mansi, XVI, 424 sqq.

[11] The most recent and fullest discussion to date of these texts can be found in J. A. Munitiz, "Synoptic Greek Accounts of the Seventh Council," *REB,* 32 (1974), 147–86, esp. 150–53. It is to be noted that, for the ecumenical councils, *SV* appears not to have used any of the known shorter treatises. (Postscript: see now also H. J. Sieben, *Die Konzilsidee der alten Kirche* [Paderborn etc., 1979], chap. 5, esp. pp. 372–77).

[12] See text, notes 11 and 16.

2. THE MANUSCRIPTS

The extant manuscripts of *SV* fall into two main groups, designated *g* and *b*, representing two branches of the tradition.

Those in group *g* are the following:

D = Andros, Μονὴ τῆς Ἁγίας 88, XIII–XIV cent., paper, 417 folios. S. P. Lampros, Κατάλογος τῶν ἐν τῇ κατὰ τὴν Ἄνδρον Μονῇ τῆς Ἁγίας κωδίκων, in Φιλολογικὸς Σύλλογος Παρνασσός, Ἐπετηρίς 2 (1898), 211–20.

The codex consists mainly of canonical works, including the canons of various councils. *SV* appears on fols. 339ᵛ–357ʳ, and the complete treatise of 166 chapters has been copied. The scribe was reasonably careful, stayed close to his exemplar, and, with a few exceptions (e.g., chaps. 47 line 1; 115 line 8), did not deliberately change the text.

L = *Laurentianus Plut. 86,6;* XII cent., vellum, 112 folios. A. M. Bandini, *Catalogus codicum graecorum bibliothecae Laurentianae,* III (Florence, 1770), 293–96.

The MS is composed of theological works including pieces by Nemesius of Emesa, Anastasius of Antioch, and John Damascene. *SV* (fols. 57ʳ–72ʳ) ends at chapter 162 line 19 ἅπαντες; in other words it stops with the Eighth Ecumenical Council, the last synod mentioned in the title, and omits the final four chapters.

G = Μετόχιον τοῦ Παναγίου Τάφου 410, XIII cent., paper, 35 folios. A. Papadopoulos-Kerameus, Ἱεροσολυμιτικὴ Βιβλιοθήκη, IV (Saint Petersburg, 1899), 365–67.

In addition to part of a nomocanonical collection the present MS (the survivor of a larger book) preserves three synodical documents: (a) a treatise of the well-known type on the seven ecumenical councils[13] which begins with the words Χρὴ γινώσκειν πάντα χριστιανὸν κτλ., (b) a short chronology of synods (*Inc.* Ἰστέον ὅτι ἡ ἔκθεσις τῶν συνόδων οὐ γέγονε κατὰ τὴν τάξιν κτλ.), (c) *SV* (fols. 5ʳ–13ᵛ), the same length as L, ending at the Eighth Council. Due to the loss of leaves, however, the greater part of chapter 162 (lines 3 κυρίου–19 ἅπαντες) has not been preserved in the original hand but was supplied in the margins much later (nineteenth century?).

The parent of LG represents, in a sense, a revision of the text by someone who saw fit to exclude the last four chapters; to omit or combine chapters (80–81, 124, 126–27); and to add, leave out, substitute, or transpose words and phrases throughout the treatise. Among the many changes are several sound emendations which have been accepted, as in the following

[13] Cf. Munitiz, *op. cit.*, 153.

chapter-line references: 29, 2; 30, 2; 32, 2; 44, 1; 45, 3; 48, 11; 49, 5; 52, 8; 59, 7; 60, 3; 89, 2; 133, 1; 139, 2.

Group *b* consists of the following:

A = *Sinaiticus gr. 482 (1117),* XIV cent., paper, 372 folios. V. Beneševič, *Catalogus codicum manuscriptorum graecorum qui in monasterio Sanctae Catharinae in Monte Sina asservantur,* I (Saint Petersburg, 1911), 266–93; v. J. Darrouzès, in *REB,* 24 (1966), 25–39.

A large MS by various hands whose first half is occupied by the nomocanon, the collection of canons, and the commentaries of Theodore Balsamon, while the second contains a miscellany of texts including imperial *novellae,* canonical and synodical decisions, patriarchal letters, and three treatises on synods: Germanus, *De haeresibus et synodis* (257^{v}–264^{v}); an anonymous description of ecumenical and selected local councils (311^{r}–324^{v}); *SV,* all 166 chapters (357^{v}–365^{r}). The section of the MS from 340^{r} to 372^{v} was badly damaged by moisture, and a later hand (designated A^{s} in the apparatus) went over many of the affected parts in an effort, often unsuccessful, to retrace the obliterated writing. Toward the end of *SV* the original scribe (364^{r}–365^{r}), pressed for time or space, began to compress his writing and even resorted to pruning words (cf. the following chapter-line references: 152, 9; 154, 10; 155, 2; 157, 1 and 4–5; 160, 5; 162, 2 and 3; 165, 1 and 4). Otherwise he stayed close to the exemplar and made few copying errors.

C = *Vaticanus gr. 419,* XIV cent., paper, 330 folios. R. Devreesse, *Codices Vaticani graeci,* II (Vatican City, 1937), 131–34.

The greater part of the MS (fols. 9–312) consists of homilies by Saint Basil, along with extracts from Anastasius of Sinai and John Chrysostom, while the last two quaternions (fols. 313^{r}–330^{r}) contain three short works written by two different hands: (1) a fourteenth-century *Notitia metropolitarum et archiepiscoporum throno Constantinopolitano subditorum* (313^{r}–313^{v}); (2) Nicephorus Chumnus against Plotinus on the soul (315^{r}–326^{r}); (3) *SV* (326^{v}–330^{r}). Only part of the text, however, is preserved, since the MS comes to a halt at chapter 47 line 1 ἐπίσκοπος. The abrupt ending can be explained by Devreesse's claim that folios 325–30 had been left blank originally and were later filled by a contemporary hand. As far as it goes, this is a straightforward copy of *SV* with some scribal errors.

E = Andros, Μονὴ τῆς Παναχράντου 7, XIV cent., paper, 134 folios. S. P. Lampros, Κατάλογοι κωδίκων ἐν ταῖς μοναῖς τῆς νήσου Ἄνδρου Ἁγίῳ Νικολάῳ καὶ Παναχράντῳ, in Φιλολογικὸς Σύλλογος Παρνασσός, Ἐπετηρίς 3 (1899), 27–30.

The codex is a varied mixture of canonical, legal, theological, and epistolary texts, including pieces by Pope Leo I, John Pediasimos, and Michael Attaleiates. *SV,* all 166 chapters, appears on fols. 40^{r}–60^{r}, framed on three sides by extracts from Epiphanius' *Panarion* written in the same hand. The copyist was not content with the text of *SV* as he found it; he tried his hand at emendation (e.g., chapter-line references 35, 3; 37, 11; 53, 3; 145, 1), left out or added words (e.g., chapter-line references 8, 3; 12, 3; 13, 3; 42, 1; 73, 7; 93, 1), and incorporated material from the treatise on ecumenical and local councils which is also found in MS A.[14] It is a document which, after the description of the Seventh Council, adds the Synodicon of Orthodoxy (with prologue) and the Tome of Union (with prologue). From it E grafted on to *SV* part of its title, substituted its longer account of Paul of Samosata for chapter 27, borrowed some phrases (chaps. 77 line 15; 84 line 3), and added at the end as an extra chapter the Tome of Union preceded by its prologue.

The rest of group *b* consists of a dozen copies in Western libraries, mainly of the sixteenth century, and designated VOTMNSBWXYZU; six of these (BWXYZU) are not independent.

V = *Vaticanus gr. 1137,* XIV cent. (?), paper, 74 folios.

A codex by various hands containing a medley of items including the following: extracts from the Mosaic Law, apostolic canons, some letters, a fragment on the Patriarchs Tarasius and Nicephorus, a treatise on marriages, and *SV* (fols. 51ʳ–74ᵛ). The last page of the MS has suffered damage, and the text of *SV* ends at chapter 162 line 16 ὅροις, showing that at least one leaf has been lost.[15]

O = Oxford, *Bodl. Laudianus* 26, late XVI cent. (*ca.* 1584), paper, 465 folios. H. O. Coxe, *Catalogus codicum manuscriptorum Bibliothecae Bodleianae,* I (Oxford, 1853), 507–8.

A MS written by Andreas Darmarios with these contents: On the Eighth Ecumenical Council (879–80) "from the discourse of (John) Beccos"; the acts of the Eighth Council; *SV* (fols. 122ʳ–196ʳ); sermons of Athanasius and his disputation against Arius; the dialogue of Basil and Gregory the Theologian and their exposition of the orthodox faith. The text of *SV* ends abruptly at chapter 160 line 9 διέπεμψε.[16]

T = Turin, *Biblioteca Nazionale cod. gr. 119,* late XVI cent., paper, 43 folios. J. Pasini; *Codices manuscripti bibliothecae regii Taurinensis Athenaei,* I (Turin, 1749), 227–28.

[14] Folios 311ʳ–324ʳ; see p. xvii *supra.*

[15] The existence of this copy and *Sinaiticus gr. 1726* (U) was kindly pointed out to us by Father Joseph Munitiz.

[16] With the scribe's comment ἐξίτηλον ἦν τὸ τέλος ὑπὸ τῆς ἀρχαιότ(ητος). Such remarks by Darmarios, well known for his tricks, should be taken with a pinch of salt. This is almost certainly the copy sold to J. Pappus; see p. xxii *infra.*

A small codex by Darmarios.[17] Contents: a short explanation of the names given to the books of the Pentateuch and of the Hebrew words in the Books of Kings (1–3^{v}); *SV* (4^{r}–32^{v}); rhetorical prolegomena of John Doxopater (35–43). The text of *SV* ends, without comment, at the same place as O (chap. 160 line 9).

MNS are three further codices by Darmarios in each of which *SV* stops short at chapter 159 line 17 καθαίρεσιν.

M = Munich, *Monacensis gr. 245,* A.D. 1571, paper, 43 folios. J. Hardt, *Catalogus codicum manuscriptorum graecorum bibliothecae regiae Bavaricae,* III (Munich, 1806), 23–24.

It consists of *SV* alone and was written, according to the subscription, in March 1571 at Valladolid.

N = Madrid, *Biblioteca Nacional 0.88* (Iriarte, 94), A.D. 1571, paper, 45 folios. E. Miller, *Bibliothèque royale de Madrid. Catalogue des manuscrits grecs* (*Supplément au Catalogue d'Iriarte*), in *Notices et extraits des manuscrits de la Bibliothèque Nationale,* XXXI, pt. 2 (Paris, 1886), 106–7.

Darmarios tells us in the subscription of this codex, which contains nothing more than *SV,* that he finished the copy in Madrid on 9 April 1571. This time, however, he decided to give *SV* an author, inserting after the title (1^{r}) ὑπὸ γεωργίου χωματιανοῦ.

S = Saragossa, *Cabildo de la Santa Iglesia Mayor del Pilar 1310,* late XVI cent., paper, approx. 40 folios. A. Martin, *Rapport sur une mission en Espagne et en Portugal. Notices sommaires des manuscrits grecs d'Espagne et de Portugal,* in *Nouvelles archives des missions scientifiques et littéraires,* 2 (Paris, 1892), 217.

Besides the *Synodicon Vetus* the MS has a short treatise entitled Περὶ τοῦ ἀρχηγοῦ τῶν Σαρακηνῶν Μωαμὲτ τοῦ Ἐμουχαμέτ. Here a different candidate for the author of *SV* is produced: πονηθέντι (sic) τῷ κυρίῳ μανουήλῳ τῷ ἀκροπολίτῃ (1^{r}).[18]

B = Rome, *Vallicellianus 133 (X),* XVII cent. (before 1648), paper. E. Martini, *Catalogo di manoscritti greci esistenti nelle biblioteche italiane,* II (Milan, 1902), 202; H. Laemmer, *De Leonis Allatii codicibus qui Romae in bibliotheca Vallicellana asservantur* (Freiburg im Breisgau, 1864), 7–10.

Written by Leo Allatius, this MS contains, apart from *SV* (fols. 1–16), apostolic canons and canons of certain ecumenical and local councils (in Greek and Latin). The text of *SV,* ending at chapter 162 line 19 ἅπαντες, is

[17] He twice asserts ownership: κτῆμα ἀνδρέου δαρμαρίου καὶ τῶν φίλων (fol. 4^{r}) and ἀνδρέου δαρμαρίου κτῆμα· εὖ τάδ' ἐγράφετο (fol. 32^{v}).

[18] It was not possible to study this copy in detail because of almost illegible photographs.

copied directly from V. In the margins Allatius has noted several variant readings, most of them taken from a close relative of LG (if not from L itself), which also provided him with the final lines of chapter 162, missing in V; the remaining variants are from the edition of Pappus.[19]

W = Turin, *Biblioteca Nazionale cod. gr. 366,* late XVI cent., paper, 248 folios. J. Pasini, *Codices manuscripti bibliothecae regii Taurinensis Athenaei,* I (Turin, 1749), 382–83.

Contents: extracts from Church Fathers on the Song of Songs; homilies of Gregory of Nyssa on the eight beatitudes; a treatise of Saint Maximus; *SV* (fols. 180–206); a short treatise on synods; a fragment of Pseudo-George Codinus, *De officiis*. This copy of *SV,* giving 160 chapters, was made directly from T.[20]

XYZ are copies by the sixteenth-century scribe Camillus Venetus, which are now preserved in three Ambrosian manuscripts. X is an immediate copy of W, Y is from X, and Z from Y.

X = Milan, *Ambrosianus gr. 899* (*C 259 inf.*), paper, 357 folios. A. Martini and D. Bassi, *Catalogus codicum graecorum bibliothecae Ambrosianae,* II (Milan, 1906), 1003–8. *SV* appears on fols. 1^{r}–23^{r}.

Y = *Ambros. gr. 704* (*Q 121 sup.*), paper, 323 folios. Martini and Bassi (*op. cit.*), 811–12. *SV* is written on fols. 81^{r}–102^{r}.

Z = *Ambros. gr. 723* (*R 115 sup.*), paper, 230 folios. Martini and Bassi (*op. cit.*), 835–36. *SV* on fols. 57^{r}–78^{v}.

U = *Sinaiticus gr. 1726,* XVII cent., paper, 222 folios. Beneševič, *op. cit.* (p. xvii *supra*), III, 170.

An immediate copy of Z by someone who wrote a number of his own corrections in the margins of the exemplar.

Sometime between the tenth and thirteenth centuries[21] an anonymous scholar revised *SV* and issued a new version (SV^2) which now survives in two manuscripts: Athos, *Dionysiou 120,* XIV cent., fols. 645^{v}–660^{v} and Vienna,

[19] In *De Octava Synodo Photiana* (Rome, 1662), 19 and 33–34, Allatius printed his text of chaps. 161–62 (not known to Pappus) together with a Latin version. It was from here that they were restored to *SV* by J. Hardouin, *Acta Conciliorum,* V (Paris, 1714), 1547–50 and thence to J. A. Fabricius and G. C. Harles, *Bibliotheca Graeca,* XII (Hamburg, 1809), 419–20 (having already appeared in the first edition of Fabricius [Hamburg, 1705–28], vol. XI).

[20] Besides reproducing its peculiar readings, the scribe copied even the marginal note of Darmarios: ἀνδρέου δαρμαρίου κτῆμα· εὖ τάδ' ἐγράφετο. See note 17 *supra.*

[21] The council treatise in *Sinaiticus gr. 482,* which incorporates several chapters of SV^2, may date from the twelfth century. At any rate, another MS of this work, *Escorialensis X.II.10,* was written in the thirteenth century.

cod. juridicus gr. 13, XVI cent., fols. 38ʳ–71ᵛ. The text is often rewritten, with obvious corrections made, wording changed, passages added and left out, and the whole comes to an en at Orthodoxy Sunday (843). Much of the new material has been taken from the works of Theodore Anagnostes, Theophanes, George the Monk, and Joseph Genesios (or a common source). The manuscript of *SV* used by the redactor was closely related to the parent of LG, though he may have had access to more than one copy; since some of the readings agree with branch *b* of the tradition. Of the several emendations by this writer the following have been adopted: μερικὴ (34, 1), σηπεδόνα (34, 4), ὃς (56, 5), ἐπινεύσει (64, 10), ἀϑῷον (102, 3). The text of the second recension, not previously published, is given in Appendix II.

The overall relationship of the manuscripts may be depicted by the following stemma:

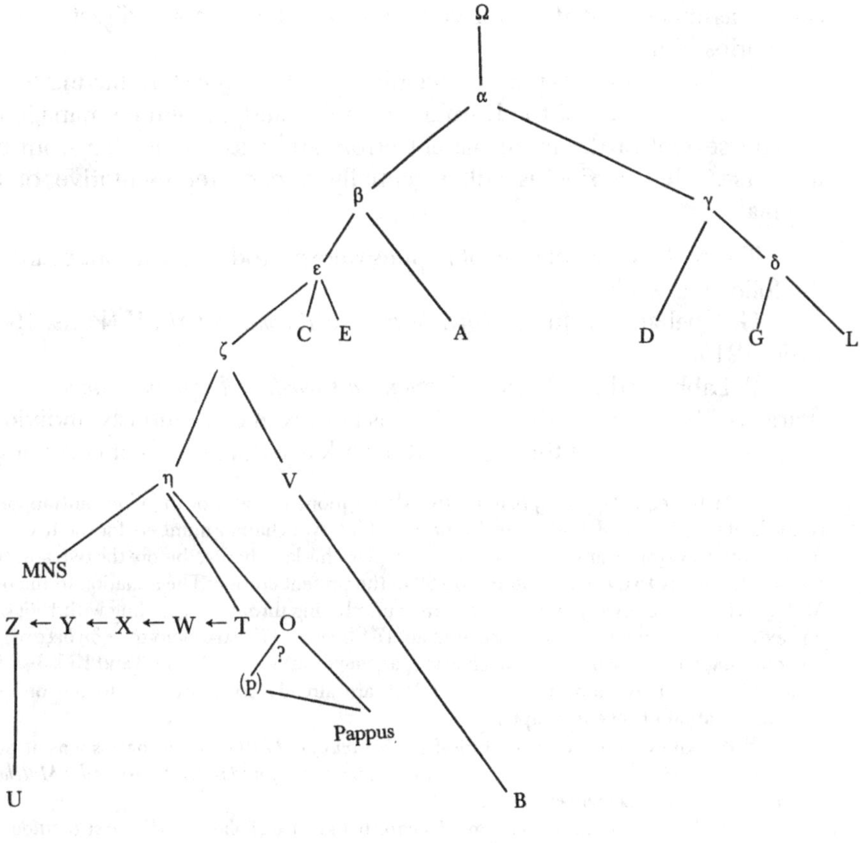

3. THE FIRST EDITION

AND ITS REPRODUCTIONS

In 1601 Johannes Pappus (1549–1610), a Lutheran theologian of Strasbourg, published the first edition of the text, chapters 1–160,[22] with a Latin translation and notes. In the preface he tells us that when, some sixteen years before,[23] Andreas Darmarios had brought several Greek manuscripts for sale, he purchased from him the *Synodicon, mole quidem exiguum, sed rerum, quae in eo tractantur, satis magnum.* This copy can hardly be any other than that now bound in the Bodleian *Laudianus 26* (O), for, aside from those which Pappus chose to correct, all its peculiarities reappear in the printed text, including the scribe's final remark, ἐξίτηλον ἦν τὸ τέλος ὑπὸ τῆς ἀρχαιότητος. But Pappus states several times in his notes that he consulted a second manuscript (p), which can no longer be traced. Since, however, it failed to provide him with readings more correct than those of O, it can be assumed that it was a very close relative, if not a direct copy by Darmarios himself.

For his edition Pappus was handicapped from the start, having to rely on the least accurate of the Darmarian copies, and, though he managed to remedy several of the more blatant errors and was seldom led from bad to worse,[24] his version is still essentially a poor representative of the original.

The text and translation of Pappus were reproduced without change in the following works:

G. Voel and H. Justel, *Bibliotheca juris canonici veteris,* II (Paris, 1661), 1166–1215.

P. Labbe and G. Cossart, *Sacrosancta Concilia ad regiam editionem exacta* (Paris, 1671, etc.). Here the text of *SV* is not given continuously, individual chapters being printed throughout the work according to their chronology.

[22] At the end Pappus appended two descriptions in Latin of the Constantinopolitan councils of 869–70 and 879–80. He also provided his own chapter numbers for the text, none being given by O (or by any of the Darmarian copies); his last chapter, before the two additions just mentioned, is 151, corresponding to 160 in the present edition. The situation in the other MSS is as follows: Only A preserves the correct numbering throughout, ending with 166; E has one extra, since it counts the sentence at chap. 154 lines 1–2 (Τελευτήσαντος – διεδέξατο) as a separate chapter; D is behind by two chapters, having omitted 129, 2–130, 3 and 135, 3–136, 3; L and G, when they come to a close at 162, are already six short, due to the omission and combination of several chapters.

[23] We know from the subscription to *Parisinus gr. 2150* that Darmarios was at Strasbourg in July 1584; see M. Vogel and V. Gardthausen, *Die griechischen Schreiber des Mittelalters und der Renaissance* (Leipzig, 1909), 21.

[24] With the notable exception of chap. 6 line 3 ὡς] ὦο OTMN: ὀκτακοσίους καὶ ἑβδομηκόντα Pappus.

J. Hardouin, *Acta Conciliorum,* V (Paris, 1714), 1491–1550 (with occasional marginal notes, some of them attributed to J. B. Cotelier). Chapters 161–62 have been added from L. Allatius, *De Octava Synodo Photiana* (Rome, 1662).[25]

J. D. Mansi, *Sacrorum Conciliorum nova et amplissima collectio,* 31 vols. (Florence, 1758–98). The chapters are scattered in several volumes, as in Labbe and Cossart.

J. A. Fabricius and G. C. Harles, *Bibliotheca Graeca,* XII (Hamburg, 1809), 360–421. Chapters 161–62 have been borrowed from Hardouin.

4. PRESENT EDITION

All the known extant manuscripts have been examined on photographs or microfilms. With few exceptions the readings peculiar to the Darmarian tradition (and Pappus) have not been noted nor have obvious errors in any one of the other copies.

In a text where many of the errors must be original it is often difficult to decide when corrections should be accepted against the consensus of the manuscripts. For this edition it has seemed best, in general, to admit them only in those cases where the faulty reading can without much effort be explained as a copyist's mistake existing already in the common archetype of *g* and *b*. When it comes to a choice between *g* and *b* for variants of equal value, the version of *g* has been preferred as a rule, since it has preserved overall a more accurate text.

It is worth noting that the writer strictly observes the rhythmical *clausula* "law," according to which there should be an even number of unaccented syllables between the last two accents preceding a pause.[26] The intervals in this text consist of either two or four syllables, and in addition there is a preference for phrase endings of the "double dactyl" type (΄˘˘΄˘˘).[27] The law can sometimes assist in deciding between variants,[28] and adherence to it accounts for strained expressions[29] and unusual word order.[30]

[25] See note 19 *supra.*

[26] Professor Westerink drew attention to this feature of *SV.* See S. Skimina, *État actuel des études sur le rythme de la prose grecque II,* EUS Supplementa, 11 (Lwów, 1930). A recent discussion of the rhythmical *clausula* in a Byzantine author will be found in R. Maisano, "La clausola ritmica nella prosa di Niceforo Basilace," *Jahrbuch der Österreichischen Byzantinistik,* 25 (1976), 87–104.

[27] The "double dactyl" rhythm, however, seldom occurs in the first 32 chapters.

[28] E.g., chap. 107 line 2.

[29] Chap. 117 line 3: ἔτι βιοῦντος ἐπάρατα.

[30] E.g., chap. 147 lines 6–7.

BIBLIOGRAPHY

Acta Archelai, ed. C. H. Beeson, GCS, 16 (Leipzig, 1906)

Alexander the Monk, *Laudatio in Apostolum Barnabam,* PG, 87(3), cols. 4087–4106

Alexander, P. J., *The Patriarch Nicephorus of Constantinople* (Oxford, 1958)

Allatius, L., *De Octava Synodo Photiana* (Rome, 1662)

Athanasius, *Apologia de fuga sua,* ed. H.-G. Opitz (Berlin, 1938)

–, *Epistula ad Afros,* PG, 26, cols. 1029–1048

–, *Epistula ad Rufinianum,* PG, 26, cols. 1179–1182

Bandini, A. M., *Catalogus codicum graecorum Bibliothecae Laurentianae,* III (Florence, 1770)

Beck, H.-G., *Kirche und theologische Literatur im byzantinischen Reich* (Munich, 1959)

Beneševič, V., *Catalogus codicum manuscriptorum graecorum qui in monasterio Sanctae Catharinae in Monte Sina asservantur,* I (St. Petersburg, 1911)

Cedrenus, *Historiarum Compendium,* ed. I. Bekker, 2 vols. (Bonn, 1838–39)

Corpus paroemiographorum graecorum, eds. E. L. a Leutsch and F. G. Schneidewin, 2 vols. (Göttingen, 1839–51)

Cotelier, J. B., *Ecclesiae graecae monumenta,* 3 vols. (Paris, 1677–86)

Coxe, H. O., *Catalogus codicum manuscriptorum Bibliothecae Bodleianae,* I (Oxford, 1853)

Cross, F. L., "History and Fiction in the African Canons," *Journal of Theological Studies,* 12 (1961), 227–47

Cyril of Alexandria, *Commentaria in Matthaeum,* PG, 72, cols. 365–474

Cyril of Scythopolis, *Vita Sabae,* ed. E. Schwartz (Leipzig, 1939)

Devreesse, R. *Codices Vaticani graeci,* II (Vatican City, 1937)

Dieten, J. L. van, *Geschichte der Patriarchen von Sergios I bis Johannes VI* (Amsterdam, 1972)

Dvornik, F., *The Photian Schism* (Cambridge, 1948)

–, "The Patriarch Photius in the Light of Recent Research," *Berichte zum XI Internationalen Byzantinisten-Kongress* (Munich, 1958)

Epiphanius, *Panarion,* ed. K. Holl, 3 vols., GCS, 25, 31, 37 (Leipzig, 1915–33)

Eusebius, *Kirchengeschichte,* ed. E. Schwartz, 2 vols., GCS, 9_1 and 9_2 (Leipzig, 1903–8)

Evagrius, *Ecclesiastical History,* eds. J. Bidez and L. Parmentier (London, 1898)

Fabricius, J. A. and Harles, G. C., *Bibliotheca Graeca XII* (Hamburg, 1809)

Genesius, *Reges,* ed. C. Lachmann (Bonn, 1834)

Georgius Monachus, *Chronicon,* ed. C. de Boor, 2 vols, (Leipzig, 1904)

Germanus, *De haeresibus et synodis,* PG, 98, cols. 39–88

Gregorius Nazianzenus, *Orationes,* PG, 35–36

Grumel, V., *Les Regestes des Actes du Patriarcat de Constantinople,* I, fasc. I, 2nd ed. (Paris, 1972); I, fasc. II (Socii Assumptionistae Chalcedonenses, 1936)

Hardouin, J., *Acta Conciliorum,* V (Paris, 1714)

Hardt, J., *Catalogus codicum manuscriptorum graecorum Bibliothecae Regiae Bavaricae,* III (Munich, 1806)

Hefele, K. J. and Leclercq, H., *Histoire des Conciles,* 8 vols. (Paris, 1907-52)

Hunger, H. (–Kresten, O.), *Katalog der griechischen Handschriften der Österreichischen Nationalbibliothek,* vol. I, pt. 2 (Vienna, 1969)

Irenaeus, *Adversus Haereses,* ed. W. W. Harvey, 2 vols. (Cambridge, 1857)

Janin, R., *La géographie ecclésiastique de l'empire byzantin.* III, *Les églises et les monastères,* 2nd ed. (Paris, 1969)
Labbe, P. and Cossart, G., *Sacrosancta concilia ad regiam editionem exacta,* 16 vols. (Paris, 1671–72)
Laemmer, H., *De Leonis Allatii codicibus qui Romae in Bibliotheca Vallicellana asservantur* (Freiburg im Breisgau, 1864)
Lampe, G. W. H., *A Patristic Greek Lexicon* (Oxford, 1961)
Lampros, S. P., *Catalogue of the Greek Manuscripts on Mount Athos,* I (Cambridge, 1895)
–, Κατάλογος τῶν ἐν τῇ κατὰ τὴν Ἄνδρον Μονῇ τῆς Ἁγίας κωδίκων, in Φιλολογικὸς Σύλλογος Παρνασσός, Ἐπετηρίς 2 (1898)
–, Κατάλογοι κωδίκων ἐν ταῖς μοναῖς τῆς νήσου Ἄνδρου Ἁγίῳ Νικολάῳ καὶ Παναχράντῳ, in Φιλολογικὸς Σύλλογος Παρνασσός, Ἐπετηρίς 3 (1899)
Liber Pontificalis, ed. L. Duchesne, 3 vols. (Paris, 1886–1957)
Maisano, R., "La clausola ritmica nella prosa di Niceforo Basilace," *JÖB,* 25 (1976), 87–104
Malalas, *Chronographia,* ed. L. Dindorf (Bonn, 1831)
Mango, C., *The Homilies of Photius* (Cambridge, Mass., 1958)
–, "The Liquidation of Iconoclasm," in *Iconoclasm,* eds. A. Bryer and J. Herrin (Birmingham, 1977)
Mansi, J. D., *Sacrorum Conciliorum nova et amplissima collectio,* 31 vols. (Florence, 1758–98)
Martin, A., *Rapport sur une mission en Espagne et en Portugal. Notices sommaires des manuscrits grecs d'Espagne et de Portugal,* in *Nouvelles Archives des Missions Scientifiques et Littéraires,* II (Paris, 1892)
Martin, E. J., *A History of the Iconoclastic Controversy* (London, 1930)
Martini, A. and Bassi, D., *Catalogus codicum graecorum Bibliothecae Ambrosianae,* II (Milan, 1906)
Martini, E., *Catalogo di manoscritti greci esistenti nelle biblioteche Italiane,* II (Milan, 1902)
Miller, E., *Bibliothèque Royale de Madrid. Catalogue des manuscrits grecs* (*Supplément au Catalogue d'Iriarte*), in *Notices et extraits des manuscrits de la Bibliothèque Nationale,* XXXI, pt. 2 (Paris, 1886)
Munitiz, J. A., "Synoptic Greek Accounts of the Seventh Council," *REB,* 32 (1974), 147–86
Nicephorus, *Opuscula historica,* ed. C. de Boor (Leipzig, 1880)
Nicephorus Callistus Xanthopulus, *Ecclesiastica Historia,* PG, 146–47
Ostrogorsky, G., *History of the Byzantine State,* trans. J. Hussey (New Brunswick, N.J., 1969)
–, "Les Débuts de la Querelle des Images," in *Mélanges Charles Diehl,* I (Paris, 1931)
Owsepian, G., *Die Entstehungsgeschichte des Monotheletismus* (Leipzig, 1897)
Papadopoulos-Kerameus, A., Ἱεροσολυμιτικὴ Βιβλιοθήκη, IV (St. Petersburg, 1899)
Pappus, J. (ed.), *Libellus Synodicus* (Argentorati, 1601)
Parthey, G., *Hieroclis Synecdemus et notitiae graecae Episcopatuum* (Berlin, 1866)
Pasini, J., *Codices manuscripti Bibliothecae Regii Taurinensis Athenaei,* I (Turin, 1749)
Philostorgius, *Kirchengeschichte,* ed. J. Bidez, GCS, 21 (Leipzig, 1913)
Photius, *Bibliotheca,* ed. R. Henry (Paris, 1959–)
–, *Homilies,* ed. B. Laourdas (Thessalonica, 1959)
–, *Contra Manichaeos,* PG, 102, cols. 15–264
Psaltes, S., *Grammatik der byzantinischen Chroniken* (Göttingen, 1913)
Rhalles, G. A. and Potles, M., Σύνταγμα τῶν θείων καὶ ἱερῶν κανόνων, 6 vols. (Athens, 1852–59)
Schwartz, E., *Publizistische Sammlungen zum Acacianischen Schisma* (Munich, 1934)
Skimina, S., *État actuel des études sur le rythme de la prose grecque,* II, EUS Supplementa 11 (Lwów, 1930)
Socrates, *Ecclesiastica Historia,* ed. R. Hussey, 2 vols. (Oxford, 1853)
Sozomenus, *Kirchengeschichte,* ed. J. Bidez, GCS, 50 (Berlin, 1960)
Stein, E., *Histoire du Bas-Empire,* 2 vols. (Paris, 1949–59)
Symeon Magister, *Chronographia,* PG, 109, cols. 663–822

Synopsis Chronica, ed. K. N. Sathas, in Μεσαιωνικὴ Βιβλιοθήκη, VII (Venice–Paris, 1894)
Theodoret, *Kirchengeschichte,* ed. L. Parmentier, GCS, 19 (Berlin, 1954)
Theodoros Anagnostes, *Kirchengeschichte,* ed. G. C. Hansen, GCS, 54 (Berlin, 1971)
Theophanes, *Chronographia,* ed. C. de Boor (Leipzig, 1883)
Vita Euthymii, ed. P. Karlin-Hayter (Brussels, 1970)
Vita Eutychii, PG, 86(2), cols. 2273–2390
Vita Ignatii, PG, 105, cols. 487–574
Vita Leonis Armeni, PG, 108, cols. 1009–1038
Vita Nicephori, in *Nicephori opuscula historica,* ed. C. de Boor (Leipzig, 1880)
Vita Nicetae, ActaSS, April, I, pp. XVIII–XXVII
Vita Nicolai Studitae, PG, 105, cols. 863–926
Vita Sabae, v. Cyril of Scythopolis
Vita Theodori Studitae, PG, 99, cols. 234–328
Voel, G. and Justel, H., *Bibliotheca juris canonici veteris,* II (Paris, 1661)
Vogel, M. and Gardthausen, V., *Die griechischen Schreiber des Mittelalters und der Renaissance* (Leipzig, 1909)
Zonaras, *Epitomae Historiarum Libri XIII–XVIII,* ed. T. Büttner-Wobst (Bonn, 1897)

LIST OF ABBREVIATIONS

ACO: *Acta Conciliorum Oecumenicorum,* ed. E. Schwartz, 4 vols. (Berlin, 1914–40)
ActaSS: *Acta Sanctorum Bollandiana*
Athanasius, *Apologia de fuga sua*: Athanasius, *Apologia de fuga sua,* ed. H.-G. Opitz (Berlin, 1938)
Cyril of Scythopolis: Cyril of Scythopolis, *Vita Sabae,* ed. E. Schwartz (Leipzig, 1939)
DHGE: *Dictionnaire d'Histoire et de Géographie Ecclésiastique*
DTC: *Dictionnaire de Théologie Catholique*
Dvornik, *Photian Schism*: F. Dvornik, *The Photian Schism* (Cambridge, 1948)
Dvornik, "Recent Research": F. Dvornik, "The Patriarch Photius in the Light of Recent Research," *Berichte zum XI. Internationalen Byzantinisten-Kongress* (Munich, 1958)
Epit. Th. A.: *Theodorus Anagnostes,* ed. G. C. Hansen, GCS, 54 (Berlin, 1971)
Eusebius: Eusebius, *Kirchengeschichte,* ed. E. Schwartz, II, pts. 1 and 2, GCS, 9_1 and 9_2 (Leipzig, 1903–8)
GCS: Die griechischen christlichen Schriftsteller der ersten [drei] Jahrhunderte
Grumel, *Regestes*: V. Grumel, *Les Regestes des Actes du Patriarcat de Constantinople,* I, fasc. 1, 2nd ed. (Paris, 1972); I, fasc. 2 (Socii Assumptionistae Chalcedonenses, 1936)
HL: K. L. Hefele and H. Leclercq, *Histoire des Conciles,* 8 vols. (Paris, 1907-52)
JÖB: *Jahrbuch der Österreichischen Byzantinistik*
Mansi: J. D. Mansi, *Sacrorum Conciliorum nova et amplissima collectio,* 31 vols. (Florence and Venice, 1759–98)
Nicephorus: Nicephorus, *Opuscula historica,* ed. C. de Boor (Leipzig, 1880)
PG: Patrologia Graeca, ed. J.-P. Migne (Paris, 1857–66)
Philostorgius: Philostorgius, *Kirchengeschichte,* ed. J. Bidez, GCS, 21 (Leipzig, 1913)
Photius, *Hom.*: Photius, *Homilies,* ed. B. Laourdas (Thessalonica, 1959)
RE: *Pauly's Real-Encyclopädie der classischen Altertumswissenschaft*
REB: *Revue des Etudes Byzantines*
Socrates: Socrates, *Ecclesiastica Historia,* ed. R. Hussey, 2 vols. (Oxford, 1853)
Sozomen: Sozomenus, *Kirchengeschichte,* ed. J. Bidez, GCS, 50 (Berlin, 1960)
SV: *Synodicon Vetus*
Theodoret: Theodoretus, *Kirchengeschichte,* ed. L. Parmentier, GCS, 19 (Leipzig, 1911)
Theophanes: Theophanes, *Chronographia,* ed. C. de Boor (Leipzig, 1883)
Vita Ignatii: Nicetas David, *Vita Ignatii,* PG, 105, cols. 487–574

LIST OF SIGNS

Sign		Manuscript	Subgroup	Group
D	=	Andros, Μονὴ τῆς Ἁγίας 88, s. XIII–XIV		*g*
L	=	Laurentianus Plut. 86,6, s. XII		*g*
G	=	Μετόχιον τοῦ Παναγίου Τάφου 410, s. XIII		*g*
A	=	Sinaiticus gr. 482 (1117), s. XIV		*b*
C	=	Vaticanus gr. 419, s. XIV		*b*
E	=	Andros, Μονὴ τῆς Παναχράντου 7, s. XIV		*b*
V	=	Vaticanus gr. 1137, s. XIV (?)	*z*	*b*
O	=	Bodleianus Laud. 26, s. XVI	*z*	*b*
T	=	Taurinensis gr. 119, s. XVI	*z*	*b*
M	=	Monacensis gr. 245, A.D. 1571	*z*	*b*
N	=	Matritensis gr. 0.88, A.D. 1571	*z*	*b*

g = consensus DLG
b = consensus A(C)E*z*
z = consensus VOTMN
SV^2 = editio altera (Athos, Dionysiou 120; Vindob., cod. jurid. gr. 13)
A^s = manus scripturam evanidam in A superscribens
Pa = ed. princeps J. Pappi (Argentorati, 1601)
HL = K. J. Hefele and H. Leclercq, *Histoire des Conciles* (Paris, 1907–52)

TEXT and TRANSLATION

ΣΥΝΟΔΙΚΟΝ ΕΝ ΕΠΙΤΟΜΗ ΑΠΑΣΑΣ ΑΠΟ ΤΩΝ ΑΓΙΩΝ ΚΑΙ ΠΑΝΕΥΦΗΜΩΝ ΤΟΥ ΧΡΙΣΤΟΥ ΑΠΟΣΤΟΛΩΝ ΓΕΓΟΝΥΙΑΣ ΟΡΘΟΔΟΞΟΥΣ ΤΕ ΚΑΙ ΑΙΡΕΤΙΚΑΣ ΠΕΡΙΕΧΟΝ ΣΥΝΟΔΟΥΣ ΜΕΧΡΙ ΤΗΣ ΟΓΔΟΗΣ ΟΙΚΟΥΜΕΝΙΚΗΣ ΜΕΓΑΛΗΣ ΑΓΙΑΣ ΣΥΝΟΔΟΥ

1.

Σύνοδος θεία καὶ ἱερὰ συναθροισθεῖσα ἐν Ἱεροσολύμοις ὑπὸ τῶν θεοδιδάκτων ἀποστόλων καὶ μυσταγωγῶν πρεσβυτέρων καὶ τῶν σὺν αὐτοῖς ἀδελφῶν, κατὰ τῶν ἐπιχειρησάντων πιστῶν Φαρισαίων κρατύνειν τὴν ἐν σαρκὶ περιτομὴν καὶ τηρεῖν τὰ νόμιμα ἔθη μετὰ τὸ εἰσδέξασθαι καθάπαξ τοὺς πιστοὺς τὴν ἐν πνεύματι καὶ ἀληθείᾳ προσκύνησιν καὶ λατρείαν, καὶ χάριτι καὶ νόμῳ δουλεύειν οἱονεὶ δυσὶ κυρίοις· ὅπερ ἀπεῖπεν ὁ τῶν ὑπὲρ νοῦν ἀγαθῶν πάροχος καὶ τῆς κατάρας τοῦ νόμου ἐξαγορασάμενος ἡμᾶς Χριστὸς ὁ θεὸς ἡμῶν. Μετὰ γοῦν τὴν τῶν ἀποστόλων σύνοδον ἐξανέστη Σίμων ὁ μάγος καὶ Κήρινθος· οὓς ἀπεκήρυξαν οἱ κορυφαῖοι τῶν ἀποστόλων, τὸν μὲν Σίμωνα Πέτρος, τὸν Κήρινθον ὁ τῆς θεολογίας ἐπώνυμος Ἰωάννης. Μετὰ τούτους ἐξανέστη Οὐαλεντῖνος, Σεκοῦνδος, Μαρκίων, Βασιλείδης, Σατορνῖνος, Καρποκράτης, Αἰβίων, Ἑρμογένης, Ἀλέξανδρος ὁ χαλκεύς, καὶ οἱ σὺν αὐτοῖς.

1: HL I_1, 2; 125 (A.D. 49) ‖ 8: Act. 15:5 ‖ 10: Joann. 4:24 ‖ 10–11: Matt. 6:24; Luc. 16:13 ‖ 12: Gal. 3:13

1: 2 ἁπάσας τὰς LG ‖ καὶ – 3 Χριστοῦ om. *z* ‖ 3 τοῦ Χριστοῦ om. LG ‖ 4 τε om. LG*z* ‖ περιέχον post Συνοδικὸν transp. *b* ‖ 4 μέχρι – 5 συνόδου] aliter E (vide praef. p. xviii) ‖ 5 οἰκ. – συνόδου] τῆς ἐπὶ τοῦ φωτίου καὶ τῇ τοῦ πάπα ἰωάννου ἑνώσει *z* ‖ ἁγίας] om. D καὶ ἁγίας ὄντως LG ‖ ante tit. τῶν σχισματικῶν τὴν πλάνην ἅπασαν βλέπε, | τὸ κρεῖττον αἱροῦ τῶν παρεγγράπτων λόγων add. C ‖ 7 ante ἀποστόλων add. ἁγίων *b* ‖ 9 ἅπαξ LG ‖ 14 τῶν ἀποστόλων om. LG ‖ μὲν om. *z* ‖ 17 ὁ χαλκεύς om. LG

SYNODICON VETUS

A synodicon containing in brief form all synods, both orthodox and heretical, which took place from the time of the holy and blessed apostles of Christ to the Eighth Great Holy Ecumenical Council.

1. A divine and sacred synod was convened in Jerusalem by the divinely instructed apostles and teaching elders and the brethren with them, against those converted Pharisees who, after the believers had fully accepted adoration and worship in spirit and truth, tried to retain circumcision in the flesh and to keep the customs of the Law, and thus to serve like two masters both Grace and the Law. This was prohibited by Christ our God, who provides us with goods beyond comprehension and who redeemed us from the curse of the Law. After the synod of the apostles, Simon Magus and Cerinthus broke away and were condemned by the chief apostles, Simon by Peter and Cerinthus by John who is called the Theologian. Subsequent rebels were Valentinus, Secundus, Marcion, Basilides, Saturninus, Carpocrates, Ebion,[1] Hermogenes, Alexander the Smith, and their followers.

[1] The writer is following the tradition which makes an individual, Ebion, the founder of the Ebionite sect. There was, however, no such person; see *DHGE, s.v.* Ébionites.

2.

Σύνοδος θεία καὶ ἱερὰ τοπικὴ δυοκαίδεκα ἐπισκόπων συναθροισθεῖσα ἐν Λουγδούνῳ μητροπόλει τῆς Γαλλίας παρὰ τὸν Ῥοδανὸν ποταμὸν ὑπὸ Εἰρηναίου τοῦ ἱερομάρτυρος, ἐπισκόπου τῆς αὐτῆς πόλεως, κατὰ τῶν προγεγραμμένων αἱρετικῶν.

3.

Σύνοδος θεία καὶ ἱερὰ τοπικὴ ἐν Ῥώμῃ δώδεκα ἐπισκόπων ὑπὸ Τελεσφόρου ἱερομάρτυρος τοῦ ταύτης πάπα συναθροισθεῖσα, κατὰ Θεοδότου ⟨τοῦ⟩ σκυτέως Βυζαντίου καὶ τῶν αὐτοῦ μαθητῶν, ὃς εἰς ἄκρον σοφίας ἐληλακὼς καὶ ἐν τῷ διωγμῷ ἐπιθύσας καὶ ἐξαρνησάμενος τὸν Χριστόν, ἐσχάτως ὑπὸ τῶν πιστῶν ὀνειδιζόμενος καὶ μὴ φέρων τὴν αἰσχύνην, εἰπεῖν ἐτόλμησεν ὁ ἀνόσιος, «ἐγὼ θεὸν οὐκ ἐξηρνησάμην, ἀλλὰ ψιλὸν ἄνθρωπον.»

4.

Σύνοδος θεία καὶ ἱερὰ τοπικὴ ἐν Ῥώμῃ, συναθροισθεῖσα ὑπὸ τοῦ μακαριωτάτου Ἀνικήτου τοῦ ταύτης πάπα καὶ Πολυκάρπου ἱερομάρτυρος ἐπισκόπου Σμύρνης καὶ ἑτέρων ἐπισκόπων δέκα, κατὰ τῶν Ἰουδαϊκῶς τῇ τεσσαρεσκαιδεκάτῃ τῆς σελήνης ἑορταζόντων τὸ θεῖον πάσχα καὶ ἑτέροις ἔθεσι καὶ τύποις τοῦτο ἐκτελούντων· ὁρίσασα τὸ μὲν φρικτὸν καὶ σωτήριον πάθος τοῦ δεσπότου ἡμῶν Ἰησοῦ Χριστοῦ καὶ θεοῦ τῇ ἁγίᾳ παρασκευῇ μυστικῶς ἐπιτελεῖν, τὴν δὲ ζωαρχικὴν ἀνάστασιν αὐτῇ τῇ μεγάλῃ καὶ περιδόξῳ κυριακῇ ἐκ παντὸς τρόπου ἄγειν.

3: HL I_1, 151–52 ‖ 2–7: cf. Epiph., *Panarion haer.*, II, 317–18; Euseb. V.27–28

4: HL I_1, 151–52 ‖ cf. Euseb. V.24, 16–17 (Iren., ed. Harvey, II, 476)

2: 1 post συναθροισθεῖσα add. θεοῦ χάριτι LG ‖ 3 τοῦ om. *z*

3: 3 τοῦ LG: om. D*b* ‖ σκυτέως om. LG ‖ καὶ om. *z* ‖ τῶν nos: τοῦ codd. ‖ μαθητοῦ codd. praeter E ‖ 5 καὶ om. LG ‖ 6 ἐξωμοσάμην LG ἀρνησάμην *z* ‖ ἀλλὰ] ἀλλ' ἢ LG ‖ ψιλὸν post ἄνθρωπον transp. *z*

4: 1 θεία καὶ ἱερὰ post Ῥώμῃ transp. LG ‖ 4 ἑορταζόντας A*z* (praeter O) ‖ 5 τόποις LG (κείμενον τύποις mg. G) ‖ ἐκτελοῦντας LG ‖ 6 καὶ θεοῦ om. LG ‖ 7 ἐκτελεῖν *z* ‖ 7–8 περιδόξω καὶ μεγάλῃ *b*

2. A divine and sacred local synod of twelve bishops was convened in Lyons, the metropolis of Gaul on the river Rhone, by the bishop of that city, Irenaeus the hieromartyr, against the aforementioned heretics.[2]

3. A divine and sacred local synod of twelve bishops was convened in Rome by the Pope of that city, Telesphorus[3] the hieromartyr, against Theodotus the Cobbler of Byzantium and his disciples. Having reached the pinnacle of wisdom, this man offered sacrifice during the persecution and denied Christ; when finally he was reproached by the faithful and could not bear the shame, the unholy wretch had the nerve to say, "It was not God that I denied, but a mere man."

4. A divine and sacred local synod[4] was convened in Rome by the most blessed Anicetus, the bishop of that city, and Polycarp the hieromartyr, bishop of Smyrna, and ten other bishops, against those who were celebrating the divine Passover according to Jewish custom on the fourteenth of the month and were performing it with other traditions and rites. It decreed the solemn commemoration on Holy Friday of the awesome and saving Passion of our Lord and God Jesus Christ and the mandatory celebration of the life-giving Resurrection on that great and glorious (Easter) Sunday.

[2] Our text is the only witness for a synod at Lyons, and it is possible that the idea was suggested by Irenaeus' well-known treatise *Adversus omnes haereses,* a detailed refutation of Gnosticism. With the exception of Hermogenes and Alexander, all of the heretics named in chap. 1 are among the Gnostics discussed by Irenaeus in his work.

[3] Theodotus was in fact condemned by Pope Victor (189–98); see HL, I_1, 132 and 152.

[4] The authenticity of this synod is suspect; see HL, I_1, 152.

5.

Σύνοδος θεία καὶ ἱερὰ τοπικὴ ἐν Ἱεραπόλει τῆς Ἀσίας συναθροισθεῖσα ὑπὸ Ἀπολιναρίου, τοῦ ταύτης ὁσιωτάτου ἐπισκόπου, καὶ ἑτέρων εἴκοσι καὶ ἓξ ἐπισκόπων, ἀποκηρύξασά τε καὶ ἐκκόψασα Μοντανὸν καὶ Μαξιμίλλαν τοὺς ψευδοπροφήτας, οἳ καὶ βλασφήμως ἤτοι δαιμονιῶντες, καθώς φησιν ὁ αὐτὸς πατήρ, «τὸν βίον κατέστρεψαν.» Σὺν αὐτοῖς δὲ κατέκρινε καὶ Θεόδοτον τὸν σκυτέα.

6.

Σύνοδος θεία καὶ ἱερὰ μερικὴ συναθροισθεῖσα ὑπὸ τοῦ ὁσιωτάτου ἐπισκόπου Ἀχελῶν Σωτᾶ καὶ ἑτέρων δώδεκα ἐπισκόπων, ἥτις ἐλέγξασα ἀπεκήρυξε τὸν σκυτέα Θεόδοτον καὶ Μοντανὸν σὺν Μαξιμίλλῃ, ὡς ὀκτὼ αἰῶνας δογματίζοντας καὶ πνεῦμα ἅγιον ἑαυτοὺς εἶναι ἐπιφημίζοντας.

7.

Σύνοδος θεία καὶ ἱερὰ τοπικὴ ἐν Γαλατίᾳ συναθροισθεῖσα ὑπὸ τῶν ὁμολογητῶν, ἀποκηρύξασα Μοντανὸν καὶ Μαξιμίλλαν, ἧς ὁ ὅρος πρὸς τοὺς ἐν Ἀσίᾳ πιστοὺς διέβη.

5: HL I_1, 127–32 (saec. II) ‖ 3–6: Euseb. V.16, 13–15 (Apolinarius)

6: HL I_1, 127–32 (saec. II) ‖ 2: cf. Euseb. V.19, 3; cf. Germ., *De haeresibus et synodis,* PG, 98, 44A

7: HL I_1, 152–53 ‖ Euseb. V.3, 4

6: 1 post μερικὴ add. ἐν ἀσία LG ‖ 2 ἀχιλῶν *b* id est Ἀγχιάλου ‖ Σωτᾶ om. LG ‖ 3 τὸν σκυτέα om. LG ‖ 4 εἶναι ἑαυτοὺς LG

7: 1 Γαλατίᾳ AEVD: γαλλία LGCOTMN, A supra lin., V mg.

5. A divine and sacred local synod was convened at Hierapolis in Asia by that city's most saintly Bishop Apollinarius and twenty-six other bishops. It denounced and excommunicated the false prophets Montanus and Maximilla who, acting blasphemously or being seized by a devil, "ended their lives," as the same father[5] puts it. Along with these the synod also condemned Theodotus the Cobbler.[6]

6. A divine and sacred particular synod was convened by Sotas, the most saintly bishop of Achelos,[7] and twelve other bishops. It refuted and condemned Theodotus the Cobbler and Montanus, along with Maximilla, for preaching eight aeons and proclaiming themselves to be the Holy Spirit.[8]

7. A divine and sacred local synod was convened in Gaul[9] by the confessors. It condemned Montanus and Maximilla, and its decision was passed on to the faithful in Asia.[10]

[5] I.e., Apollinarius, as quoted by Eusebius V.16,13.

[6] For the possibility that the Cobbler has been confused with another Theodotus, see HL, I_1, 132.

[7] That is, Anchialus in Thrace. Ἀχελός and Ἀχελῶς are later forms of Ἀγχίαλος; cf. S. Psaltes, *Grammatik der byzantinischen Chroniken* (Göttingen, 1913), 3–4; 146. The form in our text is probably meant to be genitive singular.

[8] For conflicting views on the value of the information in the present chapter, see HL, I_1, 128–30, 129 note 1. The latest attack on the credibility of *SV* in chaps. 5–7 has been made by Joseph A. Fischer, "Die antimontanistischen Synoden des 2./3. Jahrhunderts," *Annuarium Historiae Conciliorum*, 6 (1974), 241–73; *SV* is discussed on pp. 250–56. Fischer's doubts are entirely justified.

[9] On Γαλατία as the equivalent of Γαλλία, see *RE*, *s.v.* Galatia.

[10] The chapter is based on Eusebius (V.3,4), who speaks not of a synod, but of letters written by the confessors; see HL, I_1, 152–53.

8.

Σύνοδος ἀφελής, ἀνεξέταστος, μερικὴ ἐν Ἐφέσῳ μητροπόλει τῆς Ἀσίας συναθροισθεῖσα ὑπὸ Πολυκράτους τοῦ ὁσιωτάτου αὐτῆς ἐπισκόπου, ἀξιοῦσα καὶ ὁρίζουσα ἅπαντας ὥστε ἐν τῇ τεσσαρεσκαιδεκάτῃ τῆς σελήνης Ἰουδαιοπρεπῶς ἄγειν τὸ μυστικὸν πάσχα, ὡς τοῦτο ἀνέκαθεν παραλαβοῦσα βεβαιούμενον παρὰ Τιμοθέου καὶ Φιλίππου τῶν ἀποστόλων. Βίκτωρ οὖν, ὁ τῆς Ῥωμαίων ἐκκλησίας ἁγιώτατος πάπας, ἀκοινωνησίαν στέλλει Πολυκράτει τῷ ταύτης προϊσταμένῳ. Οὐ μόνον δὲ τοῦτο, ἀλλὰ καὶ συνοδικῶς τὰ περὶ τῆς τοιαύτης ἑορτῆς διεξέρχεται, καὶ σὺν αὐτῷ ἐν πλείσταις ἐπαρχίαις καὶ μέρεσι τῆς γῆς σύνοδοι συγκροτοῦνται καὶ συμφώνως ὁρίζουσι. Ταῦτα δὲ Κομόδου βασιλεύοντος γέγονε.

9.

Σύνοδος θεία καὶ ἱερὰ τοπικὴ ἐν Ῥώμῃ συναθροισθεῖσα ὑπὸ τοῦ μακαριωτάτου αὐτῆς πάπα Βίκτορος καὶ ἑτέρων ἐπισκόπων δεκατεσσάρων, ἀπαγορεύουσα Ἰουδαϊκῶς τελεῖν τῇ τεσσαρεσκαιδεκάτῃ τῆς σελήνης τὸ θεῖον καὶ μυστικὸν πάσχα, ἀλλ' ἐν μόνῃ τῇ μεγάλῃ καὶ ζωοδοτικῇ κυριακῇ.

10.

Σύνοδος θεία καὶ ἱερὰ τοπικὴ συναθροισθεῖσα ἐν Ἱεροσολύμοις ὑπὸ Ναρκίσσου τοῦ ταύτης τρισμακαρίστου ἀρχιεπισκόπου καὶ ἑτέρων ἐπισκόπων δεκατεσσάρων, ὑπὲρ τοῦ μυστικοῦ πάσχα ὁρίσασα κατὰ τοὺς ἁγιωτάτους Ἀνίκητον καὶ Βίκτορα.

8: HL I_1, 141; 151 (ca. 196) ‖ 1–5: Euseb. V.24, 1 sqq.; V.23, 1 ‖ 5–7: Euseb. V.24, 9 ‖ 7–9: Euseb. V.23, 2–3

9: HL I_1, 141; 150 (ca. 196) ‖ Euseb. V.23, 2–3

10: HL I_1, 141; 150 ‖ Euseb. V.23, 2–3

8: 2 πολυκάρπου *b* ‖ 3 ὥστε ἐν om. E ὡς ἂν LG ‖ 4 ἰουδαϊκῶς E ‖ 7 πολυκάρπω *b* ‖ τοῦτο om. LG ‖ 8 τῆς αὐτῆς *z*

9: 3 ἀπαγορεύσασα A*z*

10: 2 τρισμάκαρος *z* ‖ ἀρχιεπισκόπου] ἐπισκόπου A

8. A simple, uncritical particular synod[11] was convened at Ephesus, the metropolis of Asia, by Polycrates, the most saintly bishop of that city. It decreed and defined that all should celebrate the mystical Passover in the Jewish manner on the fourteenth of the month, this being a tradition originally instituted by the apostles Timothy and Philip. Victor, then, the most holy Pope of the Roman Church, sent an excommunication to Polycrates, the president of this synod. Not only that, but he also submitted the question of the feast to conciliar examination, and in conjunction with him synods were summoned in very many provinces and parts of the world, which ruled in agreement with him. These events took place during the reign of Commodus.

9. A divine and sacred local synod was convened in Rome by Victor, the most blessed Pope of that city, and fourteen other bishops. It decreed that the sacred and mystical Passover should not be celebrated in the Jewish manner on the fourteenth of the month, but only on the great life-giving (Easter) Sunday.

10. A divine and sacred local synod was convened in Jerusalem by Narcissus, that city's thrice-blessed archbishop, and fourteen other bishops. On the question of the mystical Passover it ruled in accordance with the most holy Anicetus and Victor.

[11] Chaps. 8–15, each describing a synod which ruled on the Easter question, must have been taken from Eusebius V.23–24. The only real difference is that *SV* gives the numbers of participating bishops; however, these can hardly be more than pure fiction.

11.

Σύνοδος θεία καὶ ἱερὰ τοπικὴ συναθροισθεῖσα ἐν Καισαρείᾳ τῆς Παλαιστίνης, Πύργου Στράτωνος παρά τισιν ἐκ παλαιοῦ καλουμένης, ὑπὸ Θεοφίλου τοῦ αὐτῆς ὁσιωτάτου ἐπισκόπου καὶ ἑτέρων δώδεκα ἐπισκόπων, ὑπὲρ τοῦ ἁγίου πάσχα ὁρίσασα ὡσαύτως.

12.

Σύνοδος θεία καὶ ἱερὰ τοπικὴ ἐν Λουγδούνῳ τῆς Γαλλίας συναθροισθεῖσα ὑπὸ Εἰρηναίου τοῦ ταύτης ἁγιωτάτου ἐπισκόπου καὶ ἑτέρων δέκα καὶ τριῶν ἐπισκόπων, ὁρίσασα ὑπὲρ τοῦ θείου καὶ μυστικοῦ πάσχα ὁμοίως.

13.

Σύνοδος θεία καὶ ἱερὰ τοπικὴ συναθροισθεῖσα ἐν Κορίνθῳ ὑπὸ Βακχυλλίδου τοῦ αὐτῆς ὁσιωτάτου ἀρχιεπισκόπου καὶ ἑτέρων δέκα καὶ ὀκτὼ ἐπισκόπων, ὁρίσασα περὶ τοῦ μακαρίου πάσχα ὡσαύτως.

11: HL I_1, 141; 150 ‖ Euseb. V.23, 2–4

12: HL I_1, 141; 151 ‖ Euseb. V.23, 2–4

13: HL I_1, 141 ‖ Euseb. V.23, 2–4

11: 2 παρὰ — καλουμένης om. *z* ‖ ἔκπαλαι LG ‖ καλουμένου C evan. A ‖ 3 ὁσιωτάτου] ἁγιωτάτου *z* ‖ ἀρχιεπισκόπου L ‖ ἐπισκόπων LG: ἀρχιεπισκόπων DACE om. *z*

12: 1 Λουγδούνῳ] κορίνθω (ex cap. 13, 1 ut vid.) C ‖ 3 ὑπὲρ] περὶ LG ‖ θείου καὶ μυστικοῦ om. E

13: 2 Βακχυλλίδου AC: -ιλλίδ- D*z* -υλίδ- E -ιλίδ- LG recte Βακχύλλου ‖ ἀρχιεπισκόπου] ἐπισκόπου LG ‖ 3 ὁρίσασα] δηλοῦσα A^s ‖ μακαρίου om. E

11. A divine and sacred local synod[12] was convened at Caesarea in Palestine, also called by some from ancient times Pyrgos Stratonos, by the most saintly bishop of that city, Theophilus, and twelve other bishops. It issued a similar decree concerning the holy Passover.

12. A divine and sacred local synod was convened at Lyons in Gaul by that city's most holy Bishop Irenaeus and thirteen other bishops, which decreed likewise concerning the divine and mystical Passover.

13. A divine and sacred local synod, convened in Corinth by the most saintly archbishop of that city, Bacchyllides,[13] and eighteen other bishops, issued the same decision on the blessed Passover.

[12] The author has misunderstood the text of Eusebius (V.23,3) and has made two synods (see previous chap.) from one which was jointly led by Theophilus of Caesarea and Narcissus of Jerusalem.

[13] Eusebius gives the form Bachyllus, which must be accepted as correct.

14.

Σύνοδος θεία καὶ ἱερὰ τοπικὴ ἐν Ἀσίᾳ συναθροισθεῖσα ὑπὸ Πλασμᾶ τοῦ ὁσίου καὶ ἑτέρων δεκατεσσάρων ἐπισκόπων, περὶ τοῦ ἁγίου πάσχα ὁρίσασα ὁμοίως.

15.

Σύνοδος θεία καὶ ἱερὰ τοπικὴ ἐν Ὀσροήνῃ, ὑφ' ἣν καὶ ἡ Ἔδεσσα καὶ ἡ τῶν Ἀδιαβηνῶν γῆ, συναθροισθεῖσα ὑπὸ δέκα καὶ ὀκτὼ ἐπισκόπων, ὧν ὁ προκαθεζόμενος οὐ δεδήλωται, περὶ τοῦ σεβασμίου πάσχα ὡσαύτως ὁρίσασα, Κομόδου βασιλεύοντος.

16.

Σύνοδος θεία καὶ ἱερὰ τοπικὴ ὀκτωκαίδεκα ἐπισκόπων συναθροισθεῖσα ἐν τῇ Μεσοποταμίᾳ ἐπὶ Κομόδου τοῦ βασιλέως, περὶ τοῦ ἁγίου πάσχα ὁμοίως ὁρίσασα, ἧσπερ οὐδεὶς τῶν ἱστορικῶν ἐδηλοποίησε τὸν προκαθεζόμενον.

14: HL I_1, 141; 151 ‖ Euseb. V.23, 2–4

15: HL I_1, 141; 151 ‖ Euseb. V.23, 2–4

14: 1 τοπικὴ om. LG ‖ recte Πάλμα ‖ 1–2 τοῦ ὁσίου om. LG

15: 1 τοπικὴ om. LG ‖ ὑφ' ἣν καὶ ἡ Ἔδεσσα CE*z*, *SV*[2]: τῇ καὶ ἐδέσσῃ *g*A ‖ 1–2 καὶ ἡ τῶν Ἀδιαβηνῶν (βυδιανῶν C) γῆ CE*z*, *SV*[2]: καὶ τῆς ἀβιδιανῶν γῆς (mg. γρ. ἀδιαβηνῶν) D καὶ τῆς ἀβυδιανῶν γῆς A καὶ τῶν ἀδιαβηνῶν γῆ LG ‖ 3 προκαθήμενος *z* ‖ σεβασμίου] θείου *z*

16: 1 post τοπικὴ add. ὑπὸ *z* ‖ 3 ἧς τὸν προκαθεζόμενον οὐδεὶς τῶν ἱστορικῶν ἐδήλωσεν *b*

14. A divine and sacred local synod, convened in Asia by the saintly Plasmas[14] and fourteen other bishops, decreed likewise on the holy Passover.

15. A divine and sacred local synod was convened in Osrhoene, which includes both Edessa and the Adiabene region, by eighteen bishops, whose president has not been recorded. It decreed in the same way on the sacred Passover. (The synod took place) during the reign of Commodus.

16. A divine and sacred local synod of eighteen bishops, convened in Mesopotamia[15] in the time of the Emperor Commodus, issued a similar decree on the holy Passover. None of the historians has recorded the name of its president.

[14] A mistake for Palmas.

[15] A synod of Mesopotamia is not mentioned by Eusebius, but we may not be too far off the mark in supposing that the writer took his cue from the phrase κατὰ τὴν Ὀσροηνὴν καὶ τὰς ἐκεῖσε πόλεις (V.23,4), Osrhoene being in fact between the two rivers.

17.

Σύνοδος θεία καὶ ἱερὰ τοπικὴ συναθροισθεῖσα ὑπὸ τοῦ πολυμαθοῦς Ὠριγένους ἐν Βόστρᾳ τῆς Ἀραβίας, ἥντινα Ἡσαΐας πάλαι Βόσθρον ὠνόμασεν ἐπώνυμον οὖσαν Βοσόρας τῆς μητρὸς τοῦ θεσπεσίου Ἰώβ, ἐπὶ διορθώσει τοῦ ἱεροσοφιστοῦ Βυρίλλου, τοῦ τῆς αὐτῆς πόλεως ἐπισκόπου, εἰς τὸ τοῦ σκυτέως Θεοδότου φρόνημα παρασυρέντος καὶ αὖθις παλινδρομήσαντος πρὸς τὴν ὀρθόδοξον πίστιν ταῖς παραινέσεσιν Ὠριγένους.

18.

Σύνοδος θεία καὶ ἱερὰ τοπικὴ ἐν Ἀραβίᾳ, συναθροισθεῖσα ὑπὸ Ὠριγένους καὶ ἑτέρων ἐπισκόπων δεκατεσσάρων, ἐπὶ τῇ τῶν πιστῶν διορθώσει ἔκ τινος λοιμώδους αἱρέσεως ἀναφανείσης συμφθείρεσθαι τὰς ψυχὰς τοῖς σώμασι καὶ πάλιν συνανίστασθαι οἰηθέντων, τῇ παραινέσει δὲ Ὠριγένους προκαθεζομένου τὴν πλάνην ἀποθεμένων.

19.

Σύνοδος θεία καὶ ἱερὰ τοπικὴ συναθροισθεῖσα ἐν Ῥώμῃ ὑπὸ Βίκτορος τοῦ ἁγιωτάτου πάπα καὶ ἑτέρων ἐπισκόπων δεκατεσσάρων, ἀποκηρύξασα Θεόδοτον, Αἰβίωνα καὶ Ἀρτέμονα, τοὺς οὐχ ἧττους Ἰουδαίων τῇ πίστει· οὗτοι γὰρ ἀρχηγοὶ γεγόνασι Παύλου τοῦ Σαμοσατέως καὶ Νεστορίου.

17: HL I_1, 162–63 (ca. 244) ‖ Euseb. VI.33, 1–3 ‖ 2: Is. 63:1 ‖ 3: Job 42:17^{c} (cf. I Mac. 5:26)

18: HL I_1, 163–64 (inter A.D. 244–49) ‖ Euseb. VI. 37

19: HL I_1, 151–52 ‖ cf. (?) Euseb. V.28, 1; 6

17: 2 ἀρραβίας *b* ‖ Βόσθρον D: βώσθρον LG βόθρον CE*z*, SV^2 evan. A Βοσὸρ Is. 63:1 ‖ 4 βηρυλλίου LG κυρίλλου *z* ‖ τοῦ σκυτέως om. LG ‖ 5 πρὸς] εἰς *b*

18: 1 ἀρραβία AC*z* ‖ 3 ante ἀναφανείσης add. καὶ ἐπὶ μήκιστον διαδοθείσης LG ‖ 5 ante Ὠριγένους add. τοῦ *z*

19: 1 τοπικὴ] μερικὴ LG ‖ ὑπὸ] ἐπὶ codd. praeter V ‖ 3 ἀρτέμωνα *g* ‖ ἧττον *b* ‖ 4 τοῦ om. LG

17. A divine and sacred local synod was convened by the very learned Origen at Bostra in Arabia—called Bosthros of old by Isaiah, after Bosora the mother of inspired Job—to discuss the correction of the hierosophist Byrillus, the bishop of that city, who, having been drawn into the error of Theodotus the Cobbler, was persuaded by Origen to return to the Orthodox faith.

18. A divine and sacred local synod was convened in Arabia by Origen and fourteen[16] other bishops concerning the correction of those faithful who, because of a pestilential heresy which had broken out, held that the soul perishes with the body and that both are resurrected together, but who had abandoned their error on the advice of Origen, the presiding bishop.

19. A divine and sacred local synod[17] was convened in Rome by Victor, the most holy Pope, and fourteen other bishops, which condemned Theodotus, Ebion, and Artemon, men no less (unorthodox) in belief than Jews, being the originators of the heresies of Paul of Samosata and Nestorius.

[16] The number of bishops given, of which Eusebius (VI.37) knows nothing, should be regarded with suspicion; cf. note 11 *supra*.

[17] HL (I_1, 151–52) include this and the following synod among doubtful or imaginary councils of the second century.

20.

Σύνοδος θεία καὶ ἱερὰ τοπικὴ συναθροισθεῖσα ἐν Ῥώμῃ ὑπὸ τοῦ μακαριωτάτου πάπα Βίκτορος, ἀποκηρύξασα Σαβέλλιον καὶ Νόητον, τοὺς ἐπὶ τῆς τρισυποστάτου θεότητος συναλοιφὴν καὶ συναίρεσιν ὑποστάσεων πρεσβεύοντας, καὶ Οὐαλεντῖνον, τὸν σὺν πολλοῖς ἀτοπήμασι καὶ οὐράνιον τὸ σῶμα τοῦ Χριστοῦ δογματίζοντα.

21.

Σύνοδος θεία καὶ ἱερὰ τοπικὴ πατέρων μακαρίων ἐν Ῥώμῃ συναθροισθεῖσα ὑπὸ Κορνηλίου τοῦ μακαριωτάτου πάπα καὶ ἑτέρων δεκαοκτὼ ἐπισκόπων, ἀποκηρύξασα Ναυάτον παγίδα τῶν μετανοεῖν ἑλομένων καὶ βρόχον γενόμενον.

22.

Σύνοδος θεία καὶ ἱερὰ τοπικὴ ἐν Καρθαγένῃ, τῇ Νεαπόλει τῆς Ἀφρικῆς καλουμένῃ, συναθροισθεῖσα ὑπὸ τοῦ ἱερομάρτυρος Κυπριανοῦ γενομένου αὐτῆς ἐπισκόπου καὶ ἑτέρων ὀγδοήκοντα τεσσάρων ἐπισκόπων, ἀποκηρύξασα Ναυάτον ὡς τὴν μετάνοιαν τοῖς πταίουσιν ἀποκλείοντα.

20: HL I_1, 151–52

21: HL I_1, 169 (ca. 251) ‖ cf. Euseb. VI.43, 2 sqq.

22: HL I_1, 167–68 (A.D. 251) ‖ cf. Euseb. VI.43, 3

20: 3 συναλειφὴν LG

21: 1 μακαρίων] ἑξήκοντα LG ‖ 3 ἑλομένων] βουλομένων *b*

22: 1 τῇ] τῇ καὶ LD ‖ 3 καὶ – ἐπισκόπων] om. LG καὶ ἑτέρων π′ ἐπισκόπων καὶ δ′ D ‖ 4 τὴν μετάνοιαν post πταίουσιν transp. LG ‖ κλείοντα *z*

20. A divine and sacred local synod[18] was convened in Rome by the most blessed Pope Victor, which condemned Sabellius and Noetus for claiming that in the Godhead of three Persons there is a confusion and contraction of the Persons. And (it denounced) Valentinus, who, in addition to many other irregularities, was teaching that Christ's body is heavenly.

21. A divine and sacred local synod of blessed fathers was convened in Rome by the most blessed Pope Cornelius and eighteen[19] other bishops, which condemned Nauatus,[20] who had become a snare and a trap for those who had chosen to repent.

22. A divine and sacred local synod was convened at Carthage, called Neapolis in Africa, by the hieromartyr Cyprian, who had become its bishop, and eighty-four[21] other bishops; it condemned Nauatus for refusing repentance to the lapsed.

[18] See previous note.

[19] The number in Eusebius is 60, which would explain the reading of manuscripts L and G.

[20] That is, Novatus or, as he is more commonly known, Novatian.

[21] Eusebius (VI.43,3) does not say how many bishops took part. However, the number 84 is also given by Zonaras in his comment on the Canons; see G. A. Rhalles and M. Potles, Σύνταγμα τῶν θείων καὶ ἱερῶν κανόνων (Athens, 1852–59), III, 1.

23.

Σύνοδος θεία καὶ ἱερὰ τοπικὴ ἐν Ἀντιοχείᾳ συναθροισθεῖσα ὑπὸ Δημητριανοῦ τοῦ ταύτης ἁγιωτάτου ἐπισκόπου, καθελοῦσα Ναυάτον ὡς ὄντα φιλαμαρτήμονα.

24.

Σύνοδος θεία καὶ ἱερὰ μερικὴ ἐν Ἀλεξανδρείᾳ συναθροισθεῖσα ὑπὸ τοῦ ὁμολογητοῦ Διονυσίου τοῦ ταύτης ἀρχιερέως, ἀποκηρύξασα Σαβέλλιον τὸν ἀντίθετον.

25.

Σύνοδος θεία καὶ ἱερὰ τοπικὴ συναθροισθεῖσα ἐν Ἀλεξανδρείᾳ ὑπὸ τοῦ προειρημένου Διονυσίου, καταδικάσασα καὶ ἀποκηρύξασα μετὰ θάνατον Νεποτιανὸν ἐπίσκοπον Αἰγύπτου καὶ Κήρινθον, ὡς διαβεβαιουμένους καὶ πλείστους ἐξαπατῶντας ἐν τῇ ἐπιγείῳ Ἱερουσαλὴμ τοῦ Χριστοῦ εἶναι τὴν βασιλείαν καὶ τὴν χιλιονταετηρίδα δογματίζοντας, καὶ πρὸς τούτοις βουθυσίας καὶ μηλοσφαγίας νομοθετοῦντας.

23: HL I_1, 169 (A.D. 252) ‖ Euseb. VI.46, 3–4

24: cf. (?) Euseb. VII.6, 1

25: HL I_1, 193–94 (ca. 255) ‖ cf. Euseb. VII.24, 1; 25, 2–3

24: 3 ἀντίθεον D ἄθεον LG cf. cap. 33, 10

25: 3 immo Νέπωτα ‖ κίρινθον LG κόρ- C ‖ 5 καὶ^{2} om. *z*

23. A divine and sacred local synod was convened at Antioch by Demetrianus, the most holy bishop of the city, and denounced Nauatus for his attachment to sin.

24. A divine and sacred particular synod[22] was convened in Alexandria by that city's archpriest Dionysius the confessor, which condemned the antithetical Sabellius.

25. A divine and sacred local synod was convened at Alexandria by the aforementioned Dionysius, which denounced and condemned posthumously Nepotianus,[23] the bishop of Egypt, and Cerinthus,[24] for leading many astray by proclaiming the kingdom of Christ to be in the earthly Jerusalem, for teaching Millenarianism, and also for prescribing the sacrifice of oxen and sheep.

[22] The idea of a synod would seem to depend on a letter of Dionysius, quoted by Eusebius (VII.6,1), in which the heresy of Sabellius is discussed.

[23] The correct form of the name is Nepos.

[24] For an account of the synod see HL, I_1, 193–94. The name of Cerinthus does not appear to have been raised during the discussions, and our writer has taken a certain liberty in his interpretation of Eusebius VII.25,1–3.

26.

Σύνοδος θεία καὶ ἱερὰ τοπικὴ ἐν Ῥώμῃ συναθροισθεῖσα ὑπὸ Στεφάνου τοῦ ἱερομάρτυρος πάπα, ἀποκηρύξασα τοὺς ἐν τῇ Ἀφρικῇ συνόδῳ παραλόγως ἐπικεχειρηκότας ἀναβαπτίζειν τοὺς ἐκ πάσης αἱρέσεως προσερχομένους τῇ καθολικῇ ἐκκλησίᾳ.

27.

Σύνοδος θεία καὶ ἱερὰ τοπικὴ ἐν Ἀντιοχείᾳ συναθροισθεῖσα, ἧς ἔξαρχος ἦν Ἕλενος ὁ Ταρσοῦ ἐπίσκοπος, Θεόδωρος ὁ Μοψουεστίας, ὁ θαυματουργὸς Γρηγόριος Καισαρείας Πόντου, Ἀνατόλιος Λαοδικείας ὁ ἱερόσοφος, οὗτινος οἱ περὶ τοῦ πάσχα κανόνες ἐμφέρονται, καὶ Μαλχίων Ἀντιοχείας ὁ ἱερώτατος· καθελοῦσα καὶ ἀποκηρύξασα Παῦλον τὸν Σαμοσατέα, μηδὲν ἧττον Ἄννα καὶ Καϊάφα περὶ Χριστοῦ πρεσβεύοντα.

28.

Σύνοδος θεία καὶ ἱερὰ μερικὴ συναθροισθεῖσα ἐν τῇ Μεσοποταμίᾳ ὑπὸ Ἀρχελάου ἐπισκόπου Καρχάρων καὶ Διοδώρου ἱερέως, κατὰ Μάνεντος τοῦ ἐρεβώδους καὶ Διοδωριάδου πρεσβυτέρου, ἥτις πολυτρόπως τούτους ἐλέγξασα ἀπεκήρυξεν.

26: HL I_1, 175–76 (ca. 256)

27: HL I_1, 199–200 (A.D. 269) ‖ 4 κανόνες ἐμφέρονται: cf. Euseb. VII.32, 13 sqq.

28: HL I_1, 205

27: ad hoc caput in E vide praef. xviii ‖ 2 Θεόδωρος — 3 Πόντου] θεόδωρος καὶ ὁ θαυματουργὸς γρηγόριος LG ‖ 4 ἐκφέρονται *z* ‖ 6 περὶ nos ἐπὶ codd.

28: 2 κατὰ] κατὰ τοῦ C

26. A divine and sacred local synod, convened in Rome by Pope Stephen the hieromartyr, condemned the bishops of the African synod who had unlawfully attempted (to establish) rebaptism for those returning to the Catholic Church from every heresy.

27. A divine and sacred local synod was convened in Antioch under the leadership of Bishop Helenus of Tarsus, Theodore of Mopsuestia,[25] Gregory Thaumaturgus of Caesarea in Pontus, Anatolius the hierosophist of Laodicea, whose canons on Easter are extant, and the most saintly Malchion of Antioch. It deposed and condemned Paul of Samosata for teaching about Christ no better than Annas and Caiaphas.

28. A divine and sacred particular synod[26] was convened in Mesopotamia by Archelaus, bishop of Carchar, and the priest Diodorus, against the infernal Manes and Diodoriades, a presbyter;[27] it roundly refuted and condemned these men.

[25] Theodore of Mopsuestia (*ca.* 350–428) is an obvious slip, already detected in the parent of manuscripts L and G; Eusebius (VII.30,2) does mention a Theodore among the participants, though without specifying his see.

[26] What, if anything, took place in Mesopotamia was more of a debate than a synod; see HL, I_1, 205 note 7.

[27] The text is certainly corrupt here, and the phrase καὶ Διοδωριάδου πρεσβυτέρου must be out of place. According to the account in the so-called *Acta Archelai,* ed. C. H. Beeson, GCS, 16 (Leipzig, 1906), 64, Manes had fled to the village of Diodori where his strange teaching began to worry a local devout presbyter named Diodorus, who reported the matter to Bishop Archelaus. Photius (*Contra Manichaeos* I, PG, 102, 44C), though following the tradition which calls him Trypho, also mentions the presbyter's piety: ἱερῷ μὲν ἀνδρί, τὸν δὲ τοῦ πρεσβυτέρου διέποντι βαθμόν. Hence, one might suppose that the text of *SV* has been corrupted from something like Διοδώρου τοῦ ἱεροῦ Διοδωριάδου πρεσβυτέρου. The redactor of SV^2 was already working along these lines, having written Διοδώρου ἱερέως Δωριάδος (sic) πρεσβυτέρου.

29.

Σύνοδος θεία καὶ ἱερὰ τοπικὴ συναθροισθεῖσα ἐν Ῥώμῃ ὑπὸ Μιλτιάδου τοῦ ἁγιωτάτου πάπα καὶ Μάρκου τοῦ ὁσιωτάτου κατὰ Κικιλλιανοῦ ἐπισκόπου Καρθαγένης, ἐπὶ τῇ ἑνώσει τῶν ἐπισκόπων. Ταύτην τοίνυν καὶ τὴν ἐν Ἀρελάτῳ προστάξας συγκροτηθῆναι ὁ μέγας βασιλεὺς Κωνσταντῖνος, ἀπάρας ἀπὸ τῶν ἑσπερίων ἐπὶ τὰ ἑῷα χωρία ἀμεταστρεπτὶ ἄπεισι, μὴ τεθεακὼς Σίλβεστρον ἐπίσκοπον ἐν τῷ θρόνῳ Ῥώμης, ἀλλ' ἐπὶ Μιλτιάδου ἀναχωρήσας· ὅθεν ἀληθέστερόν ἐστι κρατεῖν μὴ βεβαπτίσθαι αὐτὸν ἐν Ῥώμῃ, ἀλλ' ἐν Νικομηδείᾳ.

30.

Σύνοδος θεία καὶ ἱερὰ τοπικὴ ἐν Ἀρελάτῳ ὑπὸ Χρήστου συναθροισθεῖσα τοῦ ὁσιωτάτου ἐπισκόπου Συρακουσίων τῆς Σικελίας κατὰ τοῦ προειρημένου Κικιλλιανοῦ ἐπισκόπου Καρθαγένης, ἐπὶ τῇ ἑνώσει τῶν ἐπισκόπων.

31.

Σύνοδος θεία καὶ ἱερὰ τοπικὴ δυοκαίδεκα ἐπισκόπων συναθροισθεῖσα ἐν Ἀγκύρᾳ τῆς Γαλατίας, ἧς ἐξῆρχε Μάρκελλος τῆς αὐτῆς ἐπίσκοπος καὶ Ἀγρικόλαος Καισαρείας Καππαδοκίας, κανονικῶς τυπώσασα τὴν διόρθωσιν τῶν ἐν τῷ διωγμῷ παραπεσόντων.

29: HL I_1, 272–74 (A.D. 313) ‖ 1–3: cf. Euseb. X.5, 18–20 ‖ 7–8: cf. cap. 41, 1–3

30: HL I_1, 275–98 (A.D. 314) ‖ cf. Euseb. X.5, 21–24

31: HL I_1, 298–326 (A.D. 314)

29: 2 κατὰ LG: καὶ D*b* ‖ καικιλι- aut κεκιλι- codd. Euseb. (X.5, 18 sqq.) ‖ 3 ἐπὶ] καὶ LG ‖ 5 χωρεῖ L, SV^2 ‖ ἄπεισι om. LG ‖ 7 μὴ] μήτε LG

30: 1 Χρήστου L: χρηστοῦ GD χριστοῦ *b* ‖ 2 συρακουσῶν LG ‖ κατὰ LG: καὶ D*b* ‖ 3 Καρθαγένης om. *z* ‖ ἐπὶ τῇ] καὶ LG

31: 2 ἐξῆρχον LG ‖ 4 παραπεπτωκότων LG

29. A divine and sacred local synod was convened at Rome by the most holy Pope Miltiades and the most saintly Marcus against Cicillianus, the bishop of Carthage, on the union of the bishops. After the great Emperor Constantine ordered this synod and that of Arles to be summoned, he left the West and went off to the East without returning. So he did not see Bishop Sylvester on the throne of Rome, having left during the papacy of Miltiades. For this reason it is more accurate to maintain that he was not baptized in Rome, but in Nicomedia.[28]

30. A divine and sacred local synod was convened in Arles by Chrestus, the most saintly bishop of Syracuse in Sicily, against the aforementioned Cicillianus, bishop of Carthage, on the union of the bishops.

31. A divine and sacred local synod of twelve bishops was convened at Ancyra in Galatia under the leadership of Marcellus,[29] the bishop of that city, and Agricolaus of Caesarea in Cappadocia, which prescribed in canons the correction of those who had lapsed during the persecution.

[28] According to a well-known legend, which probably arose in the fifth century, Constantine was baptized and cured of leprosy by Pope Sylvester in Rome. The story may also have been the basis for the Donation of Constantine. (See *New Catholic Encyclopedia, s.v.* Constantine I). The compiler will have none of this.

[29] Other texts make Vitalis of Antioch the president; cf. Mansi, II, 527 note 1 and the treatise in *Sinaiticus gr. 482* (311^{r}). See also HL, I_1, 301.

32.

Σύνοδος θεία καὶ ἱερὰ τοπικὴ εἴκοσι καὶ τριῶν ἐπισκόπων, ὧν ἐξῆρχε Βιτάλιος, συναθροισθεῖσα ἐν <Νεο>καισαρείᾳ τοῦ Πόντου, περὶ τῶν ἐν τῷ διωγμῷ ἐπιθυσάντων ἢ ἐξομοσαμένων ἢ εἰδωλοθύτων γευσαμένων· ἢ καὶ πρὸς τὴν διαφορὰν τῆς παραβάσεως ἀναλόγως καὶ τὴν διόρθωσιν κανονικῶς διετύπωσεν.

33.

[Πατρικίου †Ἀραραίου† τοῦ μάκαρος ἐκ τοῦ λόγου αὐτοῦ τοῦ ἐπιλεγομένου Ὠκεανοῦ·] Μελέτιον τοίνυν ἐπίσκοπον Θηβαΐδος, ἐν τῷ διωγμῷ θύσαντα καὶ ἐπὶ μυρίοις ἑτέροις φωραθέντα ἐγκλήμασιν, ὁ μακαριώτατος Πέτρος ὁ Ἀλεξανδρείας ἐπίσκοπος, πρὶν ἢ τὸν τοῦ μαρτυρίου στέφανον ἀναδήσασθαι, καθεῖλε καὶ τῆς Χριστοῦ ἐκκλησίας ἐξέωσε· καὶ Ἄρειον διάκονον, ὡς τὸ ἑτεροούσιον πρεσβεύοντα ἐπὶ τοῦ θεοῦ λόγου καὶ τὸ «ἐξ οὐκ ὄντων» καὶ τὸ «ἦν ποτε ὅτε οὐκ ἦν» ὁ υἱὸς τοῦ θεοῦ καὶ πατρός, διακονεῖν καθάπαξ κεκώλυκε. Πέτρον δὲ ἐν κυρίῳ τελειωθέντα Ἀχιλλᾶς διαδέχεται, καὶ Ἄρειον, τῇ αἱρέσει καὶ φιλαρχίᾳ κρατούμενον καὶ τοῖς Μελετίου τολμήμασιν ἀντιθέτως συμπράττοντα, δελεασθεὶς χειροτονεῖ πρεσβύτερον καὶ τοῦ ἐν Ἀλεξανδρείᾳ διδασκαλείου προΐστησιν. Ἀχιλλᾶν δὲ οὐ μετ' οὐ πολὺ ὁσίως τελειωθέντα ὁ τῶν ἀποστολικῶν δογμάτων ὑπέρμαχος

32: HL I_1, 326–34 (inter A.D. 314–325)

33: 2–5: cf. *Epit. Th. A.*, 5, 28–30 ‖ 4–5: Thdrt. I.2, 8 ‖ 6–11: cf. *Epit. Th. A.*, 4, 29–32 ‖ 7: cf. Thdrt. I.9, 4 ‖ 12–13: cf. Thdrt. I.2, 8; 12; I.2, 9

32: 2 συναθρ. — Πόντου] καὶ βασιλεὺς (sic pro βασίλειος) ἀμασείας ἐν νεοκαισαρείᾳ τοῦ πόντου συναθροισθεῖσα E (vide praef. xviii) ‖ Νεοκαισαρείᾳ corr. LG (E): καισαρείᾳ DAC*z* ‖ 3 ἐξομοσαμένων] ἐξομολογησαμένων D

33: 1 Ἀραραίου LG: ἀραρέου D ἀραρσίου ACVOTMN ‖ λόγου — 2 Ὠκεανοῦ] ἐπιλεγομένου ὠκεανοῦ λόγου LG ‖ tit. om. E, SV^2 seclusimus ‖ 1 τοῦ^3 om. C ‖ 4 ὁ om. LG ‖ ἀρχιεπίσκοπος LG ‖ 5 ἀναδήσεται *g* ‖ 10 ἀντιθέως LG ‖ 12 μετ' οὐ] μετὰ *z* (excepto V), SV^2

32. A divine and sacred local synod of twenty-three bishops, headed by Vitalius, was convened at Neocaesarea in Pontus, to deal with those who during the persecution offered sacrifices or abjured or ate meat sacrificed to idols. It prescribed in canons correction according to the degree of transgression.[30]

33. [From the homily of blessed Patricius †Araraios† entitled "Ocean":][31] Before he received the martyr's crown, Peter, the most blessed bishop of Alexandria, deposed and excommunicated from Christ's Church Meletius, the bishop of Thebais, who had sacrificed during the persecution and had been found committing countless other misdeeds. He also barred outright the deacon Arius from performing his office for teaching that the Word of God is of a different substance, that the son of God the Father was created "out of nothing," and that "there was a time when he did not exist." After his death in the Lord, Peter was succeeded by Achillas, who was deceived into ordaining Arius a priest and making him head of the school in Alexandria,[32] despite the fact that Arius was dominated by heresy and love of power and was defiantly joining Meletius in his rebellious acts. Not long afterward,[33] Achillas died a holy death and was succeeded by Alexander, the

[30] The canons of Neocaesarea say nothing about those who lapsed during persecution; the writer is probably confusing this synod with the previous one of Ancyra; see HL, I_1, 327.

[31] This most puzzling title may have made its way into the text from the margin; though, even as a marginal comment, it is difficult to understand, since most of the material in the chapter is clearly taken from Theodoret and the *Epit.Th.A.*

[32] The false statement that Arius was appointed head of the Alexandrian school is to be blamed on the epitomator of Theodore Anagnostes, who had misread the text of Theodoret; see *Epit.Th.A.*, 4.

[33] One would not hesitate to correct οὐ μετ' οὐ πολὺ to οὐ μετὰ πολὺ were it not that the phrase is to be found more than once in other writers; e.g., *Vita Euthymii*, ed. P. Karlin-Hayter (Brussels, 1970), 67 line 3 and 93 line 21; *Vita Nicolai Studitae*, PG, 105, 908A; Germanus, *De haeresibus et synodis*, PG, 98, 53B and 61C; Nicephorus Callistus, PG, 146^2, 193D; SV^2 41, 2–3; 51, 1.

Ἀλέξανδρος διαδέχεται. Ἄρειος γοῦν ὡς μὴ προκριθεὶς Ἀλεξάνδρου μειζόνως τῇ φιλαρχίᾳ ἀλαζονεύεται, καὶ ἀποσπάσας τῆς ἐκκλησίας Εὐζώϊον τὸν διάκονον, Ἀειθαλᾶν, καὶ ἑτέρους τινάς, κατὰ τῆς ἐκκλησίας καὶ Ἀλεξάνδρου φατριάζειν ἀπήρξατο, κρατῦναι πειρώμενος τὸ ἑτεροούσιον. Ὁ δὲ μακαριώτατος Ἀλέξανδρος πολλαῖς νουθεσίαις χρησάμενος ἐπὶ τὴν ἀποστολικὴν διάταξιν ἔρχεται τὴν λέγουσαν «αἱρετικὸν ἄνθρωπον μετὰ μίαν καὶ δευτέραν νουθεσίαν παραιτοῦ», ἰδὼν ἐκείνων καθόλου τὸ ἀνεπίστροφον.

34.

Σύνοδος θεία καὶ ἱερὰ <**μερική**>, (μερικὴ δέ, ὡς φέρε εἰπεῖν, ἐστὶ τῶν προσφάτως εὑρισκομένων ἐπισκόπων συνέλευσις), ἥτις συγκληθεῖσα ἐν Ἀλεξανδρείᾳ ὑπὸ Ἀλεξάνδρου τοῦ μάκαρος ἀπεκήρυξε καὶ ἀναθέματι καθυπέβαλεν, ὡς ἐμμένοντας τῇ ἀπειθείᾳ καὶ σηπεδόνα τῇ ἐκκλησίᾳ προσάγοντας, Ἄρειον καὶ Εὐζώϊον, Ἀχιλλᾶν, Ἀειθαλᾶν, Λούκιον, Σαρμάτιον, Ἰούλιον, Μηνᾶν, Ἄρειον ἕτερον καὶ Ἑλλάδιον, καὶ τὴν αὐτῶν καθαίρεσιν πανταχοῦ ἐξαπέστειλεν. Εἰς ἣν ὑπογράφουσιν ἐπίσκοποι Λιβύης καὶ Πενταπόλεως, Συρίας καὶ Λυκίας, Καππαδοκίας καὶ Ἀσίας, καὶ Ἀλέξανδρος ὁ Κωνσταντινουπόλεως. Γράφει δὲ καὶ Ἄρειος τὰ συμβάντα πρὸς τὸν Νικομηδείας Εὐσέβιον καὶ τὸν ἐκείνου Παλαιστίνης ὁμόφρονα καὶ συνώνυμον, οἳ ὁμονοήσαντες τῇ ἀσεβείᾳ κατὰ Ἀλεξάνδρου καὶ τῆς Χριστοῦ ἐκκλησίας δυνάμει καὶ κακουργίᾳ πολλῇ παρατάττονται. Ὅθεν ὁ φιλόχριστος βασιλεὺς Κωνσταντῖνος συγκροτηθῆναι θεσπίζει τὴν σύνοδον.

16–17: cf. Thdrt. I.2, 12 ‖ 18–19: Tit. 3:10

34: HL I_1, 363–72 (ca. 320) ‖ 5–7: Thdrt. I.4, 61–62 ‖ 7–9: Thdrt. I.4, 59 ‖ 9–12: cf. Thdrt. I.4, 63 sqq.

---

17 μακαρίτης LG ‖ 18 τὴν — 19 παραιτοῦ om. LG ‖ 19 ἀνεπίστρεφον E

34: 1 μερική *SV^2*: om. cett. ‖ 2 προσφάτως] προσφόρως LG ‖ post εὑρισκομένων add. καὶ προχείρως *b SV^2* ‖ 4 σηπεδόνα *SV^2* Pa: -ας codd. ‖ 5 καὶ om. LG*z* ‖ ἀχιλλέα *g* ‖ σαρμάτην LG ‖ 9 καὶ om. *z* ‖ 13 κροτηθῆναι LG ‖ post σύνοδον add. τῷ κʹ ἔτει τῆς βασιλείας E

champion of apostolic doctrine. Then Arius, since he had been passed over in favor of Alexander, was driven by his ambition to acts of greater arrogance, and, having seduced from the Church the deacon Euzoius, Aeithalas, and certain others, he began to conspire against the Church and Alexander in an effort to establish the doctrine of "different substance." The most blessed Alexander issued numerous admonitions, but when he realized that those people were completely inflexible, he had recourse to the Apostle's order which says "After a first and second warning reject a heretic."[34]

34. A divine and sacred <particular> synod—particular being, we might say, a gathering of recently[35] found bishops—was convoked in Alexandria by the blessed Alexander; it condemned and placed under anathema, for persisting in disobedience and for bringing putrefaction on the Church, Arius, Euzoius, Achillas, Aeithalas, Lucius, Sarmatius, Julius, Menas, another Arius, and Helladius, and their deposition was sent to every place, having been subscribed to by the bishops of Libya, Pentapolis, Syria, Lycia, Cappadocia, Asia, and by Alexander (the bishop) of Constantinople. Arius also wrote of the events to Eusebius of Nicomedia and to that man's namesake and fellow thinker from Palestine; these two, sharing the impiety, marshalled themselves with vehemence and great wickedness against Alexander and the Church of Christ. For this reason the Christ-loving Emperor Constantine decreed that the council be summoned.

[34] By contrast, Theodoret (I.2,12) claims that Alexander was guided by the text of Matthew 5:29 on the scandalizing eye.

[35] προσφάτως here is a problem, and the attempted solution in L and G (προσφόρως) is no help. The context would seem to demand a meaning close to "found at short notice" or "readily available," which would also explain the addition of καὶ προχείρως in group *b*.

35.

Σύνοδος θεία καὶ ἱερὰ οἰκουμενικὴ πρώτη τῶν τριακοσίων δέκα καὶ ὀκτὼ θεοφόρων πατέρων συναθροισθεῖσα ἐν τῇ Νικαέων μητροπόλει τῆς Βιθυνῶν ἐπαρχίας, ἧς ἐξῆρχον προκαθεζόμενοι Βίτων καὶ Βικέντιος πρεσβύτεροι, τὸν τόπον ἐπέχοντες Σιλβέστρου τοῦ πάπα Ῥώμης καὶ τοῦ διαδόχου αὐτοῦ Ἰουλίου, Ἀλέξανδρος Ἀλεξανδρείας, Μακάριος Ἱεροσολύμων, Εὐστάθιος Ἀντιοχείας, ἐκ προσώπου Μητροφάνους Κωνσταντινουπόλεως Ἀλέξανδρος πρεσβύτερος, Ὅσιος ὁ Κουρδούβης ἐπίσκοπος, καὶ Κωνσταντῖνος ὁ ἐν χριστιανοῖς βασιλεῦσιν ἀπόστολος. Ἥτις ἁγία σύνοδος τὸ ὁμοούσιον ἐπὶ τῆς ἁγίας τριάδος ἁρμόσασα καὶ τὸ θεῖον καὶ μυστικὸν πάσχα ὁρισαμένη, ἐξέθετο κατὰ πάσης αἱρέσεως τὸ θεουργὸν τῆς πίστεως μάθημα, Ἀρείου, Σαβελλίου, Φωτεινοῦ, Παύλου τοῦ Σαμοσατέως, Μάνεντος, Οὐαλεντίνου, Μαρκίονος, καὶ τῶν σὺν αὐτοῖς. Ἀποκηρύττει δὲ καὶ τὸν τῆς Θηβαΐδος Μελέτιον μετὰ τῶν χειροτονιῶν αὐτοῦ καὶ τὸν Νικομηδείας Εὐσέβιον· τὰς ἐνδιαθέτους βίβλους καὶ ἀποκρύφους τοιῷδε τρόπῳ καταδήλους ποιήσασα· ἐν γὰρ τῷ οἴκῳ τοῦ θεοῦ κάτω παρὰ τῇ θείᾳ τραπέζῃ αὐτὰς παραθεμένη, προσηύξατο εὑρεθῆναι τὰς θεοπνεύστους ἐπάνω τὸν κύριον ἐξαιτησαμένη καὶ τὰς κιβδήλους (ὃ καὶ γέγονεν) ὑποκάτωθεν.

36.

Ἀλεξάνδρου τοίνυν τοῦ πάπα Ἀλεξανδρείας μετὰ πενταμηνιαῖον χρόνον τοῦ ἀναστρέψαι ἀπὸ Νικαίας πρὸς κύριον ἐκδημήσαντος, Ἀθανάσιος τὴν προεδρίαν ἀξίως εἰσδέχεται. Οἱ δὲ προρρηθέντες κακόδοξοι μεμαθηκότες μεγάλως ἐτάκησαν, πείρᾳ τὸν ἄνδρα γινώσκοντες, καὶ ὡς φόνιον τῷ

35: HL I_1, 386–632 (A.D. 325) ‖ 1–11: cf. Geo. Mon. 509, 3–16 ‖ 6–7: cf. Phot. *Biblioth.*, cod. 88 (Gel. Cyz. II.5, 4)

36: HL I_2, 654–55 (A.D. 334) ‖ 1–3: cf. Thdrt. I.26, 1 ‖ 3–4: Thdrt. I.26, 3 ‖

35: 1 οἰκουμενικὴ πρώτη σύνοδος mg. AC (et sim. DENO) ‖ 3 Βίτων] βίκτωρ E ‖ 4 ἐπέχοντος A ἔχοντες C ‖ 6 post Μητροφάνους add. ἀρχιεπισκόπου LG ‖ 8 post ἐπίσκοπος (et post ἀπόστολος) additamentum in E (vide praef. p. xviii) ‖ 9 ἁρμόσασα] τρανώσασα LG ‖ 12 μαρκίωνος *g* ‖ καὶ^2 om. *g* ‖ 13 τῆς om. LG

36: 3 ἀξίως post Ἀθανάσιος transp. LG ‖ μεμαθηκότες — 4 καὶ om. E

35. The divine and sacred First Ecumenical Council of three hundred and eighteen God-inspired fathers was convened at Nicaea, metropolis of the province of Bithynia. Its presiding leaders were the presbyters Vito and Vicentius taking the place of Rome's Pope Sylvester and his successor Julius, Alexander of Alexandria, Macarius of Jerusalem, Eustathius of Antioch, the presbyter Alexander representing Metrophanes of Constantinople, Hosius the bishop of Cordoba, and Constantine the apostle among Christian emperors. This holy council attached the term "consubstantial" to the Holy Trinity, fixed the time of the divine and mystical Passover, and set forth the divinely inspired teaching of the Creed against all heretics, Arius, Sabellius, Photinus, Paul of Samosata, Manes, Valentinus, Marcion, and their followers. It condemned also Meletius of Thebais, along with those ordained by him, and Eusebius of Nicomedia. The canonical and apocryphal books it distinguished in the following manner: in the house of God the books were placed down by the holy altar; then the council asked the Lord in prayer that the inspired works be found on top and—as in fact happened—the spurious on the bottom.[36]

36. Five months after his return from Nicaea, Alexander, the pope[37] of Alexandria, departed to the Lord, and Athanasius worthily received the presidency. But when that unorthodox group which we have mentioned learned this, they were greatly distressed, since they knew the man from experience,

[36] Since the story is related only by *SV,* it is not possible to know if it belongs to an older tradition or where our author might have come across it.

[37] Cf. Nil Doxapatres, Τάξις τῶν πατριαρχικῶν θρόνων (in G. Parthey, *Hieroclis Synecdemus et notitiae graecae episcopatuum* [Berlin, 1866], 265–308), 282: ἔσχεν ἐξ ἔθους παλαιοῦ ὁ μὲν Ῥώμης ἰδικῶς καλεῖσθαι πάπας, ὁμοίως καὶ Ἀλεξανδρείας πάπας.

φιλοχρίστῳ βασιλεῖ Κωνσταντίνῳ τοῦτον ἀναδιδάσκοντες, <ἐν Καισαρείᾳ Παλαιστίνης σύνοδον> κατ' αὐτοῦ γενέσθαι παρώτρυναν. Ἀθανάσιος γοῦν δι' Εὐσέβιον τὸν αὐτῆς ἐπίσκοπον ἐκεῖσε μὴ παραγενόμενος, προδήλως αὐτῷ ἔκπαλαι καὶ τῇ ἀληθείᾳ χρηματίσαντα δυσμενέστατον, ἡ μανικὴ ἄπρακτος διελύετο σύνοδος. Ὅθεν καὶ μᾶλλον οἱ ἀσεβεῖς κακουργοῦσι καὶ τὸν θυμὸν τοῦ εὐσεβοῦς βασιλέως ἀνάπτουσι καὶ τὰ κατὰ τὸν πολύαθλον Ἀθανάσιον συνοδικῶς ἐν Τύρῳ κριθῆναι παρασκευάζουσι διατάξασθαι.

37.

Εὐσέβιος δὲ ὁ Νικομηδείας ταῖς πιθανολογίαις βουκολήσας τὸν αὐτοκράτορα, ὡς ἐν τάξει θέας τῶν παρὰ τῆς μακαρίας Ἑλένης πρὸς δόξαν Ἰησοῦ Χριστοῦ τοῦ ἀληθινοῦ θεοῦ ἡμῶν οἰκοδομηθεισῶν ἐν Ἱερουσαλὴμ ἐκκλησιῶν (προεχουσῶν πολλῶν θεαμάτων, ὧν τὰ μεγέθη Ἑλλήνων παῖδες ἱστορίαις παραδεδώκασιν) ὀχήματι ἐπιβάς, καὶ ἀριθμὸν πλεῖστον ἐπισκόπων καὶ συγκλητικῶν λογάδων ἐπισυρόμενος, τὴν Τύρον κατέλαβεν, Ἀθανασίῳ πραγματευόμενος τὴν ἐκβολὴν καὶ καθαίρεσιν· καὶ σύνοδον συκοφαντίας ἀνάμεστον κατὰ τοῦ θείου συμβόλου καὶ Ἀθανασίου τοῦ μάκαρος ἐν αὐτῇ συνεκρότησε, πόρνην παραστησάμενος τῷ ἀθῴῳ κατήγορον. Ἀθανασίου δὲ τὴν συσκευὴν διὰ Τιμοθέου πρεσβυτέρου καθολικῶς διελέγξαντος, ἐπὶ τὴν ἐκκοπὴν τῆς χειρὸς Ἀρσενίου τοῦ Μελιτιανῶν διακόνου <ἐτράποντο>. Πλὴν καὶ ἐν τούτῳ συκοφάντας αὐτοὺς παραστήσας ὁ μακάριος Ἀθανάσιος διὰ τῶν

5–8: Thdrt. I.28, 2–4; *Epit. Th. A.*, 21, 32–34; Soz.II.25, 1 ‖ 8–9: cf. Phot., *Hom.*, 144, 6 (ed. Laourdas) ‖ 9–11: Thdrt. I.28, 3–4

37: HL I_2, 656–66 (A.D. 335) ‖ 1 sqq.: Thdrt. I.21, 1–2 ‖ 9–14: Thdrt. I.30, 2–11 ‖ 9–11: cf. Phot., *Hom.*, 144, 12–15; 144, 25 sqq. (cf. *Epit. Th. A.*, 22, 19–26) ‖

---

5 ἀναδιδάξαντες *b* ‖ ἐν — 6 σύνοδον add. Pa (sim. *SV*[2]) σύνοδον ἐν καισαρείᾳ τῆς φιλίππου post κατ' αὐτοῦ habent LG ‖ 6–7 ἀθανασίου - - - παραγενομένου LGE cf. cap. 58, 6–7 ‖ 6–7 δι' Εὐσέβιον om. *b* ‖ 7 τὸν αὐτῆς ἐπίσκοπον om. D ‖ τὸν — ἐκεῖσε om. E ‖ προδήλως — 8 δυσμενέστατον] om. E προδήλου αὐτῷ καὶ τῆς ἀληθείας ἔκπαλαι χρημ. δυσμ. LG ‖ 10 τὰ om. C

37: 3 ἀληθινοῦ om. LG ‖ 4 ἐκκλησιῶν ante ἐν transp. *b* ‖ 5 δεδώκασιν LG ‖ ἀριθμοῦ LG ‖ πλεῖστον L, post corr. G: πλείστων D*b* ‖ 10 post Τιμοθέου add. τοῦ L ‖ 11 ἐτράποντο nos (cf. Phot. *Hom.* 144, 27, ed. Laourdas): μετέβησαν οἱ κατήγοροι LG βαδίζουσι E ‖ 12 συκοφαντίας AC

and, representing him to the Christ-loving Emperor Constantine as a murderer, they urged that there take place <a synod> against him <in Caesarea Palestine>. But when Athanasius did not show up there because of Eusebius, the bishop of that city who had been his obvious and real enemy for a long time, the mad synod broke up without taking any action. After this, those impious men resorted to even greater misdeeds; they touched off the pious Emperor's anger and persuaded him to order that the charges against the much afflicted Athanasius be examined by a synod in Tyre.

37. But Eusebius of Nicomedia beguiled the Emperor with his persuasive arguments, and, on the pretext of visiting in Jerusalem the churches built by the blessed Helen for the glory of Jesus Christ our true God—churches surpassing many spectacles whose greatness pagan historians have described—he took to a vehicle and, bringing along a very large number of bishops and prominent senators, came to Tyre to work for the expulsion and deposition of Athanasius. There he convoked a totally slanderous synod against the divine symbol and the blessed Athanasius, bringing forward a prostitute with accusations against the innocent man. And when Athanasius with the help of the presbyter Timothy completely refuted the trumped-up charge, they <turned> to the amputation of the Meletian deacon Arsenius' hand. However, even though the blessed Athanasius proved them liars in this also by show-

δύο χειρῶν Ἀρσενίου τῆς ὑποδείξεως, οὐκ ἐδυσώπησεν αὐτοὺς λωφῆσαι τοῦ φονώδους φρονήματος· ἀλλ' ὑπ' αὐτῶν ἀναθεματίζεται καὶ ὡς κακοῦργος ἐκβάλλεται, Ἄρειος δὲ καὶ Εὐζώϊος εἰς κοινωνίαν εἰσδέχονται. Ἀθανάσιος μέντοι τὰ κατ' αὐτοῦ θεασάμενος ἐπὶ καταλύσει τῆς πίστεως τυρευόμενα φυγὰς ἐν Κωνσταντινουπόλει πρὸς τὸν φιλόχριστον βασιλέα κατήντησε, τὰ τῆς συκοφαντίας αὐτῷ ἐξηγούμενος. Οἱ δὲ περὶ τὸν Εὐσέβιον ἐπὶ τὴν θέαν τῶν Ἱεροσολύμων χωροῦντες καὶ τὰ ἐγκαίνια, τὸν Νικαίας Θεόγνιον καὶ τὸν Περίνθου Θεόδωρον, Νάρκισσον, καὶ Μάριν Χαλκηδόνος, μετὰ καὶ συμμορίας ὁμόφρονος κατὰ τοῦ θεόφρονος Ἀθανασίου ἐν τῷ Μαρεώτῃ ἐξέπεμψαν, ᾧτινι ἐκ τῆς πλησιοχώρου λίμνης καλουμένης Μαρίας τὸ ἐπώνυμον πρόσκειται· ἔστι γὰρ ἀκολούθως οὕτως: Αἴγυπτος, Θηβαῒς ἡ ἄνω καὶ κάτω, Μαρεώτης, Αὔγασις, Μαρμαρική, Λιβύη, Πεντάπολις, Ἀφρική, Βαρβαρία, Βοιωτία, Γάδειρα, Ὠκεανός.

38.

Θεόγνιος τοίνυν ἐν τῷ Μαρεώτῃ μετὰ τοῦ συνεδρίου τῆς ἀσεβείας γενόμενος, Ἰσχυρίωνα, τὸν αὐτοχειροτόνητον Μαρεώτου ἐπίσκοπον κατήγορον τοῦ θεοφόρου Ἀθανασίου ἐν τῇ παρ' αὐτοῖς συνόδῳ προεστήσατο, κατὰ τοῦ μὴ παρόντος δεχόμενος τὰ ἐγκλήματα βέβαια.

13–15: cf. Theoph., 31, 24–27 (*Epit. Th. A.*, 22, 23; 22, 26–27) ‖ 17–18: cf. Theoph., 32, 1–2; Thdrt. I.30, 11 ‖ 19–23: Thdrt. I. 30, 11–12

38: HL I_2, 662–66 (A.D. 335) ‖ 1–4: cf. Soz. III.23, 1; Thdrt. I.30, 11–12

---

14 φονώδους] λυσσώδους *b* ‖ 16 ἐπὶ] ἐπὶ τῇ ACE ‖ ἐπὶ – τυρευόμενα om. *z* ‖ 18 αὐτῶν *b* ‖ τῶν om. LG ‖ 19 θεόγνιν DE ‖ τὸν om. LG ‖ 20 πειρίνθου DE (cf. cap. 77, 11) ‖ καὶ[2] om. *b* ‖ 22–23 πρόσκειται τὸ ἐπώνυμον *b* ‖ 24 Αὔγασις] immo Αὔασις

38: 1 θεόγνις DE

ing that Arsenius had two hands, he could not convince them to give up their bloodthirsty scheme. They anathematized and excommunicated him on grounds of immorality, and received Arius and Euzoius into communion. But Athanasius, seeing the charges contrived against him to the detriment of the faith, fled to Constantinople, where he went to the devout Emperor and reported to him the slanders. The Eusebian group, on the other hand, set out for Jerusalem for the sight-seeing and consecration and dispatched to the Mareotis against the godly-minded Athanasius, Theognius of Nicaea, Theodore of Perinthus, Narcissus, Maris of Chalcedon, and a party of fellow thinkers. This area (Mareotis) takes its name from the adjacent lake Maria, and it comes in the sequence as follows: Egypt, Thebais Upper and Lower, Mareotis, Augasis,[38] Marmarica, Libya, Pentapolis, Africa, Barbaria,[39] Boeotia,[40] Gades, Ocean.

38. Theognius, then, coming to Mareotis along with the impious assembly, put forward at their synod[41] Ischyrion, the self-appointed bishop of Mareotis, to give evidence against the godly Athanasius, and accepted as true the charges made against him in his absence.

[38] A mistake for Αὔασις, also spelled Ὦασις or Ὄασις. The place meant is probably Ὄασις μικρά in Egypt, as distinct from Ὄασις μεγάλη in Lower Thebais.

[39] Most likely this refers to Tripolis Barbaria, which was subject to Alexandria; see Nil Doxapatres, *op. cit.*, 276–77.

[40] Probably a corruption of some place-name in North Africa.

[41] The delegation sent to Mareotis acted more as a commission of enquiry than as a decision-making synod; see HL, I_2, 662.

39.

Οὐ μὴν δέ, ἀλλὰ καὶ ὁ Νικομηδείας Εὐσέβιος ἀπάρας μετὰ τὴν θέαν καὶ τὰ ἐν Ἱεροσολύμοις ἐγκαίνια ἐπὶ τὴν Ἀντιόχειαν παραγίνεται, καὶ σύνοδον κατὰ τοῦ θείου συμβόλου καὶ Εὐσταθίου συνέστησε τοῦ παμμάκαρος, πλέξας Σαβελλισμὸν αὐτῷ καὶ μοιχείαν· δι' ὧν καθαίρεσιν ἐψηφίσατο καὶ ἐκ τοῦ βασιλέως κατάκρισιν ἐξορίας ἐν τῷ Ἰλλυρικῷ παρεσκεύασε. Μόνον τοῦ ἑταιρικοῦ γυναίου ἔχοντος ἐν ἀγκάλαις τὸ βρέφος καὶ Εὐσταθίου εἶναι διομνυμένου τοὺς ὅρκους λήθη καλύψαι οὐκ ἴσχυσε· νόσῳ γὰρ καὶ μακροτάτη κλινοβατίᾳ περιπεσόντος, κλῆρος καὶ λαὸς ἐξαγορεύοντος ἤκουον ἣν παρὰ τῶν αἱρετικῶν χρυσίου κατὰ Εὐσταθίου τοῦ μακαρίου ποσότητα ἔλαβεν, ἐπὶ τῶν ὅρκων φάσκοντος μὴ διαμαρτεῖν, ὡς ἔοικε, τοῦ ὀνόματος, Εὐσταθίου σπέρμα τοῦ χαλκέως τοῦ ἐπιδειχθέντος βρέφους καθάπαξ ὑπάρχοντος.

40.

Οἱ γοῦν περὶ τὸν Νικομηδείας Εὐσέβιον καὶ οἱ ἐν τῷ Μαρεώτῃ, ἐλθόντες εἰς τὸ Βυζάντιον, εὗρον τὸν ἅγιον Ἀθανάσιον Κωνσταντῖνον τὸν εὐσεβέστατον βασιλέα αἰτούμενον ἐπὶ τὴν ἐν Τύρῳ συκοφαντίαν κανονικὴν γενέσθαι ἐπὶ τοῖς διαβλήτορσιν ἐπεξέλευσιν· καὶ πρὸς τοὺς ἑαυτῶν φωλεοὺς καταπτήξαντες οἱ ἀνήμεροι θῆρες κατέδυσαν. Εὐσέβιος δὲ ἀναιδῶς φρυαττόμενος κατ' αὐτοῦ, ὄνομα φέροντας ἐπισκόπων τέσσαρας συκοφάντας παρέστησεν, οἳ περὶ σιτοπομπείου καὶ τῶν λοιπῶν ὅρκοις τὰς λοιδορίας ἐκύρωσαν, τὸν βασιλέα συνοδικῶς ἐν Κωνσταντινουπόλει τὰ κατὰ τὸν ἀοίδιμον πείσαντες Ἀθανάσιον ἐξετασθῆναι· ὃ καὶ γέγονε, συνεδρίου αἱρετικῶν κατὰ τοῦ θείου συμβόλου πάντα λίθον κινήσαντος, καὶ Ἀθανάσιον τὸν ἀνεύθυνον εἰς Τρίβεριν τῆς Γαλλίας ἐξόριστον κατακρίναντος, καὶ τὸν ὅσιον Κοματᾶν, καὶ Εὐφρατᾶν Ἀνταράδου, Εὐπρέπιον Ἀδριανουπόλεως, καὶ Λούκιον τὸν ὁμολογητήν, ὃς τελειοῦται ἐν ταῖς ἁλύσεσι, καὶ Μάρκελλον τὸν Ἀγκύρας, ὡς ἀνθρωπολάτρην, καθάραντος.

39: HL I_2, 641–47 (A.D. 330) ‖ 4: cf. Phot., *Hom.*, 143, 12 ‖ 4–5: *Epit. Th. A.*, 23, 32–33; Theoph., 28, 12–14 (Thdrt. I.21, 9–22, 1) ‖ 5–11: Thdrt. I.22, 3 ‖ 6: cf. Phot., *Hom.*, 142, 20

40: HL I_2, 667–78 (A.D. 335) ‖ 1–11: *Epit. Th. A.*, 24, 27–25, 29 (Thdrt. I.31, 4–5; Theoph., 32, 4 sqq.) ‖ 12–14: Thdrt. II.15, 8 (Athanas., *Apol. de fuga sua* 3)

39: 3 μάκαρος *b* ‖ 9 Εὐσταθίου post μακαρίου transp. *b* ‖ μακαρίτου LG

40: 1 οὖν LG ‖ 4 ἐπὶ om. LG ‖ ὑπεξέλευσιν LG ‖ 6 ἐπισκόπων LGC: -ου D*z* -ους A[s]E ‖ 8 τοῦ βασιλέως LG ‖ 10 θείου] ἁγίου *b* ‖ 12 Κοματᾶν D, *SV*[2]: κομετᾶν C κοματὸν LG κιματᾶν *z* κεματᾶν A[s] ‖ 14 καθάραντες *b*

39. Furthermore, after the sight-seeing and dedication, Eusebius of Nicomedia left Jerusalem and came to Antioch where he assembled a synod against the divine symbol and the all-blessed Eustathius with fabricated charges of Sabellianism and adultery. The council used these charges to depose Eustathius and obtained from the Emperor his condemnation and banishment to Illyricum. However, the prostitute who, while holding the child in her arms, had sworn that Eustathius was the father, was not able to keep her oath secret. For, having fallen ill and being confined to bed for a very long time, she confessed before clergy and laity about the sum of gold she had received from the heretics (to give evidence) against the blessed Eustathius; but she claimed that in her oaths she swore correctly, as it would appear, about the name, since the child exhibited was indeed the offspring of one Eustathius the Smith.

40. The followers of Eusebius of Nicomedia, then, and those who were at Mareotis came to Byzantium where they found the holy Athanasius requesting the most pious Emperor Constantine to have canonical punishment meted out to those who made false accusations at the slanderous synod in Tyre; whereupon the wild beasts went slinking off to their dens and hid themselves. Eusebius, however, continuing his shameless and arrogant attack on the man, produced four false witnesses, bearing the title of bishop, who sanctioned with oaths their calumnies about the corn provision and the rest, and they persuaded Constantine to have the affair of the glorious Athanasius examined by a synod. This took place, and the heretical assembly left no stone unturned in its attack on the divine symbol; it condemned the innocent Athanasius to exile at Trier in Gaul and deposed the saintly Comatas, Euphrates of Antaradus,[42] Euprepius[43] of Adrianople, Lucius the confessor, who died in his chains, and Marcellus of Ancyra on the charge of anthropolatry.

[42] The names are garbled; as often, our writer has not managed to copy his source correctly (in this case Theodoret II.15,8, quoting Athanasius, *Apologia de fuga sua,* chap. 3).

[43] The correct name is Eutropius. It should be pointed out, however, that the form Euprepius already appears in one of the witnesses to the text of Theodoret, namely, the unpublished *Tripartita* of Theodore Anagnostes in *Marcianus gr. 344* (fol. 108^v).

41.

Κωνσταντῖνος μὲν οὖν ὁ ἐν χριστιανοῖς βασιλεῦσιν ἀπόστολος διὰ τῆς ἐξορίας τὴν σωτηρίαν Ἀθανασίῳ πραγματευσάμενος, ἐλθὼν ἐπὶ Νικομήδειαν καὶ ἀσθενείᾳ περιπεσὼν ἐβαπτίσατο. Καὶ μέλλων ἐκδημεῖν πρὸς τὸν κύριον ἐνδιαθήκως ἀνακληθῆναι τῆς ἐξορίας τὸν θεσπέσιον διετύπωσεν Ἀθανάσιον· Κωνσταντῖνον καὶ Κώνσταντα τοὺς υἱοὺς αὐτοῦ τῶν ἐῴων Ῥωμαίων, ἐκ Ῥώμης ἀπάραντας, τῆς βασιλείας ἀντέχεσθαι, καὶ Κωνστάντιον ἀπὸ Ἀντιοχείας εἰς Ῥώμην ὁμοίως ἀντιπορεύεσθαι. Ἀλλὰ τῆς διαθήκης φαλσευθείσης ὑπὸ Εὐσταθίου τοῦ πρεσβυτέρου καὶ ἐπιτρόπου, κεκρυμμένου Ἀρειανοῦ χρηματίζοντος, Κωνστάντιος βασιλεὺς τῆς ἑῴας ἀναγορεύεται· καὶ τῶν ἀδελφῶν αὐτοῦ ἐν Ῥώμῃ ὀρθοδοξούντων, μόνος εἰς τὸ ἀρειανικὸν κατωλίσθησε φρόνημα. Εὐθὺς γὰρ οἱ περὶ τὸν Νικομηδείας Εὐσέβιον αὐτῷ κατὰ τοῦ μακαριωτάτου Παύλου προσέρχονται σὺν πολλαῖς διαβολαῖς καὶ τοῦτο ὑφαίνοντες, ὡς «δίχα τῆς σῆς, βασιλεῦ, διαγνώσεως, Ἀλεξάνδρου τελειωθέντος, εἰς τὸν θρόνον Κωνσταντινουπόλεως ἑαυτὸν ἐγκαθίδρυσεν.» Ὁ δὲ συνέδριον αἱρετικῶν ἐν Κωνσταντινουπόλει συγκροτηθῆναι κατὰ τοῦ θείου συμβόλου διαταξάμενος, Παῦλον τὸν ὁμολογητὴν ἐκβληθῆναι τῆς ἐκκλησίας ἐκέλευσε καὶ ἀντεισαχθῆναι τὸν πρώην Βηρυτοῦ, Νικομηδείας Εὐσέβιον.

42.

Σύνοδος αἱρετικὴ ἐν Ἀντιοχείᾳ τῆς Συρίας τῶν ἐνενήκοντα καὶ ἑπτὰ ἐπισκόπων συνελθόντων, λόγῳ μὲν καὶ προφάσει τῶν ἐγκαινίων τῆς Κωνσταντινιακῆς ἐκκλησίας, ἓν ὑπαρχούσης τῶν θεαμάτων, σκοπῷ δὲ καὶ πράγματι κατὰ τοῦ θείου συμβόλου καὶ Ἀθανασίου τοῦ γενναιόφρονος· ἥσπερ

41: HL I_2, 687–91 (A.D. 338 aut 339) ‖ 2–3: cf. Thdrt. I.32, 1 ‖ 3–11: cf. Phot., *Hom.*, 152–53; *Epit. Th. A.*, 26, 29 sqq. ‖ 11–17: cf. Soz. III.4, 2–3; Socr. II.7; *Epit. Th. A.*, 29, 21–26

42: HL I_2, 702–36 (A.D. 341) ‖ 1–8: cf. Soz. III.5, 1–2 ‖ 2–4: cf. Socr. II.8 ‖

41: 2 Ἀθανασίῳ om. LG ‖ 3 καὶ[1] om. *g* ‖ ἐβαπτίσατο] deletum habet L om. G ‖ τὸν om. C ‖ 5 τοὺς υἱοὺς αὐτοῦ om. LG ‖ 10 ἐν Ῥώμῃ om. *z* ‖ τὸ om. D ‖ 13 ὡς om. LG ‖ 15 αἱρετικὸν LG ‖ συγκροτηθέντος *z* κροτηθῆναι G

42: 1 αἱρετικὴ] ἢ μικτή supra scr. E ‖ 3 καὶ om. G

41. Constantine, then, the apostle among Christian emperors, having brought about Athanasius' safety by sending him into exile, came to Nicomedia where he fell ill and was baptized. Just before he departed for the Lord, he stipulated in his will that the holy Athanasius be recalled from exile; that his sons Constantine and Constans leave Rome to become emperors of the Eastern Romans; and that Constantius likewise leave Antioch for Rome. The will, however, was falsified by its trustee, Eustathius[44] the presbyter, a disguised Arian, and Constantius was proclaimed emperor of the East. While his brothers remained orthodox in Rome, he alone fell into the Arian heresy. For he was immediately approached by the party of Eusebius of Nicomedia who brought charges against the most blessed Paul; and among numerous calumnies they fabricated the following for the emperor, "without Your Majesty's consent he placed himself on the throne of Constantinople after Alexander's death." Whereupon, Constantine, having summoned by decree a heretical assembly against the holy symbol (of faith), ordered Paul the Confessor to be excommunicated from the Church and Eusebius of Nicomedia, formerly of Berytus, to be installed in his place.

42. A heretical synod of ninety-seven bishops convened at Antioch in Syria on the expressed pretext of dedicating Constantine's church, one of the marvels,[45] but really for the purpose of attacking the holy symbol (of faith) and the noble-minded Athanasius. The synod was presided over by Eusebius

[44] According to Photius, *Hom.*, 152 line 18, following Gelasius, the name of the Arian presbyter was Eutocius; see C. Mango, *The Homilies of Photius* (Cambridge, Mass., 1958), 261 note 2; 262 note 5. While *SV* may reflect a different tradition, it is more likely that the form Eustathius is a corruption.

[45] Compare the description in Malalas, Bonn ed. (1831), 324 lines 9–10, τὸ (κτίσμα) τῆς μεγάλης ἐκκλησίας τὸ μέγιστον καὶ ἓν ὂν τῶν θεαμάτων. Of the church Photius, *Hom.*, 153 lines 24–25, says μέγα γάρ τι χρῆμα καὶ ἀξιολογώτατον ὁ ἐν Ἀντιοχείᾳ περιώνυμος ναός.

ἐξῆρχον ὁ Νικομηδείας Εὐσέβιος, καὶ Παλαιστίνης Ἀκάκιος, <καὶ> Καισαρείας Καππαδοκίας Διάνιος Ἀστέριον ἔχων τὸν Καππαδόκην φιλόσοφον. Οἳ καὶ τὸ ἅγιον μεταποιήσαντες σύμβολον ἐν Ἀλεξανδρείᾳ Γρηγόριον ἐξαπέστειλαν, ὅστις ἐπιστὰς σὺν τετρακισχιλίοις ὁπλίταις τὸν μακάριον ἐξεδίωξεν Ἀθανάσιον· καὶ αὐτὸς λυμαίνεσθαι τὴν ἐκκλησίαν κατέσπευσεν. Οἱ γοῦν περὶ Εὐσέβιον Ἀρειανοὶ τῆς συνόδου κρατοῦντες, κἂν ὑπῆρχον ἐν αὐτῇ πατέρες ὀρθόδοξοι, τὸ θεῖον πάσχα κατὰ τὴν ἁγίαν ἐν Νικαίᾳ ὁρίζουσι σύνοδον καὶ τοὺς ἐμφερομένους ἤδη κανόνας ἐξέθεντο.

43.

Παῦλον τοίνυν ἐν Ῥώμῃ καὶ Ἀθανάσιον ὁ μακάριος πάπας Ἰούλιος καὶ Κώνστας ὁ εὐσεβέστατος βασιλεὺς θεασάμενοι τοὺς οἰκείους θρόνους ἀποδεδώκασι. Διόπερ οἱ ἑτερόδοξοι καὶ αὖθις ἐν Ἀντιοχείᾳ κατὰ τοῦ θείου συμβόλου συναθροίσαντες σύνοδον Παῦλον καὶ Ἀθανάσιον ἀπεκήρυξαν, καθαψάμενοι πλεῖστα Ἰουλίου ὡς μὴ καλῶς αὐτοῖς ἀντικανονίσαντος.

44.

Κώνσταντος γοῦν καὶ Ἰουλίου διὰ τὸ ἅγιον σύμβολον τοῖς αὐτοῦ συμμαχούντων συνίστορσιν, ἡ ἀληθὴς καὶ σωτήριος πίστις ηὐξάνετο. Ὅθεν καὶ φάλαγξ αἱρετικὴ πάλιν ἐν Ἀντιοχείᾳ κατὰ τοῦ θείου συμβόλου συρρεύσασα Φωτεινὸν καὶ Σαβέλλιον καὶ Μάρκελλον Ἀγκύρας ἀνεθεμάτισε, καὶ εἰς Ῥώμην ὅρον ἐκθεμένη τῆς πίστεως ἐξαπέστειλεν, ὃν οἱ ἑσπέριοι καὶ Ἰούλιος οὐ προσήκαντο.

6–7: cf. Soz. II.33, 4 ‖ 7: cf. *Epit. Th. A.*, 30, 29 ‖ 10–11: cf. Phot., *Hom.*, 153, 30–31 ‖ 11–12: cf. *Epit. Th. A.*, 31, 21–22

43: HL I_2, 695–96 (A.D. 340) ‖ 1–5: cf. Socr. II.15, 1–5 (*Epit. Th. A.*, 32, 27 sqq.; 34, 13 sqq.)

44: HL I_2, 828–30 (A.D. 344) ‖ 2–6: cf. *Epit. Th. A.*, 34, 25 – 35, 18 (Socr. II.19–20)

---

5 καὶ[1] om. E ‖ καὶ[2] D, Pa ‖ 10 οὐν LG ‖ post περὶ add. τὸν LG ‖ κἂν τε LG ‖ 11 πατέρες] κρατοῦντες *z* (ex lin. 10)

43: 5 ἰούλιον - - - ἀντικανονίσαντα LG

44: 1 κώνστα LG ‖ αὐτοῦ LG: αὐτῶν D*b* ‖ 2 συμμαχούντων *g*: -οῦντος ACE -οῦντες *z* ‖ καὶ om. *z* ‖ 6 προσήκατο CEOTMN, evan. A

of Nicomedia, Acacius of Palestine, <and> Dianius of Caesarea in Cappadocia, accompanied by Asterius, the Cappadocian philosopher. They changed the holy symbol and dispatched Gregory to Alexandria, who, having appeared with four thousand infantry, drove out the blessed Athanasius and then himself proceeded quickly to harm the Church. The Eusebian group of Arians, controlling the synod despite the presence of orthodox fathers, fixed the sacred Passover according to the holy Council of Nicaea and issued the already well-known canons.

43. After Paul and Athanasius had been seen in Rome by blessed Pope Julius and the most pious Emperor Constans, they were restored by them to their own thrones. This led the heterodox to convene once again a synod in Antioch against the holy symbol, in which they denounced Paul and Athanasius and most severely attacked Julius on the grounds that he had no right to issue rulings contrary to theirs.

44. Constans, then, and Julius, having joined forces with its supporters on behalf of the holy symbol, the true and saving creed gained strength. On this account a heretical contingent gathered once more against the divine symbol in Antioch, where they anathematized Photinus, Sabellius, and Marcellus of Ancyra, and issued a definition of faith which, when sent to Rome, was rejected by the Western bishops and by Julius.

45.

Κώνστας δὲ ὁ θειότατος Κωνστάντιον τὸν ἀδελφὸν αὐτοῦ θεασάμενος εὐριπόφρονα καὶ τοῖς Ἀρειανοῖς χαριζόμενον, δηλοποιεῖ σύνοδον ἁγίαν ἐν Σαρδικῇ τῇ μητροπόλει τῶν Ἰλλυριῶν καὶ Δακῶν ἀθροισθεῖσαν ἐξετάσαι τὰ κατὰ Παῦλον καὶ Ἀθανάσιον· ἐν ᾗ συνῆλθον ἀπό τε Ῥώμης καὶ τῶν Σπανιῶν, Γαλλίας, Ἰταλίας, Καμπανίας, Ἀφρικῆς, Σαρδανίας, Δαρδανίας, Μακεδονίας, Θεσσαλίας, Παννονίας, Μυσίας, Ἀχαΐας, Ἠπείρου, Θρᾴκης, Εὐρώπης, Ἀσίας, Καρίας, Βιθυνίας, Ἑλλησπόντου, Φρυγίας, Πισσιδίας, Καππαδοκίας, Εὐξείνου Πόντου, Κιλικίας, Φρυγίας ἄλλης, Παμφυλίας, Λυδίας, νήσων Κυκλάδων, Αἰγύπτου, Θηβαΐδος, Λιβύης, Γαλατίας, Παλαιστίνης, Ἀραβίας, τριακόσιοι ἑβδομήκοντα καὶ ἓξ λογάδες ἐπίσκοποι, ὧν ἐξῆρχον Ὅσιος ὁ Κουρδούβης ἐπίσκοπος Ἀβραμιαῖος καὶ Πρωτογένης ὁ ταύτης ἀρχιεπίσκοπος. Ἣ τὸ ὑγιὲς τρανώσασα μάθημα προσεδέξατο Παῦλον καὶ Ἀθανάσιον, εἰς παντελῆ καθαίρεσιν Γρηγόριον τὸν Ἀλεξανδρείας ἀποκηρύξασα, Κυντιανὸν Γάζης καὶ τὸν Ἀγκύρας Βασίλειον μὴ κοινωνεῖν αὐτοῖς καὶ ἐπισκόπους οὐκ ὀνομάζεσθαι παρὰ παντὸς πιστοῦ κατακρίνασα, ὡς τυραννικῶς τῶν θρόνων κρατήσαντας. Θεόδωρον δὲ τὸν Ἡρακλείας καὶ Παλαιστίνης Ἀκάκιον, Στέφανον Ἀντιοχείας καὶ τὸν Σιγδούνου Ἰσαάκιον, Μηνοφάντην Ἐφέσου καὶ τὸν Μυσίας Οὐάλεντα, ἀπεκήρυξε μόνον, καὶ τὸν Κιλικίας Γεώργιον· οὕστινας μετὰ θάνατον ἀπεβάλετο, παρὰ τοῦ Κωνσταντινουπόλεως Ἀλεξάνδρου καταδίκους τὸ πρὶν ἐξιχνεύσασα.

45: HL I_2, 737–812; 819–23 (A.D. 343) ‖ 2–4 et 10–12: cf. *Epit. Th. A.*, 35, 19 sqq. (Socr. II.20) ‖ 4–10: cf. Thdrt. II.8, 1 ‖ 11: cf. Soz. III.12, 6 ‖ 13–20: cf. Thdrt. II.8, 32–33

45: 1 αὐτοῦ om. LG ‖ 3 Σαρδικῇ] σάρδει aut σάρδη codd. praeter LG (cf. cap. 47, 3) ‖ τῇ om. L ‖ 4–5 ἱσπανιῶν LG ‖ 5 Δαρδανίας om. C ‖ 6 Παννονίας LG: παιονίας D*b* ‖ ἠπείρων LG ‖ 7 ἑλισ(-ης- D)πόντου *g* ‖ πισιδίας LGE ‖ 8 Εὐξείνου om. LG ‖ 10 ἀρραβίας *b* ‖ 11 Ὅσιος om. LG ‖ ὁ[1] om. *z* ‖ κορδούβης LG ‖ ἐπίσκοπος om. LG ‖ 13 τὸν om. LG ‖ 15 κρίνασα *z* ‖ 17 Σιγδούνου AELG: συγγισούνου (sic) C συγ(γ)ιδό(-ού- V)νου *z* σιγκιδόνος D forma rectior Συγγιδούνου ‖ ἰσάκιον LG ‖ 19 οὕστινας] ὧντινων LG ‖ μετὰ] καὶ μετὰ LG ‖ ἀπεβάλλετο *b* ‖ 20 τὸ om. C

45. When the most divine Constans observed that his brother Constantius was fickle-minded and was currying favor with the Arians, he ordered a holy synod convened at Sardica, the metropolis of Illyricum and Dacia, to examine the cases of Paul and Athanasius. The participants came from Rome, Spain, Gaul, Italy, Campania, Africa, Sardinia, Dardania, Macedonia, Thessaly, Pannonia, Moesia, Achaea, Epirus, Thrace, Europe, Asia, Caria, Bithynia, Hellespont, Phrygia, Pisidia, Cappadocia, Euxine Pontus, Cilicia, Phrygia Secunda, Pamphylia, Lydia, the Cyclades Islands, Egypt, Thebais, Libya, Galatia, Palestine, and Arabia, and numbered three hundred and seventy-six prominent bishops, led by Hosius, the Abraham-like bishop of Cordoba, and by Protogenes, archbishop of Sardica. The synod proclaimed clearly the sound creed; it received Paul and Athanasius into communion; and it denounced and stripped completely of their offices Gregory of Alexandria, Quintianus of Gaza, and Basil of Ancyra under the sentence that they should not be communicated with or be addressed as bishops by any of the faithful, since they had taken over their thrones like tyrants. On the other hand, Theodore of Heracleia, Acacius of Palestine, Stephanus of Antioch, Isaacius of Singidunum, Menophantes of Ephesus, Valens of Moesia,[46] and George of Cilicia were merely deposed. The council excommunicated them posthumously, having discovered that they had previously been condemned by Alexander of Constantinople.

[46] *SV* has failed to copy correctly the text of Theodoret II.8,33 (quoting the synod's letter) which has Οὐρσάκιον ἀπὸ Συγγιδούνου τῆς Μυσίας καὶ Οὐάλεντα τὸν ἀπὸ Μυρσῶν τῆς Παννονίας.

46.

Οἱ γοῦν Ἀρειανοὶ διὰ τὸν Παῦλον καὶ Ἀθανάσιον ἀποσχίσαντες, παρασύναγμα ἐν Φιλιππουπόλει ἐπισκόπων ἑξήκοντα ἐποιήσαντο, καὶ δύσφημον ὅρον ἐκθέμενοι Παῦλον καὶ Ἀθανάσιον ἀπεκήρυξαν.

47.

Διόπερ Κουρδούβης ἐπίσκοπος ὁ πανόσιος σύνοδον θείαν καὶ ἱερὰν ἐπισκόπων ἐν τῇ οἰκείᾳ πόλει προσκαλεσάμενος τὸ θεουργὸν ἐτράνωσε μάθημα, κατακρίνας οὓς ἡ ἐν Σαρδικῇ ἀπεκήρυξε σύνοδος καὶ οὓς πάλιν ἐδικαίωσε προσδεξάμενος.

48.

Ἀλλὰ καὶ ὁ εὐσεβέστατος Κώνστας εἰς Ἀντιόχειαν ἐκ Ῥώμης πρὸς Κωνστάντιον τὸν ἴδιον ἀδελφόν, ἐκδικῶν Παῦλον καὶ Ἀθανάσιον, ἐξαπέστειλε δύο αἰδεσιμωτάτους ἐπισκόπους καλουμένους Εὐφρατᾶν καὶ Βικέντιον, μεθ' ὧν καὶ τὸν φιλόχριστον στρατηγέτην ὀνομαζόμενον Σάλιβον. Στέφανος δὲ ὁ ἄθεος, ὁ Ἀντιοχείας ἐπίσκοπος, αἱρετικῶν συνέδριον συκοφαντίας μεστὸν ποιησάμενος, χαμαιτύπην διά τινος νεανίου νυκτὸς πρὸς τοὺς εὐλαβεῖς ἐπισκόπους Ῥωμαίων εἰσήγαγεν, ὅπερ Σάλιβος ῥαδιουργηθὲν ὑπὸ Στεφάνου διήλεγξε. Διὸ ἡ συνελθοῦσα σύνοδος, καθελοῦσα Στέφανον Ἀρειανόν, Λεόντιον ἀντεχειροτόνησεν ἐκτομίαν αὐτόχειρα· ὃς τὸν «καὶ» σύνδεσμον ἐπὶ τῆς τοῦ υἱοῦ δοξολογίας τινὰς τίθεντας ἐνσημηνάμενος, καὶ τὴν «δι' οὗ» ἄλλους πρόθεσιν, ἑτέρους τὴν «ἐν» «τῷ πατρὶ» προσαρμόζοντας, σιγῇ τὸ τέλος τῆς δοξολογίας ἐπλήρου, μόνον ἐκφωνῶν «εἰς τοὺς αἰῶνας τῶν αἰώνων.»

46: HL I_2, 813–19 (A.D. 343) ‖ cf. *Epit. Th. A.*, 35, 24–26; 36, 28–29 (Socr. II.20 sqq.)

47: 1–4: cf. Phot., *Hom.*, 159, 8–10 (ed. Laourdas); *Epit. Th. A.*, 37, 10–12

48: HL I_2, 827–34 (A.D. 344) ‖ 1–9: Thdrt. II.8, 54–10, 2 ‖ 9–13: Thdrt. II.24, 1–3

47: 1 post Διόπερ add. καὶ ὁ D ‖ ad ἐπίσκοπος desinit C ‖ 3 ἐν om. *z*

48: 4 Σάλιβον AELG, mg. D: -ίνον D -ῖνον *z*, supra lin. A recte Σαλιανόν ‖ 5 ὁ^{2} om. LG ‖ 8 συνελθοῦσα] συναχθεῖσα *z* ‖ ante Στέφανον add. τὸν LG ‖ 10 τοῦ om. E ‖ τεθέντας AE ‖ 11 δι' οὗ ἄλλους LG: διὰ ἄλλην D*b* ‖ ante σιγῇ add. αὐτὸς LG

46. The Arians, then, having broken off (from the rest) because of Paul and Athanasius, formed a rival assembly of sixty[47] bishops in Philippopolis; and issuing a blasphemous definition (of faith), they denounced Paul and Athanasius.

47. For this reason the all-holy[48] bishop of Cordoba (Hosius) summoned a divine and sacred synod of bishops in his own city, proclaimed the divinely inspired creed, condemned those whom the synod at Sardica had denounced, and received back those it had absolved.[49]

48. The most pious Constans, too, in his effort to vindicate Paul and Athanasius, dispatched from Rome to his own brother Constantine at Antioch two most venerable bishops, Euphratas and Vicentius by name, accompanied by the devout general Salibus. But Stephen, the ungodly bishop of Antioch, having organized a completely slanderous assembly of heretics, employed a young man to infiltrate a prostitute among the devout Roman bishops during the night, (a trick) which Salibus denounced as having been devised by Stephen. On this account the assembled synod[50] deposed the Arian Stephen and appointed in his place the self-castrate Leontius. This man, noting that some were using the conjunction "and" in the doxology of the Son, others the preposition "through," and others applying "in" to "the Father,"[51] passed over the end of the doxology silently, voicing only the words "for ever and ever."

[47] *Epit.Th.A.*, 35, line 21 (agreeing with Socrates II.20 and Sozomen III.12,7) numbers the Eastern bishops at 76, Theophanes (43 line 18) at 36.

[48] The word πανόσιος is a pun on the name Ὅσιος.

[49] The claim that Hosius held a synod of his own (at Cordoba, according to *SV*) is found also in Photius, *Hom.*, 159, and in the *Epit.Th.A.*, 37, lines 10–12 which read: ὁμοίως δὲ καὶ Ὅσιος ὁ Κουδρούβης ἰδίᾳ συναγαγὼν καθεῖλε τοὺς αὐτούς· ἐπὶ δὲ Παύλῳ καὶ Ἀθανασίῳ τὰ αὐτὰ τοῖς ἐν Σαρδικῇ συνελθοῦσιν ἐτύπωσε. But as Hansen (*ibid.*, 37) points out, this passage of the *Epit.Th.A.* is based on a misunderstanding by Theodore of Sozomen III.12,1–3.

[50] The present synod is probably the same as that described in chap. 44; see HL, I_2, 828.

[51] "Father" is an error for "(Holy) Spirit"; cf. Theodoret II.24,3 and Philostorgius III.13. The reason may have been a misreading of $\overline{\pi\rho\iota}$ from $\overline{\pi\rho\iota}$.

49.

Κώνσταντος οὖν τοῦ φιλοχρίστου διὰ Σαλίβου Κωνσταντίῳ πόλεμον ἀπειλήσαντος, εἰ Παύλῳ καὶ Ἀθανασίῳ τοὺς ἰδίους θρόνους ἀποδοῦναι διαναβάλλοιτο, σύνοδος θεία καὶ ἱερὰ τοπικὴ ἐν Ἱεροσολύμοις ἠθροίζετο, Μάξιμον τὸν ὁμολογητὴν καὶ μακάριον ἐκ τοῦ πάλαι διωγμοῦ ἀγκύλην καὶ ὀφθαλμὸν τῶν δεξιῶν μερῶν ἀφῃρημένον ἔξαρχον τῆς ἁγίας πόλεως ἀρχιεπίσκοπον ἔχουσα· ἣ τὸ σωτηριῶδες μάθημα βεβαιώσασα Παῦλον καὶ Ἀθανάσιον ἀπεδέξατο.

50.

Ἀθανασίου τοίνυν καὶ Παύλου τιμίως πορευομένων πρὸς τὰ ἴδια ποίμνια, τῆς ἀσεβείας οἱ πρόμαχοι σύνοδον ἐν Ἱεροσολύμοις αἱρετικὴν συνεκρότησαν καὶ τὸν μὲν ὁμολογητὴν ἀπεβάλοντο Μάξιμον, τὸν δὲ κατηχητὴν ὡς Ἀρειανὸν ἐχειροτόνησαν Κύριλλον· ὃν ἡ ἐπὶ Δαμάσου ἐν Ῥώμῃ καὶ ἡ ἐπὶ Νεκταρίου ἐν Κωνσταντινουπόλει πολλοῖς ἐπαίνοις ἐξαίρουσι σύνοδοι. Καὶ Ἀκάκιος ὁ Καισαρείας τῆς Φιλίππου, Εὐσεβίου τοῦ Παμφίλου φοιτητὴς καὶ διάδοχος, χάριν πρωτείων τοῦ θρόνου τοῦτον ἐξήλασεν.

49: HL I_2, 836 (A.D. 346) ‖ 1–3: cf. *Epit. Th. A.*, 36, 29–31 ‖ 3–7: cf. *Epit. Th. A.*, 39, 22–29; Phot., *Hom.*, 159, 12–15 ‖ 4–5: cf. Thdrt. II.26, 6

50: 2–3: cf. *Epit. Th. A.*, 47, 27–28 (Socr. II.38, 2) ‖ 6–7: cf. *Epit. Th. A.*, 49, 23–25; Thdrt. II.26, 6–7

49: 1 κώνστα γοῦν LG ‖ 2 παῦλον καὶ ἀθανάσιον *g* ‖ 3 διαναβάλοιτο LG ‖ 4 καὶ μακάριον om. LG ‖ 5 τῶν δεξιῶν LG: τὸν δεξιὸν D*b* ‖ μερῶν] μηρὸν *b* ‖ 7 προσεδέξατο *b*

50: 3 ἀπεβάλοντο *g*: -άλετο E -άλλετο A*z* ‖ 6 τῆς om. LG ‖ Παμφύλου DA^s *z*: -ίλου LGE ‖ 7 τοῦτον om. LG ‖ ἐξήγαγεν *b*

49. After the Christ-loving Constans, then, had sent Salibus to threaten Constantius with war, if he hesitated to restore their own thrones to Paul and Athanasius, a divine and sacred local synod was convened in Jerusalem, presided over by the holy city's archbishop, the blessed confessor Maximus, who had been left both hamstrung and blind on the right side[52] in the old persecution. It confirmed the saving creed and received back Paul and Athanasius.

50. When Athanasius, then, and Paul returned with honor to their own flocks, the champions of impiety assembled a heretical synod in Jerusalem, expelled Maximus the Confessor, and elected (in his place) Cyril the Catechist, since he was an Arian. Cyril was exalted with great praise by the synods in Rome under Damasus and in Constantinople under Nectarius, but Acacius of Caesarea Philippi, the pupil and successor of Eusebius of Pamphilus, banished him from his throne in the dispute over leadership.

[52] Compare Theodoret II.26,6: τόν τε γὰρ δεξιὸν ὀφθαλμὸν ἀφῄρητο καὶ τῆς ἀγκύλης ἐστέρητο τῆς δεξιᾶς.

51.

Ἀντάραντος οὖν Μαγνεντίου καὶ τὸν μακάριον Κώνσταντα πατάξαντος, μεμαθηκὼς ὁ Κωνστάντιος Γάλλον μὲν τὸν ἀδελφὸν Ἰουλιανοῦ τοῦ παραβάτου ἀναγορεύσας καίσαρα τῶν ἑῴων φροντίζειν ἐκέλευσεν· αὐτὸς δὲ μετὰ μεγίστης δυνάμεως δι' Εὐρώπης ἐχώρησε τοὺς πολεμίους χειρούμενος καὶ ταῖς ἐκκλησίαις κλόνον προσφέρων οὐ μέτριον. Ὅθεν καὶ κελεύει σύνοδον αἱρετικὴν ἐν Σερμίῳ ἀθροίζεσθαι, προφάσει μὲν Φωτεινοῦ τοῦ ἐπισκόπου αὐτῆς ὄντος ἀνθρωπολάτρου καὶ ἄφρονος, ἀληθείᾳ δὲ κατὰ τοῦ θείου συμβόλου καὶ Ἀθανασίου τοῦ γενναιόφρονος. Ἥτις ὅρον πίστεως ἐξέθετο ἄθεον φύσιν ἢ οὐσίαν ἐπὶ θεοῦ λέγειν ἀπαγορεύοντα, ὅντινά φασιν [ἐπὶ τοῦ παραβάτου Ἰουλιανοῦ] Μάρκον ἐκθέσθαι τὸν Ἀρεθούσιον, παρὰ τῶν Ἀρεθουσίων πολλὰ παθόντα διὰ τὸν κύριον ἐπὶ Ἰουλιανοῦ τοῦ παραβάτου, οὗ τὰς σάρκας μακαρίας ὁμοῦ καὶ ἀθλίας ὁ θεολόγος ἔφη Γρηγόριος.

52.

Μετὰ γοῦν τὴν σύνοδον ταύτην Κωνστάντιος ἐν Μεδιολάνῳ πόλει τῆς Ἰταλίας ἑτέραν γενέσθαι διαταξάμενος τοὺς ἑσπερίους ἐπισκόπους συνήθροισεν· ἥτις ἁγία θεόπνευστος σύνοδος, μὴ ἀνασχομένη τοῦ βασιλέως καὶ τῆς Ἀρειανικῆς οὐ φροντίσασα φάλαγγος, ἀνατρέψαι τὸ θεῖον σύμβολον καὶ τὴν ἐν Τύρῳ κυρῶσαι Ἀθανασίου καθαίρεσιν ἀπηρνήσατο. Διὸ τοὺς ἐξάρχους αὐτῆς ἐξορίᾳ Κωνστάντιος κατεδίκασε, τὸν τῶν ἀποστολικῶν διδαχῶν κήρυκα τὸν Ῥώμης πάπαν Λιβέριον, πρὸς τὸν αὐτοκράτορα πολλοῖς ἐλέγχοις τὸ τηνικαῦτα χρησάμενον, τοὺς Γαλλιῶν μητροπολίτας Παυλῖνον καὶ Διονύσιον, τὸν Ἰταλίας μητροπολίτην Εὐσέβιον τὸν μακάριον καὶ Λουκίφερ τὸν Σαρδανίας τῆς νήσου ἀρχιεπίσκοπον.

51: HL I_2, 852–62 (A.D. 351) ‖ 2–3: cf. *Epit. Th. A.*, 42, 25–27 ‖ 4–5: cf. Thdrt. II.15, 1–2 ‖ 6–10: cf. *Epit. Th. A.*, 42, 32–43, 9 ‖ 10–12: cf. *Epit. Th. A.*, 58, 4–6 ‖ 12 Γρηγόριος: *Or.* 4.89 (PG, 35, 620B)

52: HL I_2, 872–77 (A.D. 355) ‖ 1–7: Thdrt. II.15, 2–3 ‖ 7–10: Thdrt. II.15, 4 (Athanas., *Apol. de fuga sua* 4) ‖ 7–8: cf. Thdrt. II.15, 10 sqq.

51: 1 κώνσταν LG ‖ 3 ἐκέλευσε φροντίζειν *b* ‖ 5 καὶ^2 om. LG ‖ 7 ὄντος om. LG ‖ 9 post φασιν add. τὸν E ‖ ἐπὶ — 10 Ἰουλιανοῦ] post Ἀρεθούσιον transp. LG seclusimus ‖ 11 ἐπὶ — παραβάτου A*z*: om. E*g*

52: 1 οὖν LG ‖ τὴν σύνοδον om. LG ‖ 2 ἐπισκόπους om. *z* ‖ 3 post ἁγία add. καὶ LG ‖ 6 τὸν om. LG ‖ 7 πάπαν om. LG ‖ τὸν^2 om. *z* ‖ 8 παυλῖνον LG: παῦλον D*b* ‖ 9 μητροπολίτην om. E ‖ 10 τῆς om. LG

51. When Constantius, then, learned of Magnentius' rebellion and his murder of the blessed Constans, he named as Caesar Gallus, Julian the Apostate's brother, and commanded him to take charge of the East, while he himself traveled through Europe with a very great force, defeating his enemies and causing not a little turmoil for the churches. Whereupon, he ordered a heretical synod summoned at Sirmium, allegedly against Photinus, bishop of that city, an anthropolatrist and fool; the real targets, however, were the holy symbol (of faith) and the noble-minded Athanasius. The synod issued an ungodly creed which forbade the predication of nature or substance in God. It is said to have been composed by Marcus of Arethusa who suffered much at the hands of the Arethusians for the Lord's sake during the reign of Julian the Apostate; Gregory the Theologian described his flesh as being at once blessed and wretched.[53]

52. After this synod Constantius ordered another to convene in Milan, Italy, where he assembled the western bishops. This holy and divinely inspired synod, not giving in to the emperor and not heeding the Arian forces, refused to change the holy symbol (of faith) or to confirm Athanasius' excommunication at Tyre. Because of this, Constantius condemned the synod's leaders to banishment; namely, Liberius, the Pope of Rome and herald of apostolic teachings who made many charges against the Emperor at that time; the metropolitans of Gaul, Paulinus and Dionysius;[54] the blessed Eusebius, metropolitan of Italy; and Lucifer, the archbishop of the island of Sardinia.

[53] Gregory (PG, 35, 620B) in fact says . . . τὴν βρῶσιν τῶν μακαρίων ἐκείνων σαρκῶν, οὐ γὰρ ἀθλίων ἂν εἴποιμι.

[54] The text of Theodoret II.15,4 (quoting Athanasius, *Apologia de fuga sua,* chap. 4) has not been read accurately: Παυλῖνος ὁ τῆς μητροπόλεως τῶν Γαλλιῶν καὶ Διονύσιος ὁ τῆς μητροπόλεως τῆς Ἰταλίας.

53.

Τούτων ἐξορισθέντων ἐνδελεχισμῷ τῶν ἑτεροδόξων Κωνστάντιος ἐν Ἀριμήνῳ σύνοδον ἁγίων ἐπισκόπων ἑσπερίων διακοσίων συγκροτηθῆναι προσέταξε καὶ τῶν περὶ Εὐδόξιον Γερμανικίας βραχυτελῶν ἀρειοφρόνων· ἥτις θεία καὶ ἱερὰ σύνοδος τὸ θεῖον κυρώσασα σύμβολον ἀνεθεμάτισεν Ἄρειον καὶ τοὺς ἐκείνου συνίστορας, ὅπερ οἱ ἑτερόδοξοι, Εὐδόξιος καὶ Οὐρσάκιος, Οὐάλης, Δημόφιλος καὶ Γρηγόριος οὐ προσήκαντο, καὶ διὰ τοῦτό γε τῆς συνόδου ἀπεκηρύχθησαν· ὕστερον μέντοι γνησίως μετανοήσαντας Οὐάλην τε καὶ Οὐρσάκιον, καίπερ Ἀθανασίου συκοφάντας δεινοὺς χρηματίσαντας, ὡς ἐπισκόπους ἐδέξατο. Καὶ ἔνιοι ταύτην καὶ τὴν ἐν Νικαίᾳ διὰ τοὺς εὑρεθέντας αἱρετικοὺς ἐν αὐταῖς κακῶς διασύρουσιν.

54.

Οἱ γοῦν περὶ Εὐδόξιον τῆς ἀσεβείας ὑπέρμαχοι δόκιμοι Εὐσεβίου συνάρσει πείθουσι τὸν Κωνστάντιον ἐν Νίκῃ τῆς Θρᾴκης κατὰ τοῦ θείου συμβόλου σύνοδον αἱρετικῆς συστήσασθαι φάλαγγος, εἰς ἅπαν ἐξάραντα τὸ ὁμοούσιον πίστεως ὅρον ἐκθέμενοι, εἰς ὃν οἱ μὲν δέει, οἱ δὲ φενακισμῷ, τῶν ὀρθοδόξων ὑπέγραψαν· ὧν οἱ συνθέσθαι μὴ βουληθέντες εἰς τὰς ἐσχατιὰς τῆς οἰκουμένης ἐξόριστοι διεπέμφθησαν.

53: HL I_2, 934–55 (A.D. 359) ‖ 1–2: cf. Thdrt. II.18, 1 ‖ 2: cf. Thdrt. II.23, 5 ‖ 4–5: cf. Thdrt. II.18, 3 ‖ 5–6: Thdrt. II.23, 4 (Athanas., *Epist. ad Afros* 3–4, PG, 26, 1033)

54: HL I_2, 941–43 (A.D. 359) ‖ 1–4: Thdrt. II.21, 1 ‖ 4–6: Thdrt. II.21, 7

53: 1 ἐνδελεχησμῶ codd. praeter LG ‖ ἑτεροδόξων] ὀρθοδόξων *b* ‖ 3 περὶ] πρὸς *z* ‖ βραχυτελεῖς ἀρειόφρονας codd. praeter E ‖ 5 συνίστορας] ὁμόφρονας LG ‖ Εὐδόξιος] εὐσέβιος *b* ‖ 6 Οὐάλης om. *z* ‖ καὶ[2] om. *b* ‖ 9 ἐδέξαντο *b* ‖ καὶ[1] GOTMN: κἂν cett. ‖ Νικαίᾳ] immo Νίκῃ (cf. cap. 54) ‖ 10 ἐν αὐταῖς κακῶς om. LG ‖ διασύρωσιν AED

54: 1 οὖν LG ‖ 3 ἐξάραντα] ἐξῆραν LG

53. After the banishment of these men, Constantius, at the insistence of the heterodox,[55] ordered a synod to convene at Rimini which was composed of two hundred holy western bishops, and the followers of Eudoxius of Germanicia whose support of Arius was short-lived. Confirming the holy symbol (of faith), this divine and sacred synod anathematized Arius and his sympathizers. But the symbol was rejected by the heterodox, Eudoxius, Ursacius, Valens, Demophilus, and Gregory,[56] for which reason they were expelled from the synod. Later, however, Valens and Ursacius, though fierce slanderers of Athanasius, had a genuine change of mind and were accepted back as bishops. On account of the heretics they contained, there are some who unjustly disparage this synod and that of Nicaea.[57]

54. The followers of Eudoxius, then, those outstanding[58] champions of impiety, with the support of Eusebius, persuaded Constantius to assemble a synod of the heretical phalanx at Nice in Thrace against the divine symbol, and they issued a definition of faith from which the term "consubstantial" was eradicated altogether. Of the orthodox some were frightened, others cheated, into subscribing to it, while those who refused to accept it were banished to the remotest corners of the world.

[55] Theodoret (II.18,1) states clearly that the Arian opponents of the Nicene Creed persuaded Constantius to summon the synod; hence the choice of ἑτεροδόξων over ὀρθοδόξων.

[56] There is no Gregory among those named by Theodoret II.23,4 (quoting Athanasius *Epist. ad Afros* 3–4, PG, 26, 1033).

[57] Νικαίᾳ can only be an error (perhaps scribal) for Νίκη, the synod described in the next chapter.

[58] Meant sarcastically.

55.

Τὸν ὅρον τοίνυν τοῦτον τῶν ἑσπερίων πατέρων καθυποβαλλόντων τοῖς πρέπουσιν ἀναθέμασι μαθόντες οἱ ἑτερόδοξοι, συναρπάσαντες τὸν Κωνστάντιον ἐν Νικαίᾳ τῆς Βιθυνίας συνεκρότησαν σύνοδον τὸ θεῖον ἀράσασθαι σύμβολον. Ἀλλὰ πρὶν τῆς βλασφημίας ἐνάρξαιντο, θεὸς ὁ τῶν ἁγίων τριακοσίων δέκα καὶ ὀκτὼ πατέρων κατασείσας τὴν πόλιν συντετριμμένους αὐτοὺς ἐκεῖθεν ἐξέβαλε.

56.

Μεμωλωπισμένοι γοῦν διασπαρέντες οἱ ἑτερόδοξοι τὸν Κωνστάντιον ἐν Σελευκείᾳ τῆς Ἰσαυρίας ποιῆσαι παρασκευάζουσι σύνοδον, ὅρον ἐκθέμενοι παρὰ τῶν ἑσπερίων ὀρθοδόξων πολλοῖς βαλλόμενον ἀναθέμασιν· ἐν ᾗ τὸν κατηχητὴν Κύριλλον Ἱεροσολύμων ἀρχιεπίσκοπον παρὰ τῷ θείῳ Σιλβανῷ Σελευκείας ὁ Καισαρείας Φιλίππου Ἀκάκιος θεασάμενος, ὃς ποικίλαις διαβολαῖς διὰ τὴν χρυσῆν ἱερὰν στολὴν ἀποκινήσας τὸν δίκαιον τοῦ θρόνου αὐτοῦ, μυσαττόμενος τὸν Γερμανικίας Εὐδόξιον μεταστάντα εἰς Συρίας τὴν Ἀντιόχειαν μεθ' ἑαυτοῦ προσλαβόμενος, ἐν Κωνσταντινουπόλει ὥρμησε πρὸς Κωνστάντιον.

55: HL I_2, 929 (A.D. 358) ‖ 3–6: Thdrt. II.26, 1–3

56: HL I_2, 946–55 (A.D. 359) ‖ 2–9: cf. Thdrt. II.26, 4–11 ‖ 6: Thdrt. II.27, 2

55: 1 τοίνυν om. E ‖ 1 καθυποβαλόντων LG ‖ 3 ἐκρότησαν LG ‖ 4 ἀλλὰ καὶ *b* ‖ πρὶν] πρὶν ἢ LG

56: 3 παρὰ gE: περὶ A*z* ‖ 4 Κύριλλον om. LG ‖ ἀρχιεπίσκοπον om. LG ‖ 5 θεασάμενος — 7 Γερμανικίας om. *z* ‖ 5 ὃς *SV*[2]: ὡς cett. ‖ 7 τὸν Γερμ. — 8 Ἀντιόχειαν] εὐδόξιον ἀντιοχείας LG

55. When this definition, then, had been subjected to fitting anathemas by the western bishops, the heterodox learned of their action, and winning over Constantius, they summoned a synod to Nicaea[59] in Bithynia to execrate the divine symbol. But before they could begin their blasphemy, the God of the three hundred and eighteen holy fathers shook the city with an earthquake and drove them contrite out of there.

56. When the defeated heterodox, then, had dispersed, they persuaded Constantius to assemble a synod at Seleucia in Isauria and issued a definition of faith which the western bishops subjected to many anathemas. In this council, seeing the catechist Cyril, archbishop of Jerusalem, siding with the holy Silvanus of Seleucia, Acacius of Caesarea Philippi, who with various calumnies had removed the just man (Cyril) from his throne on account of the holy golden robe,[60] became disgusted, and taking along with him Eudoxius of Germanicia, who had transferred to Antioch in Syria, he set out for Constantius in Constantinople.

[59] The writer is following Theodoret (II.26,1–3), who alone of all the main sources states that the bishops actually assembled for the abortive synod at Nicaea rather than at Nicomedia. The chapter is chronologically out of place, since the synod attempted to meet in 358, before that of Rimini (chap. 53); see HL, I_2, 929. Again, the compiler has been led by the narrative of Theodoret.

[60] The wording leaves no doubt that *SV* has read the version of the story given by Theodoret (II.27,2), and not that of Sozomen (IV.25,3–4).

57.

Ὁ δὲ βασιλεὺς τῇ δυάδι τῆς ἀσεβείας φενακιζόμενος ἐν Βυζαντίῳ αἱρετικὴν συνεκρότησε σύνοδον, πολλῇ δυνάμει σπουδάσασαν τοῦ θείου συμβόλου καταγωνίσασθαι· καὶ οὐχ ἡ τυχοῦσα στάσις ἐντεῦθεν μεταξὺ τῶν ἑτεροδόξων καὶ ὀρθοδόξων παρηκολούθησεν· ὁ γὰρ μακαρίτης Ἀντιοχείας Εὐστάθιος ἐκ τοῦ παρ' αὐτοῖς ἐκτεθέντος ἀσεβοῦς τόμου ἀνόμοιον λέγοντας τὸ «ἐξ οὗ» τῷ «δι' οὗ» τὸν ἄθεον Εὐσέβιον διήλεγξε καὶ Ἀέτιον. Τέλος καθελοῦσα ὡς μὴ λέγοντα κτίσμα τὸν υἱὸν τοῦ θεοῦ Μακεδόνιον, ἀλλ' εἰς τὸ θεῖον πνεῦμα καὶ μόνον προσκρούοντα καὶ ἀλλότριον αὐτὸ φάσκοντα εἶναι παντελῶς τῆς θεότητος, ἀντεισάγει εἰς Βυζάντιον τὸν ἐκ Γερμανικίας μετελθόντα εἰς Ἀντιοχείαν Εὐδόξιον τὸν παμμίαρον, ἤδη τοῦ δυσσεβοῦς Εὐσεβίου τὸν βίον τελέσαντος καὶ τοῦ ὁμολογητοῦ Παύλου πρὸς κύριον ἐκδημήσαντος. Πρὸς τούτοις ἀνεθεμάτισε καὶ τὸν διάκονον Ἀλεξανδρείας Ἀέτιον, τὸν ἀρχηγὸν Εὐνομίου καὶ Θεοφρονίου διδάσκαλον.

58.

Μετὰ δὲ ταῦτα μαθὼν ὁ Κωνστάντιος τοὺς Πέρσας πολιορκεῖν τὸ Νιτζίβιον ἐπ' Ἀντιόχειαν ὥρμησε, καὶ Σαβωρίου ἀναχωρήσαντος αὐτὸς εἰς ἅπαν ἐξᾶραι τὸ ὁμοούσιον φρυαττόμενος καὶ τὸ ἑτεροούσιον κηρύξαι σύνοδον συνεκρότησε. Τοῦ δὲ θρόνου Ἀντιοχείας χηρεύοντος, Ἀρειανοί τε καὶ οἱ ὀρθόδοξοι Σεβαστείας τῆς Ἀρμενίων ἀρχιεπίσκοπον Μελέτιον προχειρίζονται. Ὁ δὲ βασιλεὺς τὴν ἑρμηνείαν τοῦ «κύριος ἔκτισέ με ἀρχὴν ὁδῶν αὐτοῦ» παρὰ τῶν ἐπισκόπων ἰδιοσυστάτως ἐξαιτησάμενος, πλείστων

57: HL I_2, 956–59 (A.D. 360) ‖ 1–4: cf. Thdrt. II.27, 1–4 ‖ 4–6: Thdrt. II.27, 5–7; 13 ‖ 6–9: cf. Thdrt. II.6, 1–2

58: HL I_2, 960 (A.D. 361) ‖ 1–2: Thdrt. II.30, 1 sqq. (*Epit. Th. A.*, 53, 19 sqq.) ‖ 3–5: Thdrt. II.31, 1–5 (*Epit. Th. A.*, 53, 25–29) ‖ 6–7: Thdrt. II.31, 6 (Prov. 8:22)

57: 1 εὐσεβείας ut vid. A ‖ 3 οὐχ ἡ] οὐ LG ‖ 4–5 εὐστάθιος ἀντιοχείας *z* ‖ 6 τῷ] τὸ LG*z* ‖ Εὐσέβιον] immo Εὐδόξιον; cf. cap. 53, 5 lect. *b* ‖ διήλεγχε LG ‖ 9 ἀντεισάγει] ἀντιχειροτονεῖ δὲ LG ‖ εἰς Βυζάντιον om. LG ‖ κατελθόντα *b* ‖ 12 τὸν[1] om. LG

58: 1 ὁ om. LG ‖ 5 οἱ om. *b* ‖ ἀρμενίας *z*

57. But the emperor, deluded by this impious pair,[61] convoked a heretical synod in Byzantium, which was eager to attack with great force the divine symbol. Whereupon, no ordinary conflict ensued between the heterodox and orthodox. For the blessed Eustathius of Antioch refuted the ungodly Eusebius[62] and Aetius on account of the statement contained in the impious document issued by them which said that "of whom" differs from "through whom." Finally, after it condemned Macedonius who refused to call the Son of God a creature, attacking only the Holy Spirit and describing Him as completely distinct from the Godhead, the synod brought to Byzantium in his place the utterly abominable Eudoxius of Germanicia who had transferred to Antioch, the unholy Eusebius by now having completed his life and Paul the Confessor having departed to the Lord. In addition to these, it also anathematized Aetius, the deacon of Alexandria who had been Eunomius' leader and Theophronius' teacher.

58. When later on Constantius learned of the Persian siege at Nisibis, he set out for Antioch, where, following the withdrawal of Sapor, he summoned a synod in his great eagerness to eradicate once and for all (the formula) "of one substance" and proclaim "of different substance." Since the throne of Antioch was vacant, the Arians and orthodox chose Meletius, the archbishop of Sebaste in Armenia. But when the Emperor requested the bishops to interpret in the sense of 'separate existence' the text "The Lord created me in the beginning of his ways," and when a very large number had impiously adhe-

[61] That is, Acacius and Eudoxius; see the previous chapter.

[62] This is an error for Eudoxius. Furthermore, only Aetius admitted to being the author of the anomoean document, while Eudoxius, having denied any involvement, was shortly afterward appointed patriarch of Constantinople; see Theodoret II.27,5–22.

δυσσεβῶς προσελθόντων Μελέτιος ὀρθοδόξως ἐκθέμενος μεγαλοφώνως ὁμοούσιον τὴν ἁγίαν τριάδα ἐκήρυξε· καὶ τοῦ ἀρχιδιακόνου τὸ στόμα τούτου φιμώσαντος, ἐκεῖνος διὰ τῶν δακτύλων τὸ θεουργὸν ἐκήρυξε μάθημα· ὅπερ οἱ κακόδοξοι θεασάμενοι, Σαβελλισμὸν αὐτῷ πλέξαντες ἐξορίᾳ παρέπεμψαν, καὶ τὸν σὺν Ἀρείῳ ἀναθεματισθέντα Εὐζώϊον προχειρίζονται, ὑφ' οὗ καὶ νοσήσας Κωνστάντιος βαπτισθεὶς τὸν βίον κατέλιπεν.

59.

Αὐτοκράτωρ τοίνυν Ῥωμαίων Ἰουλιανὸς ὁ παραβάτης γενόμενος τοὺς ὑπὸ Κωνσταντίου ἐξορισθέντας ἐπισκόπους προσχήματι συμπαθείας ἀνεκαλέσατο. Ἀθανάσιος οὖν ὁ μακάριος ἐν Ἀλεξανδρείᾳ συναθροίσας τοὺς ἀφεθέντας ἐπισκόπους ἐκ τῶν ἀλύσεων συνοδικῶς τὰ ἐν Νικαίᾳ δογματισθέντα ἐκύρωσε καὶ τὴν Ἀρειανικὴν ἀνεθεμάτισεν ἀθεότητα· ἐπισκόπους δὲ τοὺς μέχρι τότε τῇ πλάνῃ ἐμμείναντας μετανοοῦντας εἰς κοινωνίαν δεξάμενος ἱερουργεῖν διεκώλυσεν.

60.

Ὁμοίως δὲ καὶ Μελέτιος ὁ ἀοίδιμος ἀναλαβὼν Εὐσέβιον καὶ Λουκίφερ τὸν ἐν Ἀντιοχείᾳ τοῖς Εὐσταθιανοῖς Παυλῖνον χειροτονήσαντα καὶ πολλὰς καινοτομίας παραδεδωκότα τῷ ὑπ' αὐτοῦ διδασκομένῳ ποιμνίῳ, καὶ αὐτὸς θρόνον τὸν ἑαυτοῦ καταλαμβάνει τὴν Ἀντιόχειαν· ἐν ᾗ τοὺς ἐκ Συρίας καὶ Φοινίκης ἀρχιερεῖς συλλεξάμενος τὰ ἐν Νικαίᾳ συνοδικῶς ἀνεκήρυξεν.

9–10: *Epit. Th. A.*, 53, 30–32 ‖ 11–12: *Epit. Th. A.*, 54, 23–25 ‖ 12–13: cf. *Epit. Th. A.*, 55, 22–25; Philostorg. VI.5

59: HL I_2, 963–67 (cf. cap. 61) (A.D. 362) ‖ 2–3: cf. *Epit. Th. A.*, 57, 1–2 (Socr. III.1,48); Thdrt. III.4, 1 ‖ 3–5: *Epit. Th. A.*, 58, 9–10 (Soz. V.12, 1–3) ‖ 6–7: cf. Athanas., *Epist. ad Rufinianum*, PG, 26, 1180C

60: HL I_2, 967–68 (A.D. 362) ‖ 1–4: cf. Thdrt. III.4–5 ‖ 4–5: cf. Soz. VI.4, 6 (Socr. III.25, 7–10)

---

8 δυσσεβῶν LGOTMN ‖ 9 ἁγίαν] παναγίαν LG ‖ ante τὸ στόμα add. χειρὶ LG ‖ 12 εὐδόξιον *z* ‖ 13 κατέλοιπεν A^sV καταλέλοιπεν DE

59: 3 γοῦν LG ‖ 4 ἀφαιρεθέντας A^s ‖ 5 ἀθεότητα] φάλαγγα LG ‖ 7 διεκώλυσεν LG: διεκέλευσεν cett.

60: 3 αὐτοῦ LG: -ῶν D*b* ‖ τὸ - - - διδασκόμενον ποίμνιον LG ‖ 4 τὴν] καὶ τὴν A^s ‖ 5 ἐκήρυξεν *z*

red, Meletius expounded the orthodox doctrine and loudly proclaimed the consubstantiality of the Holy Trinity. Even when the archdeacon blocked his mouth, he proclaimed the divinely-inspired creed by means of his fingers. Witnessing this, the heterodox party plotted a charge of Sabellianism against him, banished him to exile, and appointed Euzoius who had been anathematized along with Arius. Constantius fell ill, was baptized by this Euzoius, and departed from life.

59. When Julian the Apostate, then, became emperor of the Romans, he feigned compassion and recalled the bishops banished by Constantius. Whereupon, the blessed Athanasius, gathering at Alexandria the bishops released from bondage, confirmed by means of a synod[63] the teachings of Nicaea and anathematized the Arian impiety. And while he received back into communion on repenting those bishops who had persisted in the error until then, he barred[64] them from their priestly functions.

60. Likewise, the illustrious Meletius, having received Eusebius and Lucifer, the one who had ordained Paulinus for the Eustathian group in Antioch and had introduced many novel teachings to the fold under his instruction, he himself took possession of his throne at Antioch. Here he assembled a synod of the bishops from Syria and Phoenicia and proclaimed the teachings of Nicaea.

[63] This chap. and chap. 61 are really describing one and the same synod; the writer may well have been misled by the two separate references to the synod in the *Epit. Th. A.*, 58 line 9 ff. and 59 line 17 ff.

[64] διεκώλυσεν is one of the several sound corrections made by the person responsible for the version of *SV* found in manuscripts L and G. Cf. Athanasius, *Epist. ad Rufinianum*, PG, 26, 1180C and HL, I_2, 964.

61.

Ἔτι γε μὴν καὶ ὁ πολύαθλος Ἀθανάσιος τοὺς ὑπ' αὐτὸν ἀρχιερεῖς ἐν Ἀλεξανδρείᾳ προσκαλεσάμενος ἀναθεματίζει συνοδικῶς τὸν ἄνουν Ἀπολινάριον, καὶ τὴν σάρκα Χριστοῦ τοῦ θεοῦ ἡμῶν ἔμψυχον, νοεράν, λογικήν, κατὰ τοὺς παλαιοὺς πατέρας εὐσεβῶς ἀνεκήρυξε· καθ' ὃν χρόνον καὶ Ἰουλιανὸς ὁ παραβάτης ἐν Περσίδι ἀνῄρητο.

62.

Ἰουβιανοῦ δὲ σὺν θεῷ βασιλεύσαντος καὶ εἰς Ἀντιόχειαν καταντήσαντος, ὁ Καισαρείας τῆς Παλαιστίνης Ἀκάκιος καὶ πλεῖστοι σὺν ἐκείνῳ ἐπίσκοποι λίβελλον εὐσεβείας ἐκθέμενοι πρὸς τὸν ἀγαθὸν σκοπὸν τοῦ βασιλέως ἐπιδεδώκασιν.

63.

Ὁ δὲ θειότατος Ἰουβιανὸς αὐτοκράτωρ ἀποστείλας εἰς Ἀλεξάνδρειαν Ἀθανασίῳ, τὸν ἀπαράλλακτον ὅρον τῆς ἀληθοῦς ὀρθοδοξίας ἐζήτησεν. Ὃς συναγαγὼν τοὺς λογάδας τῶν ἐπισκόπων Αἰγύπτου, Θηβαΐδος καὶ Λιβύης, ὅρον συνοδικὸν πλήρη ἀληθείας καὶ χάριτος Ἰουβιανῷ τῷ φιλοχρίστῳ ἀπέστειλεν οὐ μετὰ πολὺ ἐκ τῶν ἐπιγείων πρὸς τὰ οὐράνια μετελθόντι βασίλεια.

61: HL I_2, 963–67 (cf. cap. 59) (A.D. 362) ‖ 3–4: cf. *Epit. Th. A.*, 59, 17 sqq.

62: HL I_2, 972–73 (A.D. 363) ‖ 2–4: cf. *Epit. Th. A.*, 62, 20–23

63: HL I_2, 971–72 (A.D. 363) ‖ 1–2: cf. *Epit. Th. A.*, 62, 14–16 (Thdrt. IV.2, 3–4) ‖ 3–5: Thdrt. IV.2, 5–3, 1; *Epit. Th. A.*, 62, 16–17

61: 2 ἄνουν] ἄνομον A^s ‖ 4 post παλαιοὺς add. ἁγίους LG ‖ 5 ὁ παραβάτης om. LG

62: 2 Καισαρείας τῆς om. LG

63: 1 Ἰουβιανὸς om. LG ‖ ὁ αὐτοκράτωρ *z* ‖ 4 συνοδικῶς πλήρης LG ‖ 5 μετελθόντα *z*

61. Furthermore, the much-afflicted Athanasius, having summoned the bishops under him to a synod[65] in Alexandria, placed the "mindless"[66] Apolinarius under anathema and, following the ancient fathers, he piously proclaimed the flesh of Christ our God to be endowed with soul, mind, and reason. It was at this time also that Julian the Apostate was killed in Persia.

62. When Jovian became emperor by the grace of God and had come to Antioch, Acacius of Caesarea Palestine and a large number of bishops with him issued a statement of orthodoxy which they submitted to comply with the emperor's pious views.

63. The most divine Emperor Jovian, sending (a letter) to Athanasius in Alexandria, requested from him the "exactly like" formula of true orthodoxy. Athanasius, summoning the leading bishops of Egypt, Thebais, and Libya, dispatched a synodical statement full of truth and grace to the Christ-loving Jovian, who not long afterward passed from the earthly to the heavenly kingdom.

[65] See note 63 *supra*.

[66] Referring to Apolinarius' teaching that Christ is ἄνους; cf. Theodoret V.9,19.

64.

Οὐαλεντινιανοῦ τοίνυν τοῦ αὐτοκράτορος τὸν ἴδιον ἀδελφὸν Οὐάλεντα βασιλέα τῶν ἑῴων Ῥωμαίων ἀναγορεύσαντος καὶ πρὸς τὴν Ῥώμην ἀπαίροντος ἐν Μεδιολάνῳ συνηθροίζετο σύνοδος, ὅπως Εὐδόξιον τὸν ἐκεῖσε γεγονότα ἐπίσκοπον, Ἀρειανὸν καὶ πνευματομάχον ὑπάρχοντα, καὶ μετὰ θάνατον ἀναθέματι καθυποβάλλη τῷ πρέποντι, θεόφρονα δὲ ποιμένα τῷ θρόνῳ ἐγκαθιδρύσειεν. Ἀρειανῶν τοιγαροῦν ἐπὶ τούτοις στασιαζόντων, Ἀμβρόσιος κατέλαβεν ὁ τῆς πόλεως ἔπαρχος ἀναστεῖλαι τὸν θόρυβον. Τὸ δὲ ἄθροισμα τῶν ἑτεροδόξων αὐτὸν θεασάμενον καὶ τῶν πιστῶν τὴν κραυγὴν ἀπωσάμενον ἐπίσκοπον ἀνηγόρευσεν· ὃν ἡ συνελθοῦσα θεία σύνοδος ἐπινεύσει τοῦ βασιλέως κατασχοῦσα ἐμύησε τῷ ἁγίῳ βαπτίσματι. Καὶ χειροτονηθέντος αὐτοῦ τοιοῦτον ὕμνον ὁ βασιλεὺς τῷ θεῷ πάντων ἐπ' ὄψεσιν ἀνεπέμψατο, «χάρις σοι δέσποτα παντοκράτορ καὶ σῶτερ ἡμέτερε, ὅτι τῷδε τῷ ἀνδρὶ ἐγὼ μὲν σώματα, σὺ δὲ ψυχὰς ἐνεχείρισας, καὶ τὰς ἐμὰς ψήφους δικαίας ἀπέφηνας.»

65.

Αὐτίκα γοῦν οἱ τῆς ἀληθείας παρρησιασταὶ πρὸς Οὐαλεντινιανὸν ἐποιήσαντο δέησιν ἐν Τυάνοις ἀθροισθῆναι ὀρθόδοξον σύνοδον, ὡς ἂν τὰ ἐν Νικαίᾳ δογματισθέντα κυρώσειεν· ἐν ᾗ Γρηγόριος Ναζιανζοῦ, ὁ τοῦ θεολόγου πατήρ, καὶ ὁ Καισαρείας Καππαδοκίας ὑπῆρχεν Εὐσέβιος, ὁ Μελιτηνῆς Ὀτρήϊος καὶ ἄλλοι πολλοὶ ἐνθέου ζήλου ἀνάμεστοι. Ὁ πάπας τοίνυν Ῥώμης Λιβέριος πρὸς αὐτοὺς ὀρθοδοξίας τόμον ἀπέστειλε καὶ χαρᾶς μεγίστης ἐνέπλησεν. Οὐάλης δὲ ὑπὸ Εὐδοξίου ἐν τῷ βαπτίζεσθαι ὅρκοις τὸν ἀρειανισμὸν κρατύνειν διαβεβαιωσάμενος τοὺς συνελθόντας ἐκεῖσε ἀπήλασεν.

64: (A.D. 374) ‖ 1–14: cf. Thdrt. IV.6, 1–7, 5 ‖ 11–14: *Epit. Th. A.*, 70, 13–16

65: HL I_2, 979 (A.D. 367) ‖ 2–5: *Epit. Th. A.*, 65, 4–6 ‖ 6–7: *Epit. Th. A.*, 65, 6–7; Soz. VI.12, 2–3 ‖ 7–9: cf. Theoph., 57, 5–7; Thdrt. IV.12, 4–13, 1

64: 2 ἑῴων om. *z* ‖ Ῥωμαίων om. LG ‖ 3 συναθροίζεται *z* ‖ Εὐδόξιον] recte Αὐξέντιον ‖ 5 καθυποβάλλη Az: -βάλη LGE -βαλλομένη D ‖ 6 τούτω LG ‖ 8 θεασάμενον post πιστῶν transp. LG ‖ 10 ἐπινεύσει *SV*[2] (corrigens ut vid.): ἐπ' ὄψεσι codd. (ex lin. 11?) ‖ ἁγίῳ om. LG ‖ 12 ἐνεπέμψατο *z* ‖ 13 τὰ σώματα - - - τὰς ψυχὰς *b*

65: 1 γοῦν] τοίνυν LG ‖ 3 δογμ.] συναθροισθέντα *b* ‖ 5 πολλοὶ] πλεῖστοι LG ‖ Ὁ — 6 Λιβέριος] λιβέριος γοῦν LG ‖ 9 ἀπέλυσε(ν) E*z* evan. A

64. After the Emperor Valentinian proclaimed his own brother Valens emperor of the Eastern Romans and had gone to Rome, a synod was convened in Milan[67] to place under a suitable anathema, after his death, Eudoxius,[68] the Arian and enemy of the Spirit, who had been bishop there, and to install on the throne a pious pastor. The Arians raised trouble over these proposals, and Ambrose, the city eparch, came on the scene to control the commotion. But when the heterodox crowd saw him, they proclaimed him bishop, disregarding the cries of the orthodox. He was then taken by the divine synod assembled there and initiated into holy baptism with the approval of the Emperor. And, following his ordination, the Emperor in the sight of all offered up this song of praise to God, "Thanks be to Thee, Lord, Our Savior Almighty; I entrusted to this man men's bodies, Thou their souls, and Thou hast shown my choice to be a just one."

65. Straightaway the supporters of the truth requested Valentinian to summon an orthodox synod at Tyana in order to confirm the teachings of Nicaea. It was attended by Gregory Nazianzus, the father of the theologian, Eusebius of Caesarea Cappadocia, Otreius of Melitene, and many others who were filled with divine zeal. The Roman Pope Liberius sent them a statement of orthodoxy, which pleased them immensely. But Valens, who had taken an oath at his baptism by Eudoxius to support Arianism, expelled[69] the bishops assembled there.

[67] Because he is following the text of Theodoret (IV.6,1 ff.), the compiler has placed this synod of Milan (374) far out of chronological order; cf. note 59 *supra*.

[68] A mistake for Auxentius.

[69] The writer has apparently misread his source and has taken as a reference to Tyana an account which describes how Valens, at the instigation of Eudoxius, prevented a projected orthodox synod at Tarsus; see Sozomen VI.12,4–5 and *Epit.Th.A.*, 65 lines 6–9.

66.

Μετὰ ταῦτα Εὐσεβίου τοῦ Καισαρείας Καππαδοκίας τελειωθέντος ὁ μέγας Βασίλειος ὑπὸ πάντων εἰς τὸν θρόνον ψηφίζεται· καὶ τοὺς ἐκ τῆς ὑπερορίας ἀνακληθέντας προσκαλεσάμενος, τὸν Σαμοσατέα Εὐσέβιον καὶ Λουκίφερ τὸν Σάρδεων καὶ τὴν σὺν αὐτοῖς ὀρθόδοξον σύνοδον, ἀρχιερεὺς ὑπ' αὐτῶν προχειρίζεται καὶ ἀναθεματίζει Διάνιον τῆς αὐτῆς πρὸ Εὐσεβίου ἐπίσκοπον, Ἀστέριον, Εὐνόμιον καὶ Θεοφρόνιον τοὺς Καππαδόκας.

67.

Λιβερίου τοίνυν πάπα Ῥώμης τελειωθέντος τοῦ μάκαρος Δάμασος ἀξιοπρεπῶς προχειρίζεται, ὁ πάντα λέγειν καὶ πράττειν ὑπὲρ τῶν ἀποστολικῶν δογμάτων αἱρούμενος· ὃς αὐτίκα σύνοδον ἐνενήκοντα πατέρων συνήθροισε, καὶ ἀναθεματίσας Αὐξέντιον τὸ θεῖον ἐτράνωσε μάθημα, ὅρον εὐσεβείας ἐκθέμενος, ὃν πρὸς Ἰλλυριοὺς ἀπέστειλεν.

68.

Ἀλλὰ καὶ δευτέραν ὁ αὐτὸς πανίερον ὑπὲρ τοῦ ὁμοουσίου κατὰ Αὐξεντίου συνεκρότησε θεοσύλλεκτον σύνοδον.

67: HL I_2, 980 (A.D. 369?) ‖ 1–3: Thdrt. V.2, 2 ‖ 3–5: Thdrt. II.22, 1–2

68: HL I_2, 981 (A.D. 374)

66: 1 ante Εὐσεβίου add. τοῦ AOTMN ‖ Καππαδοκίας om. LG ‖ 2 εἰς τὸν θρόνον om. LG ‖ 4 τὸν] τῶν DEV ‖ Σάρδεων] recte Σαρδόνος (i.e., Σαρδανίας) cf. cap. 52, 10 ‖ ante ἀρχιερεὺς add. ἐν τῷ θρόνῳ LG

67: 1 ante πάπα add. τοῦ LG ‖ 5 ἐξαπέστειλεν D

68: 2 θεόλεκτον D

66. Later, following the death of Eusebius of Caesarea Cappadocia, Basil the Great was unanimously elected to the throne. And summoning those who had been recalled from banishment, Eusebius of Samosata, Lucifer of Sardis, and the synod of orthodox bishops with them,[70] he was appointed archpriest by them. Then he placed under anathema the Cappadocians Dianius, who was Eusebius' predecessor at Caesarea, Asterius, Eunomius, and Theophronius.

67. After the death of the Roman Pope, the blessed Liberius, Damasus was worthily elected, a man ready to say and do everything in support of apostolic teachings. He immediately assembled a synod of ninety bishops and, anathematizing Auxentius, he proclaimed the divine creed and issued a statement of orthodoxy which he sent to the Illyrians.

68. This same man also convoked a second most holy and divinely assembled synod against Auxentius in defense of consubstantiality.

[70] There is no other evidence for this synod, and Mansi (III, 453) regards it as a fiction.

69.

Ὁμοίως δὲ καὶ οἱ πρεσβεύοντες ἐξ ἑῴας τὸ ὁμοούσιον Οὐαλεντινιανῷ προσῆλθον σύνοδον ἐν Λαμψάκῳ αἰτούμενοι, κυρῶσαι τὰ ἐν Νικαίᾳ καὶ ἀποκηρύξαι τὸν Ἡρακλείας Πειρίνθου Ὑπάτιον. Συνελθόντες οὖν καὶ μῆνας δύο ἐκεῖσε τελέσαντες, ἄκυρα μένειν τὰ ἐν Κωνσταντινουπόλει πεπραγμένα Εὐδοξίῳ καὶ Ἀκακίῳ ψηφίζονται καὶ τὴν ἐν Σελευκείᾳ πίστιν κρατεῖν ἀφρόνως θεσπίζουσιν. Ὅπερ Οὐάλης πυθόμενος τὰ γεγονότα πάντα συνέχεε, τοὺς ἐπισκόπους ὅλους ἐξορίᾳ δεξιωσάμενος καὶ τὰς ἐκκλησίας τῷ Εὐδοξίῳ παρέδωκε.

70.

Καὶ οἱ ἐν Φρυγίᾳ δὲ Ἀετιανοὶ σύνοδον ἐν Πούζῃ τῇ κώμῃ ποιήσαντες ὥστε μετὰ Ἰουδαίων ἐκτελεῖν τὸ πάσχα ὅρον ἐκτίθενται· ὃν κρατύνας Σαββάτιος πολλοὺς τῶν Βυζαντίων συνήρπασε, παρ' οὗ καὶ Σαββατιανοὶ μέχρι καὶ σήμερον λέγονται.

71.

Οὐαλεντινιανὸς γοῦν ὁ μέγας τοῖς ὀρθοδόξοις τῆς πίστεως προτερήμασι θεσπίζει ἐν τῷ Ἰλλυρικῷ θείαν γενέσθαι καὶ πανίερον σύνοδον, ἣ τὴν ἐν Νικαίᾳ πίστιν καλῶς ἐβεβαίωσεν, ἀναθεματίσασα Πολυχρόνιον, Τηλέμαχον, Φαῦστον, Ἀσκληπιάδην, Κλεόπατρον, καὶ Ἀμάντιον· ἑαυτῆς δὲ τόμον ἐν Ἀσίᾳ, Καρίᾳ, Φρυγίᾳ ἐπισκόποις Ἀρειανοῖς διεπέμψατο, καὶ ὁ φιλόχριστος βασιλεὺς ὡσαύτως ἐξ ἴσου τὸ ἴδικτον.

69: HL I_2, 974–75 (A.D. 364) ‖ 1–8: *Epit. Th. A.*, 63, 7–9; 63, 11–17

70: (A.D. 374?) ‖ 1–4: *Epit. Th. A.*, 71, 15–18; cf. Theoph., 62, 17–20

71: HL I_2, 982–83 (A.D. 375) ‖ 2–3: *Epit. Th. A.*, 70, 19–20; cf. Thdrt. IV.7, 6 ‖ 4–5: Thdrt. IV.9, 9 ‖ 5–6: *Epit. Th. A.*, 70, 20–21; cf. Thdrt. IV.6–7

69: 3 recte Ὑπατιανόν ‖ 4 μένειν] μὲν εἶναι *Epit. Th. A.*, 63, 12 ‖ 7 ἐξορίᾳ om. LG ‖ 8 τῷ om. E

70: 1 Ἀετιανοὶ] cf. Αὐτιανῶν cod. b Theoph., 62, 17 immo Ναυατιανοὶ ‖ Πούζῃ] rectius Πάζῳ ‖ τῇ om. LG ‖ 3 καὶ om. G*z* ‖ 4 καὶ] τῆς A^s

71: 1 ὀρθοδόξοις] ὀρθοῖς LG ‖ 5 post Καρίᾳ add. καὶ LG

69. In like manner also the Eastern advocates of consubstantiality approached Valentinian and requested a synod in Lampsacus[71] to confirm the teachings of Nicaea and to condemn Hypatius[72] of Heraclea Perinthus. They convened, then, and after spending two months there, they decreed that the acts of Eudoxius and Acacius in Constantinople should remain invalid and unwisely decided to retain the creed of Seleucia. On learning this, Valens reversed every one of their decisions, welcoming all the bishops to exile, and handed over the churches to Eudoxius.

70. And the Aetians[73] in Phrygia held a synod at the village of Pouze, where they issued a decree to allow the celebration of Easter according to Jewish practice. By supporting this decision, Sabbatius drew many adherents from among the Byzantines, and these people to this very day are called Sabbatians after him.

71. The great Valentinian, then, authorized the leading orthodox defenders of the creed to hold a divine and all-holy synod in Illyricum, which nobly confirmed the Nicene creed, anathematizing Polychronius, Telemachus, Faustus, Asclepiades, Cleopatrus, and Amantius. It passed on a decree of its own to the Arian bishops of Asia, Caria, and Phrygia, while the Christ-loving Emperor likewise did the same with his edict.

[71] This synod of 364 should properly have its place after chap. 63.

[72] The compiler has not understood correctly his source, almost certainly the *Epit. Th.A.*, 63 line 7 ff. Hypatian (to give him his right name), far from being a target, was in fact the bishop who had been chosen by his colleagues to request the synod from Valentinian; see Sozomen VI.7,1–2. The cause of the error could easily have been the phrase διὰ Ὑπατίου in *Epit. Th.A.* (63 line 7), our writer misreading it as διὰ Ὑπάτιον.

[73] This should be Novatians (Ναυατιανοί), and the correct name of the village is Pazus. According to Sozomen (VI.24,6) the synod took place around the time that Ambrose became bishop of Milan (374).

72.

Ἀθανασίου τοίνυν τοῦ πανιέρου μετελθόντος γῆθεν πρὸς τὰ οὐράνια, Πέτρος, ὁ πολλὰ συνιδρώσας αὐτῷ, ψήφῳ ἐκείνου τοῦ θρόνου διάδοχος γίνεται· ὃν οἱ τῆς κιβδήλου δόξης ἐχόμενοι τὴν Ἀλεξάνδρειαν καταλαβόντες, Ἑλληνικῇ χειρὶ ἐξελαύνουσι, τὸν λύκον Λούκιον ἀντεισάξαντες. Πέτρος δὲ τὴν Ῥώμην κατέλαβε, καὶ ὁ πάπας Δάμασος αὐτὸν προσλαβόμενος ἐν Ῥώμῃ σύνοδον θείαν καὶ ἱερὰν συνεκρότησεν, ἣ τὸν ἄνουν Ἀπολινάριον Στέφανόν τε τὸν μαθητὴν αὐτοῦ ἀνεθεμάτισε καὶ τὸν φόνιον Λούκιον.

73.

Τῶν μαθητῶν δὲ τοῦ Εὐσταθίου Ἀρμενίας τὴν οἰκείαν λύμην διανεμόντων εἰς πλείονας (Δαδόη γὰρ τοῦ Μεσσαλιανῶν μετεῖχον φρονήματος παλίμβουλοι καὶ ταῖς γνώμαις ὑπάρχοντες ἀμφιτάλαντοι, καθὼς ὁ ἐκείνων διδάσκαλος θεὸν τὸν ποιήσαντα ἄρσεν καὶ θῆλυ ἐκ τῆς κατηγορίας τοῦ γάμου ἐνδιαβάλλοντες), ἡ ἐν Γάγγραις ἁγία συνήθροιστο σύνοδος, φέρουσα †Δίον† τὸν πάνυ αὐτῆς προκαθήμενον· ἥτις ὅρον θεόπνευστον ἐξενέγκασα πρὸς ἀδελφοὺς τοὺς ἐν Ἀρμενίᾳ ἐξέπεμψεν.

72: HL I_2, 984 (A.D. 376) ‖ 1–2: *Epit. Th. A.*, 68, 9–10 ‖ 2–3: Thdrt. IV.20, 1–2 ‖ 4–5: Thdrt. IV.21, 1–3; cf. *Epit. Th. A.*, 68, 12–13; 68, 15–16 ‖ 6–7: ? Thdrt. V.10, 5

73: HL I_2, 1029–45 (ca. A.D. 341?) ‖ 1 et 5: cf. *Epit. Th. A.*, 37, 17–18 ‖ 1–2:? Thdrt. IV.11, 3–4 ‖ 2: cf. *Epit. Th. A.*, 71, 5–7

72: 2 ψήφοις *b* ‖ 5 ὁ om. *z* ‖ 7 τε] γε LG, fort. D

73: 2 Μεσσαλιανῶν D: μεσαλ- LG μασσαλ- *b* ‖ 3 παλίμβολοι E ‖ 5 γάγγρα *b* ‖ συνήθροιστο LG: συναθροισθεῖσα D*b* ‖ 6 Δίον] leg. Εὐσέβιον? ‖ 7 post ἐξέπεμψεν add. κἀκείνους κανονικῶς ἀνεθεμάτισεν E

72. When the all-holy Athanasius, then, passed from earth to heaven, he was succeeded on the throne, in accordance with his own wishes, by Peter who had been his companion in many sufferings. But the adherents of the spurious doctrine came to Alexandria and, driving Peter out with the help of a pagan force, they installed the wolf Lucius[74] in his place. Then Peter went to Rome where he was received by Pope Damasus, who summoned a divine and sacred synod there. It placed under anathema the "mindless"[75] Apolinarius, Stephen[76] his disciple, and the violent Lucius.

73. Since the followers of Eustathius of Armenia were spreading their peculiar corruption to many—for they were fellow thinkers of the Messalian Dadoes, being fickle and ambivalent in their teachings and, like the master of these people, they slandered God, the creator of male and female, by attacking the institution of marriage—the holy synod of Gangra[77] was convened with the illustrious †Dios†[78] presiding. It issued a divinely inspired decree and sent it to the brethren in Armenia.

[74] The play on words between λύκος (wolf) and Λούκιος is lost in translation; cf. Georgius Monachus, *Chronicon*, ed. C. de Boor, II (Leipzig, 1904), 552 lines 9–11.

[75] See note 66 *supra*.

[76] Stephen would appear to be a mistake for Timothy; see Theodoret V.10,5.

[77] The date of the synod of Gangra is much disputed; see HL, I_2, 1029ff. Its place in *SV* may have been determined by the fact that *Epit. Th. A.* (71 line 5ff.) discusses the Messalians just after the synod of Illyricum.

[78] The name Eusebius has been suggested for the corrupt reading of the manuscripts; see HL, I_2, 1031.

74.

Ούάλης μὲν οὖν ἐν Θρᾴκῃ Γότϑοις συμβαλών, ὑπ᾽ αὐτῶν εἰς †χαλκίδα† πυρίκαυστος ἐν ἀχυρῶνι γενόμενος, πρὸς τὸ αἰώνιον πῦρ ἐξεδήμησε, καὶ Γρατιανός, Οὐαλεντινιανοῦ τελευτήσαντος ἐν Χριστῷ τῷ ϑεῷ ἡμῶν τοῦ πατρὸς αὐτοῦ, ἑσπερίων καὶ τῶν ἑῴων αὐτοκράτωρ γενόμενος, τοὺς ἐν ἐξορίᾳ εὐσεβεῖς ἐπισκόπους ἀνεκαλέσατο. Καϑ᾽ ὃν χρόνον καὶ ὁ μακάριος Δάμασος ἐν Ῥώμῃ ἁγίαν συγκαλεσάμενος σύνοδον κατὰ Ἀρειανῶν καὶ πνευματομάχων καὶ ἄλλων πλείστων αἱρέσεων, ϑεῖον ὅρον κεφαλαίων ἐκϑέμενος ἐν Θεσσαλονίκῃ πρὸς τὸν Παυλῖνον ἀπέστειλεν, ἐκ ϑείας οἰκονομίας πανταχοῦ τὰ μέγιστα διανύσαντα· προσκυνεῖν γὰρ τριάδα πάντας ἔπεισεν ὁμοούσιον.

75.

Ἀλλὰ καὶ Μελέτιος ἀνακληϑεὶς ὁ ἀοίδιμος ἐν τῷ οἰκείῳ ϑρόνῳ Ἀντιοχείας ϑείαν καὶ ἱερὰν συνεκαλέσατο σύνοδον, ἣ τὸ ϑεοποιὸν κυρώσασα σύμβολον καὶ ἀναϑεματίσασα Μάρκελλον, Φωτεινόν, καὶ Ἀπολινάριον, ὅρον ϑεῖον πρὸς Δάμασον καὶ τοὺς ἱεράρχας τῆς ἑσπέρας ἀπέστειλε.

74: HL I_2, 985–86 (A.D. 380) ‖ 1: cf. *Epit. Th. A.*, 75, 14 ‖ 1–2: cf. Cedren. (ed. Bonn.), I, 549, 17–22 (Zonar. XIII [ed. Bonn.], 16, 24–25) ‖ 3–5: Thdrt. V.1–2 (Theoph., 66, 20–22) ‖ 8: Thdrt. V.11, 1 sqq. ‖ 9–10: Thdrt. V.3, 10 sqq.

75: ? HL I_2, 985 (A.D. 379)

74: 3 οὐλεντιανοῦ A^s οὐαλεντίνου *z* ‖ 3–4 τῷ ϑεῷ ἡμῶν] ἰησοῦ LG ‖ 4 τῶν — 5 γενόμενος] τῶν ἑώων ῥωμαίων γενόμενος αὐτοκράτωρ LG ‖ 7 αἱρετικῶν *z* ‖ 7–8 ὅρον ϑείων *b*

75: 4 τοὺς ἑσπερίους ἱεράρχας LG

74. While attacking the Goths in Thrace, Valens was burned to death by them in a chaff house at †chalcis†[79] and departed to the everlasting fire. Then Gratian, since his father Valentinian had (already) died in Christ our God, became emperor of West and East, and he recalled those pious bishops who had been banished. Around this time also, the blessed Damasus summoned a holy synod in Rome against Arians, enemies of the Spirit, and numerous other heretics and issued a divine decree in chapters which he sent to Paulinus in Thessalonica. It accomplished great things everywhere, thanks to divine dispensation, for it persuaded all to worship a consubstantial Trinity.

75. After his recall the renowned Meletius summoned a divine and sacred synod to his own see at Antioch which, confirming the deifying symbol (of faith) and placing under anathema Marcellus, Photinus, and Apolinarius, sent a divine decree to Damasus and the Western bishops.

[79] Even if Χαλκιδική is meant, we are still far from the real site of Valens' fiery death, Adrianople.

76.

Γρατιανοῦ τοίνυν κατὰ Γότθων στρατοπεδεύσαντος καὶ Θεοδόσιον τὸν ἐπ' ἀδελφῇ γαμβρὸν αὐτοῦ στρατηγὸν ἀναδείξαντος, εἰρήνευον οἱ πολέμιοι καὶ τροπαιοφόρος πρὸς τὸν κρατοῦντα ὁ στρατηγέτης ἐπάνεισι. Διὸ Γρατιανὸς ὁ θειότατος ἀμοιβῇ πρεπούσῃ τιμήσας τὸν μέγιστον Θεοδόσιον τοῦ οἰκείου αὐτοῦ πατραδέλφου τὴν ἡγεμονίαν διέπειν ἐκέλευσεν (ἥνπερ Κωνστάντιος καὶ Οὐάλης Ἀρειανοῖς χαριζόμενοι ἐλυμήναντο) καὶ βασιλέα τῶν ἐῴων Ῥωμαίων προεχειρίσατο, Δαμάσῳ προστάξας τῷ πάπᾳ ἐν Ἀκυλίᾳ συστήσασθαι σύνοδον· ἧς ἐξῆρχον ὁ Μεδιολάνου Ἀμβρόσιος καὶ ὁ Θεσσαλονίκης Ἀχόλιος. Ἥτις ἁγία σύνοδος ἐκθεμένη τόμον παραινέσεως γέμοντα ὡς ἂν οἰκουμενικὴ γένοιτο σύνοδος, πρὸς Θεοδόσιον τὸν εὐσεβέστατον βασιλέα σὺν ἀξιοπίστοις ἀνδράσιν ἀπέστειλε· Ῥωμαῖοι γὰρ καὶ οἱ τῆς Σπανικῆς Γαλλίας τῆς αἱρετικῆς λύμης ὑπῆρχον ἀλώβητοι, (Σπανογαλλίας, Ἰταλίας, Καμπανίας, Δαλματίας, Καλαβρίας, Σαρδανίας, Ἀφρικῆς, ἄλλης Σαρδανίας, Μακεδονίας, Ἑλλάδος, Θεσσαλίας, Εὐρώπης, Ἠπείρου, Σκυθίας, Πανονίας, Μυσίας, Βρεττανίας, Δακίας, Δαρδανίας, Ἀχαΐας, καὶ ὅσοι τῶν ἑσπερίων τῇ Γρατιανοῦ βασιλείᾳ ὑπέκειντο.)

77.

Θεοδοσίου δὲ τοῦ ἀληθῶς ἐν θεοσεβείᾳ μεγάλου τὴν βασιλίδα καταλαβόντος Κωνσταντινούπολιν, Ἀγελίου Ἀρειανῶν καὶ Γρηγορίου τοῦ θεολόγου τῶν ὀρθοδόξων ἐν Βυζαντίῳ ἐξάρχοντος, ἡ τῶν ἑκατὸν πεντήκοντα θεοφόρων πατέρων οἰκουμενικὴ ἁγία δευτέρα συνήθροιστο σύνοδος, ἧς ἐξῆρχον προκαθεζόμενοι ὁ Ἀλεξανδρείας Τιμόθεος, Κύριλλος

76: HL II_1, 49–52 (A.D. 381) ‖ 1–3: cf. Thdrt. V.5, 1–4 (Zonar. XIII [ed. Bonn.], 17, 9–16) ‖ 4–5: cf. Thrdt. V.5, 3 ‖ 5–6: cf. (?) Thdrt. V.7, 2 ‖ 7 ἐν Ἀκυλίᾳ - - - 8 σύνοδον: cf. Thdrt. V.9, 9 ‖ 11–12: cf. (?) Thdrt. V.6, 4

77: HL II_1, 1–48 (A.D. 381) ‖ 2 Ἀγελίου Ἀρειανῶν: cf. Soz. VII.12, 9 (Socr. V.10, 24) ‖ 3–7: *Epit. Th. A.*, 77, 26–78, 7

76: 3 ὁ om. D ‖ 4 ὁ θειότατος om. *z* ‖ 5 οἰκείου αὐτοῦ om. LG ‖ 6 χαριζόμενος LG ‖ καὶ^2 om. LG ‖ 7 τῷ πάπᾳ om. LG ‖ recte Ἀκυληίᾳ ‖ 9 τόμον ἐκθεμένη LG ‖ 11 ἀνδράσιν] ἱεράρχαις D ἀρχιεράρχαις LG ‖ 14 Ἀφρικῆς — 15 Δαρδανίας om. *b*

77: 1 ἀληθοῦς E ‖ 2 Ἀγελίου — 3 ἐξάρχοντος om. LG ‖ 4–5 σύνοδος συνήθροιστο *z*

76, 77

76. When, in the course of his campaign against the Goths, Gratian proclaimed his brother-in-law Theodosius general, the enemy made peace, and the general returned triumphant to the victorious Emperor. For this reason the most divine Gratian, honoring the mighty Theodosius with a fitting reward, instructed him to assume command of the part ruled by his own paternal uncle, which had been contaminated by the Arian-pleasers, Constantius and Valens, and he made him emperor of the East Romans and ordered Pope Damasus to convene a synod in Aquileia. It was presided over by Ambrose of Milan and Acholius of Thessalonica. This holy synod issued a statement strongly urging that an ecumenical council take place and sent it, in the care of trustworthy men, to the most pious Theodosius. For the Romans and the people of Spanish Gaul[79a] were not infected with the heretical disease; i.e., those of Spanish Gaul,[79a] Italy, Campania, Dalmatia, Calabria, Sardinia, Africa, lesser Sardinia, Macedonia, Greece, Thessaly, Europe, Epirus, Scythia, Panonia, Moesia, Britain, Dacia, Dardania, Achaia, and the rest of Emperor Gratian's Western subjects.

77. After Theodosius, the truly great in piety, came to the imperial city of Constantinople, where Agelius[80] was leader of the Arians and Gregory the Theologian of the orthodox, the holy Second Ecumenical Council of one hundred and fifty godly bishops was assembled. Its presiding leaders were Timothy of Alexandria, Cyril of Jerusalem—who had by this time separated

[79a] Perhaps Σπανικὴ Γαλλία and Σπανογαλλία mean Spain and Gaul.

[80] Agelius was not an Arian but a Novatian, and the leader of the Arians at this time was Demophilus; see Socrates V.10,24 (Sozomen VII.12,9).

Ἱεροσολύμων ἤδη ἀποσχίσας Σιλβανοῦ καὶ τῶν σὺν αὐτῷ πνευματομάχων ἕξ τε καὶ τριάκοντα, καὶ ὁ φιλόχριστος βασιλεὺς Θεοδόσιος. Ἥτις ἁγία σύνοδος Βιθυνοὺς Εὐσέβιον καὶ Θεόγνιον, Πατρόφιλον καὶ Ἀέτιον ἀπεκήρυξε Παλαιστινούς, Παυλῖνον τε καὶ Γρηγόριον Φοίνικας, Θεόδοτον καὶ Γεώργιον Κιλικίας, Νάρκισσον καὶ Ἀθανάσιον, Μηνοφάντιον Ἐφέσου, καὶ τὸν Πειρίνθου Θεόδωρον, Μάρκελλον Ἀγκύρας καὶ Ἀπολινάριον, Μάξιμόν τε καὶ τὴν αὐτοῦ χειροτονίαν ἀργεῖν καθόλου θεσπίσασα. Καθ' ὃν χρόνον καὶ τὸν ἐν ἁγίοις Σαμοσατέα Εὐσέβιον Γρατιανὸς τῆς Θρᾳκικῆς ἐξορίας ἀφέμενος πρὸς τὸ ἴδιον ποίμνιον ἐξαπέστειλε, καὶ πρὸς τὴν πύλην τῆς πόλεως εἰσερχόμενον ἄνωθεν γυνὴ κεράμῳ Ἀρειανὴ ἐθανάτωσεν.

78.

Ἀλλ' οὔπω τῆς αἱρετικῆς φλογὸς εἰς ἅπαν ἀποσβεσθείσης, Γρατιανοῦ τοῦ εὐσεβοῦς ἀναιρεθέντος καὶ τῶν κακοδόξων ἐν τῇ Γραικίᾳ βατταριζόντων, Δάμασος ὁ πανίερος ἐν Ῥώμῃ σύνοδον συστησάμενος, ὅρον θεῖον ἐξέθετο καὶ πρὸς τὴν ἀθροιζομένην ἐν Κωνσταντινουπόλει ἁγίαν σύνοδον ἀπέστειλεν.

79.

Ὅνπερ οἱ ταύτης δεξάμενοι ἔξαρχοι, ὁ Βυζαντίου Νεκτάριος καὶ ὁ Ἀλεξανδρείας Θεόφιλος, μετὰ τῶν συμπαρόντων συνοδικῶς ἀναθέματι καθυπέβαλον τοὺς ἐπιμένοντας Ἀρειανούς, Παυλιανούς, Ἀπολιναριαστάς, Μαρκελλιανοὺς καὶ Φωτεινιανούς, καὶ ὅρον ἐκθέμενοι πανσεβάσμιον ἅμα ἀρχιερεῦσι πρὸς τὸν μακάριον ἐξαπέστειλαν Δάμασον.

---

8 Βιθυνοὺς – 11 Θεόδωρον: Thdrt. V.7, 1 ‖ 12: *Epit. Th. A.*, 78, 24 ‖ 13–15: *Epit. Th. A.*, 76, 20–23; Thdrt. V.4, 7–8

78: HL II$_1$, 57–63 (A.D. 382) ‖ 3–5: cf. *Epit. Th. A.*, 79, 26–31; Thdrt. V.8, 10 sqq.

79: HL II$_1$, 53–56 (A.D. 382) ‖ 1: Thdrt. V.8, 10 ‖ 3–5: cf. Thdrt. V.9, 1; 9, 19

---

7 ἁγια] θεία LG ‖ 9–10 immo Θ. καὶ Γ. Λαοδικείας, Κίλικας Ν. καὶ Α. vel sim. ‖ 14 τῇ πύλῃ LG ‖ 15 ἐξερχόμενον *b* ‖ post ἐθανάτωσεν additamentum in E (vide praef. p. xviii)

78: 5 ἀπέστειλε σύνοδον LG

79: 3 ἀπολιναριστάς DOTMN

from Silvanus and his thirty-six enemies of the Spirit—and the Christ-loving Emperor Theodosius. This holy council condemned Eusebius and Theognius of Bithynia, Patrophilus and Aetius of Palestine, Paulinus and Gregory of Phoenicia, Theodotus and George of Cilicia,[81] Narcissus and Athanasius, Menophantius of Ephesus, Theodore of Perinthus, Marcellus of Ancyra and Apolinarius, and Maximus along with those ordained by him, barring them completely from the ministry. At this time Gratian recalled from exile in Thrace and returned to his own flock Eusebius of Samosata, now among the saints, whom, as he was approaching the city gate, an Arian woman struck from above with a tile and killed.

78. The flame of heresy, however, had not yet been completely extinguished; so, after the murder of the pious Gratian and while the unorthodox continued their nonsense in Greece, the all-holy Damasus, having brought together a synod in Rome, issued a godly definition and sent it to the holy synod[82] assembled in Constantinople.

79. When this definition had been accepted by the presidents of the synod, Nectarius of Byzantium and Theophilus[83] of Alexandria, along with those present, they proceeded to anathematize by conciliar decision those persisting in the heresies of Arius, Paulinus, Apolinarius, Marcellinus, and Photinus. And issuing an all-holy definition, they sent it in the care of bishops to the blessed Damasus.

[81] The names have been confused; see Theodoret V.7,1.

[82] That is, to the synod of 382 described in the next chapter.

[83] A mistake, since Theophilus only became bishop of Alexandria in 385 after Timothy.

80.

Θεοδοσίου γοῦν καὶ Νεκταρίου μεθαρμοσθέντων πρὸς τὰ οὐράνια, τοῦ μὲν τὴν βασιλείαν ὁ υἱὸς Ἀρκάδιος διαδέχεται, Γρατιανοῦ δὲ ὁ ἀδελφὸς Ἀρκαδίου Ὁνόριος. Ἐν οἷς χρόνοις ἐν Καρθαγένῃ σύνοδος τοπικὴ θεία καὶ ἱερὰ συναθροίζεται, διακοσίων εἴκοσι ἑπτὰ πατέρων συνέλευσιν φέρουσα, κατὰ εἰδώλων, Δονατιστῶν, καὶ ἄλλης ἑκάστης αἱρέσεως καὶ τῶν ἐν τοῖς τόποις ἐκείνοις ἀτόπων σφαλμάτων τὰς πράξεις ποιήσασα· ἧς ἡγεῖτο Αὐρήλιος ὁ Καρθαγένης ἐπίσκοπος. Καὶ κανόνας ἱεροὺς ἐκθεμένη καὶ θείους, ἕως καιρῶν τοῦ μικροῦ Θεοδοσίου διήρκεσε.

81.

Νεκταρίου δὲ τῆς ἀρχιερωσύνης τὸν θρόνον θείῳ νεύματι ἐκληρώσατο πρεσβύτερος Ἀντιοχείας Συρίας Ἰωάννης ὁ μέγας Χρυσόστομος· καθ' οὗ διαβολαὶ παρὰ τῶν κρατούντων οὐχ ἥκιστα καὶ φθονούντων οὐχ αἱ τυχοῦσαι γενόμεναι, συνέδριον πονηρὸν τριάκοντα καὶ τριῶν ἐπισκόπων συνέστησαν καὶ ὑπόδικον ἐξορίᾳ κατέκριναν.

82.

Ἀλλ' οὐ μετὰ πολὺ τὴν βασιλίδα Κωνσταντινούπολιν τῆς ἀληθείας πρόμαχος ἑξήκοντα ἐπισκόπων κατέλαβε σύνοδος καὶ τὸν ἅγιον συκοφαντηθέντα Χρυσόστομον τῷ αὐτοῦ θρόνῳ ἀποκατέστησε· καὶ πάλιν ἀδικηθέντα καὶ ἀπὸ τῆς Κομανικῆς ἐξορίας ἀναδραμόντα πρὸς τὰ οὐράνια Ἀρσάκιος διαδέχεται, Ἀττικὸς ἐκεῖνον, καὶ τοῦτον Σισίννιος.

80: HL II_1, 97–211

81: HL II_1, 137–50 (A.D. 403) ‖ 3–5: cf. Socr. VI.15

82: HL II_1, 150–54 (A.D. 404) ‖ 1–4: cf. Cedren. (ed. Bonn.), I, 576, 14–23; 581–82; Thdrt. V.34, 6–8

80: 2 Γρατιανοῦ — 8 διήρκεσε om. LG (capp. 80 et 81 coniunctis) ‖ 4 πατέρων] ἐπισκόπων D ‖ 5 τοῖς om. *z* ‖ 6 ἀτόπων correximus: ἀτόποις codd. ‖ 7 Αὐρήλιος D: ἀβρήλ- E αὐρίλ(λ)- *z* ἀβρίλλ- A[s] ‖ ὁ om. D

81: 1 Νεκταρίου — ἐκληρώσατο] τοῦ δὲ τὴν ἀρχιερωσύνην LG (vide ad cap. 80, 2–8) ‖ 3 οὐχ ἥκιστα om. LG ‖ 4 γινόμεναι A ‖ 5 κἀτεδικάσαντο LG

82: 3 αὐτοῦ om. LG ‖ 5 ἀττικὸς δὲ DG ‖ σισίνιος DG

80. When Theodosius, then, and Nectarius had been translated to heaven, the former was succeeded as emperor by his son, Arcadius, while Gratian's place was taken over by Honorius, the brother of Arcadius. At this time a divine and sacred local synod[84] was convened in Carthage, a gathering of two hundred and twenty-seven bishops, and it took action against idols, Donatists, every other heresy, and the errors of irregularity in those parts. The synod was led by Aurelius, bishop of Carthage, and, issuing holy and divine canons, it lasted[85] until the time of Theodosius the Younger.

81. The episcopal throne of Nectarius was inherited in accordance with God's will by the great John Chrysostom, presbyter from Antioch in Syria. He became the target of severe slanderous attacks from those in power, not least because of their resentment, and they convened an evil assembly of thirty-three bishops, put him on trial, and condemned him to exile.

82. But, not long afterward, a synod of sixty bishops, champions of the truth, assembled in the imperial city of Constantinople and restored the unjustly accused Chrysostom to his throne. Then he, after he had been wronged again and had gone up to heaven from exile at Comana, was succeeded by Arsacius, and this man by Atticus and he by Sisinnius.

[84] Since as many as ten synods met and issued canons at Carthage under Aurelius, it is not possible to say which one the writer has in mind. It may well be that his source was in fact referring to the last of the series, that of the year 419, which as early as the sixth century was given sole credit for a set of 133 canons, 127 of which had really been issued by the preceding synods; see F. L. Cross, "History and Fiction in the African Canons," *The Journal of Theological Studies,* XII (1961), 227–47, esp. 233ff. The council treatise in *Sinaiticus gr. 482* (312^v) even makes the synod of 419 take place during the reign of Arcadius and Honorius.

[85] This could be the writer's way of acknowledging that the series of synods under Aurelius continued to issue canons after the time of Arcadius into the reign of Theodosius II, thereby constituting, in his mind, a single council.

83.

Καὶ Νεστόριος ἐξ Ἀντιοχείας ὁ φρενοβλαβὴς πρεσβύτερος διαδέχεται τὸν Σισίννιον· ὃς τῆς ἀληθείας τὸν λόγον παρίθυνε, θεοτόκον λέγειν τὴν παναγίαν παρθένον Μαρίαν μὴ προσιέμενος καὶ τὴν καθ' ὑπόστασιν ἕνωσιν τοῦ σωτῆρος τῶν ὅλων Χριστοῦ δοξάζειν οὐκ ἀνεχόμενος· καθ' οὗ Κύριλλος ὁ μέγας ἀγωνισάμενος σύνοδον θείαν καὶ ἱερὰν ἐν Ἀλεξανδρείᾳ συνήθροισεν, ἥτις ὅρον κεφαλαίων δυοκαίδεκα ἐκθεμένη τῷ Νεστορίῳ ἀπέστειλεν. Ὅντινα μᾶλλον ἀποσεισάμενος τῇ κιβδήλῳ ἑαυτὸν δόξῃ προστέθεικε, τῆς ἐκκλησίας ταράττων τὸ σύστημα.

84.

Ὅπερ θεωρῶν βασιλεὺς ὁ μικρὸς Θεοδόσιος ἐν Ἐφέσῳ τῶν διακοσίων μακαρίων πατέρων τρίτην οἰκουμενικὴν σύνοδον συγκροτηθῆναι ἐκέλευσεν, ἧς ἐξῆρχε Κύριλλος ὁ τῶν ἀποστόλων συνήγορος· Ἰωάννης δὲ ὁ Ἀντιοχείας Συρίας καὶ οἱ σὺν αὐτῷ Νεστορίῳ χαριζόμενοι οὐκ ἀπήντησαν. Ἡ δὲ ἁγία σύνοδος χρονοτριβοῦσα καὶ λοιμοῦ γενομένη κατάβρωμα τέλος Νεστόριον ἀπεκήρυξε, καθυποβαλοῦσα τῷ πρέποντι ἀναθέματι, θεοτόκον τὴν ἁγίαν παρθένον Μαρίαν κηρύξασα καὶ τὴν καθ' ὑπόστασιν ἕνωσιν τοῦ σωτῆρος τῶν ὅλων Χριστοῦ τοῦ θεοῦ ἡμῶν.

83: HL II_1, 264–78 (A.D. 430) ‖ 4–6: cf. Niceph. Call. XIV.33 (PG, 146, 1164D–1165A) ‖ 6 ὅρον: Mansi, IV, 1081–84

84: HL II_1, 287–375 (A.D. 431) ‖ 1–4: cf. Theoph., 89, 20 sqq. ‖ 5: cf. Niceph. Call. XIV.34 (PG, 146, 1169D)

83: 2 σισίνιον DG ‖ 5 post ἀγωνισάμενος add. ἄριστα LG ‖ 7 ἑαυτὸν om. LG ‖ 8 προσέθηκε *b*

84: 1 Ἅπερ A^s ‖ 2 κροτηθῆναι LG ‖ 3 post συνήγορος additamentum in E (vide praef. p. xviii) ‖ ὁ^2 om. LG ‖ 4 Συρίας om. LG ‖ 5 λιμοῦ codd. praeter A ‖ 6 ἀναθέματι ante καθυποβ. transp. *b* ‖ 8 Χριστοῦ ante τῶν transp. *b* ‖ τοῦ] καὶ *b*

83. And Sisinnius was followed by Nestorius, the mad presbyter of Antioch, who distorted the word of truth by refusing to acknowledge the all-holy Virgin Mary as the Mother of God and by denying the doctrine of the hypostatic union of Christ, the savior of all. Having engaged him, the great Cyril convened a divine and sacred synod[86] in Alexandria, which issued and sent to Nestorius a decree of twelve articles. But he refused to accept this and kept to his spurious teaching, disturbing the community of the Church.

84. When the Emperor Theodosius the Younger became aware of this, he ordered the Third Ecumenical Council of two hundred blessed bishops to be convened in Ephesus, which was presided over by Cyril, the supporter of the apostles. But John of Antioch in Syria and his followers, in order to please Nestorius, did not show up. And the holy Council, after losing time and having fallen victim to a plague, finally condemned Nestorius and imposed on him a suitable anathema, proclaiming the holy Virgin Mary to be the Mother of God and Christ our God, the savior of all, to be hypostatically one.

[86] *SV* is one of the few documents which make explicit reference to this synod; for the others see HL, II_1, 264 note 3.

85.

Ἰωάννης γοῦν μετὰ ταῦτα καὶ οἱ περὶ αὐτὸν οὐ μετρίως πρὸς τὴν ἁγίαν στασιάσαντες σύνοδον ἐν Ἀντιοχείᾳ συνέδραμον ἅπαντες καὶ θείαν καὶ ἱερὰν ποιησάμενοι σύνοδον ἀπεκήρυξαν τὸν Νεστόριον, καὶ δύο φύσεις ἐπὶ Χριστοῦ ἀσυγχύτους, ἀδιαιρέτους θεοφρόνως τρανώσαντες, τὸν ὅρον αὐτῶν πρὸς τὸν μέγαν Κύριλλον ἐξαπέστειλαν· ὃν δεξάμενος «εὐφραινέσθωσαν οἱ οὐρανοὶ καὶ ἀγαλλιάσθω ἡ γῆ» ἀνεβόησεν.

86.

Νεστορίου τοίνυν καθαιρεθέντος Μαξιμιανὸς τῷ θρόνῳ Κωνσταντινουπόλεως ἐμβιβάζεται καὶ τοῦτον Πρόκλος διαδεξάμενος, θείαν καὶ ἱερὰν ἐν Κωνσταντινουπόλει συνήθροισε σύνοδον καὶ ὅλους τοὺς ἀνθισταμένους τῇ ἁγίᾳ τοῦ θεοῦ ἐκκλησίᾳ καθυπέβαλεν ἀναθέματι.

87.

Πρὸς τούτοις ἐξ Ἀρμενίας εὐλαβεῖς τινες μοναχοὶ τὴν βασιλίδα κατέλαβον, ἀπαγγέλλοντες ὡς τὰ Θεοδώρου βιβλία τοῦ Μοψουεστίας βλασφημιῶν ὄντα ἀνάμεστα οἱ ἐν τῇ ἀνατολῇ σεμνύνουσιν ἀντὶ Νεστορίου κατέχοντες. Διὸ Πρόκλος Ἰωάννῃ τῷ Ἀντιοχείας καὶ ὁ βασιλεὺς Θεοδόσιος γράφουσι κατὰ Θεοδώρου τοῦ μιαροῦ συνοδικῶς ἀποφήνασθαι· ὁ δὲ συνέδριον ἀφελὲς ποιησάμενος, ἀνεξετάστως μηδένα μῶμον ἔχειν τὰ Θεοδώρου βιβλία Θεοδοσίῳ καὶ Πρόκλῳ ἀντέγραψε.

85: HL II_1, 399–404 ‖ 1–6: cf. Niceph. Call. XIV.35 (PG, 146, 1173A–1176B) ‖ 1–3: ? Theoph., 90, 19–23; 91, 12–16 ‖ 4–6: Theoph., 91, 19–24 ‖ 5–6: Ps. 95:11

87: HL II_1, 419–21 (ca. 438?) ‖ 1–7: cf. *Epit. Th. A.*, 96, 12–97, 2 (Theoph., 96, 2–9); v. *ACO,* II, 5, p. 112, 9 sqq.; Grumel, *Regestes,* numm. 80–81

85: 4 τὸν — 5 μέγαν] ὅρον πρὸς LG

86: 1 μαξιμῖνος *b* ‖ ante τῷ add. ἐν *b* ‖ 1–2 Κωνσταντινουπόλεως om. LG ‖ 2 ἀναβιβάζεται LG

87: 2 τὰ om. *b* ‖ 6 ἀσφαλὲς *z*

85. Later, after they had vehemently opposed the holy Council,[87] John and those with him all came together at Antioch, where they held a divine and sacred synod.[88] They condemned Nestorius, proclaimed with divine inspiration two unfused and indivisible natures in Christ, and sent their definition to the great Cyril who received it with the cry, "Let the heavens rejoice and the earth be glad."

86. After the deposition of Nestorius, Maximian was placed on the throne of Constantinople. And he was succeeded by Proclus who gathered a divine and sacred synod in Constantinople,[89] subjecting to anathema all those opposed to the holy Church of God.

87. Furthermore, certain pious monks from Armenia came to the imperial city, reporting that those in the East were following as authoritative, in place of Nestorius, the works of Theodore of Mopsuestia, which were full of blasphemies. For this reason Proclus and Emperor Theodosius wrote to John of Antioch, (instructing him) to make a synodical declaration against the abominable Theodore. But he convened a simple assembly and, without making an examination, wrote back to Theodosius and Proclus that Theodore's books were free of error.

[87] At this point the compiler skips over the intervening events. In retaliation for the deposition of Nestorius, John of Antioch and his party held a separate synod at Ephesus in which they condemned Cyril of Alexandria and Memnon of Ephesus. It was only after some years (probably in 433) that John agreed to the decisions of the Council of Ephesus against Nestorius and became reconciled with Cyril; cf. Theophanes, 90–91.

[88] As far as we know no such synod took place; the ὅρος (decision) which *SV* refers to was not a synodical document but a letter from John of Antioch to Cyril. See Theophanes, 91 lines 12–24.

[89] There is no other evidence for such a synod.

88.

Κυρίλλου τοίνυν καὶ Πρόκλου πρὸς τὴν ἀγήρω μετελθόντων λαμπρότητα, Διόσκορος τὸν μέν, τὸν δὲ Φλαβιανὸς ὁ μακάριος διαδέχεται· ὃς παρὰ τοῦ ὁσιωτάτου Εὐσεβίου τοῦ ἀρχιεπισκόπου τοῦ Δορυλαίου παρενοχλούμενος θείαν καὶ ἱερὰν ἐν Κωνσταντινουπόλει συνεκαλέσατο σύνοδον, τὰ κατὰ τὸν Εὐτυχῆ ἐξετάζουσαν τοῦ Βυζαντίου ἀρχιμανδρίτην ὑπάρχοντα, καὶ τοῦτον τῆς ἐκκλησίας ἐχώρισεν.

89.

Εὐτυχοῦς δὲ τοὺς συγκλητικούς, καὶ μάλιστα Χρυσάφιον τὸν Τζοῦπον ἐπιλεγόμενον πραιπόσιτον χρηματίζοντα, καὶ δι' αὐτοῦ ὡς μεγάλα ἰσχύοντος Θεοδόσιον τὸν βασιλέα θωπείαις ὑπονοθεύσαντος, λῃστρικὴ ἐν Ἐφέσῳ συνηθροίζετο σύνοδος, ἧς ἐξῆρχεν Ἀλεξανδρείας ὁ πάπας Διόσκορος· ἐν ᾗ Εὐτυχὴς μέσον στὰς Οὐαλεντῖνον καὶ Μάνην ἀνεθεμάτισεν ἀπροσποιήτως, κριθεὶς εὐαπόδεκτος. Φλαβιανὸς δὲ Κωνσταντινουπόλεως ὁ ἀοίδιμος καθαιρεθείς, λακτίσματι ἐπιτοπίως κτείνεται, καὶ ὁ τοῦ Δορυλαίου Εὐσέβιος ὑπὲρ Χριστοῦ ἐξορίζεται.

88: HL II_1, 518–38 (A.D. 448) ‖ 1–6: cf. *Epit. Th. A.*, 97, 11–23; Theoph., 97, 26–30; 99, 28–100, 2

89: HL II_1, 555–621 (A.D. 449) ‖ 1–8: cf. Theoph., 100, 13–31; Niceph. Call. XIV.47 (PG, 146, 1221C–1228A)

88: 2 ὁ μακάριος post διαδέχεται transp. LG ‖ 3 τοῦ^2 om. LG ‖ τοῦ^3 AED: om. LG*z* ‖ 5 τὸν om. LG ‖ τοῦ — 6 ὑπάρχοντα om. LG

89: 1 μάλιστα — 3 τὸν om. LG ‖ 1 ante Χρυσάφιον add. τὸν *z* ‖ τὸν τζεροῦπον *z* recte τὸν Τζουμᾶν ‖ 2 ἰσχύοντος LG: -οντα D*b* ‖ 4 συναθροίζεται *b* ‖ post ἐξῆρχεν scr. ὁ LG ‖ ὁ πάπας om. LG ‖ 7 ἐκτείνετο LG

88. When Cyril and Proclus, then, passed on to eternal glory, the one was succeeded by Dioscorus, the other by blessed Flavian. And Flavian, at the prodding of the most saintly Eusebius, archbishop of Dorylaeum, called together a divine and sacred synod in Constantinople to examine the teachings of Eutyches, an archimandrite of Byzantium, and excommunicated him from the Church.

89. But when Eutyches managed to seduce by flattery the senators and especially the chamberlain Chrysaphius, surnamed Tzupus,[90] and through him, because of his great influence, Emperor Theodosius, a "robber" synod was convened in Ephesus, led by Dioscorus, the pope[91] of Alexandria. Here Eutyches came forward and, without feigning, anathematized Valentinus and Manes, after being judged acceptable again. But the illustrious Flavian of Constantinople was condemned and died on the spot as the result of a kicking,[92] while Eusebius of Dorylaeum was banished for the sake of Christ.

[90] The correct form of his surname is Tzuma (e.g., Theophanes, 100 line 16).

[91] See note 37.

[92] In the version of Nicephorus Callistus (PG, 146, 1225D) and Theophanes (100 lines 30–31), with both of whose accounts *SV* shows similarities, Flavian was thrown out of the synod ὠθισμοῖς καὶ λακτίσμασι and died three days later.

90.

Λέων γοῦν πάπας ὁ μέγας τῆς Ῥωμαίων ἐκκλησίας ἐπίσκοπος τὰ ὑπὸ Διοσκόρου μαθὼν γενόμενα ἐν Ἐφέσῳ ἀνοσιουργήματα κατ' αὐτοῦ διανίσταται, καὶ σύνοδον θείαν καὶ ἱερὰν συστησάμενος ἀναθέματι αὐτὸν σὺν Εὐτυχεῖ καθυπέβαλε· κλήρῳ τε καὶ ἀξιωματικοῖς καὶ λαῷ Κωνσταντινουπόλεως τύπον ἀκοινωνησίας ἐκθέμενος ἐξαπέστειλεν.

91.

Ἔτι γε μὴν Λέων ὁ τῶν ἀποστολικῶν δογμάτων ὑπέρμαχος θείαν καὶ ἱερὰν ἐν Ῥώμῃ συγκαλεσάμενος σύνοδον, παραινέσεις ἐγγράφους τῷ φιλοχρίστῳ βασιλεῖ Μαρκιανῷ διεπέμψατο, ἐπεὶ βασιλεὺς ὁ μικρὸς Θεοδόσιος τὰ ἐπίγεια καταλέλοιπε, συνοδικῶς τὰ περὶ Φλαβιανοῦ ἐξετασθῆναι παρεγγυώμενος.

92.

Ἀλλὰ καὶ Πουλχερία ἡ εὐσεβὴς αὐγούστα διεγείρειν τὸν σύζυγον οὐ κατώκνησε σύνοδον οἰκουμενικὴν τετάρτην ἐν Χαλκηδόνι τῶν ἑξακοσίων τριάκοντα θεοφόρων πατέρων ἀθροίσασθαι· ἥτις ἁγία σύνοδος καθελοῦσα Εὐτυχῆ καὶ Διόσκορον τὰς δύο φύσεις Ἰησοῦ Χριστοῦ τοῦ θεοῦ ἡμῶν ἀδιαιρέτους καὶ ἀσυγχύτους ἐτράνωσέ τε καὶ ἀνεκήρυξεν.

90: HL II_1, 625 (A.D. 449) ‖ 1–3: cf. Theoph., 101, 5–8 ‖ 4–5: cf. *Epist. Leonis, ACO,* II, 4, pp. 21–22

91: 3–5: cf. Theoph., 105, 16–18; Niceph. Call. XV.2 (PG, 147, 13C)

92: HL II_2, 649–838 (A.D. 451) ‖ 4–5: cf. cap. 85, 3–4

90: 1 οὖν *b* ‖ πάπας om. LG ‖ τῆς τῶν *z* ‖ ἐπίσκοπος om. *b* ‖ 2 ἐν Ἐφέσῳ ἀνοσιουργήματα om. *z* ‖ 4 τε καὶ om. LG

91: 2–3 φιλοχρίστῳ om. *b* ‖ ἐπεὶ — 4 καταλέλοιπε om. LG

92: 1 τὸν σύζυγον] τὴν σύνοδον *z* (σύζυγον mg. V) ‖ 4 Ἰησοῦ om. LG ‖ 5 ἀδιαιρέτως καὶ ἀσυγχύτως *z*

90. Pope Leo, then, the great bishop of the Roman Church, having learned of the impious deeds of Dioscorus in Ephesus, was aroused against him, and convening a divine and sacred synod, he placed him along with Eutyches under anathema; and issuing a decree of excommunication, he sent it to the clergy, officials, and people of Constantinople.[93]

91. Furthermore, Leo, the champion of apostolic teachings, calling together a divine and sacred synod[94] in Rome, sent written requests to the Christ-loving Emperor Marcian—Emperor Theodosius the Younger having left this world—urging him to have the matter of Flavian examined by a synod.

92. And Pulcheria, the pious wife of the Emperor, did not hesitate to urge her husband to convene in Chalcedon the Fourth Ecumenical Council of six hundred and thirty God-inspired fathers. This holy Council, condemning Eutyches and Dioscorus, proclaimed and decreed the two indivisible and unconfused natures in Jesus Christ our God.

[93] The compiler is more than likely drawing on a letter of Leo sent to Constantinople in 449 (*ACO,* II, 4, 21–22). In the extant Greek version (printed, e.g., in J. B. Cotelier, *Ecclesiae graecae monumenta,* I [Paris, 1677], 57–59) the address is as follows: Λέων ἐπίσκοπος καὶ ἡ ἁγία σύνοδος ἡ ἐν τῇ πόλει Ῥωμαίων συναχθεῖσα κλήρῳ, ἀξιωματικοῖς καὶ παντὶ τῷ λαῷ τοῖς οἰκοῦσιν ἐν Κωνσταντινουπόλει, ἀγαπητοῖς υἱοῖς, ἐν Κυρίῳ χαίρειν. It should be noted, however, that the Pope does not mention Dioscurus or Eutyches by name but simply issues a general condemnation of those who deny the real incarnation of Christ.

[94] The compiler, finding in his source that Leo had made an official request to the Emperor for a council, assumes that this was done at a synod and so adds his usual phrase θείαν καὶ ἱερὰν . . . συγκαλεσάμενος σύνοδον.

93.

Ἀνατολίου τοίνυν τοῦ Βυζαντίου ἀρχιερέως ὑπάρξαντος καὶ Ἀπολιναρίου τὸν Διοσκόρου θρόνον κατέχοντος καὶ πρὸς κύριον ἐκδημήσαντος, Προτέριος ὁ μακάριος ἀρχιερεὺς Ἀλεξανδρείας ἐχρημάτισε. Καὶ Τιμόθεός τις μοναχὸς προσαγορευόμενος Αἴλουρος, διεγείρας Ἀλεξανδρέων τὸ φιλοσύγχυτον, ἐν τῷ βαπτιστηρίῳ παρεσκεύασεν ἀναιρεθῆναι Προτέριον· καὶ αὐτὸς Ἀλεξανδρείας τοῦ θρόνου δραξάμενος, συνέδριον συνεκρότησεν ἀθεότητος καὶ τὴν ἁγίαν ἐν Χαλκηδόνι ἀνεθεμάτισε σύνοδον.

94.

Ἅπερ Λέων ὁ μέγας φιλόχριστος βασιλεὺς μετὰ Μαρκιανὸν μαθὼν τελευτήσαντα, θείαν καὶ ἱερὰν ἐν Θεσσαλονίκῃ σύνοδον ἀθροισθῆναι ὑπὸ Εὐδοξίου τοῦ αὐτῆς ἐπισκόπου ἐθέσπισεν, ἣ Εὐτυχῆ καὶ Διόσκορον ἀνεθεμάτισε καὶ Τιμόθεον, καὶ τὴν ἁγίαν ἐν Χαλκηδόνι ἐκύρωσε σύνοδον.

95.

Ὡσαύτως καὶ Ἀνατόλιος ἐν Κωνσταντινουπόλει θεόπνευστον προσκαλεσάμενος σύνοδον, Εὐτυχῆ καὶ Διόσκορον ἀνεθεμάτισε καὶ Τιμόθεον τὸν ἐπιλεγόμενον Αἴλουρον, καὶ τὴν ἐν Χαλκηδόνι ἁγίαν ἐκύρωσε σύνοδον.

93: HL II_2, 881 ‖ 4–6: cf. *Epit. Th. A.*, 103, 22–104, 22; Theoph., 110, 24–111, 2

94: HL II_2, 881

95: HL II_2, 881 ‖ 1–4: cf. *Epit. Th. A.*, 104, 24–105, 10; Theoph., 111, 23 sqq.

93: 1 post ὑπάρξαντος add. σπουδῇ διοσκόρου μάλιστα ὡς ἀποκρισιαρίου αὐτοῦ E ‖ Ἀνατολίου – 3 ἐχρημάτισε] διοσκόρου τοίνυν καθαιρεθέντος προτέριος ὁ μακάριος ἐπὶ τὸν θρόνον ἀλεξανδρείας ἀνάγεται LG ‖ 4 καὶ Τιμόθεός] τιμόθεος δέ LG ‖ τις om. *b*

94: 1 Ὅπερ E*z* ‖ μέγας om. *z* ‖ μετὰ – 2 τελευτήσαντα] μαρκιανοῦ μαθὼν τελευτήσαντος LG ‖ 3 Εὐδοξίου] αὐξιθέου *SV*[2] recte Εὐξιθέου ‖ καὶ om. LG ‖ 4 ἀναθεματίσασα LG ‖ καὶ[2] om. LG

95: 2 ἀνεθεμάτισε om. *z* ‖ 3 Τιμόθεον – Αἴλουρον] τὸν αἴλουρον LG ‖ 3–4 ἁγίαν ἐκ. σύνοδον] σύνοδον ἐκύρωσεν *z*

93. When Anatolius, then, was archpriest of Byzantium and Apolinarius, the successor[95] to Dioscorus' throne, had departed for the Lord, the blessed Proterius became archpriest of Alexandria. And a certain monk Timothy, surnamed Aelurus (the Cat), having aroused the Alexandrian fondness of disruption, had Proterius killed in the baptistery. Then he himself seized the throne of Alexandria, convened a godless assembly,[96] and anathematized the holy Council of Chalcedon.

94. When Leo, the great and Christ-loving emperor, who had succeeded after Marcian's death, learned this, he ordered a divine and sacred synod[97] to be convened in Thessalonica by Eudoxius,[98] the bishop of that city; it anathematized Eutyches, Dioscurus, and Timothy and confirmed the holy Council of Chalcedon.

95. And Anatolius, likewise, having called together a divinely inspired synod[99] in Constantinople, anathematized Eutyches and Dioscurus along with Timothy, called Aelurus, and confirmed the holy Council of Chalcedon.

[95] Dioscurus was immediately succeeded by Proterius; the error is avoided in the second recension.

[96] The so-called συνέδριον is not attested elsewhere.

[97] This synod and the following three (chaps. 95–97) are not referred to directly by any other text. At the same time we know that Emperor Leo wrote to Anatolius of Constantinople and other bishops asking them to examine the matter of Timothy Aelurus and the Council of Chalcedon (*ACO*, II, 5, 11). The writer may well have taken his cue from the existence of such letters.

[98] The correct name is Euxitheus; SV^2 has Auxitheus.

[99] See note 97 *supra*.

96.

Ἀλλὰ καὶ Λέων πάπας Ῥώμης ὁ ἰσαπόστολος Εὐτυχῆ καὶ Διόσκορον σὺν Τιμοθέῳ συνοδικῶς καθυπέβαλεν ἀναθέματι καὶ τὴν ἐν Χαλκηδόνι ἁγίαν ἐκύρωσε σύνοδον.

97.

Ὁμοίως τε καὶ Σιμπλίκιος, Λέοντα Ῥώμης διαδεξάμενος, θείαν καὶ ἱερὰν συστησάμενος σὺνοδον Εὐτυχῆ καὶ Διόσκορον ἀνεθεμάτισε καὶ Τιμόθεον, καὶ τὴν ἁγίαν ἐν Χαλκηδόνι ἐκύρωσε σύνοδον.

98.

Τοῦ βασιλέως οὖν Λέοντος γαμβρὸν αὐτοῦ Ζήνωνα τὸν ἐπὶ θυγατρὶ Ἀριάδνῃ οἰκείᾳ ἐν Ἀντιοχείᾳ τῆς Συρίας ἐξαποστείλαντος, μοναχός τις μονῆς τῶν Ἀκοιμήτων ἐπηκολούθησεν, ὃς τῷ θρόνῳ ἐποφθαλμήσας τῆς πόλεως πείθει τὸν Ζήνωνα συνεργεῖν αὐτῷ· καὶ τῆς λώβης Ἀπολιναρίου τινὰς μισθωσάμενος τὸν θρόνον Ἀντιοχείας καθήρπασε, καὶ μιαρὰν ποιησάμενος σύνοδον προσθήκην τοῦ τρισαγίου «ὁ σταυρωθεὶς δι' ἡμᾶς» καινοτομεῖ ὁ ἀνόσιος. Ὅπερ μαθὼν αὐτοκράτωρ Λέων ὁ μέγας καὶ εὐσεβέστατος ἐξορισθῆναι αὐτὸν διετάξατο· ὃς προφθάσας εἰς τὴν μονὴν τῶν Ἀκοιμήτων κατέφυγε.

96: HL II_2, 881

98: HL II_2, 859–60 ‖ 1-9: *Epit. Th. A.*, 109, 19–110, 15; 113, 8-9

96: 1 ante πάπας add. ὁ E ‖ 2 καθυποβαλὼν LG ‖ καὶ om. LG

97: 1 τε] δὲ LG ‖ 2 σύνοδον συστησάμενος *b* ‖ 3 Τιμόθεον] τὸν αἴλουρον LG ‖ καὶ τὴν ἐν χαλκηδόνι ἁγίαν σύνοδον ἐκύρωσε *b* ‖ ἐπεκύρωσε LG

98: 1 γοῦν LG ‖ ἐπιθυγάτριον (sic) LG ‖ 2 Ἀριάδνῃ οἰκείᾳ om. LG ‖ τῆς om. LG*z* ‖ Συρίας om. LG ‖ 3 ἐποφθαλμίσας *b* ‖ 7 μέγας καὶ om. LG

96. Leo, too, the Pope of Rome and equal of the apostles, by means of a synod placed under anathema Eutyches and Dioscurus along with Timothy and confirmed the holy Council of Chalcedon.

97. And similarly Simplicius, Leo's successor in Rome, having brought together a divine and sacred synod,[100] subjected Eutyches, Dioscurus, and Timothy to anathema and confirmed the holy Council of Chalcedon.

98. When the Emperor Leo, then, sent out his son-in-law Zeno, the husband of his daughter Ariadne, to Antioch in Syria, there came in his company a certain monk from the Acoemetae monastery[101] who set his eyes on the throne of that city and persuaded Zeno to help him. And hiring some people from the heresy of Apolinarius, he seized the throne of Antioch, after which the wretch organized an impious synod[102] and changed the Trisagion hymn by adding "crucified for us." Informed of this, the most pious Emperor Leo the Elder ordered him banished. But he anticipated (the sentence) and took refuge in the Acoemetae monastery.

[100] See note 97 *supra*; the chapter is omitted by SV^2.

[101] It is puzzling why our author, who follows very closely here the *Epit.Th.A.*, 109 line 19ff., does not indicate the name of Peter the Fuller. Strange, too, is his placing of Peter in the Acoemetae monastery before his sojourn in Antioch, an item of information only otherwise preserved in an obscure text ascribed to the sixth century: Alexander the Monk, *Laudatio in Apostolum Barnabam,* PG, 87_3, 4099 (see K. Krumbacher, *Geschichte der byzantinischen Litteratur,* 2nd ed. [Munich, 1897], 164 note 3); the agreement can hardly be more than a coincidence. According to *Epit.Th.A.*, (109 line 21) Peter had been a presbyter of St. Bassa in Chalcedon. For more details, see *DTC,* XII^2, 1933, *s.vv.* Pierre le Foulon.

[102] *SV* has taken the liberty of deciding that the addition to the hymn was made at a synod; there is no hint of this either in *Epit.Th.A.* or in any other text.

99.

Ζήνωνα τοίνυν τὴν βασιλείαν τοῦ μεγάλου καὶ μικροῦ διαδεξάμενον Λέοντος Βασιλίσκος καὶ Ἀρμάτιος αὐτῆς ἀντάραντες ἐξεδίωξαν, καὶ τὴν ἐν Χαλκηδόνι σύνοδον παντελῶς ἐξοστρακίσαι προθέμενοι, τύπῳ γενικῷ Τιμόθεον ἐκ Χερσῶνος ἀνεκαλέσαντο. Ὅστις Αἴλουρος καταλαβὼν Ἀλεξάνδρειαν, Τιμόθεον τὸν Σαλοφακιόλιον μεταστήσας καὶ τοῦ θρόνου δραξάμενος, ἄθεον ποιησάμενος σύλλογον πολλοῖς ἀναθέμασι τὴν ἁγίαν ἐν Χαλκηδόνι καθυπέβαλε σύνοδον. Ταῦτα δὲ Ἀνατολίου καὶ Γενναδίου ἱεραρχῶν τοῦ Βυζαντίου τῶν ἀειμνήστων χρησαμένων τέλει τοῦ βίου καὶ Ἀκακίου κρατοῦντος ἐγένετο.

100.

Ἰωάννης δὲ Κύρου ἐπίσκοπος ὁ μακάριος τὸν Γναφέα Πέτρον καὶ πάλιν ἐν Ἀντιοχείᾳ ὁρῶν ἀθέως πολιτευόμενον καὶ Βασιλίσκου τὸ κράτος ἐρχόμενον πρὸς ἀσθένειαν, σύνοδον θείαν καὶ ἱερὰν ἐν τῇ πόλει αὐτοῦ συνεκρότησε καὶ τὸν Γναφέα Πέτρον ἀνεθεμάτισε.

101.

Καὶ Βασιλίσκον Ζήνων τὸν τύραννον χειρωσάμενος ἐν Ἀντιοχείᾳ σύνοδον ἁγίαν συναθροισθῆναι προσέταξεν, ἣ τὴν ἁγίαν ἐν Χαλκηδόνι κυρώσασα σύνοδον τὸν Γναφέα Πέτρον ἐξορίᾳ καὶ ἀναθέματι καθυπέβαλεν, ἀντ' αὐτοῦ προχειρισαμένη Στέφανον τὸν μακάριον· ὃν τάχιστα πρὸς Χριστὸν ἐκδημήσαντα Στέφανος ἕτερος διαδέχεται.

99: HL II_2, 913 ‖ 1–7: cf. *Epit. Th. A.*, 112, 11–114, 9; Theoph., 120, 1–121, 27 ‖ 2: Theoph., 124, 15 sqq.

100: HL II_2, 913

101: HL II_2, 913–14 (A.D. 478?) ‖ 1–5: Theoph., 125, 13–17 et 128, 17–18

99: 1 τοῦ μεγάλου καὶ μικροῦ λέοντος τὴν βασιλείαν διαδεξάμενον LG ‖ 2 Βασιλίσκος — ἐξεδίωξαν] βασιλίσκος ἀντάρας ἐδίωξε LG ‖ 3 προθέμενος LG ‖ 4 ἀνεκαλέσατο LG ‖ 5 recte Σαλοφακίαλον ‖ 6 σύλλογον] σύνοδον *b* ‖ ἁγίαν post Χαλκηδόνι transp. *b* ‖ 7 Ταῦτα — 9 ἐγένετο om. LG

100: 1 Γναφέα] κναφ- ubique *z* ‖ 3 ἐχόμενον *z*

101: 3 σύνοδον κυρώσασα *z*

99. Zeno, the successor to the empire of Leo the Elder and Leo the Younger, was driven out by Basiliscus and Armatius,[103] who rebelled against his rule, and they, in their efforts to condemn once and for all the Council of Chalcedon, recalled Timothy from Cherson by a general edict. This (Timothy) Aelurus came to Alexandria where, after he had removed Timothy Salophakiolus and had seized the throne, he held a godless gathering[104] and subjected the holy Council of Chalcedon to many anathemas. These events took place after Byzantium's hierarchs of eternal memory, Anatolius and Gennadius, had reached life's end and during the tenure of Acacius.

100. And John, the blessed bishop of Cyrrhus, seeing Peter the Fuller once again at his ungodly conduct in Antioch and the power of Basiliscus weakening, summoned a divine and sacred synod[105] in his own city and anathematized Peter the Fuller.

101. Following his defeat of the tyrant Basiliscus, Zeno ordered a holy synod convened in Antioch, which confirmed the holy Council of Chalcedon, banished and anathematized Peter the Fuller, and elected the blessed Stephen in his place.[106] This man very soon departed for Christ and was succeeded by another Stephen.[107]

[103] The compiler is confused; Armatius (otherwise known as Armatus or Harmatius) was sent against Zeno by Basiliscus at a later date, after the events of this chapter had taken place. The mistake has been noticed in MSS L and G.

[104] *Epit.Th.A.* (114 line 9), followed by Theophanes (121 line 22), tells us that Timothy Aelurus anathematized the Council of Chalcedon.

[105] *SV* is the only witness known for this synod.

[106] Peter the Fuller was in fact succeeded by John of Apamea, whose tenure, however, lasted only three months; see Theophanes, 125 lines 15–16; Nicephorus, 131.

[107] Our writer follows the tradition represented also by Theophanes, 128 line 17 ff. and Nicephorus, 132, according to which two Stephens held the throne of Antioch in succession; Malalas (Bonn ed.), 381, on the other hand, knows of only one. See E. Stein, *Histoire du Bas-Empire,* II, (Paris, 1949), 21 note 1, with references to both sides of the controversy.

At the same time there is an important difference between *SV* and Theophanes. While the latter maintains that Stephen[a] was charged with Nestorianism, the compiler (chap. 102), agreeing with Malalas, relates this of Stephen[b]. There is some chance, then, that *SV* here reflects more accurately than Theophanes the version of *Epit.Th.A.* (116).

102.

Οἱ γοῦν Πέτρου σπουδασταί, ὡς Νεστοριανὸν αὐτὸν διασύροντες, πείθουσι τὸν αὐτοκράτορα Ζήνωνα θείαν καὶ ἱερὰν ἐν Λαοδικείᾳ συστήσασθαι σύνοδον· ἥτις κατηγορούμενον ὑπὸ τῶν ἀθέων <ἀθῷον> εὑροῦσα τὸν Στέφανον τῷ θρόνῳ Ἀντιοχείας ἀποκατέστησεν. Οἱ δὲ τῆς κιβδήλου δόξης θεράποντες χρόνον μικρὸν ἀναμείναντες, θυμῷ ἐκ φθόνου μεγίστῳ πυρούμενοι, συρμῷ τὸν ἱερομάρτυρα Στέφανον ἀποκτείναντες εἰς τὸν παραρρέοντα Ὀρρόντην ποταμὸν κατηκόντισαν.

103.

Τιμοθέου γοῦν τοῦ Αἰλούρου ἐν Ἀλεξανδρείᾳ πρὸς ᾅδην χωρήσαντος τὸν Μογγὸν Πέτρον οἱ φιλοσύγχυτοι διάδοχον τοῦ θρόνου κατέστησαν· κληρικοὶ δὲ καὶ μοναχοὶ τῆς ἀληθείας ὑπέρμαχοι αὐτὸν ἐξεώσαντες τὸν μακάριον Ἰωάννην τὸν Ταβεννησιώτην ἀντικαθίδρυσαν. Ὅνπερ Ζήνων ὡς παρὰ γνώμην αὐτοῦ χειροτονηθέντα ἐξέωσε καὶ τὸν δυσσεβῆ Μογγόν, δοὺς τὸ ἑνωτικὸν αὐτοῦ, εἰς Ἀλεξάνδρειαν ἐξαπέστειλεν· ὃς αἱρετικὴν συστησάμενος σύνοδον τὴν ἁγίαν ἐν Χαλκηδόνι ἀνεθεμάτισε σύνοδον τὸν Κωνσταντινουπόλεως Ἀκάκιον ἔχων συμπράκτορα.

102: HL II_2, 914–15 (A.D. 478?) ‖ 1–7: Theoph., 126, 5–9; 128, 19–22 (vide *Epit. Th. A.*, 116, 3 sqq.)

103: HL II_2, 867; 919 ‖ 1–8: Theoph., 125, 19–24; 128, 28; 130, 9–18; *Epith. Th. A.*, 115, 22–29; 116, 28–117, 15 ‖ 7: *Epit. Th. A.*, 117, 24–25

102: 1 οὖν LG ‖ νεστοριανοὶ LG ‖ διασύραντες *b* ‖ 3 ἀθῷον SV^2 (ἀνεύθυνον Theoph., 126, 8-9) ‖ 5 θεραπευταὶ *b* ‖ 6 μεγίστου LG ‖ 7 ποταμὸν ὀρέντιον LG ‖ κατηκόντησαν *z*

103: 1 Τιμ. — Αἰλούρου] αἰλούρου τοίνυν LG ‖ 3 ὑπέρμαχοι] οἱ πρόμαχοι *g* ‖ 4 τὸν om. LG ‖ 5 ἀσεβῆ A^s ‖ 6 αὐτοῦ om. LG leg. αὐτῷ (cum SV^2)? ‖ 7 ἁγίαν post Χαλκηδόνι transp. *b*

102. Then, by disparaging him (Stephen) as a Nestorian, the supporters of Peter persuaded the Emperor Zeno to hold a divine and sacred synod in Laodicea. It found Stephen <innocent of> the charges brought by the godless ones and restored him to the throne of Antioch. But the servants of the spurious doctrine did not wait long and, inflamed by the strongest feelings of envy, they inflicted a violent death on the hieromartyr Stephen and cast him into the Orontes river which flowed nearby.

103. When Timothy Aelurus, then, had passed on to Hades from Alexandria, the lovers of disruption put Peter Mongus on the throne as his successor. But clergy and monks, the champions of truth, drove him out[108] and installed blessed John the Tabennesiote in his place. Zeno expelled this man on the grounds that he had been ordained against the Emperor's wishes, and, issuing his *Henoticon,* he sent Peter Mongus back to Alexandria where, abetted by Acacius of Constantinople, he convened a heretical synod and anathematized the holy Council of Chalcedon.[109]

[108] At this point *SV* takes no account of the restoration and eventual death of Timothy Salophakialos; cf. Theophanes, 125 lines 22–25; 128 lines 27–28 and *Epit.Th.A.,* 115 lines 25–29.

[109] Compare the *Epit.Th.A.,* 117 lines 24–25, which relates that Peter Mongus anathematized the Council.

104.

Ἀλλ' οἱ Κωνσταντινουπόλεως καὶ τῆς πάσης ἑῴας ὀρθόδοξοι Φίληκι τῷ πάπᾳ Ῥώμης ταῦτα διασαφήσαντες θείαν καὶ ἱερὰν παρεσκεύασαν ποιήσασθαι σύνοδον· ἣ τὸν Μογγὸν Πέτρον ἀνεθεμάτισε καὶ Ἀκάκιον, καὶ τὴν ἐν Χαλκηδόνι ἁγίαν σύνοδον ἐπεκύρωσε.

105.

Ζήνων τοίνυν ὁ βασιλεὺς χειρωσάμενος Ἴλλουν τε καὶ Λεόντιον κατὰ τῶν τῆς ἀνατολῆς ἐπισκόπων ἐχώρησε, καὶ Ἀντιοχείας τὸν Καλανδίωνα ἐξορίσας εἰς Ὄασιν τὸν Γναφέα Πέτρον πάλιν ἀποκατέστησεν· ὃς αἱρετικὴν συστησάμενος σύνοδον τὴν ἐν Χαλκηδόνι ἁγίαν ἀνεθεμάτισε σύνοδον. Καὶ σὺν πολλοῖς ἀτοπήμασιν Ἱεραπόλεως χειροτονεῖ Ξεναΐαν ἐπίσκοπον, τῷ γένει Πέρσην, ἀβάπτιστον καὶ τῆς δουλικῆς τύχης δραπέτην γενόμενον καὶ τῆς χριστιανοκατηγορικῆς αἱρέσεως ἀρχηγέτην διάπυρον· πρῶτος γὰρ πάντων Χριστοῦ τοῦ θεοῦ ἡμῶν, τῆς πανάγνου αὐτοῦ μητρὸς καὶ πάντων τῶν ἁγίων τὰς σεβασμίας εἰκόνας τῆς ἐκκλησίας ἐξέβαλεν.

106.

Ὁ γοῦν μακάριος Φίληξ τῆς πρεσβυτέρας Ῥώμης ἐπίσκοπος, μαθὼν παρὰ τῶν ὀρθοδόξων τῆς ἀνατολῆς ἱεραρχῶν τὴν Πέτρου δυσσέβειαν, διὰ Κυντιανοῦ ἐπισκόπου Ἀρκουλιανῶν θείαν καὶ ἱερὰν ποιησάμενος σύνοδον γραφῆναι καθαίρεσιν τῷ Γναφεῖ παρεσκεύασεν.

104: HL II_2, 921–22 (A.D. 483?) ‖ 1–3: cf. *Epit. Th. A.*, 119, 10–16; Theoph., 131, 23–29

105: 1: cf. Theoph., 132, 13–15 ‖ 2–9: cf. Theoph., 133, 30–134, 19

106: HL II_2, 927–30 ‖ 3–4 cf. Epist. fict. ad Petrum, *ACO*, III, 227–29

104: 1 κωνσταντινουπολῖται LG

105: 1 ἴλλον καὶ λέοντα LG ‖ 2 κλαυδίωνα *b* ‖ 3 πάλιν om. LG ‖ ἀπεκατέστησεν *z* κατέστησεν LG ‖ 5 ξενανίαν *b* ‖ 8 τῆς — μητρὸς] καὶ τῆς παναγίου μητρὸς αὐτοῦ LG ‖ αὐτοῦ om. *z* ‖ 8–9 πάντων τῶν Ez: τῶν πάντων LG πάντων AD

106: 3 κιντυνιανοῦ *b*

104. But the orthodox of Constantinople and of the entire East informed the Roman Pope Felix of these events and persuaded him to hold a divine and sacred synod, which anathematized Peter Mongus and Acacius[110] and confirmed the holy Council of Chalcedon.

105. The Emperor Zeno, then, following his defeat of Illus and Leontius, set out against the eastern bishops and, banishing Calandion from Antioch to Oasis, reinstated Peter the Fuller. This man brought together a heretical synod[111] and anathematized the holy Council of Chalcedon. Along with many other irregularities he ordained Xenaias bishop of Hierapolis, a Persian by birth, unbaptized, a runaway slave, and ardent originator of the anti-Christian[112] heresy; for he was the very first to banish from the Church the sacred images of Christ our God, of his all-holy mother,[113] and of all the saints.[114]

106. Then the blessed Felix, bishop of Old Rome, having learned of Peter's impious acts from the orthodox hierarchs of the East, organized through Quintian,[115] bishop of Arculia,[116] a divine and sacred synod and made it issue a written deposition to the Fuller.

[110] Acacius was not condemned at this time. Rather, Pope Felix wrote to him requesting the expulsion of Peter Mongus; see *Epit.Th.A.*, 119 line 16 and Theophanes, 131 lines 28–29.

[111] This appears to be based on the statement in Theophanes (134 line 7) that Peter, among many other evil deeds, anathematized Chalcedon.

[112] I.e., iconoclastic; the term is from the iconodule arsenal.

[113] The phrase τῆς πανάγνου αὐτοῦ μητρὸς seems to be an addition by *SV*.

[114] In having the word ἁγίων, the compiler agrees with Theophanes, 134 line 12, and this in contrast to two preserved fragments of the *Ecclesiastical History* of John Diakrinomenos (Mansi, XIII, 180E and *Epit.Th.A.*, 155 lines 26–27) in which Xenaias is said to have opposed representations of angels. This has led both P. Alexander (*The Patriarch Nicephorus* [Oxford, 1958], 45 note 1) and Hansen (*Epit.Th.A.*, 124 line 29) to see the ἁγίων in Theophanes as a scribal error for ἀγγέλων. Still, the evidence suggests that the chronicler already found ἁγίων in his source. (Cont. on p. 93.)

107.

Ἀλλὰ καὶ αὐτὸς Φίληξ ἐν Ῥώμῃ θείαν καὶ ἱερὰν συγκαλεσάμενος σύνοδον Πέτρῳ καθαίρεσιν τῷ Γναφεῖ ἐξαπέστειλεν.

108.

Τῷ θανάτῳ δὲ Ἀκακίου καὶ Φραυίτα προσχωρήσαντος Εὐφήμιος ὁ πανσέβαστος ἐπὶ τὸν θρόνον ἀνάγεται Κωνσταντινουπόλεως· ὅστις θείαν καὶ ἱερὰν συγκαλεσάμενος σύνοδον τὴν ἐν Χαλκηδόνι σύνοδον ἐβεβαίωσε καὶ τὰ συνοδικὰ αὐτοῦ τῷ πάπᾳ Ῥώμης ἀπέστειλεν. Ὅνπερ Φίληξ καὶ οἱ ἑσπέριοι ἀρχιεπίσκοποι ὡς μὲν ὀρθόδοξον ἄνδρα ἐδέξαντο, οὐ μὴν δὲ καὶ ὡς ἐπίσκοπον, διὰ τὸ μὴ ἐξαλεῖψαι τῶν ἱερῶν διπτύχων τοῦ ὑπὸ Φίληκος ἀναθεματισθέντος Ἀκακίου τὸ ὄνομα.

109.

Ζήνωνος γοῦν τελευτήσαντος Ἀριάδνην τὴν γυναῖκα αὐτοῦ καὶ τὴν βασιλείαν διεδέξατο Ἀναστάσιος· καὶ σύνοδον αἱρετικὴν ἐν Κωνσταντινουπόλει συστησάμενος διὰ τὴν ἁγίαν ἐν Χαλκηδόνι σύνοδον μυρίαις συκοφαντίαις ὑποβαλὼν Ἀρμενίας ἐπέκεινα ἐξώρισε τὸν Εὐφήμιον καὶ τῷ θρόνῳ ἀντικατέστησε τὸν ὁσιώτατον Μακεδόνιον.

107: HL II_2, 925 ‖ cf. Epist. Felic., *ACO*, III, 230–31

108: HL II_2, 939 (A.D. 492) ‖ 1: cf. *Epit. Th. A.*, 122, 19–21 ‖ 2–3: Theoph., 137, 11–13 (*Epit. Th. A.*, 127, 18–19) ‖ 3–7: cf. Theoph., 135, 17–19 (Niceph. Call. XVI.19 [PG, 147])

109: HL II_2, 939 (A.D. 496) ‖ 1–2: cf. Evag. III.29 ‖ 3–4: cf. Cyrill., *Vit. Sab.*, 140, 13–15 ‖ 3–5: cf. *Epit. Th. A.*, 128, 15–22 (Theoph., 140, 9–12; 19–20)

107: 1 προσκαλεσάμενος LG ‖ 2 ἀπέστειλεν *b*

108: 1 προσχωρήσαντος] sic codd. ‖ 3 σύνοδον συγκαλεσάμενος *z* ‖ τὴν] τὴν ἁγίαν LG ‖ 4 Ῥώμης om. *z* ‖ 5 ἀρχιερεῖς LG

109: 1 Ἀριάδνην — 2 Ἀναστάσιος] ἀναστάσιος ἐβασίλευσε LG ‖ 3 διὰ] καὶ D ‖ 4 Ἀρμενίας ἐπέκεινα om. LG ‖ 4–5 τῷ θρόνῳ om. LG ‖ 5 ἀντεκατέστησε LG

107, 108, 109

107. Felix himself also called together a divine and sacred synod in Rome and sent a deposition to Peter the Fuller.

108. After Acacius and Fravitas had gone to their deaths, the all-revered Euphemius was elevated to the throne of Constantinople, and having convoked a divine and sacred synod, this man confirmed the Council of Chalcedon and sent his synodical letter[117] to the Pope of Rome. Felix and the western archbishops accepted his orthodoxy but refused to recognize him as a bishop, because he had not erased from the sacred diptychs the name of Acacius, who had been anathematized by Felix.

109. When Zeno died, both his wife Ariadne and the Empire fell to Anastasius. He organized a heretical synod in Constantinople and, heaping innumerable slanders on Euphemius because of the holy Council of Chalcedon, he banished him beyond Armenia, putting on the throne in his place the most saintly Macedonius.

Surprisingly, the author of the second recension of *SV* went to the trouble of replacing the last sentence with another, which is almost identical to one of the extracts from John Diakrinomenos (*Epit.Th.A.*, 155 lines 26–27). SV^2 reads: Ἀλλ' οὗτος γε (i.e., Xenaias) τά τε ἄλλα δυσσεβῶν οὔτε Χριστοῦ τοῦ ἀληθινοῦ θεοῦ ἡμῶν οὔτε τινὸς τῶν ἀσωμάτων ἀγγέλων ἱεροτυπίας ἐν τῇ ἐκκλησίᾳ συνεχώρει ἀνατίθεσθαι.

[115] The information here and in the following chapter is not to be found in *Epit.Th.A.* or Theophanes and appears to be based on the forged letters to Peter the Fuller; see E. Schwartz, *Publizistische Sammlungen zum Acacianischen Schisma* (Munich, 1934), 291 ff.; text of letters, 135–40 and, *ACO*, III, 227–31.

SV^2 reflects more accurately the contents of the letters, characterizing that of Quintian as an admonition (παραίνεσις) and reserving the word condemnation (καθαίρεσις) for the Pope's letter.

[116] The form Ἀρκουλιανῶν is found in some manuscripts of the letter (as reported in Schwartz, *op. cit.*, 135); other readings are Ἀσκουλιανῶν and Ἐρκουλιανῶν.

[117] The dispatch of the synodical letter had nothing to do with the synod; it was sent to Rome in 490 or 491, while the synod took place in 492. See Grumel, *Regestes*, nos. 175 and 177.

110.

Ὅστις ἀφελῆ ποιησάμενος σύνοδον τὰ ἐν Χαλκηδόνι δογματισθέντα ἐγγράφως ἐκύρωσε, τὸ ἑνωτικὸν δὲ Ζήνωνος φόβῳ Ἀναστασίου παρεσιώπησε.

111.

Τοῦ Γναφέως τοίνυν Πέτρου ἀποβληθέντος Παλλάδιος τὸν θρόνον Ἀντιοχείας παρέλαβε· κἀκείνου τελειωθέντος Φλαβιανὸς διάδοχος γίνεται, καὶ σύνοδον αἱρετικὴν ποιησάμενος τὸ ἑνωτικὸν ἐδέξατο Ζήνωνος καὶ τὰς ἁγίας τρεῖς οἰκουμενικὰς συνόδους κηρύξας ἐγγράφως τὴν ἐν Χαλκηδόνι παρεσιώπησε, τῷ βασιλεῖ χαριζόμενος.

112.

Καὶ ὁ βασιλεὺς δὲ Ἀναστάσιος δι' Εὐτροπίου τριβούνου Φλαβιανῷ καὶ τῷ Ἱεροσολύμων Ἠλίᾳ ἐν Σιδῶνι σύνοδον συναθροῖσαι παρεκελεύσατο καὶ τὴν ἐν Χαλκηδόνι ἁγίαν σύνοδον ὑποβαλεῖν ἀναθέμασιν. Ἀλλὰ ταύτην Ἠλίας διέλυσεν ἄπρακτον, Εὐτροπίου συνάρσει γράμμασι πτερνίσας τὸν Ἀναστάσιον, δι' ἣν αἰτίαν τοῖς πατριάρχαις μεγάλως ὠργίζετο.

110: HL II_2, 945–47 (A.D. 499?) ‖ 1–3: cf. Theoph., 141, 19–24

111: HL II_2, 1004 (A.D. 509) ‖ 1–2: cf. Theoph., 142, 9–12 ‖ 3–5: cf. Theoph., 151, 11–14

112: HL II_2, 1015–16 (A.D. 511–512) ‖ 1–5: cf. Theoph., 153, 12–29; Cyrill., *Vit. Sab.*, 148, 9–16; 141, 16 sqq.

110: 1 post Χαλκηδόνι add. μὲν LG

111: 3 ἐδέξατο Ζήνωνος] ἐδέξαντο LG ‖ 5 τῷ om. LG

112: 2 τῷ om. LG

110. This man, having convened a simple synod,[118] confirmed in writing the doctrines of Chalcedon but made no mention of Zeno's *Henoticon* from fear of Anastasius.

111. After the expulsion of Peter the Fuller, then, Palladius took over the throne of Antioch, and he, when he died, was succeeded by Flavian. This man held a heretical synod, accepted the *Henoticon* of Zeno, and, proclaiming in writing the three Ecumenical Councils, passed over in silence that of Chalcedon, in order to gratify the Emperor.

112. Through the tribune Eutropius,[119] the Emperor Anastasius commanded Flavian and Elias of Jerusalem to assemble a synod in Sidon and place the holy Council of Chalcedon under anathema. But Elias dissolved[120] this synod before it had achieved anything, deceiving Anastasius in his letters with the support of Eutropius, thereby causing the Emperor to be greatly angered with the patriarchs.

[118] The sources do not agree on what exactly took place at this synod. For a discussion see HL, II_2, 945–47 and Grumel, *Regestes,* nos. 186 and 190.

[119] Neither Cyril of Scythopolis (141 line 16ff.) nor Theophanes, 153 line 12ff., both probably reflecting the *Epit.Th.A.,* says that Flavian and Elias were instructed to summon the synod or that the Emperor's order was relayed through Eutropius. The presiding bishops were Soterichus of Caesarea Cappadocia and Philoxenus (Xenaias) of Hierapolis.

[120] According to Theophanes (153 lines 19–20) it was dissolved by the tribune Eutropius, while Cyril of Scythopolis (148 line 12) attributes the action to Flavian and Elias.

113.

Φλαβιανοῦ δὲ καταλαβόντος τὴν Ἀντιόχειαν μοναχοί τινες ἀποσχίσται καὶ τῆς Εὐτυχοῦς λώβης οὐ μέτριοι σύνοδον ληστρικὴν ποιησάμενοι Φλαβιανὸν ἐξεδίωξαν βουκολήσαντες καὶ Σευῆρον ἀντικατέστησαν.

114.

Οὗτος οὖν σὺν διακοσίοις ἀποσχίσταις μοναχοῖς ὁ Ἀκέφαλος ἀπάρας ἐξ Ἐλευθερουπόλεως τῇ βασιλίδι προσώρμησε, κατὰ Μακεδονίου πολλὰ φρυαξάμενος. Καὶ Ἀναστασίῳ δοὺς ὅρκον ὁ ἀσυνείδητος ὡς οὐδέποτε κατὰ τῆς ἐν Χαλκηδόνι ἁγίας συνόδου κινήσειε, καὶ τοὺς ὅρκους ἐπάτησε καὶ μετὰ μιαρᾶς συνόδου ταύτην ἀνεθεμάτισεν.

115.

Ἀναστάσιος τοίνυν ὁ βασιλεὺς Μακεδόνιον τὸν Κωνσταντινουπόλεως περιβαλὼν μυρίοις ἐγκλήμασι τοῦ θρόνου ἐξεώσας ἐν Γάγγραις ἐξώρισε· καὶ οὐ μετὰ πολὺ αὐτόν τε ἀποστείλας καὶ τὸν πρὸ αὐτοῦ Εὐφήμιον, χάριν τῆς καταδρομῆς τῶν Γότθων, ὡς ἑωρακότας ἀλλήλους τοὺς πατριάρχας, ξίφει ἐτιμωρήσατο, αἱρετικὸν δὲ Τιμόθεον, Κόλωνα καὶ Λιτρόβουλον τὸν ἐπιλεγόμενον, τῇ ἐκκλησίᾳ παρέδωκεν, ὡς ὁμόφρονα καὶ τοῖς αὐτοῦ πειθαρχοῦντα βουλεύμασιν. Ὅστις ἀθεωτάτην ποιησάμενος σύνοδον κατὰ

113: HL II_2, 1016 ‖ 1–3: cf. Cyrill., *Vit. Sab.*, 148, 13–22; ?*Epit. Th. A.*, 136, 21–27; ? Theoph., 153, 29–154, 2; 156, 10 sqq.

114: 1–3: cf. *Epit. Th. A.*, 136, 21–27; Theoph., 152, 6–8 ‖ 1–2: cf. Cyrill., *Vit. Sab.*, 147, 14 ‖ 3–5: *Epit. Th. A.*, 157, 19–21 (cf. ibid., 142, 23–27)

115: HL II_2, 1016 ‖ 1–2: cf. Cyrill., *Vit. Sab.*, 140, 24–25 ‖ 3–4: cf. Theoph., 161, 28–33 ‖ 5: cf. Theoph., 155, 25–26

113: 3 σεβῆρον *b* ‖ ἀντεκατέστησαν LG

114: 1 γοῦν LG ‖ 2 ἐλευθεροπόλεως LG ‖ καὶ κατὰ LG ‖ 3 ὅρον *b* ‖ οὐδὲν ποτὲ LG

115: 2 ἐξεώσας] ἐξ ἑώας LG ‖ γάγγρα LG ‖ καὶ — 6 παρέδωκεν] αἱρετικὸν δὲ τιμόθεον ἐγκατέστησεν L om. G ‖

113, 114, 115

113. After Flavian's return to Antioch certain schismatic monks and fanatical adherents of the Eutychian heresy held a robber synod,[121] banished Flavian by trickery, and installed Severus in his place.

114. This man, then, one of the Acephali, leaving Eleutheropolis[122] with two hundred schismatic monks, set out for the imperial city, having made many insolent attacks on Macedonius.[123] And even though he had sworn to Anastasius never to attack the holy Council of Chalcedon, the unscrupulous man treated his oaths with contempt and anathematized that Council in an impious synod.[124]

115. The Emperor Anastasius, then, charging Macedonius of Constantinople with innumerable crimes and ejecting him from the throne, banished him to Gangra.[125] Not long afterward, when he had sent out (someone) to punish by the sword both Macedonius and his predecessor, Euphemius, because the patriarchs had managed to see each other due to the onslaught of the Goths, he put the heretic Timothy, surnamed Colon and Litroboulus,[126] in charge of the Church, he being of like mind and obedient to the Emperor's wishes. This man held a most ungodly synod[127] and raised a hostile voice[128] against the holy Council of Chalcedon, and having reached agreement with

[121] *SV* is the only source to mention a synod in this connection, and it is puzzling why HL (II_2, 1016) say that it was presided over by Xenaias (Philoxenus).

[122] The only other writer to mention Eleutheropolis in this context is Cyril of Scythopolis (147 line 14).

[123] The campaign against Macedonius took place before Severus became bishop of Antioch.

[124] The story of Severus' oath to Anastasius is given by John Diakrinomenos as preserved in the *Epit.Th.A.*, (157 lines 19–21; cf. 142 line 23ff.). The account of *SV* is almost identical to this, except that John Diakrinomenos says nothing about a synod; the phrase μετὰ μιαρᾶς συνόδου, then, is doubtless the compiler's own.

[125] According to Theophanes (161 line 28ff.) Macedonius had fled from his place of exile in Euchaita (whither Euphemius also had been banished [*ibid.* 155 line 23]) to Gangra, because of an attack by Huns (Goths in *SV*). The meeting between the two patriarchs is not mentioned by Theophanes but may have been in the *Epit.Th.A.*

[126] The forms and meanings of these names are problematic. Theophanes (155 line 26) gives Λιτροβούλην καὶ Κήλωνα, *Epit.Th.A.* (140 lines 12–13) has Λιτροβούλβην καὶ Κόλωνα or Λιτροβούλβιν καὶ Κίλωνα, meaning perhaps Stallion and Glutton; see Lampe, *A Patristic Greek Lexicon, s.vv.*

[127] We have no other evidence for such a synod.

[128] Literally "barked."

τῆς ἐν Χαλκηδόνι ἁγίας συνόδου ὑλάκτησε, καὶ συμφωνήσας Σευήρῳ ὁμοῦ τὰ συνοδικὰ αὐτῶν ἐκπέμπουσιν εἰς Ἱεροσόλυμα· ὧν μὴ δεχθέντων πρὸς ὀργὴν ἐξῆψε τὸν Ἀναστάσιον· διὸ τῆς ἁγίας πόλεως τὸν Ἠλίαν ἐν τῷ Ἀειλᾷ περιώρισεν, Ἰωάννην δὲ τῷ θρόνῳ ἀποκατέστησε καὶ τὰ συνοδικὰ Σευήρου καὶ Τιμοθέου ἐκεῖ διαπέμπεται.

116.

Θεοδόσιος δὲ καὶ Σάβας τῶν ὀρθοδόξων ὑπέρμαχοι καὶ τῆς ἐρήμου τῶν ἡγουμένων καὶ μοναχῶν οἱ ἀπλανεῖς ἀστέρες τῆς πίστεως, τὸ μοναδικὸν συναθροίσαντες σύστημα, τοὺς τὰ συνοδικὰ κομίσαντας τῶν ἁγίων τόπων ἐξήλασαν. Ὅπερ μαθὼν Ἀναστάσιος Θεοδόσιον καὶ Σάβαν ἐξορισθῆναι προσέταξεν· οἱ δὲ προκαταλαβόντες τὴν ἔρημον θείαν καὶ ἱερὰν μοναστῶν λογάδων συνεστήσαντο σύνοδον καὶ τέσσαρας διαμαρτυρίας πλήρεις ὀρθοδοξίας συντάξαντες, δύο τῷ βασιλεῖ Ἀναστασίῳ ἐκπέμπουσι, μίαν τοῖς ἄρχουσι, καὶ Ἰωάννῃ ἄλλην τῷ διαδόχῳ Ἠλία τοῦ θεοκήρυκος. Καθ' ὃν χρόνον ὁ τοῦ Βυζαντίου Τιμόθεος ἐτελεύτησε καὶ Μηνᾶς τὸν θρόνον παρέλαβεν.

117.

Ἀλλὰ καὶ Ὁρμίσδας διαδεξάμενος Φίληκα ὁ πάπας Ῥώμης Βιταλιανὸν καὶ Ἐνόδιον σὺν ἑτέροις διακοσίοις ἐπισκόποις εἰς τὸ Βυζάντιον ἐξαπέστειλε, Τιμοθέου ἔτι βιοῦντος ἐπάρατα· ἥντινα θείαν καὶ ἱερὰν σύνοδον ὁ βασιλεὺς Ἀναστάσιος καὶ Τιμόθεος ὁ ἀνόσιος πολυχρονίως κακῶς ἀνιάσαντες ἄπρακτον ἀπεπέμψαντο.

9–10: cf. Cyrill., *Vit. Sab.*, 148, 22–25 ‖ 10–11: cf. Cyrill., *Vit. Sab.*, 150, 7 sqq.

116: 1–4: cf. Cyrill., *Vit. Sab.*, 148, 27–149, 3; 152, 16–18 ‖ 4–5: cf. Cyrill., *Vit. Sab.*, 152, 12–16 ‖ 5–8: cf. Theoph., 162, 13–16; Cyrill., *Vit. Sab.*, 152, 16 sqq. et 158, 1–3

117: 1–5: cf. Theoph., 160, 31–161, 5 (vide *Epit. Th. A.*, 146, 10 sqq.)

---

8 ἐλάκτισε D ‖ σεβήρω *b* ‖ 10 τὸν[2] om. LG ‖ post Ἠλίαν add. ἀρχιεπίσκοπον LG ‖ 11 ἀντεκατέστησε LG ‖ σεβήρω *b*

116: 1 οἱ πρόμαχοι LG ‖ 7 συνάξαντες *z* ‖ 8 καθ' ὃν – 10 παρέλαβεν om. LG

117: 1 ὁρμίσδας *g* ‖ διαδεξάμενος Φίληκα om. LG ‖ 2 εὐόδιον codd.: corr. *SV*[2] ‖ 3 Τιμοθέου – ἐπάρατα om. LG

Severus, the two men sent their synodical letters together to Jerusalem. When these were refused,[129] Anastasius' anger was aroused, and so he banished Elias of the Holy City to Aila, establishing on the throne John, to whom the synodical letters of Severus and Timothy were then sent.

116. Theodosius and Sabas, champions of the orthodox and the fixed stars of the faith among the superiors and monks of the desert, gathered together the monastic population and drove from the holy places those bearing the synodical documents.[130] On learning this, Anastasius ordered Theodosius and Sabas banished. They, however, reaching the desert beforehand, assembled a divine and sacred synod[131] of leading monks, and having composed four declarations full of orthodoxy, they sent two to the Emperor Anastasius, one to the authorities and another to John,[132] the successor of God's herald Elias. At this time Timothy of Byzantium died, and Menas took over the throne.[133]

117. Hormisdas, the successor of Felix[134] as Pope of Rome, sent Vitalis and Enodius along with two hundred other bishops to Byzantium,[135] while Timothy was still living his accursed life. But the Emperor Anastasius and the unholy Timothy, having subjected this divine and sacred synod to prolonged and improper harassment, dismissed it before anything was accomplished.

[129] It is not possible to say why *SV* makes Severus and Timothy send their letters together to share the same fate. Cyril of Scythopolis (141 lines 1–3, cf. Theophanes, 157 lines 26–28) makes it clear that, while the condemnation of Macedonius was rejected, the *synodica* of Timothy were accepted by Elias of Jerusalem. The compiler may have overlooked the difference between the documents; see Grumel, *Regestes,* no. 194. Grumel, *ibid.,* 202–4, pays too much heed to the information given by *SV.*

[130] If the author means by this the letters to John of Jerusalem, mentioned at the end of the previous chap., he is almost certainly confused. The expulsion of the letter carriers, according to Cyril of Scythopolis (148 line 25 ff.), took place in 512 or 513 when a renewed attempt was made to have Severus accepted by Elias. John succeeded Elias in 516.

[131] Neither Cyril of Scythopolis (152 line 16 ff.) nor Theophanes (162 line 13 ff.) characterizes the gathering of monks as a synod; the words ϑείαν καὶ ἱερὰν . . . συνεστήσαντο σύνοδον must be attributed to *SV.*

[132] *SV* (like Theophanes, 162 line 16) names John of Jerusalem as the recipient of the document, but Cyril of Scythopolis (158 lines 2–3) says that it was sent to John of Constantinople, the man who succeeded Timothy in 518. Cyril is almost certainly wrong; see Hansen, *Epit. Th.A.,* p. xx.

[133] If the writer thinks, as he seems to, that Menas was the immediate successor of Timothy, he is wide of the mark, John, Epiphanius, and Anthimus having come before Menas. Cf. chaps. 117 line 1; 119 lines 6–7; 120 lines 3–5 and 12–13; 122 lines 7–8.

[134] Hormisdas was preceded by Gelasius, Anastasius, and Symmachus.

[135] The unsuccessful synod met at Heraclea; see Theophanes, 161 line 2 (cf. *Epit. Th.A.,* 146 lines 1–6).

118.

Ἀναστασίου γοῦν ἐν τῷ κοιτῶνι ὀργῇ θεοῦ τὴν μιαρὰν ψυχὴν ἀστραπῇ ἀπορρήξαντος καὶ Ἰουστίνου τοῦ εὐσεβοῦς βασιλεύσαντος, Ὁρμίσδας ὁ μακάριος πάπας Ῥώμης πλείστους ἐπισκόπους ἐν Θεσσαλονίκῃ ἀπέστειλεν, ὡς ἂν τὴν ἁγίαν ἐν Χαλκηδόνι σύνοδον συνοδικῶς βεβαιώσειεν· ἥντινα θείαν καὶ ἱερὰν σύνοδον νύκτωρ οἱ φονιώδεις ἐπελθόντες κακόδοξοι τὴν οἰκίαν ἀνῆψαν ἔνθα συνήθροιστο καὶ τοὺς ἁγίους ἡμικαύστους ἐκεῖθεν ἀπήλασαν.

119.

Ὁρμίσδας οὖν αὖθις ἐν Κωνσταντινουπόλει θείαν καὶ ἱερὰν ἐξαπέστειλε σύνοδον, καὶ τὰ ἐν Χαλκηδόνι δογματισθέντα ἐκύρωσε καὶ τὰ περὶ δύο φύσεων τοῦ μακαρίου Κυρίλλου προεκθέμενος «τὸν νοητὸν στατῆρα, τὸ βασιλικὸν νόμισμα, ᾧ ἐνενόητο διπλοῦς χαρακτὴρ ὁ Χριστὸς» διεσάφησε. Καὶ Ὁρμίσδα πρὸς κύριον ἐκδημήσαντος Ἀγαπητὸς τὸν θρόνον αὐτοῦ διεδέξατο.

120.

Ἰουστίνου δὲ τελευτήσαντος Ἰουστινιανὸς ὁ ἀνεψιὸς αὐτοῦ τὰ σκῆπτρα τῆς βασιλείας παρέλαβε· Μηνᾶ δὲ τὰ πρόσκαιρα καταλείψαντος Ἄνθιμος ὁ Τραπεζοῦντος ἐπίσκοπος τῆς Βυζαντίου ἐκκλησίας τὸν θρόνον

118: 1–2: cf. Cyrill., *Vit. Sab.*, 162, 6–9; Geo. Mon., 619, 11–15; Cedren. (ed. Bonn.), I, 636.7–8 ‖ 2: cf. Theoph., 164, 16

119: HL II_2, 1052–53 (A.D. 519) ‖ 1–2: cf. ? Theoph., 165, 12 sqq. ‖ 1–4: cf. Cedren. (ed. Bonn.), I, 683, 7–13 ‖ 3–4: cf. Cyrill., Alex., PG, 72, 429B

120: HL II_2, 1143–51 (A.D. 536)

118: 1 ὀργῇ — ἀστραπῇ] ὀργῆς θεοῦ ἀστραπῇ τὴν μιαρὰν ψυχὴν LG ‖ 2 ὀρμίσδας *g* ‖ 4 βεβαιώσοιεν LG ‖ 5 νύκτωρ ἐπελθόντες οἱ φονώδεις κακόδοξοι LG

119: 1 ὀρμίσδας codd. praeter E ‖ 2 καὶ[2] om. LG ‖ 3 προσθέμενος LG ‖ 4 τὸ νόμισμα τὸ βασιλικὸν ὦ ἐνένωτο (sic) LG ‖ ᾧ — Χριστός] ὁ ἐν ἑνότητι ἁπλοῦς χαρακτὴρ χριστὸς Cyrillus apud Cedren., I, 683, 13 ‖ 5 διεσάφησε — 6 διεδέξατο om. LG ‖ 5 ὀρμίσδα codd. praeter E

120: 2 Μηνᾶ — 4 ἐκράτησε om. LG ‖ 3 τῶν θρόνων AE

118. When Anastasius, then, had, due to the wrath of God, severed his filthy soul by lightning in his bedchamber and the pious Justin became emperor, Hormisdas, the blessed Pope of Rome, sent a large number of bishops to Thessalonica in order to confirm by a synod the holy Council of Chalcedon. This divine and sacred synod was attacked during the night by the murderous unorthodox; they set fire to the house where the bishops were gathered and drove the holy men out of there half burnt.[136]

119. Hormisdas, then, again sent a divine and sacred synod to Constantinople, where he confirmed the doctrines of Chalcedon, and after quoting the blessed Cyril's words on the two natures, "the intelligible stater, the imperial coin, on which is represented Christ's twofold character," he explained them.[137] And when Hormisdas departed for the Lord, Agapetus[138] inherited his throne.

120. On the death of Justin, his nephew Justinian took over the imperial scepter, and after Menas had left the temporal world, Anthimus,[139] the bishop of Trebizond, obtained the throne of Byzantium. And when the Goths

[136] *SV* is our only witness for this second abortive attempt by Hormisdas to confirm Chalcedon by a synod in the East; it is not possible to say what source the writer may be using.

[137] The phrase as quoted by Cedrenus, Bonn ed. (1839), I, 683 line 13 reads: ὁ ἐν ἑνότητι ἁπλοῦς χαρακτὴρ Χριστός. To be compared also is an extract from Cyril's commentary on Matthew (PG, 72, 429B): ὁ στατὴρ ὁ ἀληθινός τε καὶ νοητός, καὶ ὡς ἐν τύπῳ τῷ ἐξ ὕλης δηλούμενος, αὐτός ἐστιν ὁ Κύριος ἡμῶν Ἰησοῦς Χριστός, ὁ διπλοῦς χαρακτήρ, which tends to support the accuracy of *SV*.

[138] Between Hormisdas (514–23) and Agapetus (535–36) came Popes John I, Felix, Boniface, and John II; cf. note 133 *supra*.

[139] Anthimus was in fact the immediate predecessor of Menas; cf. note 133 *supra*.

ἐκράτησε. Καὶ τῶν Γότθων τὴν Ῥώμην καὶ τὰ περὶ αὐτὴν μελλόντων ληΐζεσθαι Ἀγαπητὸς ὁ ταύτης μακάριος πάπας τὴν βασιλίδα κατέλαβε, καὶ σύνοδον θείαν καὶ ἱερὰν ποιησάμενος Ἄνθιμον τὸν ταύτης ἐπίσκοπον, Μανιχαίου λαβόντα ὑπόνοιαν καὶ λάθρα φυγοδικήσαντα καὶ ἑαυτὸν ἀδηλοποιήσαντα, ἕως τῆς σήμερον ἀναθέματι καθυπέβαλε· καὶ τὸν θρόνον τῆς ἐκκλησίας τοῦ Βυζαντίου Εὐτύχιος μοναχὸς ἐκληρώσατο.

121.

Ἐν ᾧ καιρῷ τὰ Ὠριγένεια δόγματα ὑπό τινων τῶν Παλαιστίνης μοναχῶν ἐκρατύνοντο, καθ' ὧν ὁ μέγας Ἐφραΐμιος Ἀντιοχείας Συρίας ἀρχιεπίσκοπος θείαν σύνοδον καὶ ἱερὰν συστησάμενος ἀναθέματι τοὺς προασπιστὰς αὐτῶν κατεδίκασε.

122.

Νεστορίῳ τοίνυν τῷ δυσσεβεῖ οἱ προσκείμενοι διὰ τῶν Θεοδώρου τοῦ μιαροῦ συγγραμμάτων λανθανόντως τῆς γνώμης ἀντείχοντο. Διὸ ζήλῳ πυρούμενοι πλεῖστοι ἱεράρχαι συνοδικῶς κατέλαβον Μοψουεστίαν· οἳ τὸν κλῆρον καὶ πολιτευομένους αὐτῆς συναθροίσαντες ἐπὶ τῶν ἀχράντων εὐαγγελίων ἐξώρκισαν εἰ Θεοδώρου, τοῦ αὐτῆς γεγονότος ἀσεβοῦς ἐπισκόπου, τὸ ὄνομα ἐν τοῖς παρ' αὐτοῖς διπτύχοις ἐντέτακται· εἰπόντων δὲ «ναὶ» καὶ μὴ ἀρνησαμένων τὴν πρότασιν, ἡ ἁγία σύνοδος ταῦτα ἐγγράφως Βιργιλλίῳ τῷ ἁγιωτάτῳ πάπᾳ Ῥώμης ἀπέστειλεν· οὗτος γὰρ ἦν Ἀγαπητὸν διαδεξάμενος τὸν μακάριον.

5–7: cf. Theoph., 217, 4–9 ‖ 7–8: cf. Niceph. Call. XVII.9 (PG, 147, 240C)

121: HL II_2, 1174–78 (A.D. 542) ‖ 2–4: cf. Cyrill., *Vit. Sab.*, 191, 16–20

122: HL III_1, 38–40 (A.D. 550) ‖ 3–6: cf. Mansi, IX, 274–79 ‖ 7–8: cf. Mansi, IX, 288–89

4–5 ληΐζεσθαι μελλόντων LG ‖ 5 μακαριώτατος D ‖ 7 Μανιχαίου — 8 σήμερον om. LG ‖ 8 καὶ — 9 ἐκληρώσατο om. LG

121: 2 εὐφραίμιος DO ‖ Συρίας om. LG ‖ 3–4 τοὺς προασπιστὰς αὐτῶν om. LG ‖ 4 καθυπέβαλεν LG

122: 2 μισαροῦ (sic) *z* ‖ τὴν γνώμην A τῆς λώβης LG ‖ ζήλω θείω LG ‖ 5 ἐξώρκωσαν LG ‖ 5 αὐτῆς] αὐτῶν *z* ‖ 7 ταῦτα *b*, SV^2: πάντα *g* ‖ 8 Βιργιλλίῳ AE: βιργιλίω D βιγλίω LG βιγιλλίω *z* recte βιγιλίω ‖ οὗτος — 9 μακάριον om. LG

were on the point of plundering Rome and the surrounding area, its Pope, the blessed Agapetus, came to the imperial city,[140] where he held a divine and sacred synod[141] which subjected to anathema—in effect to this day—Anthimus, the bishop of the city, who, having come under suspicion of Manichaeism,[142] had secretly fled trial and had hid himself.[143] Then the throne of the Church at Byzantium fell to the monk Eutychius.[144]

121. At this time the teachings of Origen were being followed by certain Palestinian monks; the archbishop of Antioch in Syria, the great Ephraim, convened a divine and sacred synod[145] against them and pronounced anathema upon the leaders.

122. The adherents of the impious Nestorius, then, secretly held on to his opinions through the writings of the abominable Theodore. For this reason a large number of hierarchs, inflamed with zeal, came to Mopsuestia to hold a synod. Bringing together its clergy and lay citizens, they asked them under oath to the undefiled Gospels if the name of Theodore, the former unholy bishop of the city, was included in their diptychs. They did not deny it and answered that it was so.[146] Whereupon the holy synod sent the information in writing to the most holy Pope of Rome, Virgillius,[147] for he had succeeded blessed Agapetus.

[140] The Pope did not come to look for refuge, as *SV* implies, but had been sent by the Gothic King Theodahad to negotiate peace with Justinian; see *DHGE, s.v.* Agapet I.

[141] For a discussion of the synod see HL, II_2, 1145 ff.

[142] It is hard to say what the label is meant to convey; Theophanes, 217 lines 6–7, tells us that Anthimus was condemned for sharing the views of Severus, Julian of Halicarnassus, and the other Theopaschites.

This passage of *SV* is referred to in a marginal note of *Paris. gr. 418* (XVI cent.): . . . δηλοῖ δὲ καὶ ὁ συνοψίσας τὰς συνόδους ἁπάσας Μανιχαίων λέγων αὐτὸν (i.e., Anthimus) δεδωκέναι ὑπόνοιαν . . . . See *ACO,* III, 139.

[143] *SV* appears to be using a source which was later drawn on directly or indirectly by Nicephorus Callistus: ἐπεὶ δὲ δέει κρυπτόμενος ἀφανὴς ἦν (PG, 147, 240C).

[144] Menas (536–52) was patriarch between Anthimus and Eutychius; cf. note 133 *supra.*

[145] The words of Cyril of Scythopolis (191 lines 19–20), the only other witness for the synod, are: δημοσίῳ συνοδικῷ ἀναθέματι καθυποβάλλει τὰ Ὠριγένους δόγματα.

[146] Inexplicably *SV* gives just the opposite of the facts, all the summoned witnesses having sworn that the name of Theodore did not appear in the diptychs. See Mansi, IX, 279 ff.; HL, III_1, 40 note 3.

The author of SV^2 recognized the error and wrote: οἱ δὲ ἀπομοσάμενοι μηδαμῶς εἰδέναι τοῦτο τοῖς διπτύχοις ἐντετάχθαι ἀναμφίβολον τὴν τοῦ ζητουμένου πίστιν παρέσχον.

[147] The correct form of the name is Vigilius, and between him and Agapetus came Silverius.

123.

Ἰουστινιανὸς δὲ βασιλεὺς θεωρῶν ὁ φιλόχριστος τῶν κακοδόξων πολλὴν ἀναρριπιζομένην σκοτόμαιναν, σύνοδον ἁγίαν οἰκουμενικὴν πέμπτην ἐν Κωνσταντινουπόλει κροτηθῆναι ἐθέσπισεν, ἧσπερ ἐξῆρχον οἱ πατριάρχαι προκαθεζόμενοι Εὐτύχιος Κωνσταντινουπόλεως καὶ Ἀλεξανδρείας ὁ μέγας Ἀπολινάριος, Δόμνος Ἀντιοχείας, καὶ βασιλεὺς Ἰουστινιανὸς ὁ φιλόχριστος· Βιργίλλιος δὲ Ῥώμης παρὼν οὐ συνήδρευσε διὰ τὸ μὴ συνόδου ἀλλὰ χάριν τῆς ἐπιδρομῆς Γότθων καταλαβεῖν τὸ Βυζάντιον. Ἥτις θεία καὶ ἱερὰ σύνοδος τὰ Ὠριγένεια δόγματα καὶ τὰ Θεοδώρου Μοψουεστίας συγγράμματα καὶ τὰ Θεοδωρήτου καὶ Ἴβα κατὰ Κυρίλλου Ἀλεξανδρείας τοῦ μάκαρος ἀναθέματι καθυπέβαλε πρέποντι.

124.

Ἀλλ' ὢ τῶν ἐνέδρων τοῦ διαβόλου, πρὸς <ὅσ>α καὶ οἷα καθέστηκε καθ' ἡμῶν τῶν ἀνθρώπων ἐπεγειρόμενος· μετὰ γὰρ χρόνους τινὰς Ἰουλιανοῦ τοῦ Ἁλικαρνασέως οἱ ἀντεχόμενοι τῆς αἱρέσεως Ἰουστινιανὸν τὸν βασιλέα ὑπονοθεύσαντες πείθουσιν ἐξ οὐρανοῦ καὶ παντελῶς ἄφθαρτον εἶναι τὸ σῶμα τοῦ κυρίου ἡμῶν Ἰησοῦ Χριστοῦ καὶ θεοῦ διαβεβαιούμενοι. Δι' ἣν αἰτίαν αἱρετικὴν σύνοδον ποιησάμενος μὴ πειθόμενον αὐτοῖς Εὐτύχιον τὸν ἀοίδιμον εἰς Ἀμάσειαν κατακρίνει ἐξόριστον, καὶ Ἰωάννην Ἀντιοχέα Σχολαστικὸν τῷ θρόνῳ τῆς Βυζαντίων ἐκκλησίας ἀντικαθίστησι τῇ ἀσεβείᾳ συνθέμενον.

123: HL III_1, 68–132 (A.D. 553) ‖ 6–7: cf. Theoph., 229, 1–2; 225, 12–13

124: HL III_1, 174 (A.D. 565) ‖ 1–5: cf. Niceph. Call. XVII.29 (PG, 147, 293A–B; 296B–C); *Vita Eutych.*, PG, 86^2, 2312D; 2316B–C ‖ 4–6: cf. Theoph., 240, 31 sq. ‖ 6: cf. *Vita Eutych.*, 2320 sqq. ‖ 7–9: cf. Theoph., 240, 27–29

123: 1 ante βασιλεὺς add. ὁ *b* ‖ Ἰ. δὲ θεωρῶν ὁ φιλόχριστος βασιλεὺς LG ‖ τῶν om. LG ‖ 4 καὶ] καὶ ὁ LG ‖ 6 Ἰουστινιανὸς om. LG ‖ Βιργίλλιος AE: βιργίλιος D βίγλιος LG βιγιλλίος *z* recte βιγίλιος ‖ 9 post Θεοδώρου add. τοῦ E

124: Caput om. LG ‖ 1 ὅσα Westerink: ἃ codd. ‖ 2 ἐπεγειρόμενα D

123. But the Christ-loving Emperor Justinian, seeing a great darkness being spread around by the unorthodox, ordered the holy Fifth Ecumenical Council to be summoned in Constantinople. It was led by the presiding patriarchs Eutychius of Constantinople, the great Apolinarius of Alexandria, Domnus[148] of Antioch, and the Christ-loving Emperor Justinian. Virgillius of Rome, though present in the city, did not take part in the sessions, having come to Byzantium, not for the Council, but on account of the onslaught of the Goths. This divine and holy Council placed under a fitting anathema the teachings of Origen, the works of Theodore of Mopsuestia, and the writings of Theodoret and Ibas against blessed Cyril of Alexandria.

124. But, oh, the wiles of the devil, how many and how great are those (wiles) he resorts to in rising up against us men! For, some years later those who adhered to the heresy of Julian of Halicarnassus perverted the mind of the Emperor Justinian and persuaded him with their claim that the body of our Lord and God, Jesus Christ, came from heaven and is completely incorruptible. Holding a heretical synod[149] on this account, he condemned the renowned Eutychius to exile in Amasea for failing to agree with them and replaced him on the throne of the Byzantine Church with John Scholasticus of Antioch who acquiesced in the heresy.

[148] This should be Domninus, as corrected here and in chap. 125 by the redactor of SV^2.

[149] One might be inclined to dismiss our writer's talk of an actual synod (Theophanes, for instance, mentions none, and MSS L and G have left out the chapter) were it not that in the life of Eutychius by Eustratius there is a description of what the biographer more than once calls a συνέδριον, at which the Patriarch was condemned (PG, 86², 2320A ff.).

125.

Δόμνου τοίνυν ἐν Ἀντιοχείᾳ τελειωθέντος Ἀναστάσιος ὁ μέγας ἐν τῷ θρόνῳ ἀνάγεται, Ἀπολιναρίου τοῦ θεοσόφου Ἀλεξανδρείας δεξιὸς παραστάτης γενόμενος· ὅστις θείαν καὶ ἱερὰν σύνοδον ποιησάμενος τοὺς ἀνθισταμένους τῇ ἁγίᾳ ἐν Χαλκηδόνι συνόδῳ ἀναθέματι καθυπέβαλε.

126.

Μετὰ γοῦν τὴν Ἰουστινιανοῦ ἀποβίωσιν Ἰουστῖνος ὁ εὐσεβὴς ἐβασίλευσε, καὶ Ἰωάννου τοῦ Σχολαστικοῦ τὸν βίον τελέσαντος, Εὐτύχιον τὸν μακάριον τῆς ἐξορίας ἀνεκαλέσατο τὸν θρόνον αὐτοῦ ἀποδοὺς αὐτῷ· καὶ πρὸς κύριον ἐκδημήσαντος Ἰωάννην τὸν Νηστευτὴν ἐν Χριστῷ Ἰησοῦ ἀρχιερᾶσθαι τοῦ Βυζαντίου ἐθέσπισεν.

127.

Ἰουστίνου δὲ τὴν βασιλείαν Τιβέριος διεδέξατο, καὶ Μαυρίκιος τούτου, καὶ Μαυρικίου Φωκᾶς ὁ μισάνθρωπος· καὶ Ἰωάννου τοῦ Νηστευτοῦ τὸν θρόνον Κυριακὸς διεδέξατο, καὶ Θωμᾶς ἐκείνου, καὶ τούτου μονοθελήτης ὁ Σέργιος.

128.

Ἐξαίφνης δὲ Ἡράκλειος ἀναλαβὼν ἐκ τῆς δύσεως, Φωκᾶν ἀνελὼν τὴν βασιλείαν παρέλαβε, καὶ τὸν κατὰ Περσῶν θεόθεν ἀράμενος πόλεμον ποταμὸν τὸν Φάσιν κατέλαβεν, ἐν ᾧ τῶν Ἀκεφάλων περὶ θελημάτων καὶ

125: HL III_1, 174 ‖ 3–4: cf. (?) *Vita Eutych.*, PG, 86^2, 2324A

128: HL III_1, 336–38

125: 1 ἐν^2 om. LG

126: 2 καὶ Ἰωάννου — 5 ἐθέσπισεν om. LG

127: Ceteris omissis hoc caput cum 126 ita coniungunt LG: ἐκεῖνον τιβέριος διαδέχεται καὶ τοῦτον μαυρίκιος καὶ φωκᾶς τὸν μαυρίκιον

128: 1 ἀναβαλὼν LG ‖ 2 καὶ — 3 κατέλαβεν om. D

125. Domnus,[150] then, having died in Antioch, the great Anastasius was elevated to the throne, who was a staunch supporter of the Alexandrian theologian Apolinarius. He held a divine and sacred synod and subjected to anathema those opposed to the holy Council of Chalcedon.[151]

126. When Justinian passed away, the pious Justin became emperor, and he, after the death of John Scholasticus, recalled the blessed Eutychius from exile and gave him back his throne. On this man's departure for the Lord, Justin decreed that John, the Faster in Christ Jesus, become chief priest[152] of Byzantium.

127. Justin was succeeded as emperor by Tiberius, Tiberius by Maurice, and Maurice by Phocas the misanthrope. Cyriacus succeeded to the throne of John the Faster; Thomas came next, and he was followed by the monothelete Sergius.[153]

128. But[154] Heraclius, setting out suddenly from the West, killed Phocas and took over the Empire. And raising his holy war against the Persians, he reached the river Phasis, where one of the Acephali[155] put to him a ques-

[150] See note 148 *supra*.

[151] The only comparable reference to Anastasius' activity in support of orthodoxy is to be found in the life of Eutychius (PG, 86^2, 2324A): Πάντες γὰρ οἱ πατριάρχαι, πολλοὶ δὲ καὶ τῶν ἐπισκόπων οὐκ ἠνέσχοντο, ἐξαιρέτως οἱ τῆς Ἀνατολῆς, καθυπογράψαι εἰς ὃν ἐποίησεν ὁ βασιλεὺς λόγον περὶ τοῦ ἀφθάρτου· ἀλλ' ἔστησαν ἀνταγωνιζόμενοι συνοδικῶς καὶ ἐγγράφως, καὶ μάλιστα ὁ Θεουπόλεως ὁσιώτατος πατριάρχης Ἀναστάσιος.

[152] That is, bishop or patriarch.

[153] This and the previous chapter, giving simply the succession of emperors and patriarchs of Constantinople, serves to bring the story up to Heraclius, during whose reign begins the next series of synods.

[154] This section of the text, chaps. 128–46, deals with the Monothelete heresy and the synods which it gave rise to. The later accounts of the heresy have been carefully examined by J. L. van Dieten in his *Geschichte der Patriarchen von Sergios I bis Johannes VI* (Amsterdam, 1972), 179–218, who concludes in part (p. 204) that, for the period from Sergius' death to the Lateran synod, either *SV* (chaps. 132–38) and Theophanes (330 line 29–331 line 24) are using a common source or Theophanes is depending on an older version of *SV*. The former alternative is much more likely, there being no evidence that *SV* ever existed in an earlier form.

For the beginning of the heresy, however, *SV* and Theophanes follow two different traditions. The compiler of *SV* relies on a more accurate account which is based ultimately on documents read at the Sixth Ecumenical Council (see G. Owsepian, *Die Entstehungsgeschichte des Monotheletismus* [Leipzig, 1897], 15, 18), while Theophanes, as shown convincingly by van Dieten (*op. cit.*, 185–86) takes his version from Anastasius Sinaites.

[155] Paul, a monophysite and head of the Severian sect.

ἐνεργειῶν τις αὐτῷ πεῦσιν προσήγαγεν. Ἥντινα πεῦσιν Κύρῳ τῷ Φάσιδος ἐπισκόπῳ ἀνακοινωσάμενος, ἄμφω ἐξαπορήσαντες τῷ Κωνσταντινουπόλεως Σεργίῳ τὰ περὶ τούτου ἐγνώρισαν· ὅστις αἱρετικὸν ποιήσας συνέδριον καὶ τὰ συνοδικὰ Μηνᾶ μονομερῶς ἐπισκεψάμενος μίαν θέλησιν καὶ ἐνέργειαν ἐπὶ Χριστοῦ τοῦ θεοῦ καὶ σωτῆρος ἡμῶν εἶναι τῷ βασιλεῖ Ἡρακλείῳ ἀντέγραψεν.

129.

Ἡρακλείου δὲ τὴν βασιλίδα καταλαβόντος Κωνσταντινούπολιν, Σέργιος αἱρετικὴν συστησάμενος σύνοδον μίαν θέλησιν καὶ ἐνέργειαν ἐπὶ Χριστοῦ Ἰησοῦ τοῦ θεοῦ ἡμῶν δυσσεβῶς ἐληρώδησεν.

130.

Ἀλλὰ μὴν καὶ Κῦρος τὸν θρόνον Ἀλεξανδρείας παραλαβὼν ἐκ Φάσιδος μιαρὰν ποιησάμενος σύνοδον ἐννέα κεφάλαια τῷ Σεργίῳ ἀπέστειλε, μίαν θέλησιν καὶ ἐνέργειαν ἐπὶ Χριστοῦ Ἰησοῦ τοῦ θεοῦ καὶ σωτῆρος ἡμῶν ἐκθέμενος.

129: HL III_1, 336–38

130: HL III_1, 339–42

---

4 πεῦσιν[2] om. LG ‖ τῷ] τοῦ *g* ‖ 6 τὰ om. D ‖ ἐγνώρισεν LG

129: 2 ἐπὶ – **130:** 3 ἐνέργειαν om. D ‖ 3 ἐδογμάτισεν *z*

130: 1 μὴν καὶ] καὶ μὴν LG ‖ ἐκ] ἐκ τοῦ LG ‖ 3–4 καὶ σωτῆρος om. *b*

tion on the wills and energies. This question Heraclius communicated to Cyrus, the bishop of Phasis, and both being unable to solve it, they passed the matter on to Sergius of Constantinople. He held a heretical assembly,[156] and subjecting the synodical documents of Menas to a onesided examination, he wrote back to Emperor Heraclius that there is one will and energy in Christ our God and Savior.

129. After the return of Heraclius to the imperial city of Constantinople, Sergius held a heretical synod[157] in which he impiously proclaimed the nonsensical doctrine of one will and energy in Christ Jesus our God.

130. And Cyrus, too, who went from Phasis to take over the Alexandrian throne, held an abominable synod and sent to Sergius nine chapters[158] in which he decreed one will and energy in Christ Jesus our God and Savior.

[156] The compiler assumes that Sergius convened a synod before sending his reply to Cyrus; he may be right, but no other document supports this.

[157] There is no other evidence for the synod.

[158] Cyrus, on becoming bishop of Alexandria, did send a decree of nine propositions to Sergius (Mansi, XI, 563–68), but does not seem to have held a synod for the purpose; see HL, III_1, 342.

131

Σωφρόνιος δὲ ὁ μελίγλωσσος τῆς ἀληθείας πρόμαχος ἀρχιερεὺς Ἱεροσολύμων γενόμενος θείαν σύνοδον καὶ ἱερὰν ποιησάμενος, δύο θελήσεις καὶ ἐνεργείας τρανώσας, ἀπέστειλεν Ὀνορίῳ τῷ πάπᾳ Ῥώμης καὶ Σεργίῳ Κωνσταντινουπόλεως τὰ συνοδικὰ αὐτοῦ.

132.

Τελευτήσαντος οὖν Σεργίου Πύρρος ὁ τῆς κιβδήλου δόξης τὸν θρόνον παρέλαβε, καὶ σύνοδον αἱρετικὴν συστησάμενος τὰ δογματισθέντα ὑπὸ Σεργίου καὶ τοῦ Φάσιδος Κύρου ἐκράτυνεν.

133.

Ἀλλὰ Κολοβὸς ὁ τοῦ Βυζακίου θεόπνους ἐπίσκοπος ἀθροίσας πνευματοκίνητον σύνοδον τὰ δογματισθέντα Σεργίῳ, Κύρῳ καὶ Πύρρῳ τῷ πρέποντι καθυπέβαλεν ἀναθέματι καὶ δύο θελήσεις καὶ ἐνεργείας τοῦ σωτῆρος Χριστοῦ ἀνεκήρυξεν.

131: HL III$_1$, 365–76 (A.D. 634) ‖ 1–4: cf. Theoph., 330, 16–19

132: HL III$_1$, 391 (A.D. 639) ‖ 1–3: Theoph., 330, 29–31

133: HL III$_1$, 426–30 (A.D. 646) ‖ 1: cf. *Epist. episcop. Afric.*, Mansi, X, 920–21 ‖ 1–4: cf. Theoph., 331, 8–10

131: 1 τῆς ἀληθείας ὁ μελίγλωσσος LG ‖ πρόμαχος] πρόβολος LG ‖ 2 θεῖαν καὶ ἱερὰν σύνοδον *z* ‖ 3 post ἐνεργείας add. ἐπὶ χριστοῦ ἰησοῦ τοῦ θεοῦ ἡμῶν LG ‖ ὀνωρίω D ὠνωρίω LG ‖ 4 σεργίω τῶ LG

133: 1 κολωβὸς LG rectius Κολοῦμβος ‖ Βυζακίου LG: βυζαντίου D*b* ‖ immo Στέφανος - - - Βυζακίου (cf. cap. 134, 1–2)

131, 132, 133

131. But Sophronius, the honey-tongued champion of truth, having become archpriest of Jerusalem, brought together a divine and sacred synod, and proclaiming two wills and energies, he sent his synodical letter to Honorius,[159] the Pope of Rome, and Sergius of Constantinople.

132. When Sergius died, then, Pyrrhus, (an adherent) of the spurious doctrine, took over the throne, and convening a heretical synod,[160] he confirmed the teachings of Sergius and Cyrus of Phasis.

133. But Colobus, the divinely inspired bishop of Byzacium,[161] having assembled a synod which was moved by the Spirit, placed the teachings of Sergius, Cyrus, and Pyrrhus under a fitting anathema and proclaimed two wills and energies in Christ the Savior.

[159] Theophanes, on the other hand, makes Pope John the recipient; a good explanation for this forced error in the chronographer is given by van Dieten, *op. cit.* (*supra,* note 154), 193–94; 189–90.

[160] Van Dieten, *op. cit.,* 196, thinks that Theophanes' failure to mention expressly the synod (330 lines 29–31) may be due to his shortening of the source; it is much more probable, however, that the words σύνοδον αἱρετικὴν συστησάμενος were added by *SV.* It should also be remarked that the text on which *SV* and Theophanes depend may have been referring, not to the acceptance of the *Ecthesis* of Heraclius by Pyrrhus, but simply to the fact that he was a Monothelete like Sergius and Cyrus.

[161] In contrast to Theophanes, our writer mistakenly places the African synods (chaps. 133–36) before, instead of after, the accession of Pope John (chap. 137) and the death of Heraclius (chap. 138). He also confuses the names of Columbus and Stephen (not mentioned in Theophanes); cf. van Dieten, *op. cit.,* 196. Furthermore, HL (III_1, 429) point out that *SV* is wrong in including Pyrrhus among those anathematized by the African synods.

134.

Ὁμοίως δὲ καὶ ὁ Νουμηδίας τῆς Ἀφρικῆς ὁσιώτατος ἐπίσκοπος Στέφανος ἁγίαν συγκαλεσάμενος σύνοδον Σέργιον, Κῦρον καὶ Πύρρον ἀνεθεμάτισε καὶ δύο θελήσεις καὶ ἐνεργείας τοῦ δεσπότου ἡμῶν Ἰησοῦ Χριστοῦ καὶ θεοῦ ἐδογμάτισεν.

135.

Ὡσαύτως Ῥεπάρατος Μαυριτανίας ἐπίσκοπος ἁγιώτατος σύνοδον θείαν καὶ ἱερὰν ποιησάμενος Σέργιον, Κῦρον καὶ Πύρρον ἀνεθεμάτισε καὶ δύο θελήσεις καὶ ἐνεργείας τοῦ σωτῆρος ἡμῶν Ἰησοῦ Χριστοῦ καὶ θεοῦ ἀνεκήρυξε.

136.

Βίκτωρ δὲ ὁ Καρθαγένης ἐπίσκοπος ἀξιάγαστος ἐξ ἴσου ἁγίαν συγκαλεσάμενος σύνοδον Σέργιον, Κῦρον καὶ Πύρρον ἀνεθεμάτισε καὶ δύο θελήσεις καὶ ἐνεργείας ἐπὶ Χριστοῦ τοῦ σωτῆρος ἡμῶν διετράνωσε.

134: HL III$_1$, 426–30 (A.D. 646) ‖ 1–4: cf. Theoph., 331, 8–10

135: HL III$_1$, 426–30 (A.D. 646) ‖ 1–4 cf. Theoph., 331, 8–10

136: HL III$_1$, 429 (A.D. 646?) ‖ 1–3: cf. *Epist. Vict.*, Mansi, X, 944–49

134: 1 δὲ om. LG ‖ ὁ post Ἀφρικῆς transp. LG ‖ 2 Στέφανος] debebat Κολοῦμβος (cf. cap. 133, 1) ‖ 3 δεσπότου] σωτῆρος *b* ‖ 3–4 ἡμῶν — θεοῦ] χριστοῦ LG

135: 1 ἁγιώτατος] ὁσιώτατος *b* ‖ 1–2 θείαν σύνοδον LG ‖ 3 τοῦ — **136:** 3 ἐνεργείας om. D ‖ 3 τοῦ — Ἰησοῦ om. LG ‖ καὶ[2]] τοῦ LG

136: 1 ὁ om. LG ‖ 3 ἐπὶ — ἡμῶν] τοῦ σωτῆρος χριστοῦ LG

134. Likewise, too, Stephanus, the most saintly bishop of Numidia in Africa, having called together a holy synod, anathematized Sergius, Cyrus, and Pyrrhus and decreed two wills and energies in Jesus Christ our God and Master.

135. Similarly Reparatus, the most holy bishop of Mauretania, holding a divine and sacred synod, anathematized Sergius, Cyrus, and Pyrrhus and proclaimed two wills and energies in Jesus Christ our Savior and God.

136. And Victor, the admirable bishop of Carthage, in like manner having called together a holy synod,[162] anathematized Sergius, Cyrus, and Pyrrhus and declared two wills and energies in Christ our Savior.

[162] This synod does not appear in Theophanes, unless it be indicated by the words ἐν Ἀφρικῇ (331 line 8); the information of *SV* is based ultimately on the letter of Victor to Pope Theodore (Mansi, X, 944).

137.

Πρὸς τούτοις καὶ Ἰωάννης ὁ πάπας Ῥώμης (διαδεξάμενος γὰρ ἦν τὸν μονοθελήτην Ὀνόριον) ὁ τρισμακάριστος θείαν καὶ ἱερὰν σύνοδον ποιησάμενος Σέργιον, Κῦρον καὶ Πύρρον ἀνεθεμάτισε καὶ δύο φύσεις καὶ ἐνεργείας τοῦ δεσπότου ἡμῶν Ἰησοῦ Χριστοῦ καὶ θεοῦ ἀνεκήρυξε, καὶ πρὸς Δαβὶδ καὶ Ἡράκλειον, υἱοὺς Ἡρακλείου, τύπον εὐσεβείας ἀπέστειλεν ὕστερον.

138.

Μέλλων τοίνυν τελευτᾶν ὁ Ἡράκλειος κατέκρινεν ὅρκοις Πύρρον τὸν ἑτερόδοξον ὡς ἂν τὴν αὐτοῦ γαμετὴν Μαρτῖναν καὶ τοὺς υἱοὺς αὐτοῦ ὑπὸ Κωνσταντίνου τοῦ πρωτοτόκου υἱοῦ αὐτοῦ κακωθῆναι μὴ συγχωρήσειε, δοὺς αὐτῷ χάριν αὐτῶν καὶ χρήματα πάμπολλα εἰς ἀντίληψιν. Δι' ἣν αἰτίαν οἱ τῆς πόλεως Βύζαντος Πύρρῳ καταστασιάσαντες τοῦ θρόνου ἐξέωσαν καὶ πρὸς τὴν Ἀφρικὴν γενέσθαι φυγάδα κατηνάγκασαν· καὶ Πέτρον ὡς μονοθελήτην Πύρρου τῷ θρόνῳ ἀντικατέστησαν, καὶ τοῦτον Παῦλος τῆς αὐτῆς θρησκείας ὢν διεδέξατο. Τὴν Ἀφρικὴν δὲ Πύρρος κατέλαβε· καθ' οὗ ἐξανέστησαν Μάξιμος ὁ ἐν μοναχικοῖς αἰδέσιμος κατορθώμασι καὶ οἱ ἐκεῖσε ὄντες ἱεράρχαι θεόσοφοι. Αὐτὸς δὲ τὴν Ῥώμην καταλαβὼν ὡς πρεσβύτερος λίβελλον ὀρθοδοξίας ἐπέδωκεν. Ὃς ἐν Ῥαβέννῃ γενόμενος «ἐπὶ τὸν ἴδιον, ὡς κύων, ἐπανέστρεψεν ἔμετον.» Ὅπερ μαθὼν πάπας Ῥώμης ὁ μακαρίτης Θεόδωρος (ἦν γὰρ τὸν ὅσιον Ἰωάννην διαδεξάμενος) τὸ πλήρωμα τῆς ἐκκλησίας προσκαλεσάμενος καὶ τὸν τάφον τοῦ κορυφαίου τῶν ἀποστόλων Χριστοῦ Πέτρου καταλαβών, αἰτήσας τὸ θεῖον ποτήριον, ἐκ τοῦ φρικτοῦ καὶ ζωοδότου αἵματος Χριστοῦ ἐπιστάξας τῷ μέλανι οἰκείᾳ χειρὶ τὴν καθαίρεσιν

137: HL III_1, 393–94 (A.D. 640 aut 641) ‖ 1–4: cf. Theoph., 331, 6–8

138: HL III_1, 430 ‖ 1–4: cf. Niceph., 28, 11 sqq. ‖ 4–6: cf. Theoph., 331, 3–4 ‖ 6–8: cf. Theoph., 331, 5–6 ‖ 8–19: cf. Theoph., 331, 11–24 ‖ 11–12: *Paroem. Gr.*, I, 366 (cf. 2 Petr. 2:22; Prov. 26:11)

137: 1 ὁ om. LG ‖ διαδεξάμενος — 2 Ὀνόριον om. LG ‖ 2 θείαν σύνοδον καὶ ἱερὰν LG ‖ 3 φύσεις] θελήσεις *z* ‖ 4 τοῦ — θεοῦ] χριστοῦ LG

138: 2 αὐτοῦ[2]] αὐτῆς LG ‖ 3 κωνσταντίου *z* ‖ 4 αὐτῶ καὶ χάριν αὐτῶν E αὐτῆς χάριν αὐτῶ LG ‖ πάμπολλα om. LG ‖ 5 Βύζαντος om. LG ‖ 6 φυγὰν LG ‖ καὶ — 8 κατέλαβε om. LG ‖ 9 μοναχοῖς *b* ‖ κατορθώμασι om. *b* ‖ 10 αὐτὸς] πύρρος LG ‖ 15 Χριστοῦ om. LG

137. In addition, the thrice-blessed Pope John of Rome—for he had succeeded the monothelete Honorius— assembled a divine and sacred synod and, anathematizing Sergius, Cyrus, and Pyrrhus,[163] proclaimed two natures and energies in our Master and God Jesus Christ, and afterward he sent a decree of orthodoxy to David and Heraclius,[164] the sons of Heraclius.

138. When he was about to die, then, Heraclius bound Pyrrhus the unorthodox by an oath that he would not allow his wife Martina and sons to be wronged by his firstborn son, Constantine, giving him on their behalf a very large sum of money for support.[165] For this reason the people of Byzantium rose up against Pyrrhus, ousted him from the throne, and forced him to take refuge in Africa. In his place they put Peter on the throne, since he was a monothelete, and Paul, being of the same persuasion, succeeded Peter.[166] Pyrrhus reached Africa where he was confronted by Maximus, revered for his monastic virtues, and the local bishops full of divine wisdom. Next he arrived in Rome and submitted as a presbyter a statement of orthodoxy. Then coming to Ravenna, "he turned back like a dog to his own vomit." On learning this, the Pope of Rome, blessed Theodore—for he had succeeded John—called together the whole body[167] of the Church; going to the tomb of Peter, the leader of Christ's apostles, he requested the divine cup, and pouring some of the awesome and life-giving blood of Christ into the ink, he wrote with his own

[163] HL (III_1, 393) show how unlikely it is that Pope John anathematized these individuals by name. It is easy to see that here and in many of the previous chapters *SV* (in contrast to Theophanes) takes the meager facts from his source and fills them out with more or less identical padding.

[164] The letter of orthodoxy was sent, rather, to Constantine and Heraclonas; see HL, III_1, 393, who, however, wrongly interpret *SV* as saying that the Pope communicated the synod's decisions to Heraclius' sons.

[165] In the first part of this chapter (lines 1–4) *SV* presents a version of events quite close to that found in the *Breviarium* of Nicephorus (Nicephorus, 28 line 10ff.), while Theophanes (330 line 31 ff.) follows the tradition which represents Martina and Pyrrhus as having poisoned Constantine. It is not possible to decide which story was in the common source of *SV* and Theophanes; cf. van Dieten, *op. cit.* (*supra,* note 154), 197.

[166] Pyrrhus was in fact succeeded by Paul in 641, and Peter only came to the throne after Pyrrhus' second patriarchate in 654.

[167] Hefele and Leclercq characterize this gathering as "a kind of synod."

αὐτοῦ καὶ τῶν αὐτῷ κοινωνούντων πεποίηκε. Πύρρου δὲ τὸ Βυζάντιον καταλαβόντος καὶ Παύλου βλασφήμῳ γλώσσῃ τὸν βίον τελέσαντος οἱ γεννάδαι καὶ τολμηροὶ ἑτερόδοξοι Πύρρον πάλιν τῷ θρόνῳ ἀναβιβάζουσιν.

139.

Ἀλλὰ καὶ Μαρτῖνος ὁ ἁγιώτατος πάπας Ῥώμης διαδεξάμενος Θεόδωρον τὸν ἀοίδιμον, τοῦ θεοφόρου Μαξίμου τῷ ζήλῳ ἀναφλεγόμενος, θείαν καὶ ἱερὰν συγκαλεσάμενος σύνοδον Σέργιον, Κῦρον, Πέτρον, Παῦλον καὶ Πύρρον ἀνεθεμάτισεν, ὅρον κεφαλαιώδη ἐκθέμενος ἐν ᾧ τὰς δύο θελήσεις καὶ ἐνεργείας Χριστοῦ τοῦ θεοῦ καὶ σωτῆρος ἡμῶν ἐβεβαίωσε. Διὸ Κωνσταντῖνος αὐτὸν βασιλεύς, ὁ υἱὸς Ἡρακλείου ὁ ἐπιλεγόμενος Πωγωνάτος, ἁρπάσας πρὸς τὸ Βυζάντιον μετὰ πολλὰς τιμωρίας ἐν Χερσῶνι ἐξώρισεν· ἔτι γε μὴν καὶ τὸν γενναῖον ὕστερον συλλαβόμενος Μάξιμον, γλωσσοτομήσας τοῖς Καυκασίοις περιώρισεν ὄρεσιν.

140.

Ἀγάθων δὲ ὁ πανόλβιος πάπας Ῥώμης τὸν θρόνον Μαρτίνου διαδεξάμενος ἁγίαν συνήθροισε σύνοδον καὶ Σέργιον, Κῦρον, Πέτρον, Παῦλον καὶ Πύρρον ἀνεθεμάτισε· καὶ τρανώσας τὰς δύο θελήσεις καὶ ἐνεργείας Χριστοῦ Ἰησοῦ τοῦ θεοῦ ἡμῶν ὅρον πρὸς Λέοντα τὸν βασιλέα, υἱὸν Κωνσταντίνου τοῦ Πωγωνάτου, πατέρα δὲ Ἰουστινιανοῦ τοῦ Ῥινοτμήτου, ἐξέπεμψεν.

139: HL III_1, 434–51 (A.D. 649) ‖ 1–9: cf. Theoph., 331, 24–332, 4; 351, 17 sqq. ‖ 4 ὅρον κεφαλαιώδη: Mansi, X, 1152

140: HL III_1, 477–84 (A.D. 680) ‖ 1–3: cf. Theoph., 332, 5–8 ‖ 4 ὅρον: cf. Mansi, XI, 286–315

---

17 πεποίηται *g* ‖ Πύρρου LG*z*: κύρου A (π supra scr.), ED ‖ 18 καταλαβόντος ante Πύρρου transp. *g* ‖ 19 πάλιν om. LG

139: 2 ἀοίδιμον LG: δίδυμον D*b* ‖ τῶ ζήλω μαξίμου *b* ‖ 3 θείαν] καὶ θείαν *z* ‖ Πέτρον om. LG ‖ ante Παῦλον add. καὶ *z* ‖ 5 τοῦ χριστοῦ *b* ‖ τοῦ] καὶ *b* ‖ 6 ὁ υἱὸς Ἡρακλείου om. LG

140: 1 πάπας — Μαρτίνου] τὸν θρόνον ῥώμης LG ‖ 2 Πέτρον om. LG ‖ 4 Λέοντα — 6 Ῥινοτμήτου] κωνσταντῖνον βασιλέα ἰουστινιανοῦ τὸν πατέρα LG

hand the condemnation of Pyrrhus and those associating with him. But Pyrrhus came to Byzantium where, when Paul ended life with a blasphemous tongue, those fine and daring unorthodox raised him to the throne once more.

139. Martin, the most holy Pope of Rome and successor of the renowned Theodore, fired by the zeal of the God-inspired Maximus, called together a divine and sacred synod in which he anathematized Sergius, Cyrus, Peter,[168] Paul, and Pyrrhus and issued a decree in chapters[169] confirming the two wills and energies in Christ our God and Savior. Wherefore, the Emperor Constantine, the son of Heraclius and surnamed Pogonatus,[170] had him taken to Byzantium, subjected him to numerous punishments, and exiled him to Cherson. Later, he had the noble Maximus also seized and, having cut out his tongue, he banished him to the Caucasus mountains.

140. Agatho, the all blessed Pope of Rome, having succeeded to Martin's throne,[171] assembled a holy synod and anathematized Sergius, Cyrus, Peter,[172] Paul, and Pyrrhus; and proclaiming the two wills and energies in Christ Jesus our God, he sent a decree to the Emperor Leo,[173] the son of Constantine Pogonatus and father of Justinian Rhinotmetus.

[168] The inclusion of Peter among those condemned by the Lateran synod is due to the error in the previous chapter; see note 166 *supra*.

[169] The phrase ὅρον κεφαλαιώδη, not found in Theophanes, 331 line 28, refers to the decree of twenty chapters issued by the synod (Mansi, X, 1152).

[170] Constantine (more usually known by the diminutive form Constans) was the grandson, not the son, of Heraclius.

[171] The common source of *SV* and Theophanes (332 lines 5–6) must be responsible for their mistake of making Agatho the direct successor of Martin; Pope Eugene intervened.

[172] See note 168 *supra*.

[173] An error for Constantine IV (668–85).

141.

Ὅνπερ ὁ φιλόχριστος αὐτοκράτωρ δεξάμενος, ἁγίαν καὶ οἰκουμενικὴν ἕκτην ἐν Κωνσταντινουπόλει συγκροτηθῆναι προσέταξε σύνοδον, ἧς ἐξῆρχον προκαθεζόμενοι τοποτηρηταὶ τοῦ πάπα Ῥώμης Ἀγάθωνος Θεόδωρος καὶ Γεώργιος πρεσβύτεροι καὶ Ἰωάννης διάκονος, καὶ ὁ Κωνσταντινουπόλεως πατριάρχης Γεώργιος Πέτρον διαδεξάμενος, Θεοφάνης Ἀντιοχείας τῆς Συρίας ἀρχιεπίσκοπος, τῆς Ἀλεξανδρέων τοποτηρητὴς Πέτρος μοναχὸς καὶ πρεσβύτερος, διὰ τὸ χηρεύειν πατριαρχῶν ἐκ τῆς τῶν Ἀγαρηνῶν ἐπικρατείας αὐτὴν καὶ τὰ Ἱεροσόλυμα· κατὰ Θεοδώρου τῆς Φαρὰν ἐπισκόπου, Ὁνορίου Ῥώμης, Κύρου Ἀλεξανδρείας, Σεργίου, Πύρρου, Παύλου καὶ Πέτρου προέδρων γενομένων τῆς Κωνσταντινουπόλεως, Θεοδώρου Αἰγύπτου, Μακαρίου τοῦ ὀνομασθέντος Ἀντιοχείας, Στεφάνου τοῦ αὐτοῦ μαθητοῦ, καὶ Πολυχρονίου τοῦ νηπιόφρονος γέροντος· οὓς καθελοῦσα ἀνεθεμάτισεν· ὅρον δὲ θεῖον κατὰ τὰς ἑσπερίους συνόδους ἐξέθετο, δύο φύσεις, δύο θελήσεις καὶ ἐνεργείας τοῦ ἑνὸς Χριστοῦ Ἰησοῦ καὶ θεοῦ καὶ σωτῆρος ἡμῶν καταγγέλλοντα.

142.

Γεωργίου δὲ πρὸς κύριον ἐκδημήσαντος τοῦ παμμάκαρος Θεόδωρος αὐτὸν διεδέξατο ὁ πανσέβαστος, κἀκεῖνον ἀπὸ ἀσηκρῆτις Παῦλος ὁ πάντιμος, καὶ αὐτὸν ὁ ἱερομάκαρ ὄντως Καλλίνικος.

141: HL III_1, 472–538 (A.D. 680–81) ‖ 1–15: cf. Geo. Mon., 725, 15–726, 21; Cedren. (ed. Bonn.), I, 766, 16–767, 13; Mansi, XI, 209; 584

141: 1 ἀναδεξάμενος *z* ‖ 2 ante ἕκτην add. σύνοδον τὴν *z* ‖ κροτηθῆναι LG ‖ 3 τοῦ om. LG ‖ 4 Θεόδωρος — διάκονος om. LG ‖ 5 πατριάρχης] ἱεράρχης LG ‖ Πέτρον — 9 Ῥώμης om. LG ‖ 9 Κύρου — 13 ἀνεθεμάτισεν] ἥτις σέργιον, κῦρον, πύρρον, παῦλον, πέτρον, θεόδωρον αἰγύπτου καὶ τὸν ἀντιοχείας μακάριον, στέφανόν τε τὸν αὐτοῦ μαθητὴν πρὸς τούτοις ἀνεθεμάτισε καὶ πολυχρόνιον τὸν νηπιόφρονα γέροντα LG ‖ 9 ὀνωρίου DE ‖ 12 τοῦ μαθητοῦ αὐτοῦ *z* ‖ 14 δύο[2] om. LG ‖ καὶ om. D ‖ 15 καὶ[1]] τοῦ LG

142: Caput om. LG ‖ 2 ἀπὸ] ὁ ἀπὸ *z* ‖ ἀποασηκρῆτις E, A(?)

141, 142

141. After receiving this (decree), the Christ-loving Emperor ordered the Sixth Holy and Ecumenical Council to be convoked in Constantinople.[174] Its presiding leaders were the Roman Pope Agatho's representatives, the presbyters Theodore and George and the deacon John; George, the Patriarch of Constantinople who had succeeded Peter; Theophanes, archbishop of Antioch in Syria; Peter the monk and presbyter representing Alexandria–this city and Jerusalem being without patriarchs due to the Agarene occupation. (It was summoned) against Theodore, the bishop of Pharan, Honorius of Rome, Cyrus of Alexandria, Sergius, Pyrrhus, Paul and Peter the former patriarchs of Constantinople, Theodore of Egypt, Macarius of Antioch already mentioned,[175] his pupil Stephanus, and Polychronius "the foolish old man." Having condemned and anathematized these men, it issued a divine decree in agreement with the Western synods, which proclaimed two natures and two wills and energies in the one Christ Jesus our God and Savior.

142. After the all-blessed George departed for the Lord, he was succeeded by the all-revered Theodore, Theodore by the all-honorable Paul, the former Secretary, and this man by the truly holy and blessed Callinicus.

[174] The description of the Sixth Ecumenical Council is very close to that of Georgius Monachus, *op. cit.* (*supra,* note 74), 726 lines 2–21.

[175] This can be explained by the fact that earlier in his account George the Monk tells us that Macarius of Antioch was deposed by the Council, being replaced by Theophanes; the passage has been omitted by *SV.*

143.

Ἰουστινιανὸς τοίνυν βασίλεια τὰ πατρῷα διαδεξάμενος θείαν καὶ ἱερὰν ἐν Κωνσταντινουπόλει διακοσίων τεσσαράκοντα θεοφόρων πατέρων συνήγαγε σύνοδον, ἣ τοὺς παραλειφθέντας τῇ ἁγίᾳ πέμπτῃ καὶ ἕκτῃ συνόδοις κανόνας ἐξέθετο, καὶ πάσης Ἑλληνικῆς τε καὶ Ἰουδαϊκῆς, ἀλλά γε καὶ τῆς αἱρετικῆς παραδόσεως τὰς ἐκκλησίας ἐκάθηρε.

144.

Λεοντίου δὲ τῇ βασιλείᾳ ἐπιθεμένου καὶ ῥινότμητον Ἰουστινιανὸν ἐν Χερσῶνι περιορίσαντος Ἀρτέμιος, ὁ καὶ Ἀναστάσιος, τὸν Λεόντιον διεδέξατο. Καὶ Ἰουστινιανὸς πάλιν τὴν βασιλείαν παρέλαβε, καὶ τὸν ἀρχιεράρχην Καλλίνικον ἀπ' ὀμμάτων ποιήσας τῷ σεμνείῳ τῆς Χώρας παρέπεμψε, καὶ Κῦρον, τὸν Ἀμάστριδος τῆς νήσου ἔγκλειστον γεγονότα καὶ τῆς δευτέρας βασιλείας τὴν κατοχὴν αὐτῷ εὐαγγελισάμενον, τοῦ Βυζαντίου πατριάρχην ἀντὶ Καλλινίκου ὁ θηριότροπος ἀποκατέστησεν.

145.

Ἀλλὰ Φιλιππικός, <ὁ> καὶ Βαρδάνης, ἀπὸ Χερσῶνος ἅμα τῷ στόλῳ παραλαβὼν τὰ βασίλεια καὶ Ἰουστινιανὸν ἐν τῷ Δαματρύϊ ἀποκτείνας τοῖς ξίφεσιν, ἐν Κωνσταντινουπόλει συνέδριον μιαρὸν ποιησάμενος τῶν μονοθελητῶν ἀνεκαίνισε τὴν ἀσέβειαν καὶ τὸν ἀρχιεπίσκοπον Κῦρον ἐξέωσεν, ἐν τῇ μονῇ τῆς Χώρας ποιήσας αὐτὸν ἐγκατάκλειστον· καὶ ἀντ' αὐτοῦ Ἰωάννην ἐχειροτόνησεν.

143: HL III_1, 560–78 (A.D. 692) ‖ 1–5: cf. *Syn. Chron.*, ed. K. Sathas, in Μεσαιωνικὴ Βιβλιοθήκη, VII, 115, 5–12; Mansi, XI, 933

144: 1–2: cf. Theoph., 369, 24–26; Niceph., 39, 1–4 ‖ 4–7: cf. Theoph., 375, 13–16; Niceph., 42, 25–30

145: HL III_1, 598–99 (A.D. 712) ‖ 1–2: cf. *Epilog. Agath.*, Mansi, XII, 192; Theoph., 380, 3–381, 5; Niceph., 46, 24–47, 20 ‖ 3–6: cf. Theoph., 382, 10–15

143: 1 δεξάμενος *b* ‖ 3 παραληφθέντας LG ‖ 4 συνόδω LG

144: Caput om. LG ‖ 1 ἐπιτιθεμένου E ‖ καὶ] καὶ τὸν *z*

145: 1 ὁ] V, supra lin. add. E om. cett. ‖ καὶ Βαρδάνης om. LG ‖ ἀπὸ] ἐκ LG ‖ 5 post ἐξέωσεν add. πάλαι ἀμάστριδος γεγονότα ἡγούμενον LG ‖ ἐν τῇ μονῇ] ἐν τῷ σεμνείῳ LG ‖ ἔγκλειστον *z*

143. Justinian, then, having taken over the Empire from his father, brought together a divine and sacred synod of two hundred and forty God-bearing bishops in Constantinople, which issued the canons left out by the holy Fifth and Sixth Councils and purged the Churches of all Greek, Jewish, and heretical teaching.

144. Leontius assumed control of the Empire and banished Justinian to Cherson after cutting off his nose; Artemius, also known as Anastasius, succeeded Leontius;[176] and Justinian took over the Empire once more. He left the archbishop Callinicus without eyes and consigned him to the Chora monastery.[177] Then the bestial man installed in place of Callinicus as patriarch of Byzantium Cyrus, who had been a recluse on the island[178] of Amastris and had announced to Justinian the good news that he would obtain the Empire a second time.

145. But Philippicus, also called Bardanes, (coming) from Cherson with the fleet, took over the Empire and had Justinian put to the sword in Damatrys. Then, holding an abominable assembly in Constantinople, he revived the monothelete impiety, ousted the archbishop Cyrus, confining him in the Chora monastery, and appointed John in his place.

[176] Leontius was succeeded, rather, by Apsimar (Tiberius); cf. chap. 146.

[177] All other sources agree that this patriarch was banished to Rome; *SV* is probably confusing his fate with that of Cyrus, described in the following chapter.

[178] Following Theophanes, 375 line 14, the writer calls Amastris an island; it is, rather, a city on a promontory.

146.

Φιλιππικοῦ δὲ ὑπὸ Ἀψιμάρου ἀναιρεθέντος καὶ Ἰωάννου τοῦ δυσσεβοῦς τελευτήσαντος Γερμανὸς ὁ πανόσιος Κυζίκου ἐπίσκοπος τῷ θρόνῳ Κωνσταντινουπόλεως ἀνατίθεται. Καὶ Θεοδοσίου τοῦ ἀπὸ δυτικῶν ἐπιθεμένου τῇ βασιλείᾳ καὶ τὸν Ἀψίμαρον ἐκδιώξαντος, Γερμανὸς ὁ μακάριος σύνοδον ἑκατὸν ἀρχιερέων θείαν καὶ ἱερὰν ποιησάμενος Σέργιον, Κῦρον, Πύρρον, Παῦλον, Πέτρον καὶ Ἰωάννην ἀνεθεμάτισε καὶ Χριστοῦ Ἰησοῦ τοῦ ἀληθινοῦ θεοῦ ἡμῶν δύο φύσεις, θελήσεις καὶ ἐνεργείας ἐτράνωσε.

147.

Κόνων τοίνυν, ὁ καὶ Λέων ἐπιλεγόμενος, τὸ γένος Ἴσαυρος, τὴν βασιλείαν Θεοδοσίου διαδεξάμενος καὶ τῇ πλάνῃ Κωνσταντίνου ἐπισκόπου Νακολείας καὶ Βισὴρ πατρικίου σαρακηνόφρονος τῶν αἱρεσιαρχῶν συγχραινόμενος, μιαρὰν ἐν τῷ παλατίῳ κατὰ τῶν ἁγίων εἰκόνων ποιησάμενος σύνοδον Γερμανὸν τὸν μακάριον τὴν αὐτῶν ἠνάγκαζεν ἐκφωνῆσαι κατένεξιν. Ὁ δὲ τοῦ θεοῦ ἱεράρχης τὸ ὠμοφόριον ἐξῄει τοῦ συνεδρίου ἀποδυσάμενος· ὅντινα μὲν ὁ θηριόγνωμος τύραννος ἐν τῷ οἴκῳ αὐτοῦ περιώρισε, μετὰ μικρὸν δὲ ἐν τῷ σεμνείῳ τῆς Χώρας σὺν τῷ ἀρχιδιακόνῳ αὐτοῦ Ἀνθίμῳ ἀγχόνῃ αὐτὸν ἐθανάτωσεν· Ἀναστάσιον δὲ τὸν ἀντίθεον τῷ θρόνῳ ἀναβιβάσας τὰ ὑστερήματα Ἑλλήνων καὶ Ἰουδαίων ἐν τῇ Χριστοῦ ἐκκλησίᾳ δεινῶς ἀνεπλήρωσεν.

146: HL III$_1$, 600

147: HL III$_2$, 641–43 (A.D. 730) ‖ 2–3: cf. Theoph., 402, 9–18; 414, 27; 405, 3 ‖ 4–8: cf. Theoph., 408, 32–409, 10

146: 1 ὑπὸ Ἀψιμάρου om. LG recte Ἀρτεμίου ‖ 3 Θεοδοσίου — 5 σύνοδον] σύνοδον ἐπὶ θεοδοσίου τοῦ βασιλέως LG ‖ 4 διώξαντος *z* ‖ 6 πέτρον παῦλον *b* ‖ post Παῦλον add. καὶ LG ‖ καὶ Ἰωάννην om. LG ‖ 7 ἀληθινοῦ] ἀληθοῦς D om. LG ‖ post φύσεις add. καὶ *z*

147: 1 Κόνων — Ἴσαυρος] Λέων τοίνυν LG ‖ Κόνων — Λέων] Λέων τοίνυν, ὁ καὶ κόνων *z* ‖ 9 θηριώνυμος *b* ‖ 7 οἴκῳ — 9 ἐθανάτωσεν] ἰδίῳ οἴκῳ μέχρι θανάτου αὐτοῦ περιώρισεν LG

146. Following the murder of Philippicus by Apsimar[179] and the death of impious John, the all-saintly Germanus, bishop of Cyzicus, was placed upon the throne of Constantinople. And after Theodosius from the West assumed control of the Empire and expelled Apsimar, the blessed Germanus, having organized a divine and sacred synod of one hundred archpriests,[180] anathematized Sergius, Cyrus, Pyrrhus, Paul, Peter, and John, and proclaimed two natures, wills, and energies in Christ Jesus our true God.

147. Conon, then, also named Leo, an Isaurian by birth, succeeded Theodosius as emperor, and having been tainted by the error of the heresiarchs, Constantine, bishop of Nacolea, and Biser, the Saracen-minded patrician, he held an abominable synod[181] in the palace against the holy images, in which he compelled the blessed Germanus to proclaim an attack on them; but God's hierarch removed his pallium and left the assembly. The beastly tyrant confined him to his house, but shortly afterward he had him strangled to death in the Chora monastery along with his archdeacon Anthimus.[182] Then having elevated the adversary of God, Anastasius, to the throne, he completed in a dreadful manner in the Church of Christ what Greeks and Jews had left undone.

[179] A mistake for Artemius; cf. chap. 144 and note 176 *supra*.

[180] Our text is the only witness for this synod, and Grumel, *Regestes* no. 325, has his doubts about the information.

[181] Theophanes (408 line 32) calls this gathering a σιλέντιον, which the compiler changes to σύνοδον in his own interest; cf. HL, III_2, 641 note 3.

[182] Though other sources say that Germanus was beaten at one point, none but *SV* mentions death by strangling (see HL, III_2, 642 note 3, where the *Vita Stephani Junioris* is confused with *SV*). Germanus' tract *De haeresibus et synodis* is dedicated to "deacon Anthimus" (PG, 98, 39).

148.

Ὅπερ μαθὼν ὁ θεόληπτος πάπας Ῥώμης Γρηγόριος θείαν καὶ ἱερὰν σύνοδον συστησάμενος τοὺς εἰκονομάχους γενναίως ἀναθέματι καθυπέβαλεν, πολλοῖς καὶ σφοδροῖς ἐλέγχοις πρὸς τὸν βασιλέα χρησάμενος Λέοντα.

149.

Ὁμοίως τε καὶ Θεόδωρος ὁ τῶν Ἱεροσολύμων ἐπίσκοπος ἀθροίσας θεοσύλλεκτον σύνοδον τὰς ἁγίας ἓξ οἰκουμενικὰς συνόδους ἀριθμῷ καὶ διπτύχοις ἐκήρυξε καὶ τὴν ἀναφυεῖσαν τῶν ἁγιοκαυστῶν αἵρεσιν ἀναθέματι καθυπέβαλε.

150.

Λέοντος οὖν τελευτήσαντος Κωνσταντῖνος ὁ υἱὸς αὐτοῦ γεγονὼς τῆς βασιλείας διάδοχος Ἑλλήνων καὶ Ἰουδαίων χεῖρον τὴν Χριστοῦ ἐκκλησίαν ἐδίωξε· συγκαθεσθεὶς γὰρ Κωνσταντίνῳ διαδόχῳ Ἀναστασίου σὺν ρ′ ἐπισκόποις τῷ ματαιόφρονι ἄθεον ἐποιήσατο σύνοδον, ἐν ᾗ Χριστοῦ καὶ ἁπάντων ἁγίων τὰς σεβασμίας εἰκόνας ἀπεκάλεσεν εἴδωλα, τὰς πρεσβείας ἠρνήσατο, καὶ τὰ θεοτίμητα πυρὶ παραδέδωκε λείψανα. Ὁ γὰρ Κωνσταντῖνος οὗτος Πέργης τῆς Παμφυλίας γεγονὼς ἦν ἐπίσκοπος καὶ δι᾽ αἰσχροπραγματείας τινὰς ὑπὸ τῶν ὁμοθρήσκων αὐτοῦ ἀντέλαβε τὴν καθαίρεσιν, σχολάζων δὲ πολυτρόπως ἐφιλιώθη τῷ αὐτοκράτορι καὶ σύντεκνος αὐτοῦ ἐχρημάτισε καὶ τοῦ Βυζαντίου ἀρχιεπίσκοπος· ὅμως οὖν τῶν βλασφημιῶν αὐτοῦ ἄξιον μισθὸν ἀνταπέλαβεν ὑπὸ τοῦ συντέκνου αὐτοῦ καρατομηθεὶς προφανῶς εἰς τὸ Κυνήγιον. Καὶ Νικήτας τὸν θρόνον αὐτοῦ διεδέξατο, κἀκείνου Παῦλος ὁ Κύπριος Σαλαμινεὺς ἐκληρώσατο.

148: HL III_2, 676 ‖ 1–4: cf. Theoph., 408, 28 sqq.; 409, 14–17; 404, 5–9; Cedren. (ed. Bonn.), I, 799, 7–9; Zonar. XV: (ed. Bonn.), 4, 1

149: HL III_2, 676 (ca. 760?)

150: HL III_2, 695–705 (A.D. 754) ‖ 3–4: cf. Theoph., 427, 29 sqq. ‖ 4–5: cf. Geo. Mon., 751, 4–7 ‖ 10: cf. Theoph., 442, 15–16 ‖ 11–12: cf. Theoph., 441, 5–442, 8

148: 1 Ἄπερ A^s ‖ 3 ἐλέγχοις ante πολλοῖς transp. *b*

149: 1 ὁ τῶν *b*: ὁ D om. LG ‖ 3 καὶ om. *z*

150: 1 γοῦν LG ‖ 2 Χριστοῦ D*z*: τοῦ χριστοῦ AE om. LG ‖ 4 τοῖς (τῷ V) ματαιόφροσι(ν) *z* ‖ 6 καὶ om. D ‖ παρέδωκε *b* ‖ ὁ γὰρ — 13 ἐκληρώσατο om. LG ‖ 7 Πέργης] Συλ(λ)αίου Theoph., 428, 4

148. When he learned this, Gregory,[183] the God-possessed Pope of Rome, organized a divine and sacred synod, nobly placed under anathema the image fighters, and sent many severe criticisms to Emperor Leo.

149. In the same way, too, Theodore, the bishop of Jerusalem, having gathered a divinely-assembled synod,[184] proclaimed the Six Holy Ecumenical Councils by number and in the diptychs, and subjected to anathema the heresy of saint-burners[185] which had sprung up.

150. When Leo, then, died, his son Constantine succeeded to the Empire and persecuted the Church of Christ worse than Greeks and Jews. For, presiding with Constantine,[186] the empty-headed successor of Anastasius, he held a godless synod of one hundred[187] bishops, in which he disparaged the revered icons of Christ and all the saints by calling them idols, denied their (powers of) intercession,[188] and consigned the divinely honored relics to flames. This Constantine was formerly bishop of Perge[189] in Pamphylia and had been given his deposition by the community for certain acts of impiety. But by cleverly frequenting the Emperor's company he became his friend, co-parent, and archbishop of Byzantium. Nevertheless, he received a fitting payment for his blasphemies, being beheaded in the public view at the Cynegion by his co-parent. His throne passed to Nicetas, and this man was succeeded by Paul from Salamis in Cyprus.

[183] It is not possible to decide whether Gregory II or Gregory III is meant. The same ambiguity exists in Theophanes (408 line 28 ff.; 409 line 14 ff.), whose information *SV* repeats, adding an explicit reference to a synod. G. Ostrogorsky, "Les débuts de la querelle des images," *Melánges Charles Diehl,* I (Paris, 1930), 255 note 1, argues for Gregory III, though by his own admission (p. 254) the letters to Emperor Leo, mentioned by Theophanes (409 line 16), came from Gregory II.

[184] Theophanes (434 lines 1–5) relates how Theodore of Jerusalem, along with the Patriarchs of Alexandria and Antioch, anathematized a Syrian bishop, Cosmas, who had become an iconoclast, and a letter of Hadrian I (J. Hardouin, *Acta Conciliorum* [Paris, 1714–15], IV, 778) tells us that these same three Patriarchs sent a synodical epistle to Pope Paul I affirming their support for images. The wording of *SV,* however, suggests that the compiler is using a different source.

[185] I.e., iconoclasts; cf. note 112 *supra.*

[186] Constantine was proclaimed patriarch only at the final session of the synod (Theophanes, 428 line 2 ff.); see Grumel, *Regestes,* no. 345.

[187] SV^2 has changed this to 333, probably a variant of the number 338 given by Theophanes.

[188] This account is not accurate; see HL, III_2, 704–5; Grumel, *Regestes,* no. 345.

[189] Sylaeum, according to Theophanes. On Perge-Sylaeum see H.-G. Beck, *Kirche und theologische Literatur im byzantinischen Reich* (Munich, 1959), 173. The story about Constantine's previous deposition is not reported elsewhere and looks suspiciously like the case of Antony in chap. 155.

151.

Κωνσταντίνου τοίνυν τὴν βασιλείαν Λέων ὁ υἱὸς αὐτοῦ ὁ Χάζαρος διεδέξατο, καὶ τὴν βασιλείαν Λέοντος Κωνσταντῖνος ὁ υἱὸς αὐτοῦ μετὰ Εἰρήνης τῆς οἰκείας μητρὸς ἐκληρώσατο· οἳ θείαν καὶ ἱερὰν ἐν τῷ ναῷ τῶν ἁγίων καὶ πανευφήμων ἀποστόλων σύνοδον ποιησάμενοι, μέχρις ὥρας τετάρτης καθίσαντες ἀναθεματίσαι τοὺς εἰκονομάχους κατέσπευδον, ὅπερ γενέσθαι οὐ συνεχώρησαν οἱ σχολάριοι.

152.

Οἱ γοῦν φιλόχριστοι βασιλεῖς καὶ θειότατοι ἐξορίᾳ τοὺς σχολαρίους παιδεύσαντες ἁγίαν οἰκουμενικὴν ἑβδόμην συγκροτηθῆναι σύνοδον ἐν Νικαίᾳ τῆς Βιθυνῶν ἐπαρχίας ἐθέσπισαν· ἧς ἐξῆρχον προκαθεζόμενοι Κωνσταντινουπόλεως πατριάρχης ὁ ἐν ἁγίοις Ταράσιος τὸν Κύπριον Παῦλον διαδεξάμενος, Πέτρος καὶ Πέτρος πρεσβύτεροι Ἀδριανοῦ τοῦ ἁγιωτάτου πάπα Ῥώμης τὸν τόπον ἐπέχοντες, Ἰωάννης καὶ Θωμᾶς μοναχοὶ καὶ πρεσβύτεροι τοποτηρηταὶ πατριαρχῶν Ἀλεξανδρείας, Ἀντιοχείας, Ἱεροσολύμων, τῆς ἀνατολικῆς διοικήσεως. Ἥτις ἁγία σύνοδος τοὺς κατὰ τῆς τοῦ θεοῦ ἐκκλησίας λυττήσαντας ἀναθέματι καθυπέβαλε καὶ ὅρον ἐκθεμένη ὀρθόδοξον τὰς ἱερὰς εἰκόνας πρὸς τὴν ἀνέκαθεν δόξαν αὐτῶν ἀνεβίβασεν.

151: HL III$_2$, 756–58 (A.D. 786) ‖ 3–6: cf. Theoph., 461, 12–462, 3

152: HL III$_2$, 758–98 (A.D. 787) ‖ 1–2: cf. Theoph., 462, 5–17 ‖ 2–11: cf. Geo. Mon., 769, 10–770, 9 ‖ 4–8: Mansi, XII, 992–94

151: 1 Κωνσταντίνου — βασιλείαν] Κωνσταντῖνον LG ‖ ὁ^2] om. LG ὁ ἐκ *z* ‖ 2 ὁ om. LG ‖ 3 οἰκείας] αὐτοῦ LG ‖ 4 ante ἀποστόλων add. χριστοῦ D

152: 1 οὖν LG ‖ 2 post ἁγίαν add. καὶ D ‖ κροτηθῆναι LG ‖ 4 πατριάρχης om. *z* ‖ τὸν — 5 διαδεξάμενος om. LG ‖ 8 ἀνατολῆς LG ‖ 9 ἀναθ. καθυπέβαλε] ἀνεθεμάτισε A ‖ 10 τὰς εἰκόνας τὰς ἱερὰς E*z*

151. Constantine, then, was succeeded as emperor by his son Leo the Chazar, and his Empire was inherited by his son Constantine along with Constantine's mother Irene. And they, having organized a divine and sacred synod in the Church of the Holy and All-renowned Apostles which stayed in session until the fourth hour,[190] were eager to anathematize the image-fighters but were prevented from doing so by the imperial guards.

152. When the Christ-loving and most divine imperial rulers, then, had punished the imperial guards with exile, they decreed that the Seventh Holy Ecumenical Council be convoked at Nicaea in the province of Bithynia. The presidents who led it were the Patriarch of Constantinople, Tarasius, now among the saints, who had succeeded the Cypriot Paul; Peter and Peter, the presbyters taking the place of Adrian the most holy Pope of Rome; John and Thomas, the monks and presbyters representing the patriarchs of the Eastern provinces of Alexandria, Antioch, and Jerusalem. This holy Council placed under anathema those raging against God's Church, and issuing a decree of orthodoxy, it elevated the sacred icons to the glory they had from the beginning.

[190] Neither Theophanes nor Tarasius (Mansi, XII, 999D ff.) mentions this detail. In the short historical introduction to the Seventh Council (Mansi, XII, 991B), however, we are told that the gathering at the synod of 786 broke up ὥρας οὔσης ὡσεὶ ἕκτης.

153.

Νικηφόρου δὲ τοῦ φιλοχρίστου Εἰρήνης τὴν βασιλείαν διαδεξαμένου τῆς εὐσεβόφρονος, ἀντάρας Τοῦρκος στρατηγὸς καὶ πατρίκιος, Εἰρήνης δῆθεν τῆς βασιλίδος ἀντιποιούμενος ἐφάνη τῷ αὐτοκράτορι. Ἀλλὰ θεὸς τὴν ὁρμὴν αὐτοῦ χωρὶς διεσκέδασεν αἵματος, Ἰωσὴφ πρεσβυτέρου καὶ οἰκονόμου τῆς μεγάλης ἐκκλησίας Κωνσταντινουπόλεως μεσιτεύσαντος. Δι' ἣν αἰτίαν ὁ τρισμακάριστος Νικηφόρος πατριάρχης, Ταράσιον τὸν ἐν ἁγίοις διαδεξάμενος, θείαν καὶ ἱερὰν μερικὴν συνάρσει τοῦ βασιλέως ἐν Βυζαντίῳ συνήθροισε σύνοδον καὶ οἰκονομικῶς τὸν Ἰωσὴφ ἐδέξατο εἰς πρεσβύτερον, ὑπὸ Ταρασίου πεπαυμένον καταλειφθέντα χάριν μοιχοζευξίας Κωνσταντίνου υἱοῦ Εἰρήνης τοῦ αὐτοκράτορος. Ὅθεν ἀφελῶς τῆς Χριστοῦ ἐκκλησίας τινὲς ἀπορραγέντες πάλιν ἡνώθησαν.

154.

Τελευτήσαντος οὖν ἐν πολέμῳ Βουλγάρων Νικηφόρου τὴν βασιλείαν ὁ υἱὸς αὐτοῦ Σταυράκιος διεδέξατο, ἣν Μιχαὴλ ὁ Ῥαγγαβὲ ἐκείνου ἐπ' ἀδελφῇ Προκοπίᾳ γαμβρὸς ἐκληρώσατο. Καὶ Λέων ὁ Συραρμένιος ἐπαναστὰς ἐκράτησε τὰ βασίλεια, Ἰουδαϊκῆς τε καὶ Μανιχαϊκῆς θρησκείας

153: HL III$_2$, 1126 (A.D. 806) ‖ 2–4: cf. Theoph., 479, 15–25 ‖ 4–5: cf. *Vit. Theod. Stud.*, PG, 99, 265D ‖ 7–8: cf. *Epist. Theod. Stud.*, PG, 99, 985B ‖ 11: cf. Theoph., 494, 17–20

154: HL IV$_1$, 1–5 (A.D. 815) ‖ 1–12: cf. *Vit. Ignat.*, PG, 105, 492C–493A ‖ 6–7 et 11–12: cf. *Vit. Nicet.*, *ActaSS*, Tert. April., 37–38; *Vit. Niceph.* (ed. de Boor) 202–4

153: 2 ἀντάρας] ἐφάνη LG ‖ 3 ἐφάνη] ἀνταίρων LG ‖ 3–4 ἀλλὰ χωρὶς αἵματος θεὸς τὴν ὁρμὴν αὐτοῦ διεσκέδασεν *b* (cf. cap. 94, 1–2; 147, 6–7; 150, 3–4) ‖ 7 μερικὴν] τοπικὴν LG ‖ 8 σύνοδον ante συνάρσει transp. *z* ‖ πρεσβύτερον] τὸ πρεσβυτέριον LG an ὡς pro εἰς? ‖ 9 πεπαυμένου DOTMN

154: 1 Τελευτήσαντος – 2 διεδέξατο in cap. 153 ponent A*z* ‖ 1 γοῦν LG ‖ 2 ἣν om. LG ‖ ὁ Ῥαγγαβὲ om. LG ‖ 2–3 ἐπ' ἀδελφῇ ἐκείνου D ‖ 3 Προκοπίᾳ om. LG ‖ καὶ Λέων] omisso post ἐπαναστὰς scr. δὲ λέων E ὦ καὶ λέων D ‖ post Λέων add. στεφθεὶς ὑπὸ νικηφόρου πατριάρχου, ἐπὶ τούτου ἦν καὶ ὁ ὁμολογητὴς θεόδωρος ὁ στουδίτης *b* ‖ 3–4 ἐπαναστὰς ὁ συραρμένιος *b*

153. After the Christ-loving Nicephorus had succeeded to the Empire of the pious-minded Irene, the general and patrician Turcus rose up and confronted the Emperor in support, as he claimed, of Empress Irene. But God dissipated his attack without bloodshed, when Joseph, the presbyter and steward of the Great Church of Constantinople, acted as mediator.[191] For this reason the thrice-blessed Patriarch Nicephorus, the successor of Tarasius now among the saints, assembled in Byzantium with the Emperor's encouragement a divine and sacred particular synod[192] and, making a concession, received back to the presbyterate Joseph whom Tarasius had left suspended on account of the adulterous union of Emperor Constantine, the son of Irene. Because of this, certain people[193] foolishly broke off from Christ's church but were (later) restored to union.[194]

154. On the death of Nicephorus, then, in the Bulgarian war, his son Stauracius succeeded to the Empire, which Michael Rangabe, who was married to Stauracius' sister Procopia, inherited (next). And Leo the Syro-Armenian rose up and seized control of the Empire, becoming a refuge for the

[191] The mediation of Joseph is discussed fully by Alexander, *op. cit.* (*supra,* note 114), 85–87.

[192] Apparently two synods were held on this matter—the present one of 806, in which the priest Joseph was reinstated, and another in 809 (not mentioned by *SV*), which condemned and banished the recalcitrant Studite monks for their opposition to the dispensation granted to Joseph. See Grumel, *Regestes,* nos. 377–81; HL, III_2, 1126–27; Alexander, *op. cit.,* 87–92.

[193] The Studites.

[194] The official reconciliation came during the reign of Michael I Rangabe (811–13): see Alexander, *op. cit.,* 96–97.

ὑπάρχων κρησφύγετον· τῆς ἐξουσίας γὰρ ἀναξίως ἐπιλαβόμενος μιαρὰν καὶ ἄθεον χριστιανοκατηγορικὴν ἐν τῇ Χριστοῦ μεγάλῃ ἐκκλησίᾳ Κωνσταντινουπόλεως ἐποιήσατο σύνοδον, καὶ Νικήφορον τὸν ἐν ἁγίοις καθελών, περιορίσας ἐν τῷ μοναστηρίῳ αὐτοῦ Θεόδοτον ἀντεχειροτόνησε, Κασσιτηρᾶν καὶ Φλαβιανὸν τὸν ἐπιλεγόμενον. Καὶ τὰς ἁγίας καὶ ἱερὰς εἰκόνας καταστρεψάμενος τοὺς προσκυνητὰς αὐτῶν ἀναθέματι καθυπέβαλε καὶ δημεύσει, ἐξορίαις, λιμῷ, καὶ φυλακαῖς καὶ παντοίαις ἰδέαις θανάτου ὁ ἄθεος κατανάλωσεν, ἐκ ποδῶν σύρων καὶ πατῶν αὐχένας ὁ ἀλιτήριος.

155.

Ξίφει δὲ κυνοτρόπως τοῦ ἀληθῶς κυνολέοντος τῷ θανάτῳ προσομιλήσαντος καὶ Θεοδότου πρὸς ᾅδην χωρήσαντος Μιχαὴλ ὁ τραυλὸς τοῦ μὲν τὴν βασιλείαν, τοῦ δὲ τὸν θρόνον Ἀντώνιος μοναχὸς μονῆς τῶν Μητροπολιτῶν ἡγούμενος διεδέξατο, Πέργης τῆς Παμφυλίας προγεγονὼς καθῃρημένος ἐπίσκοπος. Καὶ Θεόφιλος υἱὸς Μιχαὴλ αὐτοκράτωρ γενόμενος, τελευτήσαντος Ἀντωνίου τὸν λεκανομάντιν πρόεδρον Ἰωάννην προχειρισάμενος μειζόνως τοῖς εὐσεβέσι τὸν διωγμὸν ἀνερρίπισε· καὶ ἄθεον ἐν Βλαχέρναις κατασκευάσας συνέδριον τοὺς προσκυνητὰς τῶν σεβασμίων εἰκόνων ἀνεθεμάτισε.

155: HL IV$_1$, 111 (A.D. 837?) ‖ 1–7: cf. *Vit. Ignat.*, 493A–D ‖ 3–5: cf. *Vit. Leon. Armen.*, PG, 108, 1025B–C

---

9 Κασσιτηρᾶν — ἐπιλεγόμενον om. LG ‖ καὶ ἱερὰς om. *z* ‖ 10 ἀναθ. καθυπέβαλε] ἀνεθεμάτισε A ‖ 11 καὶ[1] om. *b* ‖ καὶ[2] om. *b* ‖ 12 ὁ ἀλιτήριος] τῶν μακαρίων ὁ θηριόγνωμος LG

155: 1 ἀληθῶς κυνολέοντος] ἀθέου LG ‖ 2 πρὸς ᾅδην χωρήσαντος] θανόντος A ‖ 3 μοναχὸς — 4 ἡγούμενος om. LG ‖ 4 Πέργης — 5 ἐπίσκοπος om. LG

Jewish and Manichaean religions. For, having come to power unworthily, he held an abominable, godless, and anti-Christian synod in Christ's great Church in Constantinople; and deposing Saint Nicephorus and confining him in his monastery, he appointed in his place Theodotus, surnamed Cassiteras and Flavian.[195] And overthrowing the holy and sacred icons, the godless one placed their worshipers under anathema and destroyed them with fines, banishment, starvation, imprisonment, and every form of death, dragging them by the feet, and stepping on their necks, the wicked man.

155. After the veritable dog-lion (Leo) had met a dog's death by the sword[196] and Theodotus had passed on to Hades, Michael the Lisper succeeded to the Empire of the former, while the latter's throne fell to the monk Antonius, superior of the monastery of the Metropolitans and former bishop of Perge[197] in Pamphylia where he had been deposed. And when Michael's son Theophilus became emperor, he appointed as patriarch[198] on Antonius' death the dish-diviner John, thereby stirring up a more intense persecution of the orthodox. And having organized a godless assembly in Blachernae,[199] he anathematized the worshipers of the revered icons.

[195] The deposition of Nicephorus (at a synod) and the appointment of his successor, Theodotus, took place earlier in the same year, 815, and not at the synod of St. Sophia. See Alexander, *op. cit.,* 134–36; HL IV_1, 4–5. The name Flavian does not seem to be attested elsewhere.

[196] Compare *Vita Ignatii,* col. 493A: εὗρε . . . τὸν θάνατον . . . κυνὸς τρόπον τοῖς ξίφεσιν.

[197] Sylaeum, according to all other sources except *Vita Ignatii,* col. 493C; see also note 189.

[198] The Greek has πρόεδρος, a common synonym of πατριάρχης.

[199] This information is not above suspicion, as no one else mentions such a synod; cf. G. Ostrogorsky, *History of the Byzantine State* (New Jersey, 1969), 209 note 2, and Grumel, *Regestes,* no. 413. In an earlier publication, *Echos d'Orient,* 29 (1930), 99, Grumel had accepted the account of *SV* without question.

156.

Θεοφίλου τοίνυν βλασφήμως τὸν βίον τελέσαντος Μιχαὴλ ὁ υἱὸς αὐτοῦ σὺν τῇ οἰκείᾳ μητρὶ Θεοδώρᾳ τὴν βασιλείαν παρέλαβεν. Οἳ ζήλῳ θεοῦ πυρακτούμενοι τοὺς ἐν ἐξορίαις ὑπάρχοντας πατέρας ὁσίους ἀνεκαλέσαντο, καὶ σύνοδον θείαν καὶ ἱερὰν τοπικὴν ἐν τοῖς Κανικλείου ποιήσαντες Ἰωάννην μὲν τὸν μυσαρὸν τοῦ θρόνου ἐξήλασαν, Μεθόδιον δὲ τὸν ἐν ἁγίοις Κωνσταντινουπόλεως πατριάρχην προεχειρίσαντο· καὶ τὰς ἁγίας οἰκουμενικὰς ἑπτὰ συνόδους ἀποδεξάμενοι, τὰς ἱερὰς εἰκόνας ἐπὶ τὸ ἀρχῆθεν ὀφειλόμενον σέβας αὐταῖς καλῶς ἀνεστήλωσαν.

157.

Μεθοδίου δὲ τοῦ παμμάκαρος πρὸς κύριον ἐκδημήσαντος Ἰγνάτιος μοναχὸς καὶ πρεσβύτερος, υἱὸς Μιχαὴλ καὶ Νικηφόρου ἔγγονος τῶν φιλοχρίστων αὐτοκρατόρων, κανονικῶς ἐπὶ τὸν θρόνον ἀναβιβάζεται· καθ' οὗ φιλαρχίας κενοδοξίᾳ ἐπίσκοποί τινες καὶ μονάζοντες κουφιζόμενοι οὐ μετρίως χρόνῳ μακρῷ ἐστασίασαν. Οἳ καὶ Μιχαὴλ τοῦ βασιλέως λαβόμενοι τῆς κουφότητος, ἐξελαθῆναι τοῦ θρόνου ἀκρίτως ἀρχοντικῇ χειρὶ τὸν πατριάρχην Ἰγνάτιον παρεσκεύασαν, ἐν Τερεβίνθῳ τῇ νήσῳ αὐτὸν ἐξορίσαντες· καὶ ἐν τῷ παλατίῳ σύνοδον ἀφελῆ ποιησάμενοι τὸν πρωτοασηκρῆτις Φώτιον ἀρχιεράρχην προεχειρίσαντο, πολλὰ μὴ ἀκουσθέντες λόγῳ παραιτήσεως πρὸς Ἰγνάτιον πρεσβευσάμενοι.

156: HL IV_1, 112–14 (A.D. 843) ‖ 1–8: cf. Sym. Mag., PG, 109, 708D–709A; 713A ‖ 4 ἐν τοῖς Κανικλείου: cf. Genes., PG, 109, 1093A

157: HL IV_1, 252–59 (A.D. 858) ‖ 4–5: cf. (?) *Vit. Ignat.* PG, 105, 512C ‖ 5–7: ibid., 504C–505B ‖ 8–10: ibid., 509A ‖ 9–10: ibid., 505C–D

156: 1 τὸν βίον βλασφήμως *z* ‖ τελευτήσαντος LG ‖ 2 τῇ οἰκείᾳ μητρὶ] τῇ μητρὶ αὐτοῦ LG ‖ παρέλαβον *z* ‖ 3 ὁσίους πατέρας *b* ‖ 7 οἰκουμενικὰς om. LG ‖ 8 αὐταῖς om. LG

157: 1 τοῦ παμμάκαρος] τοῦ μάκαρος LG om. A ‖ 2 ἔγγονος nos: γεγονὼς D*b* ἔκγονος LG ‖ 4–5 οὐ μετρίως om. A ‖ 6 ἀκρίτως om. *z* ‖ 8–9 τὸν πρωτοασηκρῆτις om. LG ‖ 9 ἀρχιεράρχην om. LG*z* ‖ προχειρίζονται LG

156. When Theophilus, then, reached the end of his life in blasphemy, his son Michael, along with his mother Theodora, took over the Empire. These, fired with the zeal of God, recalled the holy fathers who were in exile, and having assembled a divine and sacred local synod in the Canicleiou,[200] they expelled the abominable John from the throne and appointed Saint Methodius patriarch of Constantinople.[201] And accepting the seven sacred Ecumenical Councils, they admirably restored to the holy icons the reverence due to them from the beginning.

157. Following the all-blessed Methodius' departure for the Lord, Ignatius, monk and presbyter, the son of Michael and grandson of Nicephorus, the Christ-loving emperors, was canonically[202] elevated to the throne, and against him certain bishops and monks, made light-headed by the vainglory of ambition, maintained a prolonged and vehement revolt. Seizing upon Emperor Michael's shallow-mindedness, these also managed to have the Patriarch Ignatius ousted without a trial from the throne by imperial power, banishing him to the island of Terebinthus. And having organized a simple synod[203] in the palace, they appointed as patriarch the Protoasecretis Photius, after their repeated calls on Ignatius to resign had gone unheeded.

[200] E. J. Martin, *A History of the Iconoclastic Controversy* (London, 1930), 214 note 4, is undoubtedly correct in stating that *SV* has identified (wrongly) this synod with a previous meeting at the house of the imperial official Theoktistos (κανίκλειος), which is mentioned by the historian Genesios, PG, 109, 1093A. See also C. Mango, "The Liquidation of Iconoclasm and the Patriarch Photios," in *Iconoclasm,* ed. A. Bryer and J. Herrin (Birmingham, 1977), 133. The site of the formal synod is not known, though the unpublished council treatise in *Sinaiticus gr. 482* says that it took place at Blachernae.

[201] Among the sources there is considerable disagreement on the chronological order of events; some, for instance, place the election of Methodius before the synod, others afteward, while *SV* makes it part of the proceedings. See Grumel, *Regestes,* no. 416.

[202] κανονικῶς: in the following chapter the writer stresses that Photius obtained the throne παρὰ τοὺς θείους καὶ ἱεροὺς κανόνας. Ignatius' biographer Nicetas, however, does not mention the convocation of a synod before his hero's elevation, and F. Dvornik, *Photian Schism,* 17–18, concludes that the normal canonical procedure had been set aside.

[203] The *Vita Ignatii,* col. 509A, says nothing about a synod, valid or otherwise.

158.

Φώτιος οὖν παρὰ τοὺς θείους καὶ ἱεροὺς κανόνας τοῦ θρόνου ἐπιλαβόμενος οὐκ ἐστοίχει τῷ ἡσυχάσαι οἷσπερ ὠλίσθησεν, ἀλλ' εἰς θυμὸν κινήσας τὸν αὐτοκράτορα μετὰ μυρία δεινὰ ἐξορίζει πρὸς τῇ νήσῳ Μιτυλήνῃ τὸν ἀθῷον Ἰγνάτιον· καὶ συναθροίσας πονηρευομένων ἐν Βλαχέρναις συνέδριον καθαιρεῖ μὴ παρόντα τὸν ἀδικούμενον· καὶ τοὺς ἀπαρνουμένους καθυπογράψαι τοῖς πονηροῖς αὐτοῦ νεύμασι καὶ τῆς κοινωνίας ἀντέχεσθαι πάσης κακουργίας εἰργάσατο καταγώγια, περιορίσας ἔνθα καὶ ὡς ἠβούλετο.

159.

Ἔτι γε μὴν καὶ πρὸς τὸν Ῥώμης πάπαν τὸν μακαρίτην ἐξαποστείλας Νικόλαον ἑκουσίως παραιτησάμενον διὰ γῆρας λιπαρὸν καὶ ἀσθένειαν σώματος Φώτιος ἀνεδίδασκε τὸν Ἰγνάτιον, καὶ πρὸς ἀποβολὴν τελείαν τῆς τῶν εἰκονομάχων αἱρέσεως τοποτηρητὰς πεμφθῆναι αὐτοῦ μεγάλως ἱκέτευεν, Ἰγνατίῳ δόλῳ πραγματευόμενος τὴν κατάκρισιν. Ῥοδοάλδου γὰρ καὶ Ζαχαρίου Ῥωμαίων ἐπισκόπων τοποτηρητῶν καταλαβόντων Κωνσταντινούπολιν Φώτιος ἐν τῷ ναῷ τῶν ἁγίων καὶ πανευφήμων Χριστοῦ ἀποστόλων ἀθετούντων σύνοδον ποιησάμενος, ἀγώγιμον πρὸς αὐτὴν γενέσθαι τὸν ἱεράρχην Ἰγνάτιον παρεσκεύασεν, καὶ ἑβδομήκοντα καὶ δύο

158: HL IV$_1$, 266 (A.D. 859) ‖ 3–4: cf. *Vit. Ignat.*, PG, 105, 513B–C ‖ 4–5: cf. *Epist. Styl.*, Mansi, XVI, 428E ‖ 4–8: *Vit. Ignat.*, PG, 105, 513D; *Epist. Metroph.*, Mansi, XVI, 416D ‖ 4–5 πονηρευομένων - - - συνέδριον: cf. Ps. 21:17, 25:5

159: HL IV$_1$, 272–77 (A.D. 861) ‖ 1–6: cf. *Vit. Ignat.*, PG, 105, 516A–B ‖ 7–16: ibid., 517B–520B

158: 1 γοῦν LG ‖ θείους κανόνας καὶ ἱεροὺς E ‖ 2 ἐστύχησεν (sic) LG ‖ τῷ om. LG ‖ 3 μετὰ om. *z* ‖ 4 πονηρευόμενον LG ‖ 5 μὴ] μὲν *z* ‖ 7 κακουργίας] κακουχίας LG ‖ προορίσας ut vid. A

159: 1 ἐξαπέστειλε *z* ‖ 2 γῆρας λιπαρὸν καὶ om. LG ‖ 3 ἀποβολῆς τελείας LG ‖ τῆς om. LG ‖ 4 αἱρέσεως] ὑπόθεσιν LG ‖ αὐτοῦ om. LG ‖ 5 ἱκέτευσεν *b* ‖ 6 post τοποτηρητῶν add. νικολάου LG ‖ 7 καὶ πανευφήμων] τοῦ A^s ‖ Χριστοῦ] om. LG post ἀποστόλων transp. *z* ‖ 8 ἀποστόλων post ἁγίων transp. E ‖ 9 ἱεράρχην] ἀθῷον LG

158. When Photius, then, took hold of the throne in violation of the divine and sacred canons, he was not content to confine himself to the sins he had committed, but, having moved the Emperor to anger, he banished the innocent Ignatius to the island of Mitylene after innumerable outrages. And bringing together an assembly of evildoers in Blachernae,[204] he condemned the wronged Ignatius in his absence, while those who refused to sign his wicked orders and to maintain communion with him he made receive every kind of ill treatment, confining them where and as he pleased.

159. Going even further, he sent (envoys) to the Pope of Rome, Nicholas of blessed memory, informing him that Ignatius had willingly abdicated because of advanced old age and infirmity of body, and he earnestly entreated him to dispatch his representatives for the purpose of completely eradicating the heresy of image-fighters, (all the while) paving the way by trickery for Ignatius' condemnation.[205] For, when bishops Radoaldus and Zacharias, the Roman representatives, reached Constantinople, Photius held in the Church of Christ's Holy and All-renowned Apostles a synod of those who rejected him (Ignatius) and had the hierarch Ignatius brought before it. And

[204] It is difficult to understand why *SV* places the synod in Blachernae, when all other sources say that it was held in the Church of the Holy Apostles. Dvornik, "Recent Research," 20 note 72, is hardly correct in giving more credence here to *SV*. R. Janin, *La Géographie Ecclésiastique de l'Empire Byzantin. 3. Les Églises et les Monastères,* 2nd ed. (Paris, 1969), 44, is confused in both of his references to Photian synods held in the Holy Apostles. See also Grumel, *Regestes,* no. 459.

[205] While *SV* and *Vita Ignatii* (col. 516A–B) see Photius as the prime mover in seeking a synod to condemn Ignatius, the *Life of Nicholas I* (*Liber Pontificalis,* ed. L. Duchesne, II [Paris, 1886], 155), possibly written by Anastasius the Librarian, attributes the whole initiative to Emperor Michael, and Metrophanes (Mansi, XVI, 416E) says that the Roman legates were sent on imperial request. On the motives see Dvornik, *Photian Schism,* 74–76 and "Recent Research," 21. For a further difference between the sources see Grumel, *Regestes,* no. 466.

ἀγελαίους παραστησάμενος ψευδομάρτυρας πείθει αὐτοὺς λαϊκοὺς ὄντας (ἀπειλὰς παρενείρων ταῖς ὑποσχέσεσιν) ἐπὶ πάσης θείας ὀμόσαι δυνάμεως μὴ ἐψηφίσθαι χρόνους ἕνδεκα, μῆνας τέσσαρας καὶ ἡμέρας εἴκοσιν ἐν τῷ θρόνῳ τὸν πατριάρχην διαδραμόντα Ἰγνάτιον, ἐπαναγνοὺς τῇ συνελεύσει ἀποστολικῆς αὐθεντίας ἀποτομίαν ἔχουσαν οὕτως, «εἴ τις ἐπίσκοπος κοσμικοῖς ἄρχουσι χρησάμενος δι' αὐτῶν ἐγκρατὴς ἐκκλησίας ἐγένετο, καθαιρείσθω», ἀποσιωπήσας τοῦ κανόνος τὸ ἐπαγόμενον καὶ διὰ τοῦτο μόνον αὐτοῦ ἀποφηνάμενος τὴν καθαίρεσιν.

160.

Ὅπερ μαθὼν ὁ ἐν ἁγίοις πάπας Ῥώμης Νικόλαος (οὐ γὰρ ἦν εἰκὸς λαθεῖν τὴν πᾶσαν οἰκουμένην τοσοῦτον ἔργον κακίας εἰς μέσον γενόμενον) τοὺς οἰκείους τοποτηρητὰς ἀκριβῶς ἀνακρίνας καὶ ἀπὸ τῶν στομάτων αὐτῶν δωρολήπτας εὑράμενος, καθαιρέσει διηνεκεῖ Ῥοδόαλδον καὶ Ζαχαρίαν ὑπέβαλε. Καὶ θείαν καὶ ἱερὰν σύνοδον ποιησάμενος Φώτιον ὡς μοιχὸν ἀναθεματίζει καὶ ἐπιβήτορα, τὰ εἰς αὐτὸν καὶ ὑπ' αὐτοῦ πραχθέντα ὁρίσας μένειν ἀπρόσδεκτα· καὶ ἀφορισμὸν τοῖς αὐτῷ κοινωνοῦσι Μιχαὴλ ἀποστείλας τῷ αὐτοκράτορι, Φωτίῳ, ἀρχομένοις καὶ ἄρχουσι, καὶ τοῖς λοιποῖς ὁσίοις πατριάρχαις διεπέμψατο τὰ συνοδικὰ αὐτοῦ.

14–16: can. 30, Rhalles-Potles, Σύνταγμα, II, 37

160: HL IV_1, 326–30 (A.D. 863) ‖ 3–9: *Vit. Ignat.*, PG, 105, 525C–D; cf. *Epist. Metroph.*, Mansi, XVI, 417B ‖ 4–6 et 7–8: cf. *Epist. Styl.*, Mansi, XVI, 429B–C

---

10 μάρτυρας LG ‖ 13 ἐπαναγνοὺς — 16 ἐπαγόμενον om. LG ‖ 15 γένηται *Vit. Ignat.* γένοιτο Rhall.-Potl., II, 37 ‖ 17 ἀποφηνάμενον LG ‖ ad καθαίρεσιν desinunt MNS

160: DLG AEVOT 1 Ῥώμης om. AEVOT ‖ 2 πᾶσαν om. AEVOT ‖ 4 εὑρόμενος D ‖ 5 καὶ ἱερὰν om. A ‖ ποιήσας A ‖ 7 ὁρίσας] ὁρισαμένη codd. praeter LG -άμενος coni. Pa ‖ post μένειν add. καὶ LG ‖ post κοινωνοῦσι add. εἰ μέλλουσι LG ‖ 9 διεπέμψατο AEV: διέπεμψε O, -ψα T διαπεμψάμενος LG -αμένη D ‖ ad διεπέμψατο desinunt OT, Pa

having produced seventy-two false witnesses from among the rabble, he persuaded these men, who were lay, with a combination of promises and threats to swear by every divine power that Ignatius, who spent eleven years, four months, and twenty days[206] on the throne as patriarch, had not been elected. And quoting to the gathering a stricture of apostolic authority which says, "If any bishop has come to power in his church with the help of civil rulers, let him be deposed," he passed over in silence the rest of the canon and therefore pronounced the deposition of him alone.

160. When Nicholas, the Pope of Rome who is among the saints, learned this—for an evil action of such magnitude was not likely to escape the notice of the whole world, once made public—he examined closely his personal representatives, Radoaldus and Zacharias, and discovering from their own mouths that they had accepted gifts, he placed them under perpetual condemnation.[207] And holding a divine and sacred synod, he anathematized Photius as an adulterer and intruder,[208] ruling that the actions taken in his regard and by him never be accepted. And sending a (notice of) excommunication to those in communion with him, to Emperor Michael, Photius, the authorities, and their subjects, he dispatched to the other holy patriarchs his synodical letter.

[206] The *Vita Ignatii* (col. 520A) simply says ὁ δωδεκαετῆ μικροῦ δεῖν χρόνον ἀρχιερατεύσας.

[207] The text suggests that the papal legates were condemned separately before the synod against Photius took place, and Stylianos (Mansi, XVI, 429B) clearly states that two synods were held. The usual and more likely view, however, is that the one synod of 863 took care of these matters, and in fact only one of the legates, Zachary, was judged at this time; cf. Dvornik, *Photian Schism*, 97–98 and HL, IV_1, 326ff.

[208] On these as part of a repertoire of abusive epithets employed in anti-Photian documents, see Dvornik "Recent Research," 43 note 144.

161.

Φώτιος δὲ τὸ καθ' ἑαυτοῦ γνοὺς Νικολάου τοῦ πάπα διάπυρον, Μιχαὴλ συναρπάσας βασιλέα τὸν ἀλλοπρόσαλλον, κρυφηδὸν συγγραψάμενος, ψευδοσύνοδον καὶ δῆθεν τοποτηρητὰς πατριαρχῶν τῶν λοιπῶν συστησάμενος, φωνὰς καὶ ὑπογραφὰς πάντων ἐπισκόπων, πρεσβυτέρων, διακόνων καὶ ἡγουμένων τῶν ὑπ' αὐτὸν κατεγράψατο καὶ πατρικίων, μὴ καθόλου εἰδότων πότε καὶ πῶς καὶ διὰ τί συγκεκίνηται· δι' ὧν καθαίρεσιν καὶ ἀναθεματισμὸν τῷ πάπᾳ Ῥώμης Νικολάῳ τῷ θεοσόφῳ ἀπέστειλε διὰ χειρὸς Ζαχαρίου μητροπολίτου Χαλκηδόνος καὶ Θεοδώρου Καρίας μετελθόντος εἰς Λαοδίκειαν.

162.

Ἀλλ' ἐν ὅσῳ ταῦτα ἠνύετο, Μιχαὴλ τοῦ βασιλέως θείᾳ δίκῃ τὸν βίον τελέσαντος Βασίλειος ὁ φιλόχριστος αὐτοκράτωρ μέγας Ῥωμαίων ἀναγορεύεται, καὶ ζήλῳ κυρίου πυρούμενος, ἵνα τῆς Χριστοῦ ἐκκλησίας πάντα ἐξάρῃ τὰ σκάνδαλα, θείαν καὶ ἱερὰν οἰκουμενικὴν ὀγδόην ἐν Κωνσταντινουπόλει συγκροτηθῆναι ἐθέσπισε σύνοδον. Ἧς ἐξῆρχον προκαθεζόμενοι Ἀδριανοῦ τοῦ πάπα Ῥώμης (Νικόλαος γὰρ πρὸς κύριον ἐξεδήμησε) τοποτηρηταὶ Στέφανος καὶ Δονάτος ἐπίσκοποι καὶ Μαρῖνος διάκονος, Κωνσταντινουπόλεως πατριάρχης Ἰγνάτιος, Μιχαὴλ διάκονος χαρτοφύλαξ καὶ σύγκελλος Μιχαὴλ τοῦ πάπα Ἀλεξανδρείας τὸν τόπον ἐπέχων, Θωμᾶς ἐπίσκοπος Τύρου Νικολάου Ἀντιοχείας Συρίας, καὶ Ἠλίας μοναχός,

---

161: HL IV_1, 442–49 (A.D. 867) ‖ 2–9: *Vit. Ignat.*, PG, 105, 537B–D; cf. *Epist. Metroph.*, Mansi, XVI, 417C–D

162: HL IV_1, 481–537 (A.D. 869–70) ‖ 1–3: cf. *Vit. Ignat.*, PG, 105, 540A ‖ 3–5: cf. ibid., 544B ‖ 5–12: ibid., 544C; Mansi, XVI, 309C–D

161: DLG AEV 1 δὲ] γοῦν LG ‖ 3 τῶν λοιπῶν πατριαρχῶν AEV ‖ 5 καὶ διακόνων D ‖ αὐτῶ D ‖ 6 καθόλου] καθότι AEV ‖ καθαίρεσιν] ἀπάντων καθαίρεσιν LG

162: DLG AEV 2 μέγας] om. A Ῥωμαίων μέγας V ‖ 3 ζήλῳ – 19 ἅπαντες scripsit manus recentior in G ‖ 3 κυρίου] χριστοῦ A ‖ πυρούμενος om. A ‖ Χριστοῦ om. A ‖ 5 κροτηθῆναι LG ‖ 10 Συρίας om. LG

161, 162

161. But Photius, knowing of Pope Nicholas' great anger toward him, won over the fickle Emperor Michael and, making arrangements secretly, brought together a pseudo-synod and so-called[209] representatives of the other patriarchs, in which he recorded the assents and signatures of all bishops, presbyters, deacons, and monastic superiors as well as patricians under his control, who had no idea when or how or why the assembly had taken place. He used these people to send a condemnation and anathema to the Pope of Rome, Nicholas full of divine wisdom, which was carried by Zacharias, the metropolitan of Chalcedon, and Theodore of Caria who had transferred to Laodicea.

162. While these events were taking place, Emperor Michael came to his life's end by divine justice, and the Christ-loving Basil was proclaimed Great Emperor of the Romans. And being fired with zeal for the Lord, he decreed that the divine and sacred Eighth Ecumenical Council[210] be summoned in Constantinople in order to rid Christ's Church of all the scandals. The presiding leaders were the representatives of the Roman Pope Hadrian–Nicholas having departed for the Lord–Bishops Steven and Donatus and deacon Marinus; Ignatius,[211] the Patriarch of Constantinople; Michael[212] the deacon, chartophylax, and syncellus, taking the place of Michael the Patriarch of Alexandria; Thomas, the bishop of Tyre, representing Nicholas[213] of Antioch in Syria; Elias the monk, presbyter, and syncellus for Theodosius

[209] Compare *Vita Ignatii* (col. 537B): ἐκ τῶν ἀνατολικῶν δῆθεν πατριαρχείων τοποτηρητὰς ἐπαγόμενος. On this synod see also Grumel, *Regestes,* no. 482.

[210] This council, having been annulled by the synod of 879–80, lost its ecumenical standing in the eyes of the whole Church until the eleventh century, when it became again for the Roman Church the Eighth Ecumenical Council. See Dvornik, *Photian Schism,* 309–30, and "Recent Research," 47 note 158.

[211] The compiler fails to mention that, after the accession of Basil, Photius was removed from the throne, and Ignatius was reinstated in 867.

[212] The name is wrong; the representative of Alexandria was Joseph, who appears for the first time in the acts of the ninth session; cf. Mansi, XVI, 393C and HL, IV_1, 515–16.

[213] Michael, according to *Vita Ignatii* (col. 544D); in fact the see was vacant at this period, as the acts inform us (Mansi, XVI, 18A).

πρεσβύτερός τε καὶ σύγκελλος Θεοδοσίου Ἱεροσολύμων, Βασίλειός τε καὶ Κωνσταντῖνος οἱ εὐσεβέστατοι αὐτοκράτορες. Ἥτις ἁγία σύνοδος τὰς ἁγίας οἰκουμενικὰς ἑπτὰ συνόδους καὶ τοὺς ἀνέκαθεν αὐτῶν διὰ μέσου πατέρας μακαρίους ἀνακηρύξασα, Νικολάου καὶ Ἀδριανοῦ πάπα Ῥώμης τὰ συνοδικὰ ἐπεκύρωσε, καὶ τὸν Φώτιον ἀναθεματίσασα τὰ εἰς αὐτὸν καὶ δι' αὐτοῦ καὶ ὑπ' αὐτοῦ πάντα γενόμενα δικαίοις ὅροις ἐκκλησιαστικῆς ἀπεβάλετο παραδόσεως. Καὶ οὕτω θεοπρεπῶς τετελείωτο, ἐν τοῖς δεξιοῖς μέρεσι γενομένη τῆς ἁγίας μεγάλης τοῦ σωτῆρος Χριστοῦ ἐκκλησίας ἥνπερ Σοφίαν κατονομάζειν ἀρχῆθεν ἐξεπαιδεύθημεν ἅπαντες.

163.

Μετὰ ταῦτα Φωτίου πρὸς τὸ φιλιάσαι Ἰγνατίῳ πάντα λίθον κινήσαντος, Ἰγνάτιος τὴν μὲν ἀγάπην αὐτοῦ ἀπεδέξατο, ἱερωσύνης δὲ αὐτῷ οὐ μετέδωκε λέγων «εἰ μὴ αὐτὸν οἱ Ῥωμαῖοι προσδέξονται, πρὸς οὓς ἐποίησε τὴν παροινίαν, ἐγὼ ἐξουσίαν οὐκ ἔχω δοῦναι τὴν ἄφεσιν· τὰ γὰρ εἰς ἐμὲ αὐτοῦ πταίσματα συγχωρήσειεν ὁ αἴρων τὴν ἁμαρτίαν τοῦ κόσμου Χριστὸς ὁ θεὸς ἡμῶν· πάντως γὰρ ἐὰν οἱ Ῥωμαῖοι φιλανθρωπεύσωνται εἰς αὐτόν, μετ' ἐκείνων συμπαθὴς κἀγὼ ἔσομαι.»

164.

Πρὸς κύριον δὲ τοῦ μακαρίου Ἰγνατίου ἀπάραντος Φώτιος τῆς Κωνσταντινουπόλεως ἐκκλησίας τὸν θρόνον παρέλαβε· καὶ πρὸς αὐτὸν πᾶς ἐπίσκοπος αὐτῆς ἐστασίασε, καίπερ αὐτοῦ Ἰγνάτιον τὸν μακάριον ἐν τοῖς ἱεροῖς διπτύχοις ἐπὶ τοῦ ἄμβωνος μετὰ πάντων ἁγίων ἀνακηρύττοντος καὶ τῶν πολλῶν τὴν ὀργὴν καταπαύοντος.

17–19: cf. *Vit. Ignat.*, PG, 105, 544D; Mansi, XVI, 309C

163: 1–2: cf. Mansi, XVII, 424C ‖ 3–7: cf. Mansi, XVI, 452D

164: 1–3: cf. Mansi, XVI, 452E–453A; *Vit. Ignat.*, PG 105, 569B–C

---

11 τε om. V ‖ 12 ἁγίας om. A ‖ 13 οἰκουμενικὰς om. LG ‖ αὐτῶν om. LG ‖ 15 καὶ τὸν om. LG ‖ τὰ] καὶ τὰ LG ‖ 16 πάντα om. LG ‖ ad ὅροις finit V ‖ 19 ἀρχῆθεν om. LG ‖ ad ἅπαντες desinunt LG

163: D AE 1 Μετὰ] Μετὰ δὲ D ‖ 7 κἀγὼ ἔσομαι] ἔσομαι πάντως D

164: D AE 1 post ἀπάραντος add. παραυτίκα D ‖ 4 τοῦ om. A

of Jerusalem; and Basil and Constantine the most devout Emperors. Proclaiming the seven holy Ecumenical Councils and the blessed fathers in between them from the beginning, this holy Council confirmed the *synodica* of the Roman Popes Nicholas and Hadrian, and anathematizing Photius, it rejected by just decrees of Church tradition everything done to him and through him and by him. And thus the synod ended in a godly manner, having taken place in the right-hand parts of the great Holy Church of Our Savior Christ, which we have all been taught from the beginning to call Sophia.

163. After this, Photius left no stone unturned in his efforts to show friendship to Ignatius, but, while Ignatius received his love, he did not restore him to the priesthood, saying "If the Romans,[214] who were the targets of his insults, do not receive him, I have no power to grant him pardon. As for his wrongs to me, may they be forgiven by Christ our God 'who takes away the sin of the world.' For, if the Romans show mercy toward him, I shall certainly be sympathetic along with them."

164. When the blessed Ignatius went off to the Lord, Photius took over the throne of the Church in Constantinople, and every bishop there rebelled against him, despite the fact that he proclaimed blessed Ignatius along with all the saints in the sacred diptychs[215] from the ambo and (thus) appeased the anger of most people.

[214] According to the anti-Photian Collection (Mansi, XVI, 452D), Ignatius offered to have the ban on Photius lifted by the patriarchates; Rome was not mentioned by name.

[215] See Dvornik "Recent Research," 55–56.

165.

Ἀδριανοῦ δὲ τοῦ πάπα Ῥώμης τὰ πρόσκαιρα καταλείψαντος καὶ Ἰωάννου τὸν θρόνον αὐτοῦ εὐτυχήσαντος, τοποτηρηταὶ αὐτοῦ κατέλαβον τὸ Βυζάντιον Εὐγένιος καὶ Παῦλος ἐπίσκοποι καὶ Πέτρος πρεσβύτερος· οἳ καὶ συνάρσει Βασιλείου τοῦ φιλοχρίστου ἐν Χριστῷ αὐτοκράτορος τὰ διεστῶτα ἐπισυνάψαντες Φώτιον κατέλιπον εἰρηνεύοντα, κἂν ἀψευδής ἐστιν ὁ εἰπὼν «καθὼς ἐποίησας, ἔσται σοι.»

166.

Βασιλείου γὰρ τὰ πρόσκαιρα καταλιπόντος βασίλεια Λέων τε καὶ Ἀλέξανδρος τῆς βασιλείας ἐγένοντο κάτοχοι, ἀληθῶς αἰώνιοι αὔγουστοι. Φωτίου δὲ χάριν Θεοδώρου τοῦ Σανταβαρηνοῦ τῷ αὐτοκράτορι προσκρούσαντος Λέοντι Θεόδωρος μὲν θυμῷ θεοῦ καὶ ὀργῇ τοῦ βασιλέως ἀπ' ὀμμάτων ἐγένετο, Φώτιος δὲ τῇ ἐν Κωνσταντινουπόλει ἐνδημούσῃ μερικῇ συνόδῳ παραιτήσεως ἐπιδέδωκε λίβελλον, διὰ βαθύτατον γῆρας καὶ σωματικὴν ἀσθένειαν τὰς αἰτίας ἀπαριθμούμενος· ἡ δὲ εὐμαρῶς δεξαμένη αὐτοῦ τὴν παράκλησιν, ὃ ᾐτήσατο ἀπεπλήρωσε· καὶ Στέφανον τῶν αὐτοκρατόρων ὁμοπάτριον καὶ ὁμομήτριον ἀδελφὸν ἐψηφίσατο καὶ τοῦ Βυζαντίου ἱεράρχην ἐποίησεν ἐν Χριστῷ Ἰησοῦ.

165: HL IV_1, 564–606 (A.D. 879–80) ‖ 6: cf. (?) Matt. 7:2

166: HL IV_1, 607–11 (A.D. 886) ‖ 5–8: cf. *Epist. Steph.*, Mansi, XVI, 436E

165: D AE 1 τὰ πρόσκαιρα καταλείψαντος] θανόντος A ‖ 4 ἐν Χριστῷ αὐτοκράτορος] βασιλέως A ‖ 5 συνάψαντες A ‖ post εἰπὼν add. δὲ A

166: D AE 3 σανδαβαρηνοῦ ut vid. A ‖ 3–4 fort. προσκρούοντος A ‖ 7 ἀπαριθμούμενον E ‖ 8 παράκλησιν] evan. A ‖ 10 ad ἐποίησεν finit E ‖ post Ἰησοῦ add. κυρίῳ ἡμῶν, ᾧ ἡ δόξα εἰς τοὺς αἰῶνας, ἀμήν A

165. After Adrian, the Pope of Rome, had left the temporal world and John had obtained the throne, his representatives, the Bishops Eugenius and Paul and the presbyter Peter, came to Byzantium. And these men with the support of Basil, the Christ-loving Emperor in Christ, brought the divided parties together and left Photius reconciled;[216] though the one who has said, "As you have done, so it shall be to you," spoke the truth.

166. For, after Basil's departure from the temporal realms, Leo and Alexander, the truly eternal Augusti, came into possession of the Empire; and when Photius clashed with Emperor Leo on account of Theodore Santabarenus, Theodore lost his eyes by the wrath of God and by the Emperor's anger,[217] while Photius submitted a petition of resignation to the permanent, particular synod in Constantinople, giving as the reasons extreme old age and bodily weakness.[218] For its part the synod readily accepted his request and granted what he asked. And it voted for Steven, the brother of the Emperors by the same father and mother, making him Byzantium's hierarch in Christ Jesus.

[216] The compiler of the anti-Photian Collection vigorously denies that Photius could have been pardoned by Pope John (Mansi, XVI, 453A).

[217] The fall of Photius is here linked directly to his association with Theodore Santabarenos. For details of this relationship, see *Vita Euthymii, ed. cit.* (*supra,* note 33), 37–53; also Dvornik, *Photian Schism,* 243 ff. Santabarenos' blinding is also related by *Vita Euthymii,* 9 lines 13–14.

[218] This is the only text to mention a synod concerned with the abdication. The author reflects that side of the story given to Pope Stephen by Emperor Leo; namely, that the Patriarch had resigned by choice (Mansi, XVI, 436E); the anti-Photian Stylianos, on the other hand, states bluntly that Photius was thrown out by Leo (*ibid.,* 433B). There can be little doubt that he was forced to leave the throne, going through the formality of voluntary resignation. See Dvornik, *Photian Schism,* 247; *id.,* "Recent Research," 44; *Vita Euthymii, ed. cit.,* 38 ff.

APPENDICES

APPENDIX I

The following four scholia are written in the margins of manuscript A (*Sinait. gr. 482*) by the copyist of *SV,* whose small and compressed writing has been rendered even less legible by moisture damage. That they have been deciphered to the present extent is due largely to the efforts of Professor Ihor Ševčenko (who was able to examine the MS at firsthand) and Dr. Pia Schmid. The *Panarion* or treatise against heresies, referred to in the first three of these notes, is not otherwise known.

359v (ad cap. 41) **1.** Εὕρηκα ἐν τοῖς παναρίοις ὡς ὁ Κωνσταντῖνος Παῦλον τὸν ὁμο-| λογητήν, ὃς μετὰ τὸν μέγαν Ἀλέξανδρον ἐπί|σκοπος Κωνσταντινουπόλεως ἦν, εἰς Κουκουσὸν ἐξορί|σας τῆς Ἀρμενίας, Μακεδονίῳ τὴν ἐπι|σκοπὴν παραδίδωσι (?). Ἔμεινεν οὖν ἀπὸ | τότε ἡ καθολικὴ ἐκκλησία κατεχομένη ὑπὸ τῶν Ἀ|ρειανῶν ἔτη μ′ μέχρι Θεοδοσίου τοῦ μεγάλου βασιλέως· | συνάγεται δὲ τὰ μ′ ἔτη οὕτως· Κωνσταντίου ἔτη | κδ′, Ἰουλιανοῦ τοῦ ἀποστάτου ἔτη β′, Ἰοβιανοῦ | μῆνες θ′, Βαλεντινιανοῦ ἔτη ιγ′.

362v (ad cap. 114) **2.** Γέγραπται ἐν τοῖς παναρίοις ὡς ὁ Ἀναστάσιος ἀπεχθῶς εἶχεν | πρὸς τὴν ἐν Κωνσταντινουπόλει σύνοδον. Τὴν μὲν οὖν Αἴγυπτον οἱ (?) | δυοφυσῖται εἶχον ἀπὸ Διοσκόρου χρόνων καὶ (?) τῶν | . . . . τοῦ πάπα τετολμημένων ὡς ἀνωτέρω | . . . . θέλων οὖν ὑπάγεσθαι (?) καὶ τὴν | Ἀντιοχείαν, τὸν Σευῆρον Ἀντιοχείας χειροτονεῖ. Ὃς | τῆς ἐπισκοπῆς . . . . τὴν ἐν Χαλκηδόνι | σύνοδον διέβαλε καὶ Λέοντα τὸν πάπαν Ῥώμης | καὶ κατ᾽ αὐτῶν λόγους ἔγραψαν· ἐποίει δὲ τοῦτο τὸ βού-| λημα τοῦ βασιλέως Ἀναστασίου πληρῶν (?). Ἑξαετῆ δὲ Χριστουπόλεως τὴν | ἐπισκοπὴν κατασχὼν τὴν τελευτὴν ἤκουσε (?) Ἀναστασίου· | φεύγει ἀπὸ Ἀντιοχείας εἰς Ἀλεξάνδρειαν, ἐπειδὴ | οἱ (?) . . . . Διοσκόρου τότε τῆς ἐν Ἀλε|ξανδρείᾳ ἐκράτουν.

362ᵛ (ad capp. 117–18) **3.** Γέγραπται ἐν τοῖς παναρίοις ὡς βασιλεύοντος Ἰουστίνου σύνοδοι παρα|χρῆμα γέγονασιν ἐν διαφόροις ἐπαρχίαις κατὰ Σεβήρου· | ὧν μία ἐστὶν ἐν Κωνσταντινουπόλει γενομένη ἐπὶ Ἰωάννου πατριάρχου | τὸ ἐπίκλην Καππαδόκου· ἑτέρα ἐν Ἰταλίᾳ ἐπὶ | Ὁρμίσδου πάπα Ῥώμης· ἄλλη ἐν Ἱεροσολύμοις ἐπὶ | Ἰωάννου πατριάρχου· ἑτέρα ἐν Τύρῳ, Ἐπιφανίου τότε | μητροπολίτου ὄντος ἐκεῖσε· ἄλλη δὲ ἐν Ἀπαμείᾳ | τῆς δευτέρας Συρίας ἐπὶ Παύλου μητροπολίτου. Τούτων δὲ | πάντων τὰ πρακτικὰ ἐπέμφθησαν εἰς Κωνσταντινούπολιν καὶ ἐ|δέχθησαν παρὰ τοῦ πατριάρχου τότε Ἐπιφανίου.

362ᵛ (in imo mg., ad cap. 120) **4.** Εὕρηκα ἐν τοῖς πρακτικοῖς τῆς ε' συνόδου ὅτι μετὰ τὸ Ἐπιφάνιον τελευτῆσαι τὸν πατριάρχην Κωνσταντινουπόλεως ὁ Τραπεζοῦντος Ἄνθιμος τὸν θρόνον Κωνσταντινουπόλεως ὑφήρπασεν. Ὡς δὲ ἐφωράθη ἐπὶ κακοδοξίᾳ, ὁ πάπας Ῥώμης Ἀγαπητὸς τῇ Κωνσταντινουπόλει ἐνδημ|ήσας (?) τὸ τηνικαῦτα, οὐδὲ εἰς θέαν καθάπαξ παραδέξασθαι αὐτὸν ἠβουλήθη, ἀλλὰ τὴν ὕβριν ἐκδικῶν τῶν κανόνων καὶ τῆς ὀρθῆς πίστεως, ἐξώθησεν αὐτὸν οὐ μοιχικῶς καὶ ἀθέσμως ἐπέβη θρόνου, καὶ ἐχειροτονήθη Μηνᾶς. Ἐζητήθη δὲ ὁ Ἄνθιμος ποιῆσαι τὸν ἐγ|νωσμένον τῷ ἀποστολικῷ θρόνῳ λίβελλον καὶ ἐλευθερῶσαι ἑαυτὸν πάσης αἱρετικῆς πλάνης καὶ ἐξορμῆσαι ἐπὶ τὴν Τραπεζουντίων ἐκκλησίαν ἢ τοῦτο μὴ ἀνεχόμενος τελείως κατακριθῆναι. Ἐπεὶ δὲ ἀφανὴς γέγονε, καθῃρέθη (?).

APPENDIX II

The second version of the *Synodicon Vetus* (see Introduction p. xv) is preserved in these two manuscripts:

F = *Vindobonensis jur. gr. 13,* XVI cent., paper, 347 folios. H. Hunger (– O. Kresten), *Katalog der griechischen Handschriften der Österreichischen Nationalbibliothek,* vol. I, pt. 2 (Vienna, 1969), 25–27.

Apart from canonical pieces by Th. Balsamon, M. Psellos, and *anonymi,* the codex contains writings of Nicephorus I, Gregory of Nyssa, and Alexander the Monk. SV^2 is on fols. 38ʳ–71ᵛ.

4: 3–4: cf. *ACO,* III, 135, 21 ‖ 5–8: ibid., 135, 10–13 ‖ 8–11: ibid., 132, 24–27

H = Athos, *Dionysiou 120,* XIV cent., oriental paper (?). S. P. Lampros, *Catalogue of the Greek Manuscripts on Mount Athos,* I (Cambridge, 1895), 335–38.

The book is composed of a large number of works by various authors, many of them canonical; five of the pieces are found also in F. SV^2 is item no. 39 (Lampros, *ibid.,* 337), written on fols. 645^v–660^v.

F is a slightly more accurate copy than H.

ΣΥΝΟΔΙΚΟΝ
ΕΝ ΕΠΙΤΟΜΗ ΑΠΑΣΑΣ ΤΑΣ ΑΠΟ ΤΩΝ ΑΓΙΩΝ ΑΠΟΣΤΟΛΩΝ ΓΕΓΟΝΥΙΑΣ ΟΡΘΟΔΟΞΟΥΣ ΚΑΙ ΑΙΡΕΤΙΚΑΣ ΠΕΡΙΕΧΟΝ ΣΥΝΟΔΟΥΣ ΕΩΣ ΤΗΣ ΟΡΘΟΔΟΞΙΑΣ

1. Σύνοδος θεία καὶ ἱερὰ συναθροισθεῖσα ἐν Ἱεροσολύμοις ὑπὸ τῶν θεοδιδάκτων ἀποστόλων καὶ μυσταγωγῶν πρεσβυτέρων καὶ τῶν σὺν αὐτοῖς ἀδελφῶν, κατὰ τῶν ἐπιχειρησάντων πιστῶν Φαρισαίων κρατύνειν τὴν ἐν σαρκὶ περιτομὴν καὶ τηρεῖν τὰ νόμιμα ἔθη, μετὰ τὸ εἰσδέξασθαι καθάπαξ τοὺς πιστοὺς τὴν ἐν πνεύματι καὶ ἀληθείᾳ προσκύνησιν καὶ λατρείαν, καὶ χάριτι καὶ νόμῳ δουλεύειν οἱονεὶ δυσὶ κυρίοις, βιαζομένων· ὅπερ ἀπεῖπεν ὁ τῶν ὑπὲρ νοῦν ἀγαθῶν πάροχος καὶ τῆς κατάρας τοῦ νόμου ἐξαγορασάμενος ἡμᾶς Χριστός· ἐμφέρεται γὰρ ἐν ταῖς πράξεσι τῶν ἀποστόλων ταῦτα, «ἔδοξε τοῖς πρεσβυτέροις καὶ τοῖς ἀποστόλοις σὺν ὅλῃ τῇ ἐκκλησίᾳ ἐκλεξαμένους ἄνδρας ἐξ αὐτῶν πέμψαι εἰς Ἀντιόχειαν σὺν Παύλῳ καὶ Βαρνάβᾳ Ἰούδαν τὸν καλούμενον Βαρσαβᾶν καὶ Σίλαν, ἄνδρας ἡγουμένους ἐν τοῖς ἀδελφοῖς, γράψαντες διὰ χειρῶν αὐτῶν τάδε· "Οἱ ἀπόστολοι καὶ οἱ πρεσβύτεροι καὶ οἱ ἀδελφοὶ τοῖς κατὰ Ἀντιόχειαν καὶ Συρίαν καὶ Κιλικίαν ἀδελφοῖς ἐξ ἐθνῶν χαίρειν. Ἐπειδὴ ἠκούσαμεν ὥς τινες ἐξ ἡμῶν ἐξελθόντες ἐτάραξαν ὑμᾶς λόγοις ἀνασκευάζοντες τὰς ψυχὰς ὑμῶν, λέγοντες περιτέμνεσθαι καὶ τηρεῖν τὸν νόμον, οἷς οὐ διεστειλάμεθα, ἔδοξε δὲ ἡμῖν γενομένοις ὁμοθυμαδὸν ἐκλεξαμένους ἄνδρας πέμψαι πρὸς ὑμᾶς σὺν τῷ ἀγαπητῷ ἡμῶν Βαρνάβᾳ καὶ τῷ Παύλῳ, ἀνθρώποις παραδεδωκόσι τὰς ψυχὰς ὑπὲρ τοῦ ὀνόματος τοῦ κυρίου ἡμῶν Ἰησοῦ Χριστοῦ. Ἀπεστάλκαμεν οὖν Ἰούδαν καὶ Σίλαν καὶ αὐτοὺς διὰ λόγου ἀπαγγέλλοντας τὰ αὐτά· ἔδοξε γὰρ τῷ ἁγίῳ πνεύματι καὶ ἡμῖν μηδὲν πλέον ἐπιτί-

---

1: 13–28: Act. 15:22–29

1: 2 ἀπάσας om. F ‖ 7 φαρισσαίων H ‖ 15–16 ἡγουμένας F ‖ 24–25 ἀπαγγέλλοντες H θεσθαι ὑμῖν βάρος πλὴν τῶν ἐπάναγκες τούτων, ἀπέχεσθαι εἰδωλοθύτων, αἵματος καὶ πνικτοῦ καὶ πορνείας, ἐξ ὧν διατηροῦντες ἑαυτοὺς εὖ πράξεσθε. Ἔρρωσθε."»

Σύνοδος ἡ ἐν Λουγδούνῳ. Μετὰ γοῦν τὴν τῶν ἀποστόλων σύνοδον ἐξανέστη Σίμων μάγος καὶ Κήρινθος· οὓς ἀπεκήρυξαν οἱ κορυφαῖοι, τὸν μὲν Σίμωνα Πέτρος, τὸν δὲ Κήρινθον Ἰωάννης ὁ τῆς θεολογίας ἐπώνυμος. Μετὰ δὲ τούτους ἀνέστη Οὐαλεντῖνος, καὶ Σεκοῦνδος, Μαρκίων, Βασιλείδης, Σατορνῖλος, Καρποκράτης, Ἐβιωναῖοι, Ἑρμογένης, Ἀλέξανδρος, καὶ οἱ σὺν αὐτοῖς, οἳ ἐλέγχονται μὲν ὑπὸ τῶν μαθητῶν τῶν ἁγίων ἀποστόλων· ἐξαιρέτως δὲ στηλιτεύονται ὑπὸ Εἰρηναίου τοῦ ἱερομάρτυρος Λουγδούνων.

2. Σύνοδος θεία καὶ ἱερὰ τοπικὴ κατὰ θεοῦ χάριν συναθροισθεῖσα ἐν Λουγδούνῳ, ἥτις ἐστὶ μητρόπολις τῆς Γαλλίας παρὰ τὸν Ῥοδανὸν ποταμόν, ὑπὸ Εἰρηναίου τοῦ ἱερομάρτυρος κατὰ τῶν προγεγραμμένων αἱρετικῶν, προκαθηρημένων μετὰ τῆς αὐτῆς συνόδου ὄντων δώδεκα καθῶς ὑπόκεινται, Οὐαλεντίνου, Μαρκίωνος, Σεκούνδου, Βασιλείδου, Καρποκράτου, Ἑρμογένους, Ἐβιωναίων, Σατορνίνου, Ἀλεξάνδρου, καὶ τῶν λοιπῶν.

3. Σύνοδος ἐν Ῥώμῃ ἰδική, ὑπὸ Τελεσφόρου ἱερομάρτυρος καὶ ἑτέρων ιβʹ, τοῦ ταύτης πάπα, κατὰ Θεοδότου τοῦ Βυζαντίου καὶ τοῦ αὐτοῦ μαθητοῦ, ὃς εἰς ἄκρον σοφίας ἐληλακὼς καὶ ἐν τῷ διωγμῷ ἐπιθύσας καὶ ἐξαρνησάμενος, ἔσχατον δὲ ὑπὸ τῶν πιστῶν ὀνειδιζόμενος, μὴ φέρων τὴν αἰσχύνην, εἰπεῖν ἐτόλμησεν «ἐγὼ θεὸν οὐκ ἐξωμοσάμην, ἀλλ' ἢ ἄνθρωπον ψιλόν·» παρ' οὗ οἱ λεγόμενοι Θεοδοτιανοί· ὑπόκειται Θεόδοτος καὶ Θεοδοτιανοί.

---

28 πράξεσθαι F ‖ 32 οὐαμεντῖνος codd.

2: 2 λουγδόνω H ‖ γαλίας codd.

3: 3 ἐν τῷ] αὐτῷ F

4. Σύνοδος τοπικὴ ἐν Ῥώμῃ ὑπὸ τοῦ μακαριωτάτου Ἀνικήτου τοῦ ταύτης πάπα καὶ Πολυκάρπου ἱερομάρτυρος Σμύρνης καὶ ἑτέρων ἐπισκόπων, κατὰ τῶν Ἰουδαικῶς τῇ ιδ′ ἑορταζόντων τὸ πάσχα καὶ ἑτέροις ἔθεσι καὶ τύποις τοῦτο ἐκτελούντων· ὁρίσασα τὸ μὲν φρικτὸν καὶ σωτήριον πάθος τοῦ κυρίου ἡμῶν Ἰησοῦ Χριστοῦ τῇ ἁγίᾳ παρασκευῇ μυστικῶς ἐπιτελεῖν, τὴν δὲ ζωαρχικὴν ἀνάστασιν αὐτῇ τῇ ἡμέρᾳ καὶ παραδόξῳ κυριακῇ ἐκ παντὸς τρόπου ἄγειν.

5. Σύνοδος μερικὴ ἐν Ἱεραπόλει τῆς Ἀσίας ὑπὸ Ἀπολιναρίου τοῦ ταύτης ὁσιωτάτου ἐπισκόπου καὶ ἑτέρων κς′ ἀποκηρύξασά τε καὶ ἐκκόψασα Μοντανὸν καὶ Μαξιμίλαν τοὺς ψευδοπροφήτας, οἳ καὶ βλασφήμως ἤτοι δαιμονιῶντες, καθὼς φησιν ὁ αὐτὸς πατήρ, «τὸν βίον κατέστρεψαν.» Καὶ σὺν αὐτοῖς κατέκρινεν ἡ αὐτὴ ἁγία σύνοδος καὶ Θεόδοτον τὸν σκυτέα.

6. Σύνοδος μερικὴ ἡ ἐν Ἀσίᾳ ὑπὸ τοῦ ὁσιωτάτου ἐπισκόπου Ἀχελῶν Σωτᾶ καὶ ἑτέρων ιβ′· ἥτις ἁγία σύνοδος ἐλέγξασα, ἀπεκήρυξε Θεόδοτον καὶ Μοντανὸν καὶ Μαξιμίλαν, ὡς η′ αἰῶνας δογματίζοντας καὶ πνεῦμα ἅγιον ἑαυτοὺς ἐπιφημίζοντας· ὡσαύτως δὲ καὶ Μαξιμίλαν τὴν ἀπατηλὸν καὶ ὁμόφρονα.

7. Σύνοδος τοπικὴ ἐν Γαλλίᾳ ὑπὸ τῶν ὁμολογητῶν, ἀποκηρύξασα τὸν αὐτὸν Μοντανὸν καὶ Μαξιμίλαν, ἧς ὁ ὅρος πρὸς τοὺς ἐν Ἀσίᾳ πιστούς.

8. Σύνοδος ἀφελὴς ἀνεξέταστος μερικὴ ἐν Ἐφέσῳ μητροπόλει τῆς Ἀσίας ὑπὸ Πολυκράτους τοῦ ταύτης ὁσιωτάτου ἀρχιεπισκόπου, ὁρίζουσα καὶ ἀξιοῦσα ἅπαντας ὡς ἂν τῇ ιδ′ Ἰουδαιοπρεπῶς ἄγειν τὸ μυστικὸν πάσχα, ὡς τοῦτο ἀνέκαθεν παρειληφυῖα βεβαιούμενον παρὰ Τιμοθέου καὶ Φιλίππου τῶν ἀποστόλων. Βίκτωρ οὖν ὁ τῆς Ῥώμης ἁγιωτάτης ἐκκλησίας πάπας ἀκοινωνησίαν στέλλει Πολυκράτει τῷ ταύτης ἐξάρχῳ καὶ

4: 6 ἡμέρᾳ καὶ παραδόξῳ] leg. μεγάλῃ καὶ περιδόξῳ cum SV^1

6: 4 τὴν] τὸν codd.

7: 1 γαλία codd. ‖ 3 post πιστούς intelligendum διέβη (cf. SV^1) vel sim.

8: 4 τούτου H ‖ 6 πολυκάρπω H

προϊσταμένῳ· οὐ μόνον δέ, ἀλλὰ καὶ συνοδικῶς τὰ περὶ τῆς τοιαύτης ἑορτῆς διεξέρχεται, καὶ σὺν αὐτῷ ἐν πλείσταις ἐπαρχίαις καὶ μέρεσι τῆς γῆς σύνοδοι κροτοῦνται καὶ συμφώνως ὁρίζουσι. Ταῦτα δὲ βασιλεύοντος Κομόδου τοῦ βασιλέως γέγονε.

9. Σύνοδος τοπικὴ ἐν Ῥώμῃ ὑπὸ τοῦ μακαριωτάτου πάπα Βίκτορος καὶ ἑτέρων ιδ′, ἀπαγορεύουσα κατὰ τὴν πρὸ αὐτῆς ἁγίαν σύνοδον Ἰουδαϊκῶς μὴ τελεῖν τῇ ιδ′ τὸ θεῖον καὶ μυστικὸν πάσχα, ἀλλ' ἐν μόνῃ τῇ μεγάλῃ κυριακῇ.

10. Σύνοδος τοπικὴ ἐν Ἱεροσολύμοις ὑπὸ Ναρκίσου τοῦ τρισμακαρίστου αὐτῆς ἀρχιεπισκόπου καὶ ἑτέρων ιδ′, ὑπὲρ τοῦ μακαρίου καὶ μυστικοῦ πάσχα ὁρίσασα κατὰ τοὺς μακαρίους Ἀνίκητον καὶ Βίκτορα.

11. Σύνοδος τοπικὴ ἐν Καισαρείᾳ τῆς Παλαιστίνης, ἡ παρά τισι πάλαι λεγομένη Στράτωνος πύργος, ὑπὸ Θεοφίλου τοῦ ταύτης ὁσιωτάτου ἐπισκόπου καὶ ἑτέρων ιβ′, ὑπὲρ τοῦ ἁγιωτάτου πάσχα ὁρίσασα κατὰ τοὺς προειρημένους Ἀνίκητον καὶ Βίκτορα.

12. Σύνοδος ἐν Λουγδούνῳ τῆς Γαλλίας τοπικὴ ὑπὸ Εἰρηναίου τοῦ ταὐτης ὁσιωτάτου ἀρχιεπισκόπου καὶ ἑτέρων ιγ′, ὁρίσασα ὡσαύτως περὶ τοῦ θείου καὶ μυστικοῦ πάσχα.

13. Σύνοδος τοπικὴ ἐν Κορίνθῳ ὑπὸ Βακχυλίδου τοῦ ταύτης ὁσιωτάτου ἀρχιεπισκόπου καὶ ἑτέρων ιβ′, ὁρίσασα ὡσαύτως.

14. Σύνοδος τοπικὴ ἐν Ἀσίᾳ ὑπὸ Πλάσμα καὶ ἑτέρων ιβ′, ὁρίσασα ὡσαύτως περὶ τοῦ ἁγίου πάσχα.

15. Σύνοδος τοπικὴ ἐν Ὀσρυίνῃ, ὑφ' ἣν καὶ ἡ Ἔδεσσα καὶ ἡ τῶν Ἀδιαβηνῶν γῆ, βασιλεύοντος Κομόδου, ὁρίσασα περὶ τοῦ ἁγίου πάσχα ὡσαύτως. Καὶ ἦσαν οἱ εὑρεθέντες ὁμοῦ ιη′· οὐκ ἔχω δὲ λέγειν ὅστις προεκάθητο.

12: 1 γαλίας codd.

16. Σύνοδος τοπικὴ ἐν Μεσοποταμίᾳ περὶ τοῦ ἁγίου πάσχα ὁρίσασα ὡσαύτως· οὐδεὶς δὲ τῶν ἱστορικῶν ἔφησεν ὅστις προεκάθητο, ἀλλ' ἢ μόνον ὅτι ἐπὶ τοῦ Κομόδου γεγένηται. Ἦσαν δὲ οἱ εὑρηθέντες ιη'.

17. Σύνοδος τοπικὴ ἐν Βόστρᾳ, ἥτις ἐστὶ ἐν τῇ παλαιᾷ Ἀρραβίᾳ ὑπὸ Ὠριγένους τοῦ πολυμαθοῦς, ἐπὶ διορθώσει τοῦ ἱεροσόφου Βυρίλου, τοῦ τῆς αὐτῆς πόλεως Βόστρων· ἥντινα Βόστραν ὁ Ἠσαΐας πάλαι Βόθρον ὠνόμασεν, ἐπώνυμον οὖσαν Βοσόρας τῆς μητρὸς τοῦ θεσπεσίου Ἰώβ· ὅστις Βύριλλος εἰς τὸ Θεοδότου φρόνημα μικροῦ δεῖν οὐκ οἶδ' ὅπως παρασυρείς, λόγου θᾶττον εὖ ποιῶν ἐπὶ τῇ ἀληθεῖ ὁμολογίᾳ ταῖς παραινέσεσιν Ὠριγένους παλινδρομεῖ.

18. Σύνοδος τοπικὴ ἐν Ἀρραβίᾳ ὑπὸ Ὠριγένους τοῦ πολυμαθοῦς, ἐπὶ τῇ διορθώσει τῶν ἐν Ἀρραβίᾳ πιστῶν, οἳ συμφθείρεσθαι τοῖς σώμασι τὰς ψυχὰς οἰηθέντες καὶ αὖθις ἄμφω συνανίστασθαι, ἔκ τινος λοιμώδους αἱρέσεως ἐν αὐτοῖς αὐτίκα ἀναφανείσης καὶ ἐπὶ μήκιστον διαδοθείσης, τῇ παραινέσει τοίνυν Ὠριγένους παραχρῆμα τὴν παλινῳδίαν ᾖσαν. Ὠριγένης προεκάθητο καὶ ἕτεροι ιδ'.

19. Σύνοδος μερικὴ ἐν Ῥώμῃ ἐπὶ Βίκτορος τοῦ ἁγιωτάτου πάπα καὶ ἑτέρων ιδ', ἀποκηρύξασα Θεόδοτον, Ἐβιωναίους καὶ Ἀρτέμωνα, τοὺς μικροῦ δεῖν οὐχ ἧττον τῇ πίστει Ἰουδαίους· καὶ οὗτοι γὰρ ἀρχηγοὶ γεγένηνται Παύλου καὶ Νεστορίου.

20. Σύνοδος τοπικὴ ἐν Ῥώμῃ ὑπὸ τοῦ μακαριωτάτου πάπα Βίκτορος συναθροισθεῖσα καὶ ἀποκηρύξασα Σαβέλλιον καὶ Νόϊτον, τοὺς ἐπὶ τῆς τρισυποστάτου <θεότητος> συναλειφὴν καὶ συναίρεσιν οὐσίας πρεσβεύοντας, καὶ Οὐαλεντιανὸν τὸν οὐράνιον (σὺν ἄλλοις πολλοῖς ἀτοπήμασι) τὸ σῶμα Χριστοῦ δογματίζοντα.

17: 2 Βυρίλου] sic codd. (cf. lin. 5)

18: 1 τοῦ om. F ‖ 4 ἐπιμήκιστον codd.

20: 3 θεότητος ex SV^{1}

21. Σύνοδος μακαρίων πατέρων ἐν Ῥώμῃ συναθροισθεῖσα ὑπὸ Κορνηλίου τοῦ μακαριωτάτου πάπα καὶ ἑτέρων ιη', ἀποκηρύξασα Ναυάτον τὸν τῶν μετανοεῖν ἑλομένων παγίδα καὶ βρόχον γεγονότα.

22. Σύνοδος τοπικὴ ἐν Καρθαγένῃ ὑπὸ Κυπριανοῦ τοῦ ἱερομάρτυρος συναθροισθεῖσα, ἐν Καρθαγένῃ τῆς Ἀφρικῆς, ἡ καὶ Νεάπολις λεγομένη, [τοῦ ταύτης ἐπισκόπου Κυπριανοῦ,] ἀποκηρύξασα τὸν αὐτὸν Ναυάτον ὡς τὴν μετανοίαν ἀποκλείοντα τοῖς πταίουσι.

23. Σύνοδος τοπικὴ <ἐν Ἀντιοχείᾳ> ὑπὸ Δημητριανοῦ τοῦ ταύτης ἁγιωτάτου ἐπισκόπου, ἥτις ἁγία σύνοδος καθεῖλε Ναυάτον τὸν φιλαμαρτήμονα.

24. Σύνοδος μερικὴ ἐν Ἀλεξανδρείᾳ συναθροισθεῖσα ὑπὸ Διονυσίου
(25.) τοῦ ὁμολογητοῦ, τοῦ ταύτης ἀρχιερέως <. . .> καταδικάσασα καὶ ἀποκηρύξασα καὶ μετὰ θάνατον Νεποτιανὸν ἐπίσκοπον Αἰγύπτου καὶ Κήρινθον, ὡς διαβεβαιουμένους καὶ ἀπατῶντας πλείστους ἐν τῇ ἐπιγείῳ Ἱερουσαλὴμ τὴν Χριστοῦ βασιλείαν εἶναι, καὶ τὴν χιλιονταετηρίδα δογματίζοντας, καὶ πρὸς τούτοις τὰς βουθυσίας καὶ μηλοσφαγίας νομοθετοῦντας.

26. Σύνοδος μερικὴ ἐν Ῥώμῃ συναθροισθεῖσα ὑπὸ Στεφάνου ἱερομάρτυρος πάπα, ἀποκηρύξασα τοὺς ἐν Ἀφρικῇ καὶ ἐν Συνάδοις παραλόγως ἐπικεχειρηκότας ἀναβαπτίζειν τοὺς ἐκ πάσης αἱρέσεως προσερχομένους τῇ καθολικῇ ἐκκλησίᾳ.

21: 2–3 ναβάτον H

22: 3 τοῦ – Κυπριανοῦ om. F

23: 1 ἐν Ἀντιοχείᾳ ex SV^1 ‖ 2 ναβάτον H

24: 2 lacuna (cf. SV^1)

26: 2 Συνάδοις] immo συνόδοις (τοὺς ἐν τῇ Ἀφρικῇ συνόδῳ SV^1)

27. Σύνοδος τοπικὴ ἐν Ἀντιοχείᾳ, ἧς ἔξαρχος Ἕλενος ὁ Ταρσοῦ, Θεόδωρος καὶ Γρηγόριος ὁ θαυματουργὸς λεγόμενος, Λαοδικείας Ἀνατόλιος ἱερόσοφος, οὗτινος οἱ περὶ τὸ πάσχα κανόνες ἐκφέρονται, καὶ Μαλχίων πρεσβύτερος καὶ Ἀντιοχείας ὁ ἱερός, καθελοῦσα καὶ ἀποκηρύξασα Παῦλον τὸν μηδὲν ἧττον Ἄννα καὶ Καϊάφα ἐπὶ Χριστοῦ πρεσβεύοντα, ὃς καὶ ἐκ Σαμοσάτων ὁ ἀνόσιος τὸ γένος ἦν.

28. Σύνοδος μερικὴ ἐν Μεσοποταμίᾳ ὑπὸ Ἀρχελάου τοῦ ὁσιωτάτου ἐπισκόπου Καρχάρων καὶ Διοδώρου ἱερέως Δωριάδος πρεσβυτέρου, κατὰ Μάνεντος †παρεβώδους·† ἥτις πολυτρόπως τοῦτον ἐλέγξασα ἀπεκήρυξε.

29. Σύνοδος τοπικὴ ἐν Ῥώμῃ ἐπὶ Μιλτιάδου τοῦ ἁγιωτάτου ταύτης ἐπισκόπου καὶ Μάρκου τοῦ ὁσιωτάτου καὶ Κεκιλιανοῦ ἐπισκόπου Καρθαγένης, ἐπὶ τῇ ἑνώσει τῶν ἐπισκόπων. Ταύτην τοίνυν καὶ τὴν ἐν Ἀρελάτῳ συγκροτηθῆναι ὁ μέγας Κωνσταντῖνος κελεύσας, ἀπάρας ἀπὸ τῶν ἑσπερίων ἐπὶ τὰ ἑῷα χωρεῖ ἀμεταστρεπτί, μὴ τεθεακὼς Σίλβεστρον ἐπίσκοπον ἐν τῷ θρόνῳ Ῥώμης, μήτε ἐπὶ αὐτοῦ ὑποχωρήσας, ἀλλ᾽ ἐπὶ Μιλτιάδου· ὅθεν ἀληθέστερον ἐπικρατεῖ, μὴ βεβαπτίσθαι αὐτὸν ἐν Ῥώμῃ, ἀλλ᾽ ἐν Νικομηδείᾳ.

30. Σύνοδος τοπικὴ ἐν Ἀρελάτῳ ἐπὶ Χρηστοῦ ὁσιωτάτου ἐπισκόπου Συρρακούσης τῆς Σικελίας καὶ τοῦ αὐτοῦ Κεκιλιανοῦ ἐπισκόπου Καρθαγένης ἐπὶ τῇ ἑνώσει τῶν ἐπισκόπων.

31. Σύνοδος ἐν Ἀγκύρᾳ τῆς Γαλατῶν, ἧς ἔξαρχος Μάρκελλος τῆς αὐτῆς Ἀγκύρας ἐπίσκοπος καὶ Ἀγρικόλαος Καισαρείας Καππαδοκίας, τυπώσασα τὴν διόρθωσιν τῶν ἐν τῷ διωγμῷ παραπεπτωκότων καὶ πάλιν μετανοησάντων, ἧς οἱ φερόμενοι κανόνες· ὑπῆρχον δὲ καὶ ἐν αὐτῇ πατέρες δώδεκα.

27: 4 καὶ[1] delendum ut vid. ‖ 6 σαμωσάτων codd.

28: 3 leg. τοῦ ἐρεβώδους cum *SV*[1]

29: 2 κελιανοῦ H ‖ 7 ἐπικρατεῖ] ἐστι κρατεῖν *SV*[1]

31: 2 καππαδόκου H

32. Σύνοδος ἐν Νεοκαισαρείᾳ περὶ τῶν ἐν διωγμῷ ἐπιθυσάντων ἢ ἐξομοσαμένων ἢ εἰδωλοθύτων γευσαμένων· ἥτις ἁγία σύνοδος πρὸς τὴν διαφορὰν τῆς παραβάσεως ἀναλόγως τὴν διόρθωσιν κανονικῶς διετύπωσεν, ἧς οἱ κανόνες πρόδηλοι· ὑπῆρχον δὲ πατέρες κγʹ, ὧν ἔξαρχος Βιτάλιος. Διοκλητιανοῦ τοίνυν καὶ Μαξιμιανοῦ, τοῦ καὶ Ἑρκουλίου, καὶ Μαξιμιανοῦ τοῦ Γαλερίου, Μαξιμίνου τε καὶ Μαξεντίου τῶν ἀνοσιουργῶν τυράννων αἰσχρῶς τὸν βίον καταστρεψάντων, ὁ θειότατος Κωνσταντῖνος αὐτοκράτωρ ἑῴας καὶ ἑσπερίας ἀναδείκνυται· ὃς οὐκ ἀπ' ἀνθρώπων, οὐδὲ δι' ἀνθρώπων, ἀλλ' οὐρανόθεν ἀποστολικῶς κληθείς, καὶ τὸν χριστιανισμὸν ἀσπασάμενος, ἐν τούτοις ἐκραταιοῦτο. Ἡ μὲν οὖν ἁγία ἐκκλησία τοῦ Χριστοῦ ἐγεγήθει κατὰ τὸ εἰκός, καὶ χορείας ἀνάπλεως καὶ θυμηδίας ἀνάμεστος· ὁ δὲ παμπόνηρος δαίμων καὶ τῶν εὐσεβούντων ἀλάστωρ, τεθεακὼς τὸν Ἑλληνισμὸν ἤδη ἐκποδὼν γεγονότα, ἐμφιλοχωρεῖ ἐν τοῖς τῆς χριστιανικῆς προσηγορίας μὲν ἠξιωμένοις, φιλαρχίᾳ δὲ καὶ κενῇ δόξῃ δουλουμένοις. Δηλώσει δὲ τούτους ὑποκατιὼν ὁ λόγος.

33. Μελέτιος τοίνυν ἀρχιεπίσκοπος Θηβαΐδος ἐν τοῖς διωγμοῖς ἐπιθύσας καὶ ἑτέροις ἐγκλήμασι φωραθείς, οὐκ ἐφ' οἷς ἥμαρτεν ἠρυθρία· ὁ δὲ μακαριώτατος Πέτρος τῆς Ἀλεξανδρείας ὡς ἀποστολικοῖς ἑπόμενος δόγμασι, πρὶν ἢ τὸν τοῦ μαρτυρίου στέφανον ἀναδήσηται, τοῦτον καθεῖλε καὶ τῆς ἐκκλησίας ἀπεκήρυξεν· Ἄρειον δὲ διάκονον ὄντα, ὡς ἑτερούσιον τοῦ πατρὸς πρεσβεύοντα τὸν θεὸν λόγον, καὶ τὸ «ἐξ οὐκ ὄντων» καὶ τὸ «ἦν ποτε ὅτε οὐκ ἦν» ὁ υἱὸς τοῦ θεοῦ καὶ πατρὸς τερατολογοῦντα, διακονεῖν καθάπαξ κεκώλυκε. Πέτρου δὲ μακαρίως τὸν βίον ἀπολιπόντος, Ἀχιλᾶς τοῦτον διαδέχεται· Ἄρειος δὲ τῇ αἱρέσει καὶ τῇ φιλαρχίᾳ ἔτι ἐμμένων καὶ τοῖς Μελετίου τολμήμασι συμπράττων, εἶτα δελεάσας καὶ πρός γε τὸν μακαριώτατον Ἀχιλᾶν, χειροτονεῖται ὑπ' αὐτοῦ πρεσβύτερος καὶ τοῦ ἐν Ἀλεξανδρείᾳ διδασκαλίου προΐσταται. Ἀχιλᾶ δὲ οὐ μετὰ πολὺ τελειωθέντος, Ἀλέξανδρος ὁ τῶν ἀποστολικῶν δογμάτων ὑπέρμαχος τοῦτον διαδέχεται. Ὁ δὲ προλεχθεὶς Ἄρειος, ὡς μὴ προκριθεὶς Ἀλεξάνδρου, μειζόνως τῇ φιλαρχίᾳ ἀναφλέγεται, ἀποσπάσας δὲ τῆς ἐκκλησίας Εὐζῴϊον τὸν διάκονον καὶ Ἀειθαλᾶ καὶ ἑτέρους, φατριάζει κατὰ Ἀλεξάνδρου καὶ τῆς ἐκκλησίας, κρατῦναι πειρώμενος τὸ ἑτεροούσιον. Ὁ δὲ μακαριώτατος Ἀλέξανδρος ὁρῶν ὑπὸ Ἀρείου λυμαινομένην τὴν ἐκκλησίαν καὶ τῶν σὺν αὐτῷ,

---

32: 2 ἐξομολογησαμένων F ‖ 6 γαλλερίου F ‖ 13 ἐκ ποδῶν codd. ‖ τῆς om. H

33: 3 τῆς om. H ‖ 16 κατὰ] κατὰ τοῦ H

πολλαῖς νουθεσίαις καὶ παραινέσεσι χρησάμενος, ἰδὼν τούτων τὸ ἀνεπίστροφον, ἐπὶ τὴν ἀποστολικὴν διάταξιν χωρεῖ, τὴν λέγουσαν «αἱρετικὸν ἄνθρωπον μετὰ μίαν καὶ δευτέραν νουθεσίαν παραιτοῦ.»

34. Σύνοδος ὁσίων μερική· μερικὴ δέ ἐστιν, ὡς φέρε εἰπεῖν, τῶν προσφάτως καὶ προχείρως εὑρισκομένων καὶ κληρικῶν πρόσκλησις· ἥτις ἁγία σύνοδος συγκληθεῖσα ὑπὸ Ἀλεξάνδρου τοῦ μακαρίου Ἀλεξανδρείας ἀπεκήρυξε καὶ ἀναθέματι καθυπέβαλεν ὡς ἐμμένοντα τῇ ἀπειθείᾳ καὶ σηπεδόνα τῷ σώματι τῆς Χριστοῦ ἐκκλησίας γενόμενον Ἄρειον, Εὐζώϊον, Ἀχιλᾶν, Ἀειθαλᾶ, Λούκιον, Σαρμάτιον, Ἰούλιον, Μηνᾶν, Ἄρειον ἕτερον, Ἑλλάδιον. Γράφει δὲ ὁ αὐτὸς Ἀλέξανδρος τόμον τῆς αὐτοῦ καθαιρέσεως ἁπανταχοῦ· ὅντινα τόμον ἐνυπόγραφον δεξάμενοι καὶ ἀποδεξάμενοι οἵ τε τῆς Λιβύης ἐπίσκοποι καὶ Ἀλέξανδρος ὁ Μακάριος, ἐκύρωσάν τε καὶ ἐβεβαίωσαν. Γράφει δὲ καὶ Ἄρειος πρὸς Εὐσέβιον τὸν Νικομηδείας τήν τε οἰκείαν καθαίρεσιν καὶ τὸ δυσσεβὲς φρόνημα, ὡσαύτως καὶ Εὐσεβίῳ τῷ Παλαιστινῷ, οἳ ὁμονοήσαντες τῇ ἀσεβείᾳ παρατάσσονται δυνάμει καὶ κακουργίᾳ πολλῇ κατὰ τοῦ Ἀλεξάνδρου καὶ τῆς τοῦ θεοῦ ἐκκλησίας· ὅθεν ὁ φιλόχριστος Κωνσταντῖνος σύνοδον συγκροτηθῆναι θεσπίζει ἐν Νικαίᾳ τῇ μητροπόλει· ἐν ᾗ προκαθέζεται Ἀλέξανδρος μεθ' ἑτέρων κ', καὶ καταδικάζεται Ἄρειος, Εὐζώϊος, Ἀχιλᾶς, Ἀειθαλῆς, Ἄρειος ἄλλος, Λούκιος, Σαρμάτιος, Ἑλλάδιος, Μηνᾶς, Ἰούλιος.

35. Σύνοδος οἰκουμενικὴ ἐν Νικαίᾳ τῶν τιη' πατέρων, ἧς ἡγεμόνες Βίτος, Βικέντιος πρεσβύτεροι, τὸν τόπον ἐπέχοντες Σιλβέστρου καὶ τοῦ διαδόχου αὐτοῦ Ἰουλίου, Ὅσιος ἐπίσκοπος Κουδρούβης, Ἀλέξανδρος Ἀλεξανδρείας, Μακάριος Ἱεροσολύμων, Εὐστάθιος Ἀντιοχείας, καὶ ἐκ προσώπου Μητροφάνους ἀρχιεπισκόπου Κωνσταντινουπόλεως Ἀλέξανδρος πρεσβύτερος. Ἥτις ἁγία σύνοδος τὸ ὁμοούσιον ἐπὶ τῆς ἁγίας τριάδος τρανώσασα καὶ τὸ θεῖον μυστικὸν πάσχα κατὰ τοὺς πρὸ αὐτῆς ὁρίσασα, ἐξέθετο τὸ θεουργὸν τῆς πίστεως μάθημα κατὰ πάσης αἱρέσεως, Ἀρείου, Σαβελλίου, Φωτεινοῦ, Παύλου τοῦ Σαμοσατέως, Μάνεντος, Οὐα-

---

19–20 τὸ ἐπίστροφον F

34: 6 ἀειθαλ(˜) F ‖ 10 δὲ om. F ‖ 12 ταράσσονται H

35: 2 πρεσβύτερος F ‖ 3 ὁ ὅσιος H ‖ 9 σαμωσατέως F

λεντίνου, Μαρκίωνος, καὶ τῶν σὺν αὐτοῖς. Ἀποκηρύττει δὲ ἡ αὐτὴ Μελέτιον Θηβαΐδος καὶ τὰς τούτου χειροτονίας, καὶ Εὐσέβιον τὸν Νικομηδείας καὶ τοὺς σὺν αὐτῷ. Καὶ προκάθηται ὁ βασιλεὺς Κωνσταντῖνος, Εὐστάθιος, Μακάριος, Ἀλέξανδρος, καὶ οἱ πρεσβύτεροι τῆς Ῥώμης. Τὸ δὲ σύμβολον τῶν τιη΄ πατέρων ἐξετέθη οὕτως· «πιστεύομεν εἰς ἕνα θεὸν πατέρα παντοκράτορα, ποιητὴν οὐρανοῦ καὶ γῆς, ὁρατῶν τε πάντων καὶ ἀοράτων, καὶ εἰς ἕνα κύριον Ἰησοῦν Χριστὸν τὸν υἱὸν τοῦ θεοῦ τὸν μονογενῆ, τὸν ἐκ τοῦ πατρὸς γεννηθέντα πρὸ πάντων τῶν αἰώνων, φῶς ἐκ φωτός, θεὸν ἀληθινὸν ἐκ θεοῦ ἀληθινοῦ, γεννηθέντα οὐ ποιηθέντα, ὁμοούσιον τῷ πατρί, δι᾽ οὗ τὰ πάντα ἐγένετο, τὸν δι᾽ ἡμᾶς τοὺς ἀνθρώπους καὶ διὰ τὴν ἡμετέραν σωτηρίαν κατελθόντα ἐκ τῶν οὐρανῶν καὶ σαρκωθέντα ἐκ πνεύματος ἁγίου καὶ Μαρίας τῆς παρθένου, καὶ ἐνανθρωπήσαντα παθόντα τε καὶ ἀναστάντα τῇ τρίτῃ ἡμέρᾳ καὶ ἀνελθόντα εἰς τοὺς οὐρανούς, καὶ ἐρχόμενον κρῖναι ζῶντας καὶ νεκρούς· καὶ εἰς τὸ πνεῦμα τὸ ἅγιον· τοὺς δὲ λέγοντας τὸ "ἦν ποτε ὅτε οὐκ ἦν" καὶ "πρὶν γεννηθῆναι οὐκ ἦν" καὶ ὅτι "ἐξ οὐκ ὄντων ἐγένετο," ἢ ἐξ ἑτέρας ὑποστάσεως ἢ οὐσίας φάσκοντας εἶναι, τρεπτὸν ἢ ἀλλοιωτὸν τὸν υἱὸν τοῦ θεοῦ, τούτους ἀναθεματίζει [καὶ] ἡ καθολικὴ καὶ ἀποστολικὴ ἐκκλησία.»

36. Ἄθροισις αἱρετικὴ ἐν Καισαρείᾳ τῆς Φιλίππου κατὰ τοῦ ἁγίου Ἀθανασίου. Οἱ δὲ περὶ τὸν Νικομηδείας Εὐσέβιον ὄντες σπουδασταὶ καὶ τοῦ ψεύδους συνήγοροι καὶ κατὰ τῆς εὐσεβείας δεινοὶ ὁπλῖται καὶ πολέμιοι, ὡς ἤδη καθαιρεθέντες καὶ ἐκποδὼν γεγονότες, ταράσσονται κατὰ τοῦ θείου συμβόλου· καθ᾽ ὧν διαβολὰς ποιοῦντες καὶ συκοφαντίας ἀτόπους συρράπτοντες οὐ διέλιπον τάς τε βασιλικὰς ἀκοὰς ἐνοχλοῦντες, οὐ μόνον δὲ τοῦ μεγάλου Κωνσταντίνου ἀλλὰ καὶ Κωνσταντίου τοῦ υἱοῦ αὐτοῦ· οὐ τὰς τυχούσας κακώσεις κατὰ τῶν ἀθλητῶν τῆς ἀληθείας ἐσκευάσαντο. Ἀλλ᾽ ὁ μὲν μακαριώτατος Ἀλέξανδρος μετὰ τὴν ἁγίαν σύνοδον πεντάμηνον ἐπιβιώσας, ἐν εἰρήνῃ ἐπὶ τὸ αὐτὸ ἐκοιμήθη καὶ ὕπνωσεν, Ἀθανάσιος δὲ τούτου τὴν προεδρίαν ἀξίως εἰσδέχεται. Οἱ δὲ προρρηθέντες ἑτερόδοξοι μεμαθηκότες τὴν Ἀθανασίου προχείρισιν, πολλὴν ἐν ἑαυτοῖς ἀνῆψαν τὴν κατὰ τοῦ ἀνδρὸς ὀργήν τε καὶ δυσμένειαν καὶ μιαιφονίαν·

35: 14–27: cf. Thdrt. I.12, 8; Socr. I.8, 44–45

35: 26 καὶ om. Thdrt. et Socr.

36: 4 ἐκ ποδῶν codd. ‖ 5 ὧν] leg. οὗ? ‖ 12 προχείρησιν H

καὶ ὅσας μὲν κατ' αὐτοῦ συσκευὰς ἐτεκτήναντο, τοῦτο μὲν φόνου δίκας οἱ μιαιφόνοι γραφόμενοι, τοῦτο δὲ γυναίου διαφθορὰν οἱ κατὰ τῆς εὐσεβείας ἐκπορνεύσαντες αἰτιώμενοι, τοῦτο δὲ σκευῶν ἱερῶν βεβήλωσιν οἱ τὰ ἅγια βεβηλώσαντες, τοῦτο δὲ καὶ εἰς τυραννίδα διασύροντες, καὶ ὡς τὴν κατ' ἔτος σιτοπομπίαν τὴν ἐξ Αἰγύπτου πρὸς τὴν βασιλεύουσαν τῶν πόλεων γινομένην ἀποκωλύσειν ἠπείλησε. Ταῦτα πάντα παρήσειν μοι δοκῶ, ἅτε δὴ πανταχοῦ ταῖς ἱστορίαις ᾀδόμενα καὶ τὸν ἀθλητὴν δεικνύντα πᾶσι διὰ τῆς ἐπιβουλῆς τε καὶ συκοφαντίας τῶν δυσσεβούντων περιφανῶς στεφανούμενον· καὶ τό γε βαρύτατον τῶν δυσσεβούντων καὶ ἀναισχυντότατον, ὅτι καὶ συνόδων ὀνόματι τὰς συκοφαντίας ὧν ἦσαν γεννήτορες καθυπέβαλον· καὶ συναθροίζονται μὲν πρῶτα κατὰ τοῦ ἱεροῦ καὶ θεσπεσίου ἀνδρὸς Ἀθανασίου ἐν Καισαρείᾳ τῆς Παλαιστίνης· ἔπειτα δὲ μετὰ
(37.) πλείονος τῆς παρασκευῆς ἐν Τύρῳ, οὐ κατὰ μόνου πνέοντες τοῦ ἱεροῦ
Ἀθανασίου τὸν φόνον, ἀλλὰ καὶ τὴν ἴσην γνώμην καὶ κατὰ τοῦ θείου συμ-
(38.) βόλου προτείνοντες συνηθροίσθησαν· καὶ τρίτην σύνοδον ἀθετούντων
συγκροτοῦσιν ἐν τῷ Μαρεώτῃ, τοῖς ὁμοίοις ἀσελγαίνουσαν καὶ συκοφαντίαις καὶ δυσσεβήμασιν· ἐφ' οἷς ἅπασιν αἰσχύνην μὲν ἑαυτοῖς, τῷ δὲ ἀθλητῇ τῆς ἀληθείας ἀντὶ τῆς συκοφαντίας μεγάλας τὰς εὐφημίας οἱ δυσσεβοῦντες καὶ ἄκοντες ἀνεπλέξαντο.

39. Σύνοδος αἱρετικὴ ἐν Ἀντιοχείᾳ ὑπὸ Εὐσεβίου τοῦ Νικομηδείας κατὰ τοῦ θείου συμβόλου καὶ Εὐσταθίου τοῦ μακαρίου, ἣ μισθωσαμένη καὶ αὕτη γύναιον ἑταιρικὸν εἰς ἔλεγχον καὶ συκοφαντίαν παρέστησεν· ἥτις πόρνη πάντων εἰς μέσον καταστᾶσα, βρέφος ἐν ἀγκάλαις ἔχουσα, ἔφη «ἦ μὴν Εὐσταθίου ὑπάρχει τὸ βρέφος τοῦτο·» ταύτην δὲ τὴν φωνὴν οἱ τῆς συκοφαντίας ἀρχιτέκτονες ἅρπαγμα ποιησάμενοι, μηδεμιᾶς μηδαμόθεν τῇ κατηγορίᾳ τῆς πίστεως ἐπιτεθείσης, μὴ διά τινων τεκμηρίων, μὴ διὰ μαρτύρων, μηδαμόθεν ἄλλοθεν, ἀλλ' ἐκ μόνης φωνῆς τοῦ μαχλῶντος γυναίου, καίτοι καὶ τούτου δώροις προδιαφθαρέντος ὑπ' αὐτῶν, ὅμως τὸν τοῦ θεοῦ θεράποντα Εὐστάθιον τοῦ τε θρόνου καὶ τῆς ἱερωσύνης οἱ τῆς δυσσεβείας ἐρασταὶ πικρῶς ἀπελαύνουσι, Σαβελλισμὸν αὐτῷ μετὰ τῆς μοιχείας ἐπιφημίσαντες. Ἐν δὲ ταύτῃ τῇ αἱρετιζούσῃ συνόδῳ καὶ τῶν ὀρθοδόξων παρῆσάν τινες, οἳ τῇ κατὰ τοῦ ἀνδρὸς καταδίκῃ οὐ συναπηνέχθησαν.

36: 18–19: cf. *Epit. Th. A.*, 24, 32–33

---

14 σκευὰς F ‖ 17 καὶ[1] om. H ‖ 24 καὶ[2] om. F

39: 2 ἣ] ἢ H ‖ 3 ἑταιρικὸν] αἱρετικὸν F ‖ 8 τοῦ om. F ‖ 12 αἱρετιαζούσῃ F

40. Συνέδριον αἱρετικῶν κατὰ τοῦ θείου συμβόλου καὶ Ἀθανασίου ἐν Κωνσταντινουπόλει, ὅπερ πολλαῖς συκοφαντίαις χρησάμενον ἐξορίζει τὸν ἀνεύθυνον Ἀθανάσιον εἰς Τρίβεριν τῆς Γαλλίας, καὶ τὸν ὅσιον Κοματᾶν καὶ Εὐφρατᾶν Ἀνταράδου καὶ Εὐπρέπιον Ἀδριανουπόλεως καὶ Λούκιον τὸν ὁμολογητήν, ὃς τελειοῦται ἐν ταῖς ἁλύσεσι· καθεῖλε δὲ καὶ Μάρκελλον τὸν Ἀγκύρας ὡς ἀνθρωπολάτριν.

41. Σύνοδοι αἱ γινόμεναι ἐπὶ Κωνσταντίου βασιλέως, τοῦ υἱοῦ τοῦ μεγάλου Κωνσταντίνου. Μετὰ γοῦν τὴν ἐξορίαν τοῦ ἱεροῦ Ἀθανασίου οὐ μετ' οὐ πολὺ ὁ φιλόχριστος βασιλεὺς ἐν Νικομηδείᾳ ἐξελθὼν καὶ ἀσθενείᾳ περιπεσὼν βαπτισθείς, αὐτίκα ἀπὸ τῶν ἐπιγείων ἐπὶ τὴν οὐράνιον μετοικίζεται βασιλείαν, Κωνσταντίου τοῦ υἱοῦ αὐτοῦ ὑπάρχοντος ἐν Ἀντιοχείᾳ, Κωνσταντίνου δὲ καὶ Κώνσταντος ἐν Ῥώμῃ, Κρίσπου ἤδη τελειωθέντος. Τῆς δὲ διαθήκης φαλσευθείσης τοῦ βασιλέως, Κωνστάντιος βασιλεὺς τῆς ἑῴας ἀναδείκνυται· τῶν δὲ ἀδελφῶν αὐτοῦ ἐν Ῥώμῃ ὀρθοδοξούντων, αὐτὸς μόνος εἰς τὸ Ἀρειανικὸν δόγμα παρεσύρη. Οὐ μετ' οὐ πολὺ δὲ καὶ Ἀλέξανδρος ὁ Κωνσταντινουπόλεως εἰς τὸν ἀμείνω βίον μεθαρμόζεται, καταλείψας Παῦλον τοῦ θρόνου διάδοχον. Τοῦ δὲ Κωνσταντίου ἀπὸ Ἀντιοχείας τὴν βασιλίδα καταλαβόντος, οἱ περὶ τὸν Εὐσέβιον Ἀρειανοὶ κατὰ τοῦ μακαριωτάτου Παύλου τῷ βασιλεῖ προσέρχονται σὺν πολλαῖς διαβολαῖς, καὶ τοῦτο προσθέντες, ὅτι «δίχα τῆς σῆς, βασιλεῦ, διαγνώσεως, Παῦλος ἑαυτὸν τῷ θρόνῳ καθίδρυσεν·» ὁ δὲ συνοδικῶς κριθῆναι πάντα τὰ κατ' αὐτὸν παρεκελεύσατο. Συνέδριον αἱρετικῶν ἐν Κωνσταντινουπόλει κατὰ τοῦ θείου συμβόλου καὶ Παύλου τοῦ ὁμολογητοῦ, ὑφ' οὗ συνεδρίου ὁ μὲν θεράπων τοῦ θεοῦ Παῦλος ἐκβάλλεται, ἀντεισάγεται δὲ Εὐσέβιος Νικομηδείας, ὁ πρώην Βηρυτοῦ γεγονὼς ἀναξίως ἐπίσκοπος, Κωνσταντίνου συνάρσει· καὶ γὰρ οἱ ἑτερόδοξοι θᾶττον τὴν κουφοτάτην αὐτοῦ ἐπολιόρκησαν γνώμην. Τοῦ τοίνυν μακαριωτάτου Κωνσταντίνου τὴν μεγάλην ἐκκλησίαν Ἀντιοχείας ὡς ἓν τῶν θεαμάτων ἀρξαμένου κτίζειν, Κωνστάντιος τὴν βασιλείαν παραλαβών, καὶ ταύτην πεπληρωκώς, πλείστους ἐπισκόπους πρὸς τὸν ἐγκαινισμὸν συνεκαλέσατο.

40: 3 γαλίας codd.

41: 1 αἱ om. H ‖ 2 ἱεροῦ] ἁγίου H ‖ 8 ἑῴας] ἕως H ‖ 10 καὶ] καὶ ὁ H ‖ 20 κουφότητα H

42. Σύνοδος αἱρετικὴ ἐν Ἀντιοχείᾳ τῶν ϟζʹ, λόγῳ μὲν καὶ προφάσει τῶν ἐγκαινίων, πράγματι δὲ καὶ σκοπῷ κατὰ τοῦ θείου συμβόλου καὶ Ἀθανασίου· ὁ γὰρ μακάριος Κωνσταντῖνος τελειούμενος τὸν ἅγιον Ἀθανάσιον ἀποκαταστῆναι τῷ θρόνῳ διετάξατο· ἐν ᾗ ἐξῆρχον Εὐσέβιος ὁ Νικομηδείας, Ἀκάκιος ὁ Παλαιστινός, Διάνιος ὁ Καισαρείας Καππαδοκίας, ὅστις ἔσχεν Ἀστέριον τὸν Καππαδόκην φιλόσοφον. Ἥτις σύνοδος τὸ σύμβολον μεταποιήσασα, ἀποστέλλει Γρηγόριον ἐν Ἀλεξανδρείᾳ σὺν χειρὶ βαρείᾳ κατὰ Ἀθανασίου· ὅστις ἐπιστὰς σὺν τετρακοσίοις ὁπλίταις, ἐξελαύνει μὲν τὸν μακάριον, αὐτὸς δὲ ἀδεῶς λυμαίνεται τὴν ἐκκλησίαν. Οἱ δὲ περὶ τὸν Εὐσέβιον Ἀρειανοὶ ἐν Ἀντιοχείᾳ ὁρίζουσι τὸ θεῖον πάσχα κατὰ τὴν ἁγίαν ἐν Νικαίᾳ σύνοδον, ἐξέθετο δὲ κανόνας τοὺς ἤδη ἐμφερομένους. Ἰστέον δὲ ὅτι ὑπάρχουσιν ἐν αὐτῇ καὶ ὀρθόδοξοι πατέρες, ἀλλ' ἡ φονιώδης συμμορία Εὐσεβίου ὑπερεκράτει.

43. Παῦλος τοίνυν καὶ Ἀθανάσιος τῶν ἐκκλησιῶν ἐκδιωχθέντες, καταλαμβάνουσι τὴν παλαιὰν Ῥώμην· Κώνστας δὲ τὸ τηνικάδε τὰ σκῆπτρα τῆς ἐκεῖσε βασιλείας εἶχε, τῶν δὲ ἱερῶν θρόνων τὴν ἐφορείαν Ἰούλιος ἐγκεχείριστο. Οἳ τὴν κατ' αὐτῶν γεγενημένην ἄδικον καὶ παράνομον ψῆφον ἀκριβῶς ἀναμαθόντες, ἐνδίκῳ καὶ ἱεροπρεπεῖ κρίσει τοῖς οἰκείοις τούτους ἀποκαθιστῶσι θρόνοις· διὸ οἱ ἑτερόδοξοι καὶ αὖθις ἐν Ἀντιοχείᾳ συναθροίζονται. Σύνοδος αἱρετικὴ ἐν Ἀντιοχείᾳ, κατὰ τοῦ θείου συμβόλου καὶ Ἀθανασίου καὶ Παύλου, ἥτις τούτους μὲν ἀποκηρύξασα, κατὰ Ἰουλίου δὲ πλεῖστα βατταρίσασα, τούτῳ γράμματα διαπέμπονται ὡς μὴ δεῖν τὰ αὐτῶν ὑπ' αὐτοῦ ἀντικανονίζεσθαι.

44. Τοῦ τοίνυν Ἰουλίου καὶ Κώνσταντος ὑπὲρ τοῦ θείου συμβόλου καὶ τῶν αὐτοῦ ὑπερμαχούντων, ἡ ἀληθὴς καὶ σωτήριος πίστις ἐκρατύνετο· καὶ ἡ αἱρετικὴ φάλαγξ ἐν Ἀντιοχείᾳ πάλιν ἠθροίζετο. Σύνοδος αἱρετικὴ ἐν Ἀντιοχείᾳ κατὰ τοῦ θείου συμβόλου, ἥτις ἐκθεμένη ὅρον πίστεως, ἀποστέλλει τοῦτον ἐν τῇ ἑσπερίῳ· ἀναθεματίζει δὲ ἡ αὐτὴ Φωτεινὸν καὶ Μάρκελλον Ἀγκύρας καὶ Σαβέλλιον. Ἰούλιος δὲ καὶ οἱ ἑσπέριοι, ὡς ἀνόσιον ὄντα καὶ ἄθεσμον, τὸν παρ' αὐτοῖς ὅρον οὐ προσήκαντο.

42: 4 τοῦ θρόνου H ‖ 5 παλαιστηνός H

43: 6 τούτου F ‖ 7 ἀθροίζονται H ‖ 8 τούτου F ‖ 9 βαταρίσασα codd.

44: 5 an ἑσπερίᾳ?

45. Τότε οὖν ὁ θειότατος Κώνστας ἐκ Ῥώμης δηλοῖ Κωνσταντίῳ τῷ ἀδελφῷ αὐτοῦ ἐν Σαρδικῇ γενέσθαι σύνοδον καὶ ἐξετασθῆναι τὰ κατὰ Ἀθανασίου καὶ Παύλου. Σύνοδος θεία καὶ ἱερὰ ἐν Σαρδικῇ, ἡ δὲ Σαρδικὴ μητρόπολίς ἐστιν Ἰλλυριῶν, ἔθνους Δακῶν· ἐν ᾗ τῶν μὲν ἑσπερίων τμα΄ συνελέγησαν πατέρες, τῶν δὲ ἀνατολικῶν Ἀρειανοὶ ος΄, ὧν ἐξῆρχεν ὁ Ὅσιος Κουδρούβης καὶ Πρωτογένης ὁ Σαρδικῆς ἀρχιεπίσκοπος. Ἥτις σύνοδος τὸ ὑγιὲς μάθημα τῶν πατέρων τρανώσασα, Ἀθανάσιον καὶ Παῦλον τοὺς ἀρχιερεῖς ἐδέξατο· ἀπεδίωξε δὲ Γρηγόριον τὸν Ἀλεξανδρείας καὶ Βασίλειον τὸν Ἀγκύρας καὶ Κεντιανὸν Γάζης, ὡς ἐκ τυραννίδος τοὺς θρόνους ἁρπάσαντας· ἀλλὰ τούτους μὲν καὶ κοινωνίας θείας ἀπεστέρησαν· Θεόδωρον δὲ Ἡρακλείας καὶ Ἀκάκιον Παλαιστίνης Στέφανόν τε τὸν Ἀντιοχείας καὶ Ἰσαάκιον Συγγιδούνου, Οὐάλεντα Μυσίας καὶ Μηνόφαντον Ἐφέσου καὶ Γεώργιον Κιλικίας μόνον ἀπεκήρυξαν. Ἰστέον δὲ ὅτι καὶ Ἀλέξανδρός τινας τούτων ἤδη πάλαι ἀπεκήρυξε· καὶ νῦν δὲ ἡ ἁγία σύνοδος τὸ αὐτὸ κατ' αὐτῶν διεπράξατο, τῶν μὲν ἤδη περιόντων τῷ βίῳ, τῶν δὲ καὶ μεταλλαξάντων.

46. Ὅσοις μέντοι τὸ τοῦ Ἀρείου ἐθάλπετο φρόνημα, οὗτοι δὲ ἄρα διαρραγέντες τῇ συνόδῳ ἐν Φιλιππουπόλει συνάγονται εἰς ἀριθμὸν τελοῦντες ἑξήκοντα. Σύνοδος ἐν Φιλιππουπόλει κατὰ Ἀθανασίου καὶ Παύλου τῶν ἀθλητῶν τῆς ἀληθείας· ἣ καὶ τὸν ὅρον τῆς εὐσεβείας παραχαράξασα, ἔκθεσμα κατὰ Ἀθανασίου καὶ Παύλου, ἐκκηρύκτους ποιουμένη, διετάξατο.

47. Δι' ἣν αἰτίαν καὶ ὁ Κουδρούβης Ὅσιος ἐν τῇ αὐτοῦ πόλει σύνοδον συνεκρότησε. Σύνοδος ἐν Κουδρούβῃ, ἧς ἔξαρχος Ὅσιος ὁ ταύτης ἐπίσκοπος· ἥτις τὸ θεουργὸν τῆς εὐσεβείας ἐπικυρώσασα μάθημα, σύμψηφος ἐν πᾶσι τῇ ἐν Σαρδικῇ συνόδῳ γίνεται.

45: 4–5 *Epit. Th. A.*, 35, 20–21

45: 4 τμα΄] τριακόσιοι H ‖ 6 Ἥτις] ἤτοι H ‖ 9 καὶ] ὁ F

46: 2–3 τελειοῦντες F

47: 1 post Κουδρούβης add. ὁ F ‖ 2 ὁ ὅσιος ταύτης H

48. Μετὰ δὲ τὴν ἱερὰν ταύτην σύνοδον Κώνστας ὁ εὐσεβὴς βασιλεὺς πρὸς τὸν ἴδιον διαπέμπεται ἀδελφόν, εἰς ἐκδίκησιν διαναστῆναι Ἀθανασίου καὶ Παύλου διανοούμενος· ἐπίσκοποι δὲ διηκόνουν τῷ λόγῳ, Εὐφρατᾶς καὶ Βικέντιος προσαγορευόμενοι, οἷς καὶ στρατηγὸς συναπεστάλη, Σαλῖνος τοὔνομα. Στέφανος δὲ ὁ Ἀντιοχείας τὰ Ἀρείου νοσῶν κατὰ τῶν Ῥώμης ἐπισκόπων συσκευὴν ἐδραματούργησε· τοῦ δὲ δράματος ἐκκαλυφθέντος, ὡς συκοφάντης ἀπείληφε τὰ ἐπίχειρα. Σύνοδος ἐν Ἀντιοχείᾳ αἱρετική, Στεφάνου τοῦ ταύτης αἱρεσιάρχου κατάρχοντος, ἐν ᾗ Σαλῖνος ὁ ἐκ Ῥώμης στρατηγὸς τὴν Στεφάνου κατὰ τῶν ἐπισκόπων ῥαδιουργίαν διήλεγξε· διὸ καὶ ἄκοντες τὸ τῶν αἱρετικῶν ἄθροισμα Στέφανον μὲν καθεῖλον, ἀντιχειροτονοῦσι δὲ Λεόντιον τομίαν αὐτόχειρα, τῆς Ἀρειανικῆς λύσσης οὐδὲν ἔλαττον Στεφάνου ἀνάπλεων.

49. Ὁ μέντοι βασιλεὺς Κώνστας διὰ τοῦ προονομασθέντος στρατηγοῦ Σαλίνου τὰ ἐκθέσμως ὑπὸ τῶν Ἀρειανῶν τολμώμενα μαθών, πάλιν ἐκπέμπει πρὸς τὸν ἀδελφὸν καὶ τὸν στρατηγόν, εἰ μὴ Ἀθανάσιος καὶ Παῦλος κἂν ὀψέ ποτε τῶν μυρίων κατ' αὐτῶν ἐπιβουλῶν πεπαυμένοι τοὺς οἰκείους ἀπολείψονται θρόνους, πόλεμον αὐτῷ διαπειλεῖν. Ὁ δὲ Κωνστάντιος τὸν τοῦ ἀδελφοῦ φόβον λαβὼν ἐν ὀφθαλμοῖς, δέχεται μὲν ἐπιεικῶς τὸν Ἀθανάσιον, ψηφίζεται δὲ αὐτῷ καὶ τὴν ἐν Ἀλεξανδρείᾳ κάθοδον. Ἀλλ' ὅ γε θεῖος ἀνὴρ Ἀθανάσιος πρὸς Μάξιμον τὸν τῶν Ἱεροσολύμων ἀπιών, συνόδου κρίσει λαμβάνει τὴν εἰς τὸν ἴδιον θρόνον ἀποκατάστασιν.

50. Σύνοδος τοπικὴ ἐν Ἱεροσολύμοις Μαξίμου τοῦ ὁμολογητοῦ καθαίρεσιν συσκευάσασα, ἥτις καὶ Κύριλλον ἀντεχειροτόνησε, τότε τὰ Ἀρείου πρεσβεύειν διαθρυλλούμενον, κατηχητὴν δὲ τὸν ἄνδρα ἐπίκλην ὕστερον ἡ πρᾶξις ἐπέθετο. Καὶ σημείωσαι ὅτι ἡ ἐπὶ Δαμάσου σύνοδος ἐν Ῥώμῃ ὡς ὀρθόδοξον Κύριλλον ἐπαινοῦσα παραδέχεται· ὁμοίως δὲ καὶ ἡ ἐπὶ Νεκταρίου τοπικὴ σύνοδος. Ἀκάκιος μέντοι, ὁ μαθητὴς Εὐσεβίου καὶ τοῦ θρόνου διάδοχος νῦν μὲν τοῦ ἱεροῦ Μαξίμου καταγωνίζεται.

48: 5 ὁ om. H ‖ 10 τῶν om. H

49: 9 κρίσιν H

50: 2 ἥτις] εἴ τις H

51. Οὐ μετ' οὐ πολὺ δὲ καὶ οὐ πολὺς δὲ χρόνος ἐν μέσῳ καὶ Μαγνέντιος ἐν τῇ δύσει τυραννίδι ἐπιθέμενος, Κώνσταντα τὸν βασιλέα ἀναιρεῖ· καὶ ἀναρριπίζει πάλιν τὴν οἰκείαν φλόγα τῆς ἀσεβείας κατὰ Ἀθανασίου καὶ Παύλου ἡ ἀρειανίζουσα θύελλα. Κωνστάντιος δὲ τὴν ἀναίρεσιν τοῦ ἀδελφοῦ μαθών, Γάλον μὲν τὸν ἀδελφιδοῦν καίσαρα τῶν ἐῴων προχειρίζεται, αὐτὸς δὲ Κωνσταντινουπόλεως ἀπάρας ἐπὶ τὸν κατὰ Μαγνεντίου ἐξορμᾷ πόλεμον· καὶ τῶν μὲν ἐχθρῶν οὐ πολλοῖς ἀγωνίσμασι κρατεῖ, τὸν δὲ κατὰ τῆς ἐκκλησίας ἀνακινεῖ πάλιν πόλεμον. Διὸ σύνοδον ἐν τῷ Σιρμίῳ γενέσθαι παρακελεύεται. Σύνοδος αἱρετικὴ ἐν Σιρμίῳ προφάσει μὲν κατὰ Φωτεινοῦ τοῦ ἀνθρωπολάτρου, τοῦ ταύτης ἐπισκόπου, σκοπῷ δὲ κατὰ τοῦ θείου συμβόλου καὶ Ἀθανασίου· ἥτις ἐκθεμένη ὅρον δυσσεβείας, μὴ δεῖν φάσκειν οὐσίαν ἐπὶ θεοῦ ἐδογμάτισε. Μάρκον δὲ τὸν Ἀρεθούσιον συνθεῖναι τὸν ὅρον ἔφασαν, ὃς ἐπὶ Ἰουλιανοῦ πολλὰ παθὼν ὑπὲρ εὐσεβείας, ἐν καιρῷ τῆς εὐσεβείας περὶ ταύτην ἐναυάγησε.

52. Κωνστάντιος δὲ μετὰ τὴν ἐν Σιρμίῳ πάλιν σύνοδον ἐν Μεδιολάνῳ προστάσσει γενέσθαι. Σύνοδος ἱερὰ τοπικὴ ἐν Μεδιολάνῳ ἐν ᾗ ὑπῆρχον τιε' πατέρες τῶν ἑσπερίων. Αὕτη ἡ σύνοδος οὐκ ἀνασχομένη ἀνατρέψαι τὸ θεῖον σύμβολον οὔτε μὴν κυρῶσαι τὴν ἐν Τύρῳ κατὰ Ἀθανασίου καθαίρεσιν, οὐ κατὰ τὸν θυμὸν Κωνσταντίου οὐδὲ τοῖς Ἀρειανίζουσι φίλα ἔπραττε· διὸ τοὺς ἐξάρχους ταύτης ὁ Κωνστάντιος ἐξορίᾳ καταδικάζει, Λιβέριον μὲν τὸν Ῥώμης, εἶτα Παυλῖνον τὸν τῶν Γαλλιῶν μητροπολίτην, καὶ Διονύσιον τὸν τῆς Ἰταλίας, Εὐσέβιόν τε τὸν μέγαν, καὶ Λουκίφερ τὸν Σάρδεων.

53. Τούτων δὲ ἐξορίᾳ παραδοθέντων, σύνοδος πάλιν ἐν Ἀριμίνῳ θεσπίζεται ἀθροισθῆναι, τῶν ἑτεροδόξων Κωνστάντιον ἐνοχλούντων. Λιβέριος δέ, ὥσπερ ἔφημεν, ἐξορίζεται ἀπὸ Μεδιολάνων εἰς Βέρροιαν τῆς Θρᾴκης, ἀντιχειροτονεῖται δὲ Φίληξ, ὃς τὴν μὲν ἐν Νικαίᾳ ἐδέχετο σύνοδον, τοῖς δὲ ταύτης ἐχθροῖς ἀδιαφόρως ἐκοινώνει· διὸ καὶ τῶν Ῥωμαίων οἱ ἀκριβέστεροι καθ' ἑαυτοὺς ἐκκλησίαζον. Σύνοδος ἱερὰ ἐν Ἀριμίνῳ συνελθόντων διακοσίων μὲν πατέρων ἐκ τῆς ἑσπέρας, τῶν δὲ περὶ Εὐδόξιον

51: 1 οὐμετοπολὺ (sic) H ‖ 1–2 μαγνέτιος H ‖ 3 εὐσεβείας F ‖ 6–7 μαξεντίου H ‖ 7 ἐξορμῶν F

52: 7 γαλιῶν codd.

53: 6–7 συνελθόντων post ἑσπέρας transp. H

τὸν Γερμανικίας εἰς ἀριθμὸν βραχὺν συντελούντων. Αὕτη ἡ σύνοδος τὸ θεῖον κυροῖ σύμβολον, ἀναθεματίζει δὲ Ἄρειον καὶ τοὺς ὁμόφρονας αὐτοῦ. Οἱ δὲ τὰ Ἀρείου φρονοῦντες, τοῦτον ἀναθεματίσαι μὴ βουλόμενοι, ὑπὸ τῆς ἁγίας συνόδου ἀποκηρύττονται· ὧν εἰσιν Οὐρσάκιος, Εὐδόξιος, Οὐάλης, Δημόφιλος καὶ Γρηγόριος. Καὶ ταύτην τὴν σύνοδον ὡς αἱρετίζουσαν διασύρουσιν, ἀλλ' οὐχ οὕτως ἔχει.

54. Μετὰ δὲ τὴν ἐν Ἀριμίνῳ σύνοδον οἱ περὶ Εὐδόξιον ἐν αὐτῇ καθαιρεθέντες παρασκευάζουσι Κωνστάντιον ἐν Νίκῃ τῆς Θρᾴκης πάλιν σύνοδον προστάξαι συναθροισθῆναι. Σύνοδος αἱρετικὴ ἐν Νίκῃ τῆς Θρᾴκης κατὰ τοῦ θείου συμβόλου, ἐν ᾗ κατατρίψας χρόνον συχνὸν τοὺς τῆς ἀληθείας ἀγωνιστὰς ὁ Εὐσέβιος, διὰ τὸ μὴ συμβαίνειν αὐτοὺς τῇ ἐκείνου δυσσεβείᾳ, ὕστερον ἅμα τοῖς συναιρετίζουσιν αὐτῷ πίστεως ὅρον ἐκτίθεται, ἐν ᾧ παντελῶς τὸ ὁμοούσιον ἐκβάλλεται· εἰς ὃν ὅρον οἱ μὲν φόβῳ, οἱ δὲ καὶ ἀπάτῃ δελεασθέντες, ὑπέγραψαν· ὅσοι δὲ κρείττους καὶ φόβου καὶ ἀπάτης ἐγένοντο, εἰς τὰς ἐσχατιὰς τῆς οἰκουμένης παρεπέμφθησαν.

55. Μετὰ δὲ τὴν ἐν Νίκῃ σύνοδον οἱ μὲν ἑσπέριοι πατέρες πολλοῖς ἀναθέμασιν αὐτὴν καθυπέβαλον, οἱ δὲ τῆς ἑτεροδόξου μοίρας παραπείθουσι Κωνστάντιον ἐν Νικαίᾳ τῇ μητροπόλει συγκροτηθῆναι σύνοδον ἐπὶ καθαιρέσει τοῦ συμβόλου. Καὶ δὴ συναθροισθέντων, πρὶν ἢ τὴν βλάσφημον αὐτῶν ἀνακινῆσαι γλῶσσαν, ὁ τῶν ἁγίων πατέρων θεὸς τὴν πόλιν κατασείσας, τοὺς ἐπιβούλους αὐτῆς τῆς ἀληθείας τῇ συναγωγῇ διεσκόρπισεν.

56. Οὐδὲ μετὰ ταύτην τὴν θεήλατον ὀργὴν τὸ αἱρετίζον στῖφος σωφρονισθέντες, παρασκευάζουσι πάλιν ἐν Σελευκείᾳ σύνοδον γενέσθαι. Σύνοδος αἱρετικὴ ἐν Σελευκείᾳ τῆς Ἰσαυρίας, τὸ θεῖον παραχαράττουσα σύμβολον, ἣν οἱ ἑσπέριοι πατέρες ἀναθέματι καθυπέβαλον. Ἀλλ' ἔτι τὸ αἱρετικὸν φρύαγμα μηδαμῶς τῷ θεῷ ταπεινούμενον, πάλιν παρασκευάζουσι Κωνστάντιον θεσπίσαι ἐν Σελευκείᾳ σύνοδον γενέσθαι· ἐν ᾗ καὶ ὁ

10 Οἱ δὲ] εἰ δὲ F

55: 2 καθυπέβαλλον H

56: 4 οἱ om. F

Ἱεροσολύμων Κύριλλος, ὃς διαβολαῖς καὶ τέχναις Ἀκακίου τοῦ θρόνου ἀπωσθεὶς παρὰ Σιλβανῷ τῷ Σελευκείας διέτριβε. Διαφιλονεικησάντων δὲ Κυρίλλου καὶ Ἀκακίου, ἄπρακτος μὲν μικροῦ ἡ σύνοδος διαλύεται, ἐκεῖθεν δὲ Ἀκάκιος πρὸς ἔχθραν Κυρίλλου τὸν Εὐδόξιον ἑταιρισάμενος τὴν βασιλίδα καταλαμβάνει καὶ σύνοδον ἐν αὐτῇ ἀθροισθῆναι παρασκευάζει.

57. Σύνοδος ἐν Κωνσταντινουπόλει αἱρετική, ἐν ᾗ μεταξὺ τῶν ὀρθοδόξων καὶ ἑτεροδόξων στάσεως γενομένης Εὐστάθιος καὶ Εὐσέβιος διήλεγχον τοὺς Ἀρειανοὺς ὡς τὸ «ἀνόμοιον» καὶ τὸ «ἐξ οὐκ ὄντων» πρεσβεύοντας· ἐν οἷς ὁ μάλιστα τούτων προεστὼς Ἀέτιος ἁλούς, ἐξορίᾳ καὶ ἀκόντων τῶν συναιρεσιωτῶν παραπέμπεται. Καθαιρεῖται δὲ Εὐστάθιος καὶ Εὐσέβιος ὑπὸ τῶν αἱρετικῶν, περιδρομῇ Ἀκακίου τοῦ Καισαρείας, καὶ ἕτεροί τινες.

58. Μετὰ δὲ τὴν ἐν Κωνσταντινουπόλει σύνοδον Κωνστάντιος προφάσει τοῦ πρὸς Σαβώριον πολέμου τὴν Ἀντιόχειαν καταλαβών, σύνοδον συνεγείρει κατὰ τοῦ ὁμοουσίου. Μελέτιον δὲ τὸν Σεβαστείας ἀρχιεπίσκοπον τό τε ὀρθοδοξοῦν καὶ τὸ Ἀρειανίζον, ἐπὶ τὸ αὐτὸ συνεληλυθός, ψηφίζονται τοῦ Ἀντιοχείας θρόνου πατριάρχην, ἑκάτερον μέρος πρὸς τὴν οἰκείαν δόξαν ἀποκλίνειν τὸν ἄνδρα νομίζοντες. Ὁ δέ, καταστὰς ἀρχιερεὺς Ἀντιοχείας, τρανῶς τὸ ὁμοούσιον ἐδείχθη πρεσβεύων· ὑπὲρ οὗ καὶ Σαβελλισμὸν αὐτῷ Κωνστάντιος καὶ ἡ Ἀρειανίζουσα μοίρα ἐπιφημίσαντες, τοῦτον μὲν ἐξορίᾳ παρέδωκαν, ἀντ' αὐτοῦ δὲ Εὐζώϊον, τὸν σὺν Ἀρείῳ λαβόντα τὸ ἀνάθεμα, ἐπίσκοπον προχειρίζονται. Καὶ ἡ μὲν ἐν Ἀντιοχείᾳ σύνοδος ταῦτα πραξαμένη διελύετο. Νόσῳ δὲ μετὰ ταῦτα βληθεὶς Κωνστάντιος, ὑπὸ Εὐζωΐου τοῦ Ἀρειανοῦ τὸ βάπτισμα δέχεται, εἶτα καταστρέφει τὸν βίον.

57: 2 post Εὐστάθιος add. μὲν F

58: 5 πατριάρχου F ‖ 10 ἐν om. H

59. Ἰουλιανὸς δὲ ὁ παραβάτης, ἐπὶ Κωνσταντίου ζῶντος τυραννίδι ἐπιθέμενος, κρατύνει τὴν βασιλείαν ἑαυτῷ μᾶλλον μετὰ τὸν ἐκείνου θάνατον. Καὶ οὓς Κωνστάντιος ἀρχιερεῖς ἐξορίᾳ παρέδωκε φιλανθρωπίας ἀνακαλεῖται προσχήματι, ἐν οἷς ἦσαν Εὐσέβιος ὁ ἑσπέριος, Μελέτιος Ἀντιοχείας καὶ Λουκίφερ. Τηνικαῦτα δὲ καὶ Ἀθανάσιος ἐν Ἀλεξανδρείᾳ ἅμα τοῖς ἐκ τῆς ἐξορίας ἀνακληθεῖσι σύνοδον συγκροτήσας, κυροῖ μὲν τὰ ἐν Νικαίᾳ δογματισθέντα, ἀναθεματίζει δὲ τὰ τοῖς Ἀρειανισταῖς δόξαντα· τοὺς δὲ εἰρηνεύειν μὲν τελοῦντας, μέχρι δὲ τότε τῇ πλάνῃ τῆς Ἀρειανικῆς ἐμμεμενηκότας λύσσης, εἰς κοινωνίαν μὲν μετανοοῦντας παρεδέξατο, ἱερωσύνης δὲ οὐ μετέδωκε.

(**59[a].**) Σύνοδος ἐν Ἀλεξανδρείᾳ ἐπισκόπων πλείστων ἐγένετο, ἐν ᾗ τὸ τῆς τριάδος ὁμοούσιον ἐκήρυξε καὶ ἀπαράλλακτον, καὶ ὅτι ἔμψυχος καὶ ἔννους ἡ σὰρξ ἣν ὁ θεὸς λόγος ἐκ τῆς θεοτόκου ἀνέλαβε. Φησὶ δὲ ὁ ἱστορῶν ὅτι τοῖς πάλαι σοφοῖς ἠκολούθησαν οἱ <ταῦ>τα νῦν ἐν Ἀλεξανδρείᾳ τρανώσαντες, Εἰρηναίῳ καὶ Κλήμεντι καὶ Ἀπολιναρίῳ τῷ Ἱεραπόλεως καὶ Σεραπίωνι τῷ Ἀντιοχείας· προστέθεικε τούτοις [τὸ] διὰ πολλῶν ῥημάτων καὶ Ὠριγένην· ἐν οἷς καὶ τὴν ὑπὲρ αὐτοῦ ἀπολογίαν Πάμφιλον καὶ Εὐσέβιον ἅμα λέγει ποιήσασθαι. Τὸ τῆς οὐσίας ὄνομα παρὰ τῆς ἔξω πίστεως κατὰ διαφόρων σημαινομένων [εἰς ὃ] εὑρίσκεται, τὸ δὲ τῆς ὑποστάσεως σπανίως μὲν εὕρηται, ἐπὶ δὲ τοῦ νῦν σημαινομένου οὐχ εὕρηται ὅλως παρά τινι· παρὰ μὲν Σοφοκλεῖ, ὥς φησιν, ἐπὶ τῇ ἐνέδρᾳ εὕρηται, παρὰ δὲ Μενάνδρῳ ἐπὶ τρυγίας πίθου ἢ καρυκευμάτων· οἱ δὲ νεώτεροι τῶν φιλοσόφων ἀντὶ τῆς οὐσίας νουνεχῶς τῇ λέξει τῆς ὑποστάσεως κέχρηνται. Καὶ ἡ μὲν ἐν Ἀλεξανδρείᾳ ταῦτα διεπράξατο.

59[a]: 1–14: *Epit. Th. A.*, 59, 17–60, 2

59: 1 ἐπὶ] leg. ἔτι? ‖ 9 μετανοῦντας F

59[a]: 1 post Σύνοδος add. μὲν F ‖ 2 ἐκηρύχθη *Epit. Th. A.* ‖ 4 τανῦν (sic) codd. ‖ 5 ἀπολλιναρίῳ H ‖ 6 σεραπίονι H ‖ προστέθηκε F ‖ τὸ non habet *Epit. Th. A.* ‖ 8 ἅμα] ἄμφω *Epit. Th. A.* ‖ 8–9 τῆς ἔξω] τοῖς ἔξω τῆς *Epit. Th. A.* ‖ 9 εἰς ὃ] om. *Epit. Th. A.* ‖ 10–11 ηὕρηται *Epit. Th. A.* ‖ 11 φασιν *Epit. Th. A.* ‖ ἐπὶ τῆς ἐνέδρας εἴρηται *Epit. Th. A.* ‖ 13 νουνεχῶς] συνεχῶς, et post φιλοσόφων, *Epit. Th. A.*

60. Μελέτιος δὲ Εὐσέβιον καὶ Λουκίφερα συμπαραλαβών, καταλαμβάνει τὴν Ἀντιόχειαν, καὶ τοὺς ἐκ Συρίας καὶ Φοινίκης ἀθροίσας ἀρχιερεῖς, συνοδικῶς καὶ αὐτὸς τὰ ἐν Νικαίᾳ ἐκύρωσεν. Ἰστέον ὅτι ὁ Λουκίφερ οὗτος, ὁ παραλόγως Παυλῖνον ἐν Ἀντιοχείᾳ τοῖς λεγομένοις Εὐσταθιανοῖς ἀρχιερέα χειροτονήσας, οὗτος καταλαβὼν τὴν ἑαυτοῦ ἐπισκοπήν, πολλῆς καινοτομίας τὰς ἐν αὐτῇ ἐκκλησίας ἐνέπλησε.

61. Μετὰ δὲ ταύτην ἐν Ἀντιοχείᾳ σύνοδον Ἀθανάσιος, ἐγείρας τοὺς ὑπ' αὐτὸν ἀρχιερεῖς, ἀναθεματίζει μὲν Ἀπολινάριον, τὴν δὲ σάρκα Χριστοῦ τοῦ ἀληθινοῦ θεοῦ ἡμῶν ἔμψυχον καὶ νοερὰν κατὰ τοὺς πάλαι πατέρας ἀνακηρύξας, διαλύει τὴν σύνοδον.

62. Μετὰ δὲ τὴν ἐν Ἀλεξανδρείᾳ σύνοδον Ἰουλιανοῦ τοῦ δυσσεβοῦς ἐν Περσίδι τὸν βίον ἀπορρήξαντος, Ἰουβιανοῦ δὲ τοῦ εὐσεβοῦς εἰς βασιλέα ἀναγορευθέντος, καταλαβὼν τὴν Ἀντιόχειαν Ἀκάκιος ὁ Παλαιστίνης καὶ ἕτεροι πλεῖστοι, λιβέλλους εὐσεβείας ἀντιποιούμενοι, τῷ βασιλεῖ ἐπιδιδόασι.

63. Μετὰ δὲ τὴν Ἀκακίου ἐπὶ τοῖς εἰρημένοις γενομένην σύνοδον, ὁ βασιλεὺς ἐξ Ἀντιοχείας εἰς Ἀλεξάνδρειαν ἀποστείλας, τὸν ἀπαράλλακτον ὅρον τῆς ὀρθοδοξίας παρὰ Ἀθανασίου ἐπεζήτησεν. Ἀθανάσιος δὲ τοὺς λογάδας τῶν ἀρχιερέων συναγαγών, τὸν ἐπιζητηθέντα ὅρον τῷ βασιλεῖ διεπέμψατο. Μετ' οὐ πολὺ δὲ καὶ ὁ βασιλεὺς τὴν ἐπίγειον βασιλείαν πρὸς τὴν οὐράνιον διαμείβεται.

60: 5 χειροτονίσας H

61: 1 ἐν om. F ‖ 2 ἀπολλινάριον H

62: 2 ἰοβιανοῦ H ‖ 3 βασιλέα] βασιλείαν F ambig. H ‖ 4 λιβέλους F

63: 2 τὸν] τὸ F

64. Οὐαλεντῖνος δὲ ἀντ' αὐτοῦ τὸ κράτος τῆς βασιλείας κοινῇ τῶν ὑπηκόων ψήφῳ περιβάλλεται, ὃς ὕστερον ἔδειξε κοινῇ βλαβῇ κοινωνὸν τοῦ κράτους τὸν ἀδελφὸν Οὐάλεντα προσλαβών, ἐπὶ τὰ ἑσπέρια ὥρμησεν, αὐτῷ τὴν τῆς ἑῴας ἀρχὴν χειρισάμενος. Καταλαβὼν δὲ τὰ Μεδιόλανα καὶ πολλοὺς ἀρχιερεῖς συγκαλέσας, ὥστε Εὐδόξιον μὲν τὸν γεγονότα Μεδιολάνων ἐπίσκοπον, ἅτε δὴ Ἀρειανὸν καὶ πνευματομάχον, καὶ μετὰ θάνατον τῷ ἀναθέματι παραπέμψαι, τὸν δὲ ἄξιον τῷ θρόνῳ καθιδρῦσαι. Τῶν δὲ Ἀρειανῶν στασιασάντων, ἀνεκόπη τὸ βούλημα· Ἀμβροσίου δὲ τοῦ τῆς πόλεως ἐπάρχου ἐπιστάντος, ὥστε διαλῦσαι τὴν στάσιν, ἅμα τῶν τε ἀπίστων καὶ τῶν ὀρθοδόξων τὸ πλῆθος εἰς ὁμόψηφον γνώμην συνέρχεται καὶ Ἀμβρόσιον σφῶν ἀρχιερέα καταστῆναι ἐσπούδαζον· ἡ δὲ σύνοδος ἐπινεύσει τοῦ βασιλέως βαπτίσασά τε καὶ μυήσασα τὰ θεῖα εἰς ἀρχιερέα προβιβάζει τὸν Ἀμβρόσιον. Ἐφ' ᾧ καὶ φωνὴν ἀφεῖναι τὸν βασιλέα λέγουσιν ὡς, «Χάρις σοι, δέσποτα παντοκράτορ καὶ σωτὴρ ἡμέτερε, ὅτι τῷδε τῷ ἀνδρὶ ἐγὼ μὲν σώματα ἐπίστευσα, σὺ δὲ ψυχάς, καὶ τὰς ἐμὰς ψήφους δικαίας ἀπέφηνας.»

65. Μετὰ δὲ τὴν ἐν Μεδιολάνῳ σύνοδον αἰτησαμένων τῶν εὐσεβῶν, σύνοδον ὁ βασιλεὺς ἐν Τυάνοις ψηφίζει γενέσθαι, τοῖς ἐν Νικαίᾳ δογματισθεῖσι τὸ κῦρος ἐπιψηφίζουσαν. Καὶ δὴ αὐτὴ συναθροίζεται· ἐν οἷς συνήχθησαν Γρηγόριος ὁ τοῦ θεολόγου πατὴρ καὶ Ὀτρίης ὁ Μελιτηνῆς, Εὐσέβιός τε ὁ Καισαρείας καὶ ἕτεροι. Καὶ Λιβέριος δὲ πρὸς τὴν συναθροισθεῖσαν σύνοδον τόμον ὀρθοδοξίας ἀπέστειλεν. Ἀλλ' ὅ γε Οὐάλης ὁ τῆς ἑῴας βασιλεὺς παρὰ Αὐξεντίου τοῦ Ἀρειανίζοντος τὸ βάπτισμα δεξάμενος καὶ συμφρονεῖν αὐτῷ κατὰ πᾶσαν τὴν ἀσέβειαν ἐν τῷ βαπτίζεσθαι ὅρκον ὑποσχών, τοὺς συνελθόντας ἐν Τυάνοις †σύνοδον†.

66. Εὐσεβίου δὲ τοῦ Καισαρείας τῆς Καππαδοκίας τελειωθέντος, ὁ μέγας Βασίλειος εἰς ἀρχιεπίσκοπον τοῦ θρόνου ψηφίζεται. Ὁ δὲ προσκαλεσάμενος τοὺς ἐκ τῆς ὑπερορίας ἀνακληθέντας, Εὐσέβιον λέγω τὸν Σαμοσατέα καὶ Λουκίφερα τὸν ἐκ Σάρδεων καὶ τοὺς ὑπ' αὐτοῖς, ὑπ' αὐτῶν τῷ θρόνῳ καθιδρύεται. Ἀναθεματίζει δὲ αὕτη ἡ σύνοδος Διάνιον τὸν ταύτης πάλαι πρὸ Εὐσεβίου ἀρχιεπίσκοπον, Ἀστέριόν τε καὶ Εὐσέβιον καὶ Θεοφρόνιον τοὺς Καππαδόκας.

64: 2 ὃς] ὃς ὡς H ‖ 14 σωτὴρ] sic codd. ‖ 16 ἀπέφανας H

65: 4 ὀτρίης codd. ‖ 9 σύνοδον] ἀπήλασεν *SV*[1]

67. Μετὰ δὲ τὴν ἐν Καισαρείᾳ τῆς Καππαδοκίας σύνοδον, Λιβερίου τὸν βίον ἀλλάξαντος, Δάμασος ἐν Ῥώμῃ προχειρίζεται· ὃς σύνοδον διακοσίων πατέρων ἐν Ῥώμῃ συναθροίσας, τὸ σύμβολον τρανοῖ τὸ τῆς πίστεως· ἀναθεματίζει δὲ Αὐξέντιον, καὶ ὅρον εὐσεβείας διαθέμενος, τοῖς Ἰλλυριοῖς διαπέμπεται.

68. Εἶτα πάλιν δεύτερον ἀθροίσας σύνοδον ὑπὲρ τοῦ ὁμοουσίου καὶ κατὰ τοῦ Αὐξεντίου.

69. Μετὰ δὲ ταῦτα δέονται Οὐαλεντινιανοῦ τοῦ βασιλέως οἱ τοῦ ὁμοουσίου κυρωθῆναι μὲν τὰ ἐν Νικαίᾳ, ἀποκηρυχθῆναι δὲ Ὑπάτιον τὸν Ἡρακλείας τῆς Πειρίνθου ἐπίσκοπον. Καὶ συναθροίζονται ἐν Λαμψάκῳ· δύο δὲ μῆνας κατατρίψαντες ἐν αὐτῇ, ψηφίζονται μὲν ἄκυρα εἶναι τὰ ἐν Κωνσταντινουπόλει ὑπὸ Εὐζωΐου καὶ Ἀκακίου πάλαι πεπραγμένα, κρατεῖν δὲ τὴν ἐν Σελευκείᾳ πίστιν. Ἃ διαγνοὺς Οὐάλης, πάντα μὲν τὰ ἐκεῖσε ἀνέτρεψε, τοὺς δὲ συνελθόντας ἐξορίᾳ παρέπεμψε.

70. Μετὰ δὲ τὴν ἐν Λαμψάκῳ σύνοδον οἱ ἐν Φρυγίᾳ Ἀετιανοὶ σύνοδον ἐν Πούζῃ ἀθροίζουσι, δι᾽ ἧς μετὰ Ἰουδαίων τὸ πάσχα ἐκτελεῖν δογματίζουσιν. Ὃν ὅρον Σαβάτιος κρατύνας, πολλοὺς τῶν ἐν Βυζαντίῳ συνήρπασεν, ἐξ οὗ τὸ τῶν Σαβατιανῶν προελήλυθε σύστημα.

71. Μετὰ δὲ τὴν ἐν Πούζῃ αἱρετικὴν σύνοδον Οὐαλεντινιανὸς ὁ βασιλεὺς σύνοδον ἐν τῷ Ἰλλυρικῷ γενέσθαι προστάσσει, ἣ τὴν μὲν ἐν Νικαίᾳ πίστιν ἐβεβαίωσεν, ἀναθεματίζει δὲ Πολυχρόνιον, Τηλέμαχον, Φαῦστον, Ἀσκλητιάδην, Ἀμάντιον, καὶ Κλεόπατρον· τὸν δὲ τῆς συνόδου τόμον ἐν Ἀσίᾳ τε Φρυγίᾳ καὶ Καρίᾳ Ἀρειανοῖς ἐπισκόποις ἐξαπέστειλεν. Ὡσαύτως δὲ καὶ ὁ βασιλεὺς Οὐαλεντινιανὸς ἴδικτον ποιήσας, πρὸς τοὺς αὐτοὺς διεπέμψατο.

69: 4–7: *Epit. Th. A.*, 63, 11–16

67: 5 ἰλλυρικοῖς H
68: 1 δεύτερον] sic codd. ‖ ἀθροίσας] sic codd.
69: 7 παράπεμψε F
71: 5 τε] τε καὶ H

72. Μετὰ δὲ τὴν ἐν τῷ Ἰλλυρικῷ ἁγίαν σύνοδον ὁ μὲν ἱερὸς Ἀθανάσιος εἰς τὸν ἀγήρω μετέστη βίον· Πέτρον δὲ τὸν ἐν τοῖς ὑπὲρ εὐσεβείας ἀγῶσιν αὐτῷ συνιδρώσαντα τελευτῶν ἤδη ἄξιον τῆς τοῦ θρόνου διαδοχῆς ἐμμαρτύρεται. Οἱ δὲ τῆς Ἀρειανικῆς δόξης ἔξαρχοι τὴν Ἀλεξάνδρειαν καταλαβόντες καὶ χειρὶ Ἑλληνικῇ τὸν μαρτυρηθέντα ἐξελάσαντες, Λούκιον ὁμόφρονα τῇ ἐκκλησίᾳ ἀντεκατέστησαν· Πέτρος δὲ φυγὰς ἐπὶ Ῥώμην ᾤχετο πρὸς Δάμασον. Εἶτα σύνοδος ἱερὰ τοπικὴ συνίσταται, ἥτις ἀναθεματίζει μὲν τὸν ἄνουν Ἀπολινάριον καὶ Στέφανον τὸν αὐτοῦ μαθητὴν καὶ τὸν δυσώνυμον Λούκιον.

73. Μετὰ δὲ ταύτην τὴν σύνοδον οἱ Εὐσταθίου τοῦ Ἀρμενίας μαθηταὶ τὴν ἑαυτῶν ὕλην πολλοῖς ἐσπούδασαν ἐπινέμεσθαι· καθ' ὧν σύνοδος ἐν Γάγγρᾳ συναθροίζεται, ἥτις τοὺς βδελυσσομένους τὸν ἔνθεσμον γάμον ἀναθέματι παρεπέμψατο, καὶ ὅσα ἄλλα παρὰ τοὺς τῆς ἐκκλησίας νόμους οἱ Εὐσταθιανοὶ πράττειν ἐτόλμησαν.

74. Μετὰ δὲ τὴν ἐν Γάγγρᾳ σύνοδον Οὐάλης ὁ βασιλεὺς Γότθοις συμβαλὼν κατὰ τὴν Θρᾴκην, πυρίκαυστος ὑπ' αὐτῶν γίνεται. Γρατιανὸς δὲ ὁ τῶν ἑσπερίων βασιλεὺς καὶ τῆς ἑῴας τὸ κράτος προσλαβών, τοὺς ἐν ἐξορίᾳ πάντας ἐπισκόπους ἀνακαλεῖται. Καὶ Δάμασος ὁ τῆς Ῥωμαίων ἐκκλησίας ἐπίσκοπος σύνοδον ἀθροίζει, ἥτις τὸ τῶν ἐν Νικαίᾳ κυρώσασα θεῖον σύμβολον, κατὰ πνευματομάχων καὶ ἑτέρων αἱρετικῶν δικαίαν τὴν ψῆφον ἐπήνεγκε.

75. Μετὰ δὲ τὴν ἐν Ῥώμῃ σύνοδον ὑπὸ τοῦ αὐτοῦ Γρατιανοῦ Μελέτιος πάλιν ἀνακληθείς, σύνοδον ἐν Ἀντιοχείᾳ συγκαλεῖ, ἥτις τὸ ἅγιον κυρώσασα σύμβολον, ἀνεθεμάτισεν Ἀπολινάριον, Φωτεινὸν καὶ Μάρκελλον, καὶ ὅρον διαθεμένη πρὸς τὸν ἀρχιερέα Ῥώμης ἀπέστειλε Δάμασον.

72: 9 δυσσώνυμον codd.

73: 2 ὕλην] leg. ἰλὺν? (λύμην *SV*[1])

75: 3 ἀπολλινάριον H

76. Ἀλλ' ὅ γε Γρατιανὸς ἐν πολέμοις Θεοδόσιον ἀριστεύσαντα τῆς ἑῴας βασιλέα ἀναδείκνυσι· τοῦτο μὲν ἆθλον τῶν πόνων, τοῦτο δὲ τῆς ἐπὶ τῷ πατρὶ παρανόμου πράξεως παραμυθίαν ἅμα καὶ ἀπολογίαν προβαλλόμενος.

77. Θεοδόσιος δὲ τὰ σκῆπτρα τῆς βασιλείας ἐγχειρισθεὶς σύνοδον ἐν Κωνσταντινουπόλει ἀθροίζει, ἧς ἐξῆρχε Τιμόθεος ὁ Ἀλεξανδρείας, Κύριλλος Ἱεροσολύμων ἤδη διαστὰς Σιλβανοῦ καὶ τῶν σὺν αὐτῷ λς' ὁμοφρόνων, οἳ τῇ τῶν πνευματομάχων νόσῳ κατείχοντο. Αὕτη ἡ ἁγία β' καὶ οἰκουμενικὴ σύνοδος τῶν ρν' πατέρων Εὐσέβιον καὶ Θεόγνιον τοὺς Βιθυνοὺς καὶ Πατρόφιλον καὶ Ἀέτιον τοὺς Παλαιστινούς, Παῦλον καὶ Γρηγόριον τοὺς Φοίνικας, Θεόδωρόν τε καὶ Γεώργιον, Ἀθανάσιον καὶ Νάρκισσον τοὺς Κίλικας, Μηνόφαντόν τε τὸν Ἐφέσου καὶ Θεόδωρον Πειρίνθου Ἀπολινάριόν τε καὶ Μάρκελλον Ἀγκύρας, τούτους ἅπαντας ἀποκηρύξασα, Μακεδόνιον καὶ τὴν αὐτοῦ χειροτονίαν πάσης ἱερωσύνης ἀπεγύμνωσε, καὶ τὸ ἅγιον πνεῦμα τῷ πατρὶ καὶ τῷ υἱῷ ὁμοούσιον ἀνεκήρυξεν. Ἔστι δὲ καὶ τὸ σύμβολον τῶν ρν' πατέρων οὕτως· «πιστεύομεν εἰς ἕνα θεὸν πατέρα παντοκράτορα, ποιητὴν οὐρανοῦ καὶ γῆς, ὁρατῶν τε πάντων καὶ ἀοράτων», ὡς προεγράφη. Ταύτῃ δὲ τῇ ἁγίᾳ καὶ οἰκουμενικῇ δευτέρᾳ συνόδῳ προστάξει Γρατιανοῦ τοῦ βασιλέως ἐν Ἀκυληίᾳ σύνοδος ἀθροισθεῖσα, ἧς ἐξῆρχε Δάμασος, Ἀμβρόσιος Ἀχόλιός τε ὁ Θεσσαλονίκης, κατὰ πάντα συμφώνους τὰς ψήφους ἔθετο, ὡς τοῦ ἁγίου πνεύματος ἐνεργήσαντος, ἔν τε τῇ Κωνσταντινουπόλει καὶ ἐν τῇ ἐν Ἀκυληίᾳ συστάσῃ ἁγίᾳ συνόδῳ.

78. Γρατιανοῦ δὲ τὸν βίον ξίφει λιπόντος καί τινων τὴν οἰκείαν δυσσέβειαν ἀνακινεῖν σπουδαζόντων, Δάμασος ὁ τῆς Ῥώμης ἐπίσκοπος σύνοδον ἐν αὐτῇ συγκαλεῖ, ἥτις ὅρον εὐσεβείας ἐκθεμένη πρὸς τὴν ἐν Κωνσταντινουπόλει σύνοδον ἀθροιζομένην διαπέμπει.

77: 14 ὡς προεγράφη] 35, 14 sqq.

77: 2 συναθροίζει H ‖ ὁ om. H ‖ 12 τὸ om. F ‖ 15 δευτέρᾳ om. H ‖ 18 ἐν[2] om. H ‖ συστήσῃ F

79. Σύνοδος τοπικὴ ἐν Κωνσταντινουπόλει ἐπὶ Νεκταρίου, ἧς αὐτὸς ἐξῆρχε καὶ Θεόφιλος Ἀλεξανδρείας· ἥτις ἀναϑέματι καϑυπέβαλεν Ἀρειανούς τε καὶ Παυλιανοὺς καὶ Ἀπολιναριστάς, Μαρκιανούς τε καὶ Φωτεινόν· καὶ ὅρον δὲ διατυπώσασα πρὸς τὸν μακάριον Δάμασον καὶ τὴν ἐκεῖσε σύνοδον ἀρχιερέων ὑπηρετουμένων τῷ γράμματι ἐξαπέστειλε.

80–81. Μετὰ δὲ ταύτην τὴν ἐν Κωνσταντινουπόλει σύνοδον Θεοδόσιος μὲν ὁ βασιλεὺς καὶ Νεκτάριος ὁ ἀρχιερεὺς ἐπὶ τὰ οὐράνια μεϑαρμόζονται, διαδέχεται δὲ τὸν μὲν Ἀρκάδιος υἱός, τὸν δὲ Ἰωάννης ὁ Χρυσόστομος. Τοῦ φϑόνου δὲ κατὰ τοῦ μακαριωτάτου Ἰωάννου αἰκίας πολλὰς βάλλοντος, λγ′ συνέδριον ἐν τῇ Δρυΐ, τῇ νῦν Ῥουφινιαναῖς, κατὰ τοῦ ϑείου συνιστῶσιν ἀνδρός, καὶ ὁ μὲν τοῦ ϑεοῦ ἄνϑρωπος παραυτίκα ἐξορίζεται.

82. Ἄνδρες δὲ τῆς ἀληϑείας ἐρασταὶ εἰς ἀριϑμὸν συντελοῦντες ξ′, τῶν ἔμπροσϑεν καταγνόντες καὶ συνοδικῶς τὴν ἀϑῴωσιν τῷ ϑείῳ ἀνδρὶ συμψηφισάμενοι, τῷ οἰκείῳ ϑρόνῳ ἀποκαταστῆναι παρεσκεύασαν. Ἀλλ' ὅ γε φϑόνος οὐδὲ μετὰ ταῦτα ἠρεμῶν, μᾶλλον δὲ πλέον τοῖς προτερήμασι τοῦ ἀνδρὸς ἐκκαιόμενος, ἐξορίᾳ πάλιν τὸν ἄνδρα παρέπεμψεν· ἐν ᾗ καὶ τὸν βίον λιπών, πρὸς τὰς οὐρανίους μονὰς ἀνεφοίτησε. Τοῦτον δὲ διαδέχεται μὲν Ἀρσάκιος τῆς ἐκκλησίας πρεσβύτερος, τὸν δὲ Ἀττικός, τὸν δὲ Σισίνιος, τῆς ἐκκλησίας καὶ αὐτοὶ ἱερουργοὶ χρηματίζοντες.

83. Μεϑ' ὃν Νεστόριος ὁ φρενοβλαβὴς ἐξ Ἀντιοχείας μετάκλητος γεγονώς, τῷ Κωνσταντινουπόλεως ϑρόνῳ ἐνιδρύεται· ὃς καινοτέραν τῶν ἔμπροσϑεν αἱρεσιωτῶν ὁδὸν τεμεῖν φιλοτιμησάμενος, ϑεοτόκον καλεῖν τὴν ἀληϑῶς καὶ κυρίως σαρκὶ τεκοῦσαν τὸν υἱὸν τοῦ ϑεοῦ ὁ παράφορος οὐκ ἠνέσχετο· καϑ' οὗ καὶ Κύριλλος σύνοδον ἀϑροῖσαι προήχϑη. Σύνοδος τοπικὴ ἐν Ἀλεξανδρείᾳ ὑπὸ τοῦ ϑεσπεσίου Κυρίλλου συναϑροισϑεῖσα, ἥτις

80–81: 5: cf. *Epit. Th. A.*, 89, 14

80–81: 3 post υἱός add. ϑεοδοσίου H

82: 3 ψηφισάμενοι H ‖ ἀποταστῆναι (sic) F

ὅρον ιβʹ κεφαλαίοις ἀπαρτιζόμενον ἐκθεμένη πρὸς Νεστόριον ἀπέστειλεν, ἅτινά εἰσι ταῦτα·

αʹ. Εἴ τις οὐχ ὁμολογεῖ θεὸν εἶναι κατὰ ἀλήθειαν τὸν Ἐμμανουὴλ καὶ διὰ τοῦτο θεοτόκον τὴν ἁγίαν παρθένον, γεγέννηκε γὰρ σάρκα γεγονότα τὸν ἐκ θεοῦ πατρὸς λόγον, ἀνάθεμα.

βʹ. Εἴ τις οὐχ ὁμολογεῖ σαρκὶ καθ᾽ ὑπόστασιν ἡνῶσθαι τὸν ἐκ θεοῦ πατρὸς λόγον ἕνα τε εἶναι Χριστὸν μετὰ τῆς ἰδίας σαρκός, τὸν αὐτὸν δηλονότι θεόν τε ὁμοῦ καὶ ἄνθρωπον, ἀνάθεμα.

γʹ. Εἴ τις ἐπὶ τοῦ ἑνὸς Χριστοῦ διαιρεῖ τὰς ὑποστάσεις μετὰ τὴν ἕνωσιν, μόνῃ συνάπτων αὐτὰς συναφείᾳ τῇ κατὰ τὴν ἀξίαν, ἤγουν αὐθεντίᾳ ἢ δυναστείᾳ, καὶ οὐχὶ μᾶλλον συνόδῳ τῇ καθ᾽ ἕνωσιν φυσικήν, ἀνάθεμα.

δʹ. Εἴ τις προσώποις δυσὶν ἤγουν ὑποστάσεσι τάς τε ἐν τοῖς ἀποστολικοῖς καὶ εὐαγγελικοῖς συγγράμμασι διανέμει φωνὰς ἢ ἐπὶ τῷ Χριστῷ παρὰ τῶν ἁγίων λεγομένας ἢ παρ᾽ αὐτοῦ περὶ ἑαυτοῦ καὶ τὰς μὲν ὡς ἀνθρώπῳ παρὰ τὸν ἐκ θεοῦ λόγον ἰδικῶς νοουμένῳ προσάπτει, τὰς δὲ ὡς θεοπρεπεῖς τῷ ἐκ θεοῦ πατρὸς μόνῳ λόγῳ, ἀνάθεμα.

εʹ. Εἴ τις τολμᾷ λέγειν θεοφόρον ἄνθρωπον τὸν Χριστὸν καὶ οὐχὶ δὴ μᾶλλον θεὸν εἶναι κατὰ ἀλήθειαν, ὡς υἱὸν ἕνα καὶ φύσει, καθὸ γέγονε σὰρξ ὁ λόγος, κεκοινώνηκε γὰρ παραπλησίως ἡμῖν σαρκὸς καὶ αἵματος, ἀνάθεμα.

ϛʹ. Εἴ τις λέγει θεὸν ἢ δεσπότην εἶναι τοῦ Χριστοῦ τὸν ἐκ θεοῦ πατρὸς λόγον καὶ οὐχὶ τὸν αὐτὸν ὁμολογεῖ θεὸν ὁμοῦ τε καὶ ἄνθρωπον, ὡς γεγονότος σαρκὸς τοῦ λόγου κατὰ τὰς γραφάς, ἀνάθεμα.

ζʹ. Εἴ τίς φησιν ὡς ἄνθρωπον ἐνεργεῖσθαι παρὰ τοῦ θεοῦ λόγου τὸν Ἰησοῦν καὶ τὴν τοῦ μονογενοῦς εὐδοξίαν περιῆφθαι ὡς ἕτερον παρ᾽ αὐτὸν ὑπάρχοντα, ἀνάθεμα.

ηʹ. Εἴ τις τολμᾷ λέγειν τὸν ἀναληφθέντα ἄνθρωπον συμπροσκυνεῖσθαι δεῖν τῷ θεῷ λόγῳ καὶ συνδοξάζεσθαι καὶ συγχρηματίζειν ὡς θεὸν ἕτερον ἐν ἑτέρῳ, τὸ γὰρ σὺν ἀεὶ προστιθέμενον, τοῦτο νοεῖν ἀναγκάζει, καὶ οὐχὶ μᾶλλον μιᾷ προσκυνήσει τιμᾷ τὸν Ἐμμανουὴλ καὶ μίαν αὐτῷ τὴν δοξολογίαν ἀναπέμπει καθὸ γέγονε σὰρξ ὁ λόγος, ἀνάθεμα.

83: 7 ὅρον ιβʹ κεφ.: Mansi, IV, 1081–84 (cf. *ACO,* I, 1, 5, pp. 15–25) ‖ 35 τὴν τοῦ] τὴν αὐτοῦ H

θ'. Εἴ τις τὸν ἕνα κύριον Ἰησοῦν Χριστὸν δοξάζεσθαι λέγει παρὰ τοῦ πνεύματος, ὡς ἀλλοτρίᾳ δυνάμει τῇ δι' αὐτοῦ, καὶ παρ' αὐτοῦ λαβόντα τὸ ἐνεργεῖν καὶ δύνασθαι κατὰ πνευμάτων ἀκαθάρτων καὶ τὸ πληροῦν εἰς ἀνθρώπους τὰς θεοσημείας, καὶ οὐχὶ δὴ μᾶλλον ἴδιον αὐτοῦ τὸ πνεῦμά φησι, δι' οὗ καὶ ἐνήργησε τὰς θεοσημείας, ἀνάθεμα.

ι'. Ἀρχιερέα καὶ ἀπόστολον τῆς ὁμολογίας ἡμῶν γεγενῆσθαι Χριστὸν τὸν θεὸν λέγει ἡ γραφὴ προσκεκομικέναι τε ὑπὲρ ἡμῶν ἑαυτὸν εἰς ὀσμὴν εὐωδίας τῷ θεῷ καὶ πατρί. Εἴ τις τοίνυν ἀρχιερέα καὶ ἀπόστολον ἡμῶν γεγενῆσθαι λέγει οὐκ αὐτὸν τὸν ἐκ θεοῦ λόγον, ὅτε γέγονε σὰρξ καὶ καθ' ἡμᾶς ἄνθρωπος, ἀλλ' ὡς ἕτερον παρ' αὐτὸν ἰδικῶς ἄνθρωπον ἐκ γυναικός· ἢ εἴ τις λέγει καὶ ὑπὲρ αὐτοῦ προσενεγκεῖν αὐτὸν τὴν προσφορὰν καὶ οὐχὶ μᾶλλον ὑπὲρ μόνων ἡμῶν, οὐ γὰρ ἂν ἐδεήθη προσφορᾶς ὁ μὴ εἰδὼς ἁμαρτίαν, ἀνάθεμα.

ια'. Εἴ τις οὐχ ὁμολογεῖ τὴν τοῦ κυρίου σάρκα ζωοποιὸν εἶναι καὶ ἰδίαν εἶναι αὐτοῦ τοῦ ἐκ θεοῦ πατρὸς λόγου, ἀλλ' ὡς ἑτέρου τινὸς παρ' αὐτὸν συνημμένου μὲν αὐτῷ κατὰ τὴν ἀξίαν ἤγουν ὡς μόνην θείαν ἐνοίκησιν ἐσχηκότος, καὶ οὐχὶ μᾶλλον ζωοποιόν, ὡς ἔφημεν, ὅτι γέγονεν ἰδία τοῦ λόγου τοῦ τὰ πάντα ζωογονεῖν ἰσχύοντος, ἀνάθεμα.

ιβ'. Εἴ τις οὐχ ὁμολογεῖ τὸν τοῦ θεοῦ λόγον παθόντα σαρκὶ καὶ γεγονότα ἐσταυρωμένον σαρκὶ καὶ θανάτου γευσάμενον σαρκὶ γεγονότα τε πρωτότοκον ἐκ τῶν νεκρῶν, καθὸ ζωή ἐστι καὶ ζωοποιὸς ὡς θεός, ἀνάθεμα.»

Νεστόριος δὲ τοῖς ἀπεσταλμένοις οὐκ ἐμβλέψας τῆς προτέρας εἴχετο λώβης.

84. Θεοδόσιος δὲ ὁ Ἀρκαδίου παῖς τὴν πατρῴαν ἔχων βασιλείαν, σύνοδον οἰκουμενικὴν ἐν Ἐφέσῳ ἀθροισθῆναι κελεύει. Σύνοδος οἰκουμενικὴ τῶν ἐν Ἐφέσῳ σ' πατέρων συγκροτηθεῖσα, ἧς ἐξῆρχε Κύριλλος ὁ Ἀλεξανδρείας· Ἰωάννης δὲ ὁ Ἀντιοχείας καί τινες τῶν σὺν αὐτῷ ἀνατολικῶν ἐπισκόπων τὴν παρουσίαν ἀναβαλλόμενοι χρονοτριβεῖν τε καὶ ταλαιπωρεῖν τοῖς ἐν Ἐφέσῳ καθίσταντο αἴτιοι. Ἡ δὲ οὐκ ἔτι οἷα τε οὖσα

84: 6 Ἡ] οἱ F

περιμένειν τοὺς ἑκουσίως βραδύνοντας, Νεστόριον μὲν ἀποκηρύττει, θεοτόκον δὲ τὴν τοῦ Χριστοῦ καὶ θεοῦ ἡμῶν μητέρα καὶ καλεῖσθαι καὶ προσκυνεῖσθαι ἁγιοπρεπῶς ἀνεκήρυξεν.

85. Οἱ δὲ περὶ τὸν Ἀντιοχείας Ἰωάννην ὡς παρὰ γνώμην αὐτῶν τῆς συνόδου παραλαβούσης οὐ τὴν τυχοῦσαν ἔριν ἀνεκίνησαν· πλὴν ἐν Ἀντιοχείᾳ συνδραμόντες καὶ ἐπὶ Χριστοῦ δύο φύσεις ἀσυγχύτους καὶ ἀδιαιρέτους δογματίσαντες, πρὸς Κύριλλον διεπέμψαντο. Ὁ δὲ τῆς συνόδου ταύτης τὸν ὅρον δεξάμενος καὶ λαμπρᾷ τῇ φωνῇ ἀναβοήσας τὸ «εὐφραινέσθωσαν οἱ οὐρανοὶ καὶ ἀγαλλιάσθω ἡ γῆ,» ἐγγράφως τε αὐτοῖς τὴν ἰδίαν γνώμην συμφωνοῦσαν βεβαιωσάμενος, σαφῶς τε καὶ φιλαδέλφως τὴν στάσιν διέλυσε.

86. Μετὰ δὲ τὴν Νεστορίου καθαίρεσιν Μαξιμῖνος ἀρχιεπίσκοπος Κωνσταντινουπόλεως προχειρίζεται, ὃν Πρόκλος τελευτήσαντα διεδέξατο· ὃς ἔτι τὴν ἐκκλησίαν ταραττομένην ταύτην εὑρών, συνόδῳ τὸν τάραχον ἔπαυσε. Σύνοδος ἐν Κωνσταντινουπόλει τοπική, Πρόκλου προεξάρχοντος, ἥτις ἅπαντας τοὺς ἀνθισταμένους τῇ ἁγίᾳ καὶ καθολικῇ τοῦ θεοῦ ἐκκλησίᾳ τῷ ἀναθέματι ἐπιμένοντας παρεπέμψατο.

87. Μετὰ ταύτην τὴν τοπικὴν σύνοδον ἄνδρες εὐλαβεῖς τοῦ μονάδος βίου ἐξ Ἀρμενίας ἀπάραντες καὶ τὴν βασιλίδα καταλαβόντες πόλιν, ἀνεδίδασκον ὡς τὰ Θεοδώρου βιβλία τοῦ Μομψουεστίας οἱ ἐν τῇ Ἀνατολῇ ἀντὶ Νεστορίου περιέπουσι. Θεοδόσιος δὲ ὁ βασιλεὺς ἅμα Πρόκλῳ τῷ ἀρχιερεῖ Ἰωάννῃ τῷ τῆς Ἀντιοχείας γράφουσι, συνόδῳ τὰ παρὰ τῶν μοναχῶν περὶ Θεοδώρου τοῦ Μομψουεστίας λεγόμενα δοκιμάσαι· ὁ δὲ σύνοδον μὲν συγκροτεῖ, ἀθῷον δὲ Θεόδωρον τῶν ἐπιφερομένων εὑρεθῆναι τοῖς τε πρὸς τὸν βασιλέα γράμμασι καὶ τοῖς πρὸς τὸν ἀρχιερέα διεσήμανεν. Οἱ δὲ τὴν σύνοδον ταύτην πληροῦντες τὸν ἀριθμὸν ἦσαν γʹ καὶ ἑξήκοντα.

86: 3 ταύτην om. H

87: 1 ταύτην] ταύτην δὲ H ‖ 7 φερομένων H

88. Μετὰ δὲ ταύτην τὴν ἐν Ἀντιοχείᾳ σύνοδον Κύριλλος μὲν ὁ θεσπέσιος τὸν βίον διαμείβει, διάδοχος δὲ αὐτοῦ καθίσταται Διόσκορος· ὡσαύτως δὲ καὶ Πρόκλος ὁ μακαριώτατος τὸν βίον μεταλλάσσει, ἀντ' αὐτοῦ δὲ Φλαβιανὸς ἐγχειρίζεται τὸν θρόνον. Πρὸς ὃν Εὐσέβιος ὁ τοῦ Δορυλαίου ἐπίσκοπος παραγεγονώς, τὰ κατ' Εὐτυχῆ ἀναδιδάσκει· καὶ σύνοδος τοπικὴ ἐν Κωνσταντινουπόλει ἀθροίζεται, ἥτις τὰ κατ' Εὐτυχοῦς ἐξετάσασα, τῆς ἐκκλησίας ἀποκηρύττει τὸν ἄνθρωπον.

89. Ὁ δὲ μετὰ τὴν συνοδικὴν καταδίκην πολλοὺς τῶν συγκλητικῶν θωπείαις ὑπελθών, πείθει δι' αὐτῶν Θεοδόσιον σύνοδον ἐν Ἐφέσῳ συγκροτηθῆναι. Σύνοδος ἐν Ἐφέσῳ ληστρικὴ Εὐτυχῆ μὲν ἀθῳοῦσα, Φλαβιανὸν δὲ τὸν ἅγιον καὶ Εὐσέβιον τὸν Δορυλαίου καθελοῦσα· ὧν τὸν μὲν Εὐσέβιον Διόσκορος ἐξορίᾳ παρέδωκε, τὸν δὲ ἐν ἁγίοις Φλαβιανὸν πρὸς ἐξορίαν πεμπόμενον, κατὰ τὴν ὁδὸν ὑπὸ τοῦ Βαρσουμᾶ ἐθανάτωσε.

90. Μετὰ δὲ ταύτην τὴν παράνομον σύνοδον Λέων ὁ Ῥώμης τὸν Φλαβιανοῦ θάνατον ἐκδικῶν σύνοδον ἐν Ῥώμῃ συναθροίζει, ἥτις τύπον ὑπὲρ Φλαβιανοῦ ἐκθεμένη, τῷ τε κλήρῳ Κωνσταντινουπόλεως καὶ τοῖς ἐν ἀξίᾳ καὶ τῷ κοινῷ πλήθει διεπέμψατο. Ἐκπέμπει δὲ καὶ παραινετικὸν γράμμα πρὸς Θεοδόσιον τὸν βασιλέα, στοιχῆσαι τῇ καθαιρέσει Εὐτυχοῦς καὶ Διοσκόρου, ἀθετῆσαι δὲ τὴν κατάκρισιν Φλαβιανοῦ· οὗ καὶ τὸ τῆς βασιλείας στέφος ἀλλαξαμένου, σύνοδον πάλιν ἀθροίζει ὁ τῆς Ῥώμης πάπας Λέων.

91. Σύνοδος ἰδικὴ ὑπὸ τοῦ μακαριωτάτου πάπα Λέοντος ἐν Ῥώμῃ συνελθοῦσα, ἥτις διὰ γραμμάτων παραινεῖ Μαρκιανὸν τὸν βασιλέα συνόδῳ τὰ περὶ Φλαβιανοῦ ὑποβληθῆναι.

92. Καὶ δὴ σύνοδος συγκροτεῖται οἰκουμενικὴ ἐν Χαλκηδόνι χλ' πατέρων, ἥτις Εὐτυχῆ καὶ Διόσκορον καθελοῦσα, ἐπὶ Χριστοῦ δύο φύσεις ὁμολογεῖσθαι ἀσυγχύτους καὶ ἀδιαιρέτους τρανῶς ἐδογμάτισε.

90: 6 διοσκούρου F

92: 3 ἀδιαιρέτως F

93. Μετὰ δὲ τὴν τελευτὴν Μαρκιανοῦ τοῦ εὐσεβοῦς Λέοντος τὰ Ῥωμαϊκὰ σκῆπτρα περιέποντος, Προτέριος τῷ Ἀλεξανδρείας θρόνῳ προβιβάζεται. Τιμόθεος δέ τις μοναχός, Αἴλουρος ἐπίκλην, ἐκ περιδρομῆς στάσιν κατὰ Προτερίου κινήσας, ἐκεῖνον μὲν ἀναιρεθῆναι ἐν τῷ βαπτιστηρίῳ παρασκευάζει, αὐτὸς δὲ τὸν Ἀλεξανδρείας θρόνον ἁρπάσας, τὴν ἐν Χαλκηδόνι σύνοδον ἀπεκήρυξεν.

94. Ὧν ἡ γνῶσις Λέοντι τῷ βασιλεῖ ἀνενεχθεῖσα, συνόδῳ κριθῆναι τὰ τολμηθέντα παρώρμησε. Σύνοδος ἐν Θεσσαλονίκῃ ὑπὸ Αὐξιθέου τοῦ ταύτης ἐπισκόπου συναθροισθεῖσα, ἥτις Τιμόθεον τὸν Αἴλουρον καὶ Εὐτυχῆ ἀναθεματίσασα, τὴν ἐν Χαλκηδόνι ἀνεκήρυξε σύνοδον.

95. Εἶτα θεσπίσματι Λέοντος σύνοδος ἐν Κωνσταντινουπόλει συγκροτεῖται ἧς ἐξῆρχεν Ἀνατόλιος· καὶ αὐτὴ δὲ Τιμόθεον ἀποκηρύξασα, τὴν ἐν Χαλκηδόνι ἐπεκύρωσε σύνοδον.

96. Μετὰ δὲ ταῦτα πάλιν σύνοδος ἐν Ῥώμῃ συναθροίζεται ὑπὸ Λέοντος τοῦ ταύτης πάπα· ἥτις ἐν αὐτῇ Τιμόθεον τὸν Αἴλουρον καὶ Εὐτυχῆ ἀναθεματίσασα, τὴν ἐν Χαλκηδόνι σύνοδον ἀνεκήρυξε.

98. Μετὰ δὲ ταῦτα Λέων ὁ βασιλεὺς Ζήνωνα ἀναλαβὼν ἐπὶ θυγατρὶ γαμβρόν, ἐν Ἀντιοχείᾳ ἐξαπέστειλεν. Ἀνιὼν δὲ Πέτρος τις τῆς ἐν Χαλκηδόνι ἐκκλησίας ἐπίκλην Κναφεὺς συνείπετο, ὃς ἐποφθαλμίσας τὸν Ἀντιοχείας θρόνον, πείθει Ζήνωνα συνδραμεῖν αὐτῷ ἐπὶ τῇ κατασχέσει τοῦ θρόνου. Καὶ μισθωσάμενός τινας τῆς λώβης Ἀπολιναρίου, ἁρπάζει μὲν τὸν θρόνον Ἀντιοχείας, προστίθησι δὲ τῷ τρισαγίῳ «ὁ σταυρωθεὶς δι' ἡμᾶς.» Ταῦτα δὲ Λέων ὁ βασιλεὺς ἀναμαθών, ἐξορισθῆναι τὸν Πέτρον προσέταξεν· ὁ δὲ προφθάσας τὴν ἀπειλὴν ᾤχετο φυγάς, καὶ ἐν τῇ μονῇ τῶν Ἀκοιμήτων ἐκρύπτετο.

93: 1 τὴν om. H ‖ 5 αὐτὸν F

98: 1 ζήνων codd. ‖ 3 συνείπτετο H ‖ 4 θήνωνα F ‖ 8 καὶ om. F

99. Μετὰ δὲ τὴν ἀποβίωσιν Λέοντος καὶ τοῦ ἐπ' ὀλίγον αὐτὸν διαδεξαμένου μικροῦ Λέοντος, Ζήνων ὁ τοῦ μικροῦ Λέοντος πατὴρ τῶν Ῥωμαϊκῶν αὐτοκράτωρ ἀναγορεύεται. Βασιλίσκος δὲ τυραννίδι ἐπιθέμενος καὶ Ζήνωνα φυγάδα καταστήσας, τὴν μὲν ἐν Χαλκηδόνι σύνοδον ἐξοστρακίσαι σπουδὴν ἔθετο, τύπῳ δὲ γενικῷ τὸν Αἴλουρον ἐκ Χερσῶνος ἀνακαλεῖται. Ὁ δὲ τὴν Ἀλεξάνδρειαν καταλαβών, Τιμόθεον μὲν τὸν ἐπίκλην Σαλοφακίωλον, τὰ τῆς εὐσεβείας κρατύνοντα δόγματα, τοῦ θρόνου ἐλαύνει, αὐτὸς δὲ τοῦ θρόνου γεγονὼς ἐγκρατής, τὴν ἐν Χαλκηδόνι σύνοδον ἀνακηρύττει.

100. Πέτρος δὲ ἀπὸ τῆς μονῆς τῶν Ἀκοιμήτων ἀναφανείς, τὸν τῆς Ἀντιοχείας θρόνον καταλαμβάνει. Ἰωάννης μέντοι ὁ Κύρου ἐπίσκοπος, εἰς ἀσθένειαν τὴν τυραννίδα Βασιλίσκου ῥέπουσαν ὁρῶν, κατὰ Πέτρου τοῦ Κναφέως ἀγωνίζεται. Σύνοδος τοπικὴ ὑπὸ Ἰωάννου ἐπισκόπου Κύρου συγκροτηθεῖσα, ἥτις Πέτρον τὸν Κναφέα ἀναθέματι καθυπέβαλλεν.

101. Ἐκποδὼν δὲ τοῦ τυράννου γεγονότος καὶ Ζήνωνος πάλιν τὴν ἰδίαν βασιλείαν καταλαβόντος, σύνοδος πάλιν ἐν Ἀντιοχείᾳ ἀθροίζεται, ἥτις τὴν ἐν Χαλκηδόνι ἐπικυρώσασα σύνοδον, Πέτρον ἀναθεματίζει τὸν Κναφέα, εἶτα ἐξορίᾳ παραδίδωσι. Μετὰ δὲ τὴν τούτου ἐξορίαν ἡ σύνοδος Στέφανον προχειρίζεται· μετ' οὐ πολὺ δὲ τοῦ ἀνδρὸς τὸν βίον ἀπολιπόντος, Στέφανος ἕτερος ἀντ' αὐτοῦ χειροτονεῖται.

102. Οἱ δὲ Πέτρου σπουδασταί, Νεστόριον φρόνημα τῷ Στεφάνῳ κατειπόντες, πείθουσι τὸν βασιλέα Ζήνωνα ταῖς διαβολαῖς τὸ οὖς ὑποσχεῖν καὶ σύνοδον οὗτος ὁρίζει περὶ αὐτοῦ συστῆναι. Σύνοδος τοπικὴ ἐν Λαοδικείᾳ, ἥτις ἁγία σύνοδος Στέφανον ὑπὸ αἱρετικῶν κατηγορούμενον ἀθῷον ἀποφαίνει καὶ τῷ θρόνῳ ἀποκαθίστησιν. Ἀλλ' οἵ γε τῆς ἀσεβείας θερμοὶ ζηλωταί, οὐ πολλοῦ διελθόντος χρόνου, θυμῷ καὶ ἀπονοίᾳ καθοπλίσαντες ἑαυτούς, τὸν ἰθυνόμενον ἄνδρα συναρπάσαντες καὶ σύραντες εἰς τὸν παραρρέοντα τῇ Ἀντιοχείᾳ ποταμὸν Ὀρόντην ἐναπέρριψαν.

102: 6–7: cf. *Epit. Th. A.*, 116, 23 (Theoph., 128, 22–23)

99: 3 διεπιθέμενος F ‖ 9 immo ἀποκηρύττει
101: 1 ἐκ ποδῶν codd.

103. Καὶ Αἰλούρου δὲ τοῦ Ἀλεξανδρείας καταστρέψαντος τὸν βίον, Πέτρον τὸν Μογγὸν οἱ συναιρεσιῶται τῷ θρόνῳ ἐγκαθιδρύουσιν· ἀλλ' οἵ γε τῆς ἀληθείας ἐρασταὶ τοῦτον μὲν ἐκεῖθεν ἀπήλασαν, Ἰωάννην δὲ τὸν ἐπιλεγόμενον Ταβενησιώτην ἀντεκατέστησαν. Ὁ δὲ Ζήνων ὡς παρὰ γνώμην αὐτοῦ χειροτονηθέντα τὸν μὲν ἱερὸν ἄνδρα τοῦτον ἐκβάλλει, τὸν Μογγὸν δὲ Πέτρον ἀντεισήγαγεν, ἐπιδοὺς αὐτῷ καὶ τὸ λεγόμενον ἑνωτικόν. Ὃς καταλαβὼν τὴν Ἀλεξάνδρειαν, κατὰ τῆς ἐν Χαλκηδόνι συνόδου λυττᾷ, καὶ Ἀκάκιος δὲ ὁ Κωνσταντινουπόλεως πρότερον οὐ προσιέμενος τὸν Μογγόν, εἶτα ὕστερον ἐπὶ θεραπείᾳ τοῦ βασιλέως εἰς κοινωνίαν ἀφρόνως ἐδέξατο. Σύνοδος αἱρετικὴ ἐν Ἀλεξανδρείᾳ ὑπὸ Πέτρου συγκροτηθεῖσα τοῦ Μογγοῦ, ἥτις τὴν ἐν Χαλκηδόνι σύνοδον ἐβλασφήμησεν.

104. Ἀλλ' οὐδ' οὕτως ὁ Κωνσταντινουπόλεως Ἀκάκιος τῆς πρὸς Πέτρον κοινωνίας διετειχίζετο· διὸ καὶ οἱ ἐν Κωνσταντινουπόλει ζηλωταὶ γράφουσι τὰ γεγονότα τῷ Ῥώμης Φίληκι, καὶ ἀθροίζει οὗτος σύνοδον. Σύνοδος ἀθροισθεῖσα ὑπὸ Φίληκος ἐν Ῥώμῃ, ἥτις Ἀκάκιον καὶ Πέτρον τὸν Μογγὸν ὑπὸ καθαίρεσιν ποιησαμένη, τὴν ἐν Χαλκηδόνι σύνοδον ἐπεσφράγισεν.

105. Ἀλλ' ὅ γε Ζήνων Καλαδίωνα μὲν τὸν Ἀντιοχείας ὀρθοδοξοῦντα ἐξορίζει εἰς Ὄασιν, ἀντικαθίστησι δὲ Πέτρον τὸν Κναφέα· ὅστις τὸν θρόνον δεξάμενος, πολλὰ μὲν καὶ ἄλλα τῶν ἀτόπων διεπράξατο, χειροτονεῖ δὲ καὶ Ξεναΐαν τὸν Πέρσην, δραπέτην πάλαι γεγονότα τοῦ οἰκείου δεσπότου, ὃς οὐδὲ τοῦ θείου λουτροῦ ἠξιωμένος ἐτύγχανεν. Ἀλλ' οὗτός γε τά τε ἄλλα δυσσεβῶν, οὔτε Χριστοῦ τοῦ ἀληθινοῦ θεοῦ ἡμῶν οὔτε τινὸς τῶν ἀσωμάτων ἀγγέλων ἱεροτυπίας ἐν τῇ ἐκκλησίᾳ συνεχώρει ἀνατίθεσθαι. Σύνοδος αἱρετικὴ ἐν Ἀντιοχείᾳ ὑπὸ τοῦ Κναφέως Πέτρου συστᾶσα, ἥτις κατὰ τῆς ἐν Χαλκηδόνι ἁγίας συνόδου ἐλύσσησεν.

106–107. Οἱ δὲ κατὰ τὴν ἀνατολὴν τῆς εὐσεβείας ὑπέρμαχοι τὰ τολμηθέντα τῷ Κναφεῖ Φίληκα τὸν Ῥώμης ἀναδιδάσκουσιν. Ὁ δὲ πρῶτον μὲν διὰ Κεντιανοῦ ἐπισκόπου Ἀρκουλάνων καὶ τῆς σὺν αὐτῷ συνόδου παραίνεσιν γραφῆναι τῷ Κναφεῖ παρεσκεύασεν, ὕστερον δὲ καὶ αὐτὸς συνοδικῶς καθαίρεσιν αὐτῷ διαπεπραγμένος, ταύτην αὐτῷ ἐξαπέστειλεν.

105: 6–7: cf. *Epit. Th. A.*, 155, 26–27 (vide ibid., 155, 3)

103: 4 ταβενισιώτην H

105: 1 Καλαδίωνα] sic codd.

108. Ἀκακίου δὲ τελευτήσαντος καὶ τοῦ μετ' αὐτὸν Φραβίτα, Εὐφήμιος Κωνσταντινουπόλεως χειροτονεῖται ἐπίσκοπος· ὅστις τοὺς ἐνδημοῦντας ἐπισκόπους συγκαλεσάμενος καὶ σύνοδον συγκαθίσας, τὰ ἐν Χαλκηδόνι δόγματα ἐγγράφοις ὑποσημειώσεσιν ἐπεκύρου. Γράφει δὲ καὶ πρὸς Φίληκα συνοδικὴν ἐπιστολήν· ὃς δεξάμενος ταύτην, ὀρθοδοξίαν ἐμαρτύρησεν, οὐ μὴν δὲ ὡς ἀρχιερέα προσήκατο, ἅτε δὴ μὴ ἀπαλείψαντος τῶν διπτύχων τοῦ Ἀκακίου τὸ ὄνομα, ὃν πάλαι Φίληξ ἦν ὑπὸ ἀνάθεμα ποιησάμενος.

109. Μετὰ δὲ τὴν Ζήνωνος τελευτὴν Ἀναστάσιος τὴν βασιλείαν ὑπέδραμεν, ὃς Εὐφήμιον αἰτίαις ἀδίκοις ποιῶν ἐπηρέαζε· τὸ γὰρ ὅλον αὐτοῦ τὴν ἐν Χαλκηδόνι σύνοδον ἐπεσημαίνετο. Σύνοδος τοπικὴ ἐν Κωνσταντινουπόλει Ἀναστασίου προστάξει συναθροισθεῖσα, ἥτις Εὐφήμιον τὸν ἀρχιεπίσκοπον ταύτης διὰ τὴν ἐν Χαλκηδόνι σύνοδον ἐξώσασα, Μακεδόνιον καὶ αὐτὸν ὀρθοδοξοῦντα ἀντεκατέστησε.

110. Μετὰ δὲ τὴν ἐξορίαν τοῦ μακαρίου Εὐφημίου ὁ διαδεξάμενος τοὺς ἐνδημοῦντας ἀθροίσας ἐπισκόπους, τὰ μὲν τῆς ἁγίας ἐν Χαλκηδόνι συνόδου δόγματα ἐγγράφως ἐπεσφραγίσατο, οὐ μέντοι καὶ τὸ ἑνωτικὸν ἐξεκήρυξε Ζήνωνος, ὑποστελλόμενος, τινὲς ὥς φασιν, Ἀναστασίου τὴν ἐξορίαν.

111. Μετὰ δὲ τὴν ἐκβολὴν Πέτρου τοῦ Κναφέως Παλλάδιος τὸν Ἀντιοχείας θρόνον ἐγχειρίζεται· τοῦδε τελειωθέντος Φλαβιανὸς ἀντικαθίσταται, ὃν καὶ Ἀναστάσιος ὁ βασιλεὺς τὸ ἑνωτικὸν ἀποδέξασθαι προὔτρεπε, τὸ Ζήνωνος. Ὁ δὲ συγκαλεσάμενος τοὺς ὑπ' αὐτὸν ἐπισκόπους καὶ βασιλεῖ χαριζόμενος τὸ ἑνωτικὸν μὲν ἀπεδέξατο καὶ τὰς τρεῖς οἰκουμενικὰς συνόδους ἐγγράφως ἀνεκήρυξε, τὴν ἐν Χαλκηδόνι δὲ παρεσιώπησε.

108: 7 τοῦ om. H

109: 2 αἰτίοις F

110: 1 δὲ om. F ‖ 2 χαλκηδόνου H ‖ 4–5 ἐξορίαν] ὀργήν coni. Westerink

111: 6 δὲ om. H

112. Μετὰ δὲ τὴν ἐν Ἀντιοχείᾳ ὑπὸ Φλαβιανοῦ παρανόμως συστᾶσαν σύνοδον ὁ βασιλεὺς Ἠλίᾳ τε τῷ Ἱεροσολύμων καὶ Φλαβιανῷ, οὗ πρὸ βραχέως ἐμνήσθην, δι' Εὐτροπίου τριβούνου σύνοδον ἐν Σιδῶνι ἀθροῖσαι παρεκελεύσατο, ἐκκήρυκτα τὰ ἐν Χαλκηδόνι ποιήσουσαν. Σύνοδος ἐν Σιδῶνι ὑπὸ Ἠλία καὶ Φλαβιανοῦ εὐτρεπιζομένη συστῆναι, ἀλλ' ὅ γε Ἠλίας Εὐτρόπιον ἔχων συνεργόν, ἄπρακτον αὐτὴν διελύσατο.

113. Μετὰ δὲ ταῦτα Ἀναστάσιος Ἠλίαν καὶ Φλαβιανὸν ἐν ὀργῇ ἐποιήσατο· καὶ Φλαβιανὸς καταλαβὼν τὴν Ἀντιόχειαν εὗρε τὸ σύστημα τῶν αἱρεσιωτῶν αὐτοῦ κατεπανιστάμενον, καὶ σύνοδον λῃστρικὴν τὸ αἱρετίζον ἀθροίσαντες, Φλαβιανὸν μὲν ἀπάτῃ τοῦ θρόνου ἐκβάλλουσι, Σεβῆρον δὲ ἀντικαθιστῶσιν.

114. Ὃς ὅρκον ὑποσχὼν Ἀναστασίῳ τῷ βασιλεῖ ὡς ἀκίνητα τὰ ἐν Χαλκηδόνι τηρήσει, οὕτω τοῦ θρόνου ἐπέβη. Καὶ τὸν ὅρκον ἀθετήσας, ὑπὸ ἀνάθεμα τὴν ἐν Χαλκηδόνι ποιεῖται σύνοδον Σεβῆρος ἐκεῖνος· ὃς σὺν διακοσίοις ἀποστάταις μοναχοῖς ἐξ Ἐλευθεροπόλεως ἀπάρας καὶ τὴν βασιλίδα καταλαβών, κατὰ Μακεδονίου τε τοῦ ὀρθοδόξου καὶ τῆς ἁγίας δ' συνόδου πολλοὺς ἀγῶνας ἠγωνίσατο.

115. Φλαβιανοῦ δὲ τῆς Ἀντιοχείας ὡς ἔφημεν ἀπάτῃ δελεασθέντος, Ἀναστάσιος σφόδρα κατὰ Μακεδονίου Κωνσταντινουπόλεως ἠγωνίζετο· καὶ πολλὰς ἐγκλημάτων αἰτίας ἀλόγως ἐπιγραφόμενος τοῦ θρόνου ἐξήλασε καὶ ὑπερόριον ἐν Γάγγρᾳ ἐποίησε, Τιμόθεον δὲ τὸν αἱρετικὸν ἀντ' αὐτοῦ κατέστησε. Σύνοδος αἱρετικὴ ὑπὸ Τιμοθέου κατὰ τῆς ἐν Χαλκηδόνι συνόδου· αὐτοῦ δὲ Τιμοθέου καὶ Σεβήρου τὰ συνοδικὰ αὐτῶν πρὸς τὰ Ἱεροσόλυμα πεμψαμένων, οὐδεὶς αὐτῶν ἀνασχέσθαι τῆς κοινωνίας ἠνέσχετο· διὸ περιοργὴς γεγονὼς Ἀναστάσιος, Ἠλίαν τὸν Ἱεροσολύμων ἐν τῷ Αἴλᾳ ὑπερώρισεν, Ἰωάννην δὲ τῷ θρόνῳ ἀντεκατέστησεν. Οἱ δὲ περὶ Τιμόθεον Ἰωάννῃ πάλιν τὰ συνοδικὰ διαπέμπουσι.

115: 1 ἐν ἀντιοχεία H ‖ δελεασθέντα codd. ‖ 8 περὶ ὀργῆς codd. ‖ τὸν] τῶν H

116. Θεοδόσιος δὲ καὶ Σάβας, ὧν πολὺς ἐν μοναχοῖς ὁ λόγος, ἅτε δὴ λογάδες ὄντες τῶν ἐν τῇ ἐρήμῳ καθηγουμένων, ἅπαν τὸ πλῆθος τῶν εὐσεβῶν συναθροίσαντες μοναχῶν τὰ Ἱεροσόλυμα καταλαμβάνουσι. Ταῦτα δὲ μαθὼν Ἀναστάσιος τοὺς τῆς ἀρετῆς ἀθλητὰς ἐξορίστους γενέσθαι προσέταξεν· οἱ δὲ προφθάσαντες τοὺς τῶν μοναχῶν λογάδας συναθροίζουσι. Σύνοδος ἱερὰ ἐν τῇ ἐρήμῳ συνελθοῦσα ὑπὸ Θεοδοσίου καὶ Σάβα, τῶν ἱερῶν ἀνδρῶν, ἥτις τέσσαρας διαμαρτυρίας ὀρθοδοξίας πλήρεις συντάξασα, δύο μὲν ἀποστέλλει Ἀναστασίῳ τῷ βασιλεῖ, μίαν δὲ τοῖς ἄρχουσι, καὶ μίαν Ἰωάννῃ τῷ Ἱεροσολύμων.

117. Μετὰ δὲ τὴν ἐν ἐρήμῳ τῶν ἁγίων ἀνδρῶν σύνοδον Ὁρμίσδας ὁ Ῥώμης—οὗτος γὰρ ἤδη τὴν ἐφορείαν ταύτης ἐδέδεκτο—ἀποστέλλει Ἐνώδιον καὶ Βιταλιανὸν σὺν ἑτέροις ἐπισκόποις ἐν Κωνσταντινουπόλει, ὥστε σύνοδον συγκροτηθῆναι· ἀλλ' ὅ γε βασιλεὺς καὶ ὁ Τιμόθεος πολυχρονίῳ ταλαιπωρίᾳ τοὺς ἀπεσταλμένους παρατείναντες, ἀπράκτους ἀπεπέμψαντο.

118. Ἀναστασίου δὲ τὸν βίον θεηλάτως καταστρέψαντος, Ἰουστῖνος βασιλεὺς Ῥωμαίων ἀναδείκνυται, ἐφ' οὗ Ὁρμίσδας ὁ Ῥώμης πολλοὺς ἐπισκόπους ἐν Θεσσαλονίκῃ ἐξαπέστειλεν, ὡς ἂν τὰ πάλαι ἐν Χαλκηδόνι δόξαντα ἐπιβεβαιωθείη. Τῆς συνόδου δὲ κατὰ Θεσσαλονίκην ἀθροιζομένης, οἱ τῆς αἱρέσεως ἔξαρχοι πῦρ βαλόντες νύκτωρ ἐν οἷς ἐκάθευδον δωματίοις οἱ ἀπεσταλμένοι, τὰς οἰκίας κατέκαυσαν· οἱ δὲ ἐν αὐτοῖς παρατυχόντες ἡμίκαυστοι τὸν ὄλεθρον διαφυγόντες, εἰς τὰ οἰκεῖα ὑπέστρεψαν ἄπρακτοι.

119. Μετὰ δὲ τὴν ἐν Θεσσαλονίκῃ σύνοδον Ὁρμίσδας πάλιν ἐπισκόπους πρὸς Ἰουστῖνον ἀπέστειλε. Σύνοδος ἱερὰ ἐν Κωνσταντινουπόλει, ἐν ᾗ παρῆσαν καὶ οἱ παρ' Ὁρμίσδα ἀπεσταλμένοι· ἥτις τὰ ἐν Χαλκηδόνι δογματισθέντα ἐκύρωσε, προεκθεμένη καί τινα ὧν Κύριλλος περὶ τῶν δύο Χριστοῦ διέλαβε φύσεων.

117: 2 ἐφορίαν H ‖ ἐδέδεικτο F ‖ 4 ὁ^2 om. H

118: 7 ἀπέστρεψαν F

119: 4 προεθεμένη codd.

120. Μετὰ δὲ ταύτην τὴν σύνοδον Ἰουστίνου μὲν μεταστάντος ἐκ τῶν ἐνθάδε Ἰουστινιανοῦ δὲ τοῦ ἀνεψιοῦ αὐτοῦ τὰ σκῆπτρα περιζωσαμένου τῆς βασιλείας, Ἀγαπητὸς ὁ πάπας Ῥώμης καταλαβὼν τὴν Κωνσταντινούπολιν διὰ τὴν παρὰ τῶν Γότθων γινομένην δύναμιν καὶ μέλλουσαν τῶν πραγμάτων διαφθορὰν καὶ τῆς εὐσεβείας ἐπήρειαν, σύνοδος τοπικὴ ἐν Κωνσταντινουπόλει ἐν ᾗ Ἀγαπητὸς ἐξῆρχεν ὁ πάπας Ῥώμης· ἥτις Ἄνθιμον τὸν ἐκ Τραπεζοῦντος ἐπὶ τὴν βασιλίδα μετακινηθέντα καθελοῦσα ἅμα Σεβήρῳ παραδέδωκε τῷ ἀναθέματι.

121. Εἶτα κατὰ τούσδε τοὺς καιροὺς ἐν Παλαιστίνῃ τινῶν μοναχῶν τὰ Ὠριγένους κρατυνόντων Ἐφραϊμίου τε τοῦ Ἀντιοχείας ἐπισκόπου πρὸς ταύτην ἀντικαθισταμένου τὴν νόσον, σύνοδος ἀθροίζεται ἐν Ἀντιοχείᾳ, ἧς ἐξῆρχεν Ἐφραΐμιος· ἥτις τὰ Ὠριγένους δόγματα ὑπέβαλεν ἀναθέματι.

122. Μετὰ δὲ ταύτην τὴν σύνοδον οἱ τῷ Νεστορίῳ προσκείμενοι διὰ τῶν τοῦ Θεοδώρου συγγραμμάτων τὴν ἐκείνου πάλιν ἀνενέουν αἵρεσιν· διὸ τῶν ζηλωτῶν ἐν Μοψουεστίᾳ συνάγεται σύνοδος. Σύνοδος ἐν Μοψουεστίᾳ ἥτις τοὺς ἐκεῖσε κληρικοὺς καὶ πολιτευομένους συγκαλεσαμένη ὅρκῳ τούτους κατέλαβεν, εἰπεῖν εἰ ἐπίστανται Θεοδώρου ὄνομα ἐν τοῖς διπτύχοις καταταττόμενον· οἱ δὲ ἀπομοσάμενοι μηδαμῶς εἰδέναι τοῦτο τοῖς διπτύχοις ἐντετάχθαι, ἀναμφίβολον τὴν τοῦ ζητουμένου πίστιν παρέσχον. Ἡ δὲ σύνοδος ταῦτα ἐγγράφως διεξελθοῦσα πρὸς Βιγίλιον τὸν πάπα Ῥώμης ἀπέστειλε.

123. Μετὰ δὲ ταῦτα οὐδ' οὕτως ἔληξε τὰ Ὠριγένεια δόγματα, οὔτε τὰ Θεοδώρου συγγράμματα μὴ ὑπὸ πολλῶν σπουδαζόμενα, ἀλλὰ καὶ τὰ τοῦ Θεοδωρίτου καὶ Ἴβα κατὰ τοῦ μακαρίου Κυρίλλου συγγραφέντα ἀποδοχῆς τοῖς αἱρετίζουσιν ἐνομίζετο ἄξια. Μετὰ δὲ ταῦτα Ἰουστινιανὸς ὁ βασιλεὺς οἰκουμενικὴν σύνοδον ἐν Κωνσταντινουπόλει ἀθροίζει, ἥτις τὰ

120: 2 ἐνθένδε F

121: 4 ἐφραιμένος H

122: 3 μομψουεστία (bis) H ‖ 5 εἰ om. F

123: 4 δὲ om. F

Ὠριγένους δόγματα καὶ Θεοδώρου συγγράμματα, ἔτι δὲ καὶ Θεοδωρήτου τὰ κατὰ Κυρίλλου καὶ τὴν λεγομένην Ἴβα ἐπιστολὴν ἀναθέματι παραδοῦσα, εἰρηνικῶς διαλύεται. Ταύτης δὲ ἐξῆρχεν Εὐτύχιος Κωνσταντινουπόλεως, Ἀπολινάριος Ἀλεξανδρείας, Δομνῖνος Ἀντιοχείας, Πέτρος Ἱεροσολύμων· Βιγίλιος δὲ ὁ πάπας Ῥώμης παρὼν οὐ συνήδρευεν· οὐδὲ γὰρ οὐδ' ἡ παρουσία αὐτοῦ σκοπὸν τὴν σύνοδον εἶχεν, ἀλλ' ὑπὲρ τοῦ Ῥώμης πρεσβεύσασθαι· ἄλλως δὲ καὶ φιλονεικία τις τὴν παρουσίαν ἀνέστελλε· πλὴν καὶ αὐτὸς τοῖς ὀρθοῖς ὡμοφρόνει τῆς συνόδου θεσπίσμασι.

125. Μετὰ δὲ τήν ἁγίαν καὶ οἰκουμενικὴν πέμπτην σύνοδον τὸ τέλος μὲν Δομνῖνος ὁ μακάριος διαβεβαιοῦται τοῦ βίου, Ἀναστάσιος δὲ τῷ πατριαρχικῷ θρόνῳ Ἀντιοχείας ἀντιχειροτονεῖται. Οὗτος ἀθροίσας σύνοδον τοὺς ἀνθισταμένους τῇ ἐν Χαλκηδόνι συνόδῳ παραπέμπει τῷ ἀναθέματι.

126. Μετὰ δὲ τὴν Ἰουστινιανοῦ ἀποβίωσιν βασιλεὺς Ῥωμαίων Ἰουστῖνος ἀναγορεύεται.

127. Ὃν Τιβέριος διαδέχεται καὶ Τιβέριον Μαυρίκιος· κατὰ Μαυρικίου δὲ Φωκᾶς τυραννίδι ἐπιθέμενος, ἁρπάζει τὴν βασιλείαν.

128. Ἡράκλειος δὲ ἐκ δυσμῶν ἀναχθεὶς καὶ Φωκᾶν ἀνελών, τὴν βασιλείαν περιβάλλεται. Τῶν δὲ Περσῶν ἐπὶ πόλεμον ὁρμώντων, ὁ βασιλεὺς Ἡράκλειος τὸν Φάσιν καταλαμβάνει ποταμόν, ἐν ᾧ τῶν Ἀκεφάλων τις περὶ δύο θελημάτων καὶ ἐνεργειῶν λόγους ἀνακινῶν τῷ βασιλεῖ ἐμφανίζεται. Ὁ δὲ τὸν συζητητὴν παραπέμπει Κύρῳ τῷ Φάσιδος ἐπισκόπῳ, ὡς ἂν ἀνακοινωσάμενοι ἀλλήλοις τὸ ὀρθὸν τῆς εὐσεβείας δόγμα κρατύνοιεν. Ἐν τῷ ἀμφιβόλῳ δὲ τῆς γνώσεως αὐτῶν σαλευομένης, Σεργίῳ τῷ Κωνσταντινουπόλεως τὰ περὶ αὐτῶν ὁ βασιλεὺς κατεμήνυσεν· ὁ δὲ τοῖς τοῦ μακαρίου Μηνᾶ συνοδικοῖς μονομερῶς ἐπιβαλών, μίαν θέλησιν ἐπὶ Χριστοῦ τοῦ θεοῦ ἡμῶν εἶναι καὶ ἐδογμάτισε καὶ διὰ γραμμάτων ἐδήλωσε τῷ βασιλεῖ.

13 τῆς ὀρθῆς H

125: 2 δομνῆνος H

129. Ἡρακλείου δὲ ὑποστρέψαντος πρὸς τὴν βασιλίδα, Σέργιος τὰ πρὶν αὐτῷ δόξαντα ἀφρόνως συνοδικῶς κρατύνειν ἐνεανιεύσατο. Σύνοδος αἱρετικὴ ἐν Κωνσταντινουπόλει ὑπὸ Σεργίου τοῦ ταύτης ἀρχιεπισκόπου συναθροισθεῖσα, ἥτις μίαν θέλησιν καὶ μίαν ἐνέργειαν ἀθέσμως ἐπὶ Χριστοῦ τοῦ θεοῦ ἡμῶν διωρίσατο.

130. Μετὰ δὲ τὴν Σεργίου σύνοδον Κῦρος ἐκ τοῦ Φάσιδος ἀπάρας, τὸν Ἀλεξανδρείας θρόνον παρείληφε, καὶ μίαν θέλησιν καὶ μίαν ἐνέργειαν καὶ αὐτὸς ἐπὶ Χριστοῦ τοῦ θεοῦ ἡμῶν ὁμολογήσας, ἐν κεφαλαίοις θ′ τὴν βλασφημίαν περιλαβών, Σεργίῳ ἀπέστειλε.

131. Σωφρόνιος δὲ τῶν Ἱεροσολύμων πρόεδρος ἀναδειχθείς, τοῖς δυσσεβέσιν ἀντικαθίσταται δόγμασι. Σύνοδος ἱερὰ ἐν Ἱεροσολύμοις ὑπὸ Σωφρονίου τοῦ ταύτης ἀρχιερέως συγκροτηθεῖσα, ἥτις δύο θελήσεις καὶ δύο ἐνεργείας ἐπὶ Χριστοῦ τοῦ ἀληθινοῦ θεοῦ ἡμῶν κατὰ τὰς πατρικὰς διανοίας τρανώσασα, τὰ συνοδικῶς πεπραγμένα αὐτῷ τε Σεργίῳ τῷ Κωνσταντινουπόλεως καὶ Ὀνορίῳ τῷ πάπα Ῥώμης ἀπέστειλε.

132. Μετὰ δὲ τελευτὴν Σεργίου Κῦρος ταύτης τῆς αἱρέσεως ἐρασθεὶς διάδοχος γίνεται. Σύνοδος αἱρετικὴ ὑπὸ Κύρου ἐν Κωνσταντινουπόλει, ἥτις Σεργίῳ τὰ αὐτὰ δυσφημήσασα, τοῖς προγεγενημένοις ὡς ἔδοξεν (138.) ἐπέθετο τὴν βεβαίωσιν. Ἡράκλειος οὖν τὸν βίον ἀπολιμπάνων, Πύρρον ὅρκοις ἠσφαλίσατο μὴ ἀνασχέσθαι κακωθῆναι Μαρτῖναν, ὅσα αὐτῷ ἐστι δυνατά, τὴν αὐτοῦ γεγενημένην γαμετήν, μήτε μὲν τοὺς ἐξ αὐτῆς παῖδας ὑπὸ τοῦ ἐκ τῆς προτέρας αὐτοῦ γυναικὸς γεγενημένου παιδός· Κωνσταντῖνος δὲ ἦν αὐτῷ τὸ ὄνομα. Καὶ μεγάλας λαβὼν τὰς παρὰ Πύρρου ὑποσχέσεις, χρήματα καταπιστεύει εἰς ἐπικουρίαν τε καὶ συγκρότησιν τῶν τε παίδων αὐτοῦ καὶ τῆς γυναικός. Κωνσταντίνου δὲ τοῦ υἱοῦ τοῦ Ἡρακλείου τὴν τῆς βασιλείας περιδύντος πορφύραν, οἱ τῆς πόλεως οὐ μετ᾽ οὐ πολὺν χρόνον κατεστασίασαν Πύρρου, ἄλλα τε ἐπιγραφόμενοι καὶ ὡς συνεργὸς εἴη Μαρτίνης ἐπὶ τῇ τῶν κρινόντων συγχύσει· διὸ καὶ τοῦ θρόνου ἀποστῆναι παρασκευάζουσι. Πύρρος δὲ τὴν Ἀφρικὴν καταλαμβάνει, ἐν ᾗ Μάξιμος ὁ ἐν μοναχοῖς περιβόητος καὶ οἱ ἐκεῖσε ἀρχιεπίσκοποι λόγοις συμπλακέντες, αἰσχύνεσθαι οἷς ἐφρόνει παρεσκεύαζον καὶ σύνοδον ἀθροισθῆναι σπουδάζουσι.

129: 1 ἀποστρέψαντος F (cf. 118, 7)

132: 5 αὐτῷ] αὐτοῦ F ‖ 11 μετ᾽ οὐ] μετὰ H cf. 41, 3 et 9; 51, 1; *SV*[1] 33, 12

133. Σύνοδος ἱερὰ ἐν Βυζακίῳ ὑπὸ Κολοβοῦ τοῦ ταύτης ἀρχιεπισκόπου, ἥτις τὰ παρὰ Σεργίου καὶ Πύρρου καὶ Κύρου καὶ Πέτρου τολμηθέντα ἀναθεματίσασα, δύο θελήσεις καὶ ἐνεργείας τοῦ δεσπότου Χριστοῦ καὶ θεοῦ ἡμῶν ἀνεκήρυξε.

134. Σύνοδος πάλιν ἱερὰ ἐν Νουμηδίᾳ τῆς Ἀφρικῆς συναθροισθεῖσα ὑπὸ Στεφάνου τοῦ ταύτης ὁσιωτάτου ἐπισκόπου τὰ αὐτὰ τῇ ἐν Βυζακίῳ διεθέσπισεν.

135. Ἀλλὰ καὶ ἐν Μαυριτανίᾳ ὑπὸ Ῥεπάτου τοῦ ταύτης ἀρχιεπισκόπου συναθροισθεῖσα τὰ ὅμοια ταῖς εἰρημέναις διεπράξατο.

136. Οὐ μὴν ἀλλὰ καὶ ἐν Καρθαγένῃ ὑπὸ Βίκτορος τοῦ ταύτης ἀρχιεπισκόπου συναθροισθεῖσα ὁμοίως ταῖς ἄλλαις Σέργιον, Κῦρον καὶ Πύρρον ἀποκηρύξασα, δύο θελήσεις καὶ ἐνεργείας Χριστοῦ τοῦ θεοῦ ἡμῶν ἀνακηρύττεσθαι διετράνωσε.

137. Καὶ ἐν Ῥώμῃ δὲ ὑπὸ Ἰωάννου τοῦ ταύτης ἀρχιεπισκόπου σύνοδος συναθροισθεῖσα τὰ ἴσα ταῖς προλαβούσαις διετυπώσατο· ἧς τὰ πεπραγμένα πρὸς Ἡράκλειον καὶ Δαυὶδ υἱοὺς Ἡρακλείου διεπέμφθησαν.

138. Βονιφατίου δὲ Ἰωάννην διαδεξαμένου, καὶ Βονιφατίου τὸν βίον ἀμείψαντος, τοῦ θρόνου διάδοχος Θεόδωρος γίνεται, ὃς τῆς εὐσεβείας ἦν θερμὸς ὑπέρμαχος. Ὧι καὶ Πύρρος ὁ γεγονὼς Κωνσταντινουπόλεως πατριάρχης τὴν Ῥώμην καταλαβὼν λίβελλον ὀρθοδοξίας ἐπιδίδωσι καὶ δεκτὸς εἰς κοινωνίαν καθίσταται. Ἀλλ' ἐκεῖθεν ἀπάρας καὶ πρὸς Ῥάβενναν ἐλθών, ἐπὶ τὴν ἰδίαν πάλιν δυσσέβειαν ἐπανέστρεψε. Μαθὼν δὲ

133: 2 παρὰ] περὶ F

135: 1 immo Ῥεπαράτου

136: 2 ante Κῦρον add. καὶ H

138: 1 βονυφατίου bis F

τοῦτο Θεόδωρος ὁ Ῥώμης καὶ σύνοδον ἀθροίσας, ἐγγράφως Πύρρου τὴν καθαίρεσιν ἐποιήσατο· οὐκ αὐτοῦ δὲ μόνον, ἀλλὰ καὶ ὅσοι αὐτῷ μετὰ ταῦτα κοινωνεῖν ἀνάσχοιντο. Φασὶ δὲ καὶ τὴν ἀναγραφὴν τῆς καθαιρέσεως Πύρρου τὸ φρικτὸν καὶ φοβερὸν Χριστοῦ αἷμα τῷ μέλανι κερασάμενον τὸν ἀρχιεπίσκοπον Ῥώμης ὑποστήσασθαι. Ἀλλ' ὅ γε Πύρρος, <Παύλου τὸν βίον ἀπορ>ρήξαντος, πάλιν συνδρομῇ τῶν ἀσεβούντων τὸν Κωνσταντινουπόλεως θρόνον ἐγχειρίζεται.

139. Ἐπειδὴ δὲ Θεόδωρος τὴν παροῦσαν ζωὴν πρὸς τὴν ἀτελεύτητον διελύσατο, Μαρτῖνος θείᾳ ψήφῳ προχειρίζεται. Μάξιμος δέ, οὗ καὶ πρὶν ὁ λόγος μνήμην ἔσχε, παρὼν τῇ Ῥώμῃ, Μαρτίνου πλέον τὸν ζῆλον τῆς εὐσεβείας ἀνέφλεξε. Σύνοδος ἐν Ῥώμῃ ἱερὰ ὑπὸ Μαξίμου καὶ Μαρτίνου συστᾶσα, ἥτις Σέργιον καὶ Πύρρον καὶ Κῦρον ἀναθεματίσασα, κεφαλαιώδη ὅρον διετυπώσατο, ἐν ᾧ τὰς δύο θελήσεις καὶ ἐνεργείας Χριστοῦ τοῦ θεοῦ ἡμῶν ὁμολογήσασα διετράνωσε. Μετὰ δὲ τὴν ἁγίαν καὶ τοπικὴν σύνοδον Μαρτῖνος ὁ Ῥώμης μετάπεμπτος ὑπὸ Κωνσταντίνου τοῦ βασιλέως γίνεται, καὶ πολλοῖς ἐτασμοῖς ὑποβληθεὶς καὶ κακώσεσιν, ἅτε μὴ ἀνασχόμενος τοῖς αἱρετίζουσι συμφρονεῖν, ὑπερόριος ἐν Χερσῶνι παραπέμπεται. Μετ' οὐ πολὺ δὲ καὶ Μάξιμος τοῖς αὐτοῖς ὑπὲρ εὐσεβείας ἐνδιατρίψας ἀγωνίσμασιν, ἔτι δὲ καὶ τὴν γλῶσσαν ἀποτμηθείς, πρὸς τοῖς Καυκασίοις ὄρεσιν—ἔθνος δὲ τούτοις παρῴκει τότε οἱ λεγόμενοι Σούανοι—τὴν πικρὰν ἐξορίαν ὑφίσταται.

140. Ἀλλὰ γὰρ ὡς ἔφημεν Μαρτίνου τὴν ὑπερορίαν ἐν Χερσῶνι φέροντος καταδίκην, Ἀγάθων Ῥώμης ἀρχιερεὺς προχειρίζεται, ζηλωτὴς καὶ αὐτὸς τῶν εὐσεβῶν χρηματίζων δογμάτων. Σύνοδος ἱερὰ ἐν Ῥώμῃ ὑπὸ τοῦ ἁγίου Ἀγάθωνος πάπα, ἥτις Σέργιον καὶ Κῦρον καὶ Πέτρον ἀποκηρύξασα, τὰς β' θελήσεις καὶ ἐνεργείας ἐπὶ Χριστοῦ τοῦ θεοῦ ἡμῶν ἀνεκήρυξεν· ἧς ὅρος Κωνσταντίνῳ τῷ πατρὶ Ἰουστινιανοῦ ἀναπέμπεται.

11–12 ῥήξαντος codd. suppl. Westerink (cf. 150,1–2; 154,2 et *SV*[1])

139: 12 post ἀποτμηθείς add. καὶ τὴν χεῖρα F (cf. *Theoph.*, 351, 20)

141. Ὁ δὲ εἰρημένος βασιλεὺς Κωνσταντῖνος τὸν συνοδικὸν ὅρον Ἀγάθωνος προσδεξάμενος, σύνοδον οἰκουμενικὴν συγκαλεῖται. Σύνοδος θεία καὶ οἰκουμενικὴ ἐν Κωνσταντινουπόλει συγκροτηθεῖσα ὑπὸ Γεωργίου τοῦ ταύτης ἀρχιεπισκόπου, ἥτις ἀπεκήρυξε Σέργιον, Πύρρον, Παῦλον, Κῦρον καὶ Μακάριον, Στέφανον καὶ Πολυχρόνιον Ἀντιοχείας· ὅρον δὲ θεῖον συνᾴδοντα ταῖς ἑσπερίαις συνόδοις διαθεμένη, τὰς β′ φύσεις θελήσεις τε καὶ ἐνεργείας ἀσυγχύτους καὶ ἀδιαιρέτους Χριστοῦ τοῦ θεοῦ ἡμῶν ἀνομολογεῖσθαι διετράνωσε.

143. Μετὰ δὲ ταῦτα τοῦ βασιλέως Κωνσταντίνου ἐκλελοιπότος τὸν βίον, καὶ Ἰουστινιανοῦ τοῦ υἱοῦ αὐτοῦ τὴν βασιλείαν ἔχοντος, σύνοδον ἐν Κωνσταντινουπόλει σμ′ πατέρων θεσπίσματι τοῦ βασιλέως συναθροίζονται, ἥτις οὓς παραλέλοιπε κανόνας ἡ ἁγία ε′ καὶ ς′ οἰκουμενικαὶ σύνοδοι ἀνεπλήρωσε· πρὸς δὲ τούτοις πᾶσαν Ἑλληνικὴν καὶ Ἰουδαικὴν παράδοσιν ἔτι πολλοὺς ὑποδυομένην καὶ βίον ἄλλον ἀκαθαρσίας τῆς ἐκκλησίας ἐξεκάθηρε.

145. Φιλιππικοῦ δὲ τυραννίδι ἐπιθεμένου καὶ τὴν βασίλειον ὑπελθόντος ἀρχήν, συνέδριον ἐν Κωνσταντινουπόλει ἀθροίζεται, ὅπερ Κῦρον μὲν τὸν ταύτης ἀρχιεπίσκοπον ἐκβάλλει τοῦ θρόνου· οὗτος δὲ ὁ ἀνὴρ ἀνδρῶν ἡγήσατο μοναχῶν πρότερον, ἐν τῇ Ἀμάστριδι τοὺς ἀσκητικοὺς ἀγῶνας διεξιών· ὃν ἀπελαθέντα τοῦ θρόνου ἐν τῇ τῆς Χώρας μονῇ περιορίζουσιν, Ἰωάννην δὲ ἀντ' αὐτοῦ τῷ θρόνῳ ἐγκαθιδρύουσι. Καὶ τότε τὸ πονηρὸν τοῦτο συνέδριον τὴν καλῶς ἀπομαρανθεῖσαν πάλαι δυσφημίαν ἀναζωπυρήσαντες, ἓν θέλημα καὶ μίαν ἐνέργειαν δυσσεβεῖ καὶ ἄφρονι λογισμῷ ἀνεκήρυξαν.

146. Φιλιππικοῦ δὲ ξίφει τὸν βίον λιπόντος καὶ Ἰωάννου τοῦ δυσσεβοῦς πρὸς τὰ ἐκεῖθεν ἀπαχθέντος δικαιωτήρια, Γερμανὸς ὁ Κυζίκου τῷ

143: 1 ἐκλειπόντος (sic) H ‖ 6 post ἀκαθαρσίας add. καὶ F

145: 5–6 περιορίζεται H

δευτέρῳ ἔτει τῆς βασιλείας Ἀρτεμίου, τοῦ καὶ Ἀναστασίου, σπουδῇ τῶν εὐσεβούντων τὸν θρόνον ἐγχειρίζεται, μηνὶ Αὐγούστῳ ια´ ἰνδικτιῶνος ιγ´· ἐφ' ᾧ καὶ κιτατόριν μετα<. . .> «καὶ διακόνων καὶ παντὸς τοῦ εὐαγοῦς κλήρου καὶ τῆς ἱερᾶς συγκλήτου καὶ τοῦ φιλοχρίστου λαοῦ τῆς θεοφυλάκτου ταύτης καὶ βασιλίδος πόλεως, <. . .>.» Οὗτος ὁ Γερμανός, αὐτίκα τοῦ λαβεῖν τὴν ἀρχιερατικὴν ἐφορείαν, σύνοδον ρς´ ἀνδρῶν ἐγείρει—Θεοδόσιος δὲ τότε τῇ βασιλείᾳ διέπρεπε—καὶ προσφωνεῖ τούτοις εὐσεβείας πεπληρωμένον ὅρον. Σύνοδος θεία καὶ ἱερὰ ἐν Κωνσταντινουπόλει ὑπὸ Γερμανοῦ τοῦ ταύτης ἀρχιεπισκόπου συγκροτηθεῖσα, ἥτις Σέργιον καὶ Πύρρον καὶ Κῦρον καὶ Παῦλον καὶ Πέτρον ἀποκηρύξασα, τὰς β´ θελήσεις ἐκήρυξεν.

147. Ἐπειδὴ δὲ Θεοδόσιος μὲν τῆς βασιλείου ἀρχῆς ἐξέστη, Λέων δὲ ταύτην ἀντικατέσχε, Κωνσταντῖνος ὁ Νακολίας ἐπίσκοπος καὶ Βισὴρ ἐκεῖνος, ὃς ἐπὶ συχνὸν χρόνον τοῖς τῶν Σαρακηνῶν ἐξεδιητήθη ἔθεσί τε καὶ φρονήμασι, πατρίκιος τηνικαῦτα χρηματίζων, ἀρχηγοὶ αἱρέσεων ἀνεφάνησαν, μὴ δεῖν λέγοντες προσκυνεῖν εἰκόνα Χριστοῦ, μηδέ τινι τῶν ἁγίων. Ὧν τὴν λύμην ὁ βασιλεὺς εἰσδεξάμενος, μεταλαβεῖν τῆς νόσου Γερμανὸν τὸν ἁγιώτατον ἀρχιερέα θεοῦ ἐξεβιάζετο· τοῦδε μὴ ἀνασχομένου αὐτὸς τὴν σύγκλητον καὶ τῶν ἱερέων ὅσοι μικρὰ τῆς σφῶν σωτηρίας ἐφρόντιζον συναγαγών, ἐν τῷ παλατίῳ σύνοδον καθίζει. Ὁ δὲ τοῦ θεοῦ ἀρχιερεὺς εἰς ἔσχατον κακοῦ τὴν ἀπόνοιαν αὐτοῦ βλέπων, πρὸς πᾶσάν τε θεραπείαν καὶ παραίνεσιν ἀποτεθηριωμένον ὄντα τὸν Λέοντα, ἀθῷον ἑαυτὸν τῆς τε παρ' αὐτῶν σπουδαζομένης δυσσεβείας ἀποφαίνων, ἀντὶ τοῦ ἀποτινάξασθαι τὸν κονιορτὸν δι' ἑτέρου συμβόλου πράττει τὸ αὐτό, καὶ τὸ ὠμοφόριον ἀποδυσάμενος ἔξεισι τοῦ συνεδρίου μονονουχὶ φάσκων ὡς, «τὸ αἷμα ὑμῶν ἐπὶ τὴν κεφαλὴν ὑμῶν.» Τοῦτον δὲ τὸν ἱερὸν ἄνδρα δι' ὧν ἔδρων ἀνοσίων δογμάτων οἱ τῆς ἀσεβείας ἐρασταὶ τοῦ θρόνου παρασκευάσαντες ἀποστῆναι, ἐν ἰδίῳ οἴκῳ μέχρι τῆς πρὸς τὰ ἐκεῖθεν πορείας

146: 3–7: Theoph., 384, 19–25

147: 12–13: Luc. 9:5; Matt. 10:14 ‖ 14–15: Act. 18:6

146: 3 τοῦ] ὁ F om. H ‖ 5 ᾧ] ἧ Theoph. ‖ μετὰ codd. μεταθεσίμου κτλ. Theoph. 384, 22–385, 2

147: 1 ἐξέστι F ω supra scr. (= ἐξώσθη?) H ‖ 2 ἀντικατέστη F ‖ 3 ἐξεδιετήθη (lineola sub ε[3]) F ‖ 16 εὐσεβείας F

καθείρξαντες περιώρισαν· καὶ Ἀναστάσιον ἄνδρα γαστρὸς μόνον καὶ ἡδονῆς λόγον ἔχοντα τῷ Κωνσταντινουπόλεως θρόνῳ παρὰ πάντα θεσμὸν ἐκκλησίας ἐγκαθιδρύουσι. Μετὰ μέντοι τὴν ἐξέωσιν τοῦ ἀρχιεπισκόπου Γερμανοῦ Λέων καὶ Ἀναστάσιος ὅσα τὸ Ἰουδαίων καὶ Ἑλλήνων ἔθνος ἐνυβρίσαι τῇ πίστει τῶν χριστιανῶν καθυστέρησαν, αὐτοὶ ταῦτα τῇ σφῶν παρανοίᾳ καὶ ἀσεβείᾳ ἀνεπλήρωσαν.

148. Γρηγόριος δὲ ὁ τῆς Ῥώμης ἀρχιεπίσκοπος τὴν τε τοῦ ἐν ἁγίοις Γερμανοῦ τοῦ θρόνου μαθὼν ἐκβολὴν καὶ ὅσα Λέων καὶ Ἀναστάσιος κατὰ τῆς τοῦ θεοῦ ἐκκλησίας νεανιεύονται, γενναίῳ ὑπὲρ τῆς ἐκκλησίας φρονήματι διανίσταται καὶ σύνοδον ἐν Ῥώμῃ συναθροίζει, ἥτις καὶ σφοδροῖς ἐλέγχοις γράμμασι διατυπώσασα διαπέμπεται πρὸς Λέοντα.

149. Καὶ μὴν καὶ Θεόδωρος ὁ τῆς ἐν Ἱεροσολύμοις ἐκκλησίας ἀρχιερεὺς τὸν ἴσον τῆς ἐκκλησίας ἐν ἑαυτῷ φέρων ζῆλον, τοὺς ἐκ Παλαιστίνης ἀθροισάμενος ἐπισκόπους τήν τε ἁγίαν σύνοδον τὴν πέμπτην καὶ ἕκτην ταῖς πρὸ αὐτῶν συναριθμῶν διπτύχοις ἐγκατατάττει, καὶ τὴν τῶν εἰκονομάχων αἵρεσιν ἀναθεματίζει. Σύνοδος ἱερὰ ἐν Ἱεροσολύμοις ὑπὸ Θεοδώρου τοῦ ταύτης ἀρχιεπισκόπου συναθροισθεῖσα, ἥτις τὴν τῶν εἰκονομάχων ἀνεθεμάτισεν αἵρεσιν.

150. Λέοντος δὲ τοῦ βασιλέως ἐν ἀσεβείᾳ τὴν ψυχὴν ἀπορρήξαντος, Κωνσταντῖνος ὁ παῖς καὶ τῆς ἀσεβείας καὶ τῆς ἀρχῆς θεοῦ παροράσει διάδοχος γίνεται καὶ κατὰ τῆς εὐσεβείας θερμότερον τοῦ φύσαντος ὁπλίζεται. Συνέδριον Ἰουδαϊκὸν κατὰ Χριστοῦ καὶ τῶν ἁγίων αὐτοῦ, ἐν ᾧ τοὺς ἀρχιερεῖς ἀθροίσας καὶ ἄκοντας, βαρβάρως καὶ ἀνερυθριάστως πρὸς αὐτοὺς διεξῆλθε· «θέλω καὶ κελεύω καὶ βούλομαι τὰς εἰκόνας Χριστοῦ καὶ τῶν ἁγίων εἴδωλα προσαγορεύεσθαι καὶ τοὺς προσκυνητὰς αὐτῶν ὡς εἰδωλολάτρας κολάζεσθαι.» Καὶ τὸ μὲν πρῶτον αὐτοῦ συνέδριον τοιοῦτον τὸ πέρας ἐκδέχεται. Συνέδριον ἐν Κωνσταντινουπόλει τλγ´ τῆς Ἄννα καὶ Καϊάφα μιαιφονίας ἐφάμιλλον, οὗ Κωνσταντῖνος ὁ δυσσεβὴς ἐξῆρχεν, ἐν ᾧ κατὰ τῆς εὐσεβείας ἐπαλαμᾶτο πάντα δυσσεβῶς καὶ ἀναισχύντως.

151. Μετὰ δὲ τὴν ληστρικὴν ταύτην καὶ ἄθεον σύνοδον οὐδὲν παρῆκεν ἀτόλμητον ὃ μὴ πλάνη καὶ δυσσεβείᾳ λαβοῦσα κράτος κατατολ-

---

20 ἐξέωσιν] sic codd.

μήσειεν. Ἀλλά γε μετὰ τοὺς πολλοὺς ἐκείνους καὶ ἀρρήτους κατὰ τῆς ἐκκλησίας διωγμοὺς καὶ τὸ ἀδιήγητον πλῆθος τῶν ἀτόπων ἔργων, πικρῷ θανάτῳ τὸν βίον ὁ ἀσεβὴς καταστρεψάμενος, Λέοντι τῷ υἱῷ τὴν βασιλείαν καταλείπει. Ὃς τὴν μὲν ἀσέβειαν ἔχων τοῦ πατρὸς καὶ τὴν ἄλλην ὠμότητα, καὶ λύσσαν κατὰ τῆς τοῦ θεοῦ ἐκκλησίας ὑποστελλόμενος οὕτως ἀπαλλάσσεται τοῦ βίου. Μετὰ δὲ τὴν τούτου τελευτὴν Κωνσταντῖνος ὁ παῖς καὶ Εἰρήνη τῆς εὐσεβείας γεγονότες σπουδαῖοι ἐρασταὶ καὶ τῶν προκαταρξάντων τὴν δυσσέβειαν βδελυξάμενοι, σύνοδον ἀθροίζουσιν ἐν τῷ ναῷ τῶν ἁγίων ἀποστόλων, ἥτις ἀναθέματι καθυποβάλλει τὰ τῶν ἀσεβῶν κατὰ τῶν σεπτῶν εἰκόνων βλάσφημα δόγματα καὶ τὸ ἀνέκαθεν αὐτοῖς παραδεδομένον σέβας τῇ ἐκκλησίᾳ ἀποκαθίστησι, εἰ καὶ τὸ τῶν λεγομένων σχολαρίων στῖφος τῆς προκατασχούσης αὐτοὺς εἰκονομαχικῆς λύσσης τῇ νόσῳ φλεγμαίνοντες κατὰ τῆς συνόδου ὅπλα ἄραντες, ἡμιτελῆ ταύτην διαλύσασθαι παρεσκεύασαν.

152. Ἀλλ' ὅ γε Κωνσταντῖνος καὶ Εἰρήνη τοὺς δυσσεβεῖς καὶ τυραννίδος ἐρῶντας σχολαρίους τῆς πόλεως ἐξελάσαντες, σύνοδον οἰκουμενικὴν ἐν Νικαίᾳ θεσπίζουσιν ἀθροισθῆναι. Σύνοδος θεία καὶ οἰκουμενικὴ ἐν Νικαίᾳ τῆς Βιθυνίας συγκροτηθεῖσα, ἧς ἐξῆρχε Ταράσιος ὁ ἁγιώτατος πατριάρχης Κωνσταντινουπόλεως, Πέτρος καὶ Πέτρος πρεσβύτεροι τὸν τόπον ἐπέχοντες Ἀδριανοῦ τοῦ ἁγιωτάτου πάπα Ῥώμης, Ἰωάννης καὶ Θωμᾶς πρεσβύτεροι καὶ μοναχοὶ καὶ αὐτοὶ τὸν τόπον ἀναπληροῦντες τῶν τῆς ἀνατολικῆς διοικήσεως πατριαρχῶν, Ἀντιοχείας λέγω καὶ Ἀλεξανδρείας καὶ Ἱεροσολύμων. Ἥτις ἁγία σύνοδος τοὺς κατὰ τῆς τοῦ θεοῦ ἐκκλησίας λυττήσαντας καὶ τῇ λύσσῃ ἐπιμένοντας ἀναθέματι καθυπέβαλλε, τοὺς δέ γε τὸ δυσσεβὲς μεταθεμένους φρόνημα καὶ εἰλικρινῶς προσελθόντας κοινωνοὺς καὶ ἀρχιερεῖς συμπαρεδέξατο, ὅρον τε εὐσεβείας ταῖς προλαβούσαις ἁγίαις συνόδοις συνδιαπλέξασα καὶ τὰ τῆς εὐσεβείας ἐπιτρανώσασα δόγματα, εἰρηνικὴν καὶ ἀτάραχον καὶ τὴν διάλυσιν ἔσχε.

153. Νικηφόρου δὲ τοῦ ἀπὸ γενικῶν λογοθέτου τῆς βασιλείας ἐπιβάντος καὶ σὺν τῷ υἱῷ Σταυρακίῳ βασιλεύοντος, Νικηφόρον τὸν ἀπὸ ἀσηκρητῶν ἐχειροτόνησαν οὗτοι εἰς τὸν θρόνον τῆς Κωνσταντινουπόλεως.

151: 5 λέοντα F ‖ 14 στίφος codd.

152: 8 ἀνατολῆς H ‖ 13 συνδιαπλέξαντες H

153: 3 ἀσηκρητῶν] ā(i.e., πρωτο)σηκρητῶν codd. cf. Theoph. 481, 20–21 ‖ τῆς om. H

Πλάτων δὲ καὶ Θεόδωρος, ἡγούμενοι τῆς μονῆς τῶν Στουδίου, φιλαρχίαν νοσήσαντες ὡς μέγα φρονοῦντες ἐπ' εὐλαβείᾳ, μᾶλλον ἄξιοι τοῦ θρόνου Κωνσταντινουπόλεως ἐφιλονείκησαν εἶναι, σχίσμα μελετήσαντες εἰ μὴ προχειρισθείη Θεόδωρος πατριάρχης, αἰτίαν εὔλογον δῆθεν ἔχοντες τὸ μὴ δεῖν ἀπὸ λαϊκῶν ἀθρόως εἰς ἐπισκοπὴν ἀνατρέχειν. Οὓς ὁ βασιλεὺς Νικηφόρος τῆς Κωνσταντινουπόλεως ἀπελάσαι βουληθεὶς ἀνετράπη, συμβουλευόντων τινῶν οὐκ ἐπαινετὴν ἔσεσθαι τὴν Νικηφόρου τοῦ πατριάρχου χειροτονίαν, ἐπὶ <. . .> τηλικαύτης μονῆς πεντακοσίων που μοναστῶν ὑπὸ Θεοδώρῳ τεταγμένων. Διὸ σύνοδον συγκροτήσας ὁ βασιλεὺς ἐπισκόπων μηνὶ Ἰαννουαρίου ἰνδικτιῶνος β' τρίτῳ ἔτει τῆς βασιλείας αὐτοῦ κατὰ τῶν Στουδιτῶν, ὡς μὴ κοινωνούντων Νικηφόρῳ πατριάρχῃ διὰ Ἰωσὴφ οἰκονόμον προφάσει μοιχοζευξίας, ἐξορίᾳ τούτους παρέπεμψεν ἐν τῇ Πριγκίπῳ νήσῳ, λύσας τηλικαύτην μονὴν τούς τε ὑποτακτίτας αὐτῶν διέσπειρεν.

154. Ἀλλὰ Νικηφόρου τοῦ βασιλέως μετὰ ἔτη ε' κακῶς ἐν Βουλγαρίᾳ τὸν βίον ἀπορρήξαντος, καίπερ τὸ πρότερον ἐν τῇ ἐκστρατείᾳ φανέντος ἀρίστου καὶ τοὺς Βουλγάρους τροπωσαμένου, Σταυράκιος ὁ υἱὸς αὐτοῦ μετήχθη εἰς τὴν τῆς βασιλείας ἀρχήν. Καὶ μικρόν τι διαβιοὺς ἐν αὐτῇ ὡς τετραυματισμένου ὄντος ἀπὸ τῆς πρὸς τοὺς Βουλγάρους μετὰ τοῦ πατρὸς μάχης, ἐπιλαμβάνεται τῆς βασιλείας ὁ ἐπὶ Προκοπίᾳ τῇ αὐταδέλφῃ τοῦ Σταυρακίου γαμβρὸς Μιχαὴλ ὁ Κωνσταντινουπολίτης, ὁ Ῥαγαβὲ ἐπικεκλημένος, κουροπαλάτης τυγχάνων. Εὐσεβὴς δὲ καὶ διϊθύνων τὴν βασίλειον ἀρχήν, ἐλυπεῖτο ἐπὶ τοῖς ἀποσχίζουσι τῆς ἐκκλησίας ἐφ' οἱᾳδήποτε προφάσει εὐλόγῳ, πολλά τε τὸν πατριάρχην Νικηφόρον καὶ τοὺς δυναμένους συντρέχειν τῇ κοινῇ εἰρήνῃ παρακαλῶν οὐκ ἐπαύσατο· ἐν οἷς καὶ Θεόδωρον τὸν ἡγούμενον τῶν Στουδίου καὶ Πλάτωνα καὶ Ἰωσὴφ ἀρχιεπίσκοπον Θεσσαλονίκης ἀδελφὸν Θεοδώρου ἐν φυλακαῖς πικραῖς συνεχομένους μετὰ καὶ τῶν προυχόντων τῆς κατ' αὐτοὺς μονῆς ἔσπευσεν ἑνωθῆναι· ὃ καὶ πεποίηκε. Καὶ τούτου μὲν εἰς β' ἔτη ἠρέμα διατελέσαντος ἐν τῷ κράτει, Λέων ὁ Βαρδάνης ὁ υἱὸς Βάρδα πατρικίου ὁ Ἀρμένιος, στρα-

153: 4–12: Theoph., 481, 22–29 ‖ 12–15: cf. ibid., 484, 24–28

154: 9–15: Theoph., 494, 14–20

15–16 πριγκήπω H ‖ 16 τηλικαύτη μονῆ codd. ‖ 16–17 διέσπειραν H

154: 4 μετήχθη] μετημείμφθη H ‖ 12 τῶν] τοῦ F ‖ 15 διατελέσαντα codd. ‖ 16 ὁ^{2} om. H ‖ υἱὸς Βάρδα πατρικίου deleta habet H

τηγὸς ὢν τῶν ἀνατολικῶν, ἐπέβη τῆς ἀρχῆς· τῇ γὰρ ια′ τοῦ Ἰουλίου μηνὸς ἰνδικτιῶνος ς′ ἡμέρᾳ β′ ἐστέφθη ὑπὸ Νικηφόρου πατριάρχου· ἔστεψε δὲ μετὰ δύο ἔτη καὶ Θεοδοσίαν τὴν γυναῖκα αὐτοῦ αὐγοῦσταν, ὡσαύτως Σαββάτιον τὸν υἱὸν αὐτοῦ εἰς βασιλέα, μετονομάσας Κωνσταντῖνον. Καὶ διϊθύνων τὴν βασίλειον οὗτος ἀρχὴν καὶ προσκαλεσάμενος Νικηφόρον τὸν πατριάρχην, λέγει αὐτῷ, «ἐπίδειξόν μοι τῆς τῶν εἰκόνων προσκυνήσεως τὰ δικαιώματα, ἐκ ποίας ἐγγράφου παραδόσεως τοῦτο παρειλήφαμεν, ἵνα μεμαθηκὼς ἔχω εὐφυῶς ἀπολογεῖσθαί με πρὸς τοὺς ἐνοχλοῦντάς με περὶ τούτου·» τινὲς γὰρ τῶν ἀρχόντων ἠνώχλουν τὸν βασιλέα λέγοντες, «δίκαιόν ἐστιν ἐκζητῆσαι τὸ τῶν εἰκόνων κεφάλαιον· εἰ μὴ γὰρ ἡ τούτων προσκύνησις παυθῇ, χριστιανῶν ἀνάκλησις οὐκ ἔστιν.» Ὁ δὲ πατριάρχης λέγει αὐτῷ, «κέλευσον εἰσελθεῖν τοὺς μητροπολίτας, δέσποτα, καὶ ἐπιδιδόαμέν σοι τὰς χρήσεις.» Καὶ ὃς προσεκαλέσατο αὐτοὺς ἐκ πάντων τῶν θεμάτων. Τούτων οὖν παραγενομένων καὶ τοῦ πατριάρχου τὸν τοῦ βασιλέως σκοπὸν ἀνακοινωσαμένου αὐτοῖς, ἐπιδεδώκασι τῷ βασιλεῖ τὰ πεπραγμένα τῆς ἐν Νικαίᾳ συνόδου, τῆς γενομένης ἐπὶ Εἰρήνης αὐγούστης. Ὁ δὲ βασιλεὺς χρήσεις εἰς ταῦτα εὑρηκὼς ὡς δῆθεν Γρηγορίου τοῦ θεολόγου καὶ Βασιλείου τοῦ πάνυ, βίβλους ἐζήτει τῶν δύο χρήσεων· τῶν δὲ μὴ ἐχόντων τὰς βίβλους, ἐκέλευσεν ὁ βασιλεὺς εἰσελθεῖν πάντας τοὺς ἐπισκόπους. Συμμάχους δὲ τῆς αὐτοῦ ἀσεβείας ἐκζητήσας, εὗρεν Ἰωάννην τὸν ἐπιλεγόμενον Γραμματικόν, μᾶλλον δὲ Ἰαννῆν, Σίμωνα ἄλλον καὶ λεκανομάντιν, ἐπὶ φαρμακείαις διαβεβοημένον, καὶ ἑτέρους τινὰς Ἰαννίτας καὶ Ἰαμβρίτας. Προσκαλεῖται οὖν Νικηφόρον τὸν ἀοίδιμον πατριάρχην καὶ τοὺς σὺν αὐτῷ ἐπισκόπους ἐνώπιον τῆς συγκλήτου καί φησι, «μὴ δεῖν προσκυνεῖσθαι εἰκόνας λέγεται.» Ὃν ὁ θεῖος Νικηφόρος λέγει, «εἴπατέ μοι, τὸ μὴ ὂν δύναται πεσεῖν;» Τῶν δὲ τῆς ἀσφαλείας τῆς λέξεως ἀπορηθέντων, εἶπε πάλιν ὁ ἅγιος, «ἔπεσον ἐπὶ Λέοντος καὶ Κωνσταντίνου τῶν Ἰσαύρων αἱ ἁγίαι εἰκόνες ἢ οὔ;» Τῶν δὲ κατανευσάντων εἶπεν, «οὐκοῦν ἵσταντο καί εἰσι καὶ ἀρχαῖόν ἐστι τὸ ἀναστήλωμα· τὸ γὰρ μὴ ὂν μηδὲ ἱστάμενον πῶς δύναται πεσεῖν;» Εἶτα καὶ τῶν ἄλλων ἐπισκόπων τοιαῦτά τινα ὑπὲρ τῶν εἰς ἀνατροπὴν τῆς αἱρέσεως λαλησάντων, ὁ μητροπολίτης Σάρδεων παρρησιασάμενος λέγει, «βασιλεῦ, ἀφ' οὗ Χριστὸς ἦλθεν ἐπὶ γῆς μέχρι νῦν ω′ παρῆλθον ἔτη καὶ πανταχοῦ σκιαγραφεῖται Χριστὸς καὶ ἐν εἰκόνι προσκυνεῖται· ποῖος οὖν αὐθάδης τολμήσειε τῶν τοσούτων χρόνων

17–18 ibid., 502, 29–30 ‖ 36–54: cf. Geo. Mon., 778, 10–779, 17

---

19 Θεοδοσίαν] θεοδώραν F ‖ 19–20 σαββατίκιον F recte Συμβάτιον ‖ 25 ἠνώχλουν] sic codd. ‖ 37–38 λεκανομάντην H ‖ 38 φαρμακίαις F ‖ 42 ἀσφαλείας] immo ἀσαφείας

ἀποστολικήν τε καὶ πατρικὴν παράδοσιν ἀθετῆσαι, τοῦ ἀποστόλου λέγοντος, "ἀδελφοί, ἑδραῖοι γίνεσθε καὶ κρατεῖτε τὰς παραδόσεις ἃς ἐδιδάχθητε· κἂν ἄγγελος ἐξ οὐρανοῦ εὐαγγελίζηται ὑμῖν παρ' ὃ παρελάβετε, ἀνάθεμα ἔστω."» Μεθ' οὗ καὶ Θεόδωρος ὁ τῶν Στουδίου πολλὰ ἤλεγξε τὸν βασιλέα. Ἀλλ' ἡ καθαίρεσις τῶν σεβασμίων εἰκόνων ἐκ βασιλέως θριαμβεύεται· πρὸς ἣν καὶ τὸν ἀρχιερέα Νικηφόρον ὑποσημήνασθαι κατηνάγκαζε, καὶ μηδαμῶς πειθαρχήσαντα ἀλογίστως εὐθύνει ἐξόριστον. Καὶ Θεόδωρος ᾧ ἐπίκλην Κασσιτηρᾶς τὸν πατριαρχικὸν θρόνον παρ' ἀξίαν εἰληφὼς ἐν ἡμέραις τῆς ζωοποιοῦ Χριστοῦ τοῦ θεοῦ ἡμῶν ἀναστάσεως, ἐπ' ἀδείας τῆς αἱρέσεως εἴχετο. Ὁ δὲ βασιλεὺς μονονοὺ σαφῶς τοιαῦτα τολμῶν καὶ λέγων ὅτι, «μοὶ οὐ πρὸς σοῦ γε τὸ βασιλεύειν οὔτε ὑποτετάχθαι σοι βουλήσομαι, ἀλλὰ κατανδρίζομαί σου καὶ κατεξανίσταμαι, καὶ ὥσπερ ἡττημένον σε καταλήψομαι καὶ μηδ' ὁτιοῦν τῶν ἐπὶ γῆς κατεξουσιάζοντα δεῖξαι.» Ταῦτα δὲ τὰ ῥητὰ τοῦ βασιλέως ἐκ στηλιτευτικοῦ τοῦ ἐν ἁγίοις Νικηφόρου τοῦ πατριάρχου εἰς τὸν αὐτὸν βασιλέα.

155. Ἀλλ' ὁ μὲν βασιλεὺς Λέων τῆς βασιλείας κρατήσας ἑπτὰ ἐπ' ἔτεσι καὶ μησὶ πέντε, κατὰ θεοῦ ὑψίστου ἐμμανῶς καυχησάμενος, οἰκτίστῳ μόρῳ τὸν βίον ἀπέλιπε. Μιχαὴλ δὲ ὁ Ἀμοριανὸς ἐκ τῶν δεσμῶν παρ' ἐλπίδα τὸ κράτος εἰσδύς, κατὰ τὴν ἀρχὴν τῆς αὐτοῦ βασιλείας παντελῶς ἀγροικίᾳ ἢ τῇ σκηπτουχίᾳ καλλωπιζόμενος, περὶ τῶν θείων εἰκόνων ἐδημηγόρησε τὸ ἑκάστῳ δοκοῦν ἐπεργάζεσθαι, ἀλογιστεύων δὲ μετὰ ταῦτα πρὸς διπλόην ἀποτραπείς. Καὶ τὸν εὐαγῆ Μεθόδιον ἀδίκως τυραννησάμενος, καθ' εἱρκτὴν ἐφυλάκισε περὶ τὴν νῆσον Ἀνδρέου τοῦ ἀποστόλου, καθ' ἣν ὁ Ἀκρίτας ἐγγειτόνων ἐμφανίζεται, οὗ ἀντικρὺ καταπλῆξαι τοῦτον οἰόμενος, Εὐθύμιον τὸν μητροπολίτην Σαρδιανῶν ἐξηγούμενον [ἔν τε] βουνεύροις χαλεπῶς ἐθανάτωσεν. Ἐπεβίω οὖν ὁ Μιχαὴλ τῇ βασιλείᾳ ἔτη ὀκτὼ πρὸς ἐννέα μησί. Θεόφιλος δὲ τὴν πατρῴαν ἀρχὴν κληρωσάμενος, πολυπράγμων περὶ ζητημάτων τῶν ἀποκρύφων ἐτύγχανε λίαν· ὧν χάριν καὶ Μεθόδιον τὸν ὅσιον, ἅτε σοφὸν ὄντα καὶ περὶ τὰς λύσεις αὐτῶν ἱκανῶς

55–57: Genesius (ed. Bonn.), 15, 11–14 ‖ 57–60: ibid., 16, 11–13 ‖ 64 ἐκ στηλιτευτικοῦ] Nicephori opus perditum; cf. P. J. Alexander, *The Patriarch Nicephorus of Constantinople,* 179–80; Geo. Mon., 780, 15–16

155: 1–2: Genesius, 29, 3–4 ‖ 3–4: ibid., 30, 1–2 ‖ 5–12: ibid., 50, 8–19 ‖ 12: ibid., 51, 1 ‖ 13–18: ibid., 76, 4–12

---

57 Θεόδωρος] recte Θεόδοτος ‖ 59 leg. ἡμέρᾳ ‖ τῆς] τοῦ H ‖ 60 μονονουχὶ H ‖ 61 τὸ] τῷ H ‖ 64 ἐκ] ἐκ τοῦ H

155: 7–8 τυραννισάμενος H ‖ 8 ἐφυλάκησε H ‖ περὶ] παρὰ H ‖ 9 καταπτῆξαι H ‖ 10 ἔν τε] non habet Genesius

ἔχοντα, τῆς φυλακῆς ἀνερρύσατο, συνδιάγειν αὐτῷ κατὰ τὸ παλάτιον αἱρετισάμενος, κἂν διὰ τὸ ὀρθὸν δόγμα αὐτὸν ἐμυσάττετο, καὶ ἀφρόνως τῆς ὀρθοδόξου πλεῖστα καταλαζονευόμενος πίστεως, βασιλεύσας ἔτη δώδεκα καὶ μῆνας γ'.

156. Μιχαὴλ δὲ ὁ τούτου τοῦ Θεοφίλου υἱὸς σὺν Θεοδώρᾳ τῇ μητρὶ αὐτοῦ τὰ τῆς βασιλείας εἰσδέχονται· καὶ τὰ τῆς ὀρθοδοξίας ἀνακαλύπτεται καιροῦ λαβόμενα εὐαγοῦς, τῆς στυγητῆς αἱρέσεως τῶν εἰκονομάχων διασυρείσης ἀπὸ τοῦ βασιλέως Λέοντος τοῦ Ἀμαληκίτου μέχρι χρόνων λ'. Περιπίπτει οὖν ἀρρωστίᾳ Μανουήλ, ὃς προεῖχεν ἐν ταῖς διοικήσεσι, δι' ἥσπερ ἀπέγνωστο· καθ' ἣν θεὸς παραδοξοποιῶν διανίστησι μοναχοὺς τῶν Στουδίου, ἄνδρας τῷ ὄντι ἐπισκεψομένους· ἤκουστο γὰρ ὅτι ἀπεβίω καὶ ἐπικηδείους ὕμνους προσοίσειαν. Καὶ ἐπελθόντες τῇ κλίνῃ τῶν μοναζόντων τινὲς τεθαρρηκότες θεῷ ἀναθαρροῦσι τὸν ὡς νεκρόν, ἢ μετ' ὀλίγον γενησόμενον, λέγοντες τοῦτον ἀναρρωσθῆναι. Τοῦ δὲ ἐκ βάθους ἐστενωμένης ψυχῆς μικρόν τι ἀνενεγκόντος καὶ διαπορήσαντος εἰ τοῦτο ἔσται αὐτῷ κατ' ἐλπίδα, ἐπεβόησαν ὡς, «εἴπερ ἂν ὑπόσχεσίς ἐστί σοι πρὸς θεὸν τὰς θείας εἰκόνας κατὰ τὸ ἀρχαῖον ἀνανεώσασθαι, τὴν ζωὴν εὐαγγελιζόμεθα.» Ἀπῄεσαν, καὶ τὸ εὐαγγελισθὲν συντόμως ἐπεπραγμάτευτο καὶ παραδόξως ὡς ἐξ ᾅδου ἀνέδυ, τοῦ θανάτου ἀπαλλαγείς. Ὡς οὖν ἑαυτὸν διέγνω παρ' ἐλπίδα τῆς ἀσθενείας ἀποραΐσαντα, πρὸς τὴν βασίλισσαν Θεοδώραν ὀρθοδόξως διαγωνίζεται· καὶ μετὰ πολλὰς ἀντιθέσεις καὶ λογομαχίας αἵ τε θεῖαι εἰκόνες ἀνεμορφοῦντο καὶ τῶν ἱερέων πρὸς δὲ καὶ ἀρχιερέων, τῶν μὲν μεταστοιχειουμένων τῆς δυσσεβείας, τῶν δὲ ἀνθεστηκότων τῷ εὐσεβεῖ δόγματι καὶ δικαίως ἐξωθουμένων καὶ πρό γε πάντων Ἰωάννου τοῦ δυσσεβοῦς πατριάρχου, ὃν πρόσθεν ἐδήλωσεν ὁ λόγος. Καὶ ὁ εὐσεβὴς ἀντεισάγεται Μεθόδιος, ἐν ἑαυτῷ πλεῖστα τὰ ὑπὲρ εὐσεβείας στίγματα καὶ τὴν δι' εἱρκτῆς σαπρώσης τῶν τριχῶν ψίλωσιν οἷά τινα γέρα προσκομιζόμενος. Καὶ κατὰ διωρισμένην ἡμέραν γεγονυίας συνελεύσεως, καθ' ἣν ἡ ἐκκλησία τὴν ἑαυτῆς εὐπρέπειαν ἀμφεβάλλετο, κατίασιν ἐκ τοῦ Ὀλύμπου ὄρους, Ἄθω τε καὶ τῆς Ἴδης καὶ τοῦ κατὰ Κυμινᾶν συμπληρώματος περιφανῶς τὴν ὀρθοδοξίαν κηρύσσοντες τῇ πρώτῃ κυριακῇ τῶν νηστειῶν, ἥτις λέγεται τῆς ὀρθοδοξίας.

156: 1–2: cf. Genesium, 77, 1–2 ‖ 2–17: ibid., 78, 16–79, 20 ‖ 18–21: Genesius, 80, 17–22 ‖ 21–26: ibid., 82, 3–6 ‖ 24–27: ibid., 82, 8–13

---

15 συνδιάγων H

156: 8 ἐπελθόντας H ‖ 14 Ἀπῄεσαν H Genesius: ἀπέστησαν F ‖ 16 rectius ἀπορραΐσαντα (sensu ἀναρραΐσαντα) ‖ 20 πρό] πρός H

INDICES

I: PROPER NAMES

II: TERMS AND VOCABULARY

* distinguishes unattested or rare words and forms

CORPUS FONTIUM HISTORIAE BYZANTINAE

SERIES WASHINGTONIENSIS, EDITOR JOHN M. DUFFY

DUMBARTON OAKS TEXTS

De Administrando Imperio
Constantine VII Porphyrogenitus
Gyula Moravcsik | R. J. H. Jenkins
CFHB 1 • DOT 1

Nicholas I, Patriarch of Constantinople: Letters
R. J. H. Jenkins | L. G. Westerink
CFHB 6 • DOT 2

Nicholas I, Patriarch of Constantinople: Miscellaneous Writings
L. G. Westerink
CFHB 20 • DOT 6

The Correspondence of Athanasius I, Patriarch of Constantinople
Alice-Mary Talbot
CFHB 7 • DOT 3

The Letters of Manuel II Palaeologus
George T. Dennis
CFHB 8 • DOT 4

The Synodicon Vetus
John Duffy | Thomas S. Parker
CFHB 15 • DOT 5

Letters of Gregory Akindynos
Angela Constantinides Hero
CFHB 21 • DOT 7

The Correspondence of Leo, Metropolitan of Synada and Syncellus
M. P. Vinson
CFHB 23 • DOT 8

Three Byzantine Military Treatises
George T. Dennis
CFHB 25 • DOT 9

Nikephoros, Patriarch of Constantinople: Short History
Cyril Mango
CFHB 13 • DOT 10

The Correspondence of Ignatios the Deacon
Cyril Mango | Stephanos Efthymiadis
CFHB 39 • DOT 11

The Taktika *of Leo VI*
George T. Dennis
CFHB 49 • DOT 12

The Life of Patriarch Ignatius
Nicetas David
Andrew Smithies | John M. Duffy
CFHB 51 • DOT 13

COMMENTARIES

De Administrando Imperio*: A Commentary*
R. J. H. Jenkins

A Critical Commentary on the Taktika *of Leo VI*
John F. Haldon